Citizen Politics

Citizen Politics
Public Opinion and Political Parties in Advanced Industrial Democracies

FIFTH EDITION

RUSSELL J. DALTON
UNIVERSITY OF CALIFORNIA, IRVINE

CQ PRESS

A DIVISION OF CONGRESSIONAL QUARTERLY INC.
WASHINGTON, D.C.

CQ Press
2300 N Street, NW, Suite 800
Washington, DC 20037

Phone: 202-729-1900; toll-free, 1-866-4CQ-PRESS (1-866-427-7737)

Web: www.cqpress.com

Cover design by Anne C. Kerns, Anne Likes Red, Inc.
Typesetting by BMWW, Baltimore, MD

⊗ The paper used in this publication exceeds the requirements of the American National Standard for Information Sciences—Permanence of Paper for Printed Library Materials, ANSI Z39.48-1992.

Printed and bound in the United States of America

12   11   10   09   08   1   2   3   4   5

Library of Congress Cataloging-in-Publication Data

Dalton, Russell J.
  Citizen politics : public opinion and political parties in advanced industrial democracies / Russell J. Dalton. — 5th ed.
     p. cm.
  Includes bibliographical references and index.
  ISBN 978-0-87289-537-9 (pbk. : alk. paper)   1. Political parties.   2. Political participation.
3. Democracy.   4. Public opinion.   5. Comparative government.   I. Title.

  JF2011.D34 2008
  323'.042—dc22   2008008959

To my three sons,
Penn, Mac, and Snickers

Contents

Tables and Figures

FIGURES

Preface

Experts frequently claim that history follows a circle, and if you wait long enough you will end up where you started. When I began work on the first edition of this book in the 1980s, many political scientists were openly worried about the viability of modern democracy. Claims about an imminent crisis of democracy were commonplace. Against this backdrop, the first edition of *Citizen Politics* (1988) argued that democracy was alive and well in the advanced industrial democracies, whose citizens believed in the democratic creed and wanted their governments to meet these expectations. That book presented evidence that contemporary publics were becoming more active in the political process, more likely to participate in elite-challenging activities, more likely to vote on issues and other policy criteria, and more demanding of their representatives. If democracy was in crisis, it was a crisis of institutions, not of the democratic spirit among citizens.

Events ultimately supported my contrarian perspective on democracy. The toppling of the Berlin Wall, the collapse of communism in the Soviet Union and Eastern Europe, and the spread of democracy in the 1990s created a euphoria surrounding the democratic process. Even those who had proclaimed its limits a few years earlier now trumpeted this new wave of democratization. Suddenly it seemed apparent to everyone that democracy represented the start of a new history. But I remain skeptical of fads—even those reinforcing my own views. Therefore, in revising the third and fourth editions of *Citizen Politics,* I highlighted not only the strengths of democratic processes, but also the challenges confronting contemporary democracies.

Now we have come full circle. The current conventional wisdom again claims that democracy is at risk—and the citizens are at fault. A host of distinguished scholars cite an apparently unending list of what is wrong with democracy's citizens. Too few of us follow politics, too few are voting, too many of us are cynical about politics, and too often we are intolerant of those who do not share our positions. It's déjà vu all over again, as Yogi Berra used to say.

Watching this ebb and flow of the political debate has deepened my belief that systematic research provides a corrective to the winds of punditry. Things were not so bad during the pessimistic days of the "crisis of democracy" literature, and they were not so good during the euphoria following the Berlin Wall's collapse. We understand the nature of democracy and its citizens not by watching talking heads on television, but by talking to the public, learning how they think about politics, and learning how they act on their beliefs. And while I sometimes subscribe to the line about "lies, damn lies, and statistics," in the long run systematic research can provide a deeper understanding of the true nature of citizen politics.

This book introduces students to what we know about citizens' political behavior, questions about it that remain unanswered, and the implications of findings thus far. The analyses focus on citizen politics in the United States, Great Britain, France, and Germany, with frequent comparisons to other established democracies. This edition re-engages in the debate on the vitality of contemporary democracy and argues that ongoing processes of social modernization are changing the values and behavior of the public. These changes to the status quo might be a concern to someone who longs for an idyllic past (which never existed); indeed, these changes create new challenges and tensions for the democratic process. In the end, however, if democracies successfully respond to these challenges, the democratic process will be stronger.

I hope this book is of value to several audiences. It was written primarily for classroom use in courses on comparative political parties, public opinion, and European politics. The first half (chapters 1–6) introduces the principles of public opinion and the broad contours of citizen action and citizen beliefs. The second half (chapters 7–11) covers party alignments and can be combined with other texts on political parties. The book concludes with a discussion of citizen attitudes toward democratic institutions and the political process and the choices that face the various polities.

The book is useful at the graduate level as a core text for courses on comparative political behavior or West European politics. It summarizes the existing knowledge in the field and introduces the controversies that at present divide researchers. I hope instructors find that this introductory analysis facilitates discussion of readings from primary research materials. Even senior scholars may find familiar data interpreted in new and thought-provoking ways.

MAJOR REVISIONS

The basic framework of this book and its findings have remained fairly constant since the first edition. As more data and research have become available, the trends have become clearer and more apparent. Still, this new edition has undergone more restructuring than any previous revision, including several major changes to improve the presentation.

- Important new literature on the cognitive sophistication of citizens and the implications of cognitive sophistication is included in the chapters on political sophistication and issue voting.
- New forms of political activity, such as Internet-based activism and new forms of political consumerism, are described.
- More attention is devoted to current academic debates over the decline of participation, the erosion of political support, and the implications for de-

mocracy. I offer a contrarian view on these points. (Also see Russell J. Dalton, *The Good Citizen: How a Younger Generation Is Reshaping American Politics*, CQ Press, 2008.)

- Chapters 3 and 4 are reorganized so that the book no longer separates conventional participation and protest into discrete chapters. Because protest has become conventional, chapter 3 now describes all the modes of participation and their trends over time. Chapter 4 examines which citizens use the different modes of activity.
- All the chapters are revised to present the latest research and empirical evidence, including new evidence from the Comparative Study of Electoral Systems project (module II), the 2003–2008 World Values Survey, and the International Social Survey Program. I also supply new material from the 2005 British and 2005 German national election studies.
- A new statistical primer (appendix A) is provided to give readers guidance in interpreting tables and figures. In addition, the primer serves as a reference guide for using correlation statistics to understand the relationship between two traits, such as summarizing educational differences in voting turnout.
- A new data supplement from the 2004 International Social Survey Program is included (appendix C). These data are used throughout the book, and a subset of items is available to instructors for class use. Appendix C presents a detailed list of variables, and matching *Statistical Package for the Social Sciences* (SPSS) files are available online at http://cqpress.com/cs/dalton. Computer-based research projects on public opinion enrich the subject matter of the course for students and provide them with a firsthand opportunity to understand the process of public opinion research.

ACKNOWLEDGMENTS

For five editions, this research has benefited from the advice and criticism of my colleagues, comments of students who have used this text, and insights I have gained from working with other scholars. Many colleagues offered advice, survey data, or moral support: Paul Abramson, Paul Beck, Scott Flanagan, Hans-Dieter Klingemann, Michael Lewis-Beck, Ian McAllister, Robert Rohrschneider, Hermann Schmitt, Martin Wattenberg, and Bernhard Wessels commented on the manuscript throughout the various editions. I also appreciate the reviewers for this new edition: Miki Caul Kittilson of Arizona State University and Michael D. Martinez of the University of Florida. Alix van Sickle developed the index for this book. I owe an equal debt to the students in my Citizen Politics course at the University of California, Irvine, who have used this book and shared their reactions.

It is a pleasure to collaborate with a great group of professionals at CQ Press. I want to thank the editors who worked on the project: Charisse Kiino, Allison McKay, Carolyn Goldinger, and Gwenda Larsen.

I also want to acknowledge a special debt to Ronald Inglehart. Ron was my mentor at the University of Michigan, and his provocative views about citizen politics have deeply influenced my own thinking. He has developed the World Values Survey into a global resource for social science research; many of the analyses in this book are based on World Values Survey data. I have always admired Ron's enthusiasm for social research and his creativity as a scholar. In innumerable ways, I am in his debt.

This book has a bold objective: to provide an overview of the nature of citizen politics in advanced industrial democracies. The task is clearly beyond the means of one individual, but with a little help from these friends, the resulting product begins to outline the political changes and choices that today face the citizenry in these established democracies.

Russell J. Dalton
Irvine, California

Citizen Politics

CHAPTER 1

Introduction

This is a book about you and me. As citizens, voters, protesters, campaign workers, community activists, party members, and political spectators, we are the driving force of the democratic process. The spectacle of an American party convention, the intensity of a French farmers' protest, the community spirit of a New England town meeting, or the dedication of a German environmental group create an impressive image of the democratic process.

Over the past two decades, we watched in awe as the force of "people power" tore down the Berlin Wall, dismantled apartheid in South Africa, brought democracy back to the Philippines, and created a democratization wave on a global scale. Many of the nations that were once part of the Soviet empire are now members of the European Union and offer new freedoms and liberties to their citizens. New democracies were created in East Asia and in Africa. As the democratization wave swept across the world in the 1990s, it created optimism about the democratic process, even though barely half of the world's nations have real democratic institutions and procedures. Still, some writers claimed that liberal democracy represented the "end of history" and that eventually all nations would become democratic (Fukuyama 1992). Public opinion surveys found broad public support for democracy, even in nations that lacked democratic regimes (Inglehart and Welzel 2005). Democracy had won the cold war, enriched the lives of its citizens, and seemed to represent nearly universal human values.

At the same time, however, scholars, journalists, and other observers are engaged in an active debate on the vitality of contemporary democracy. New political challenges have emerged in the established democracies, and some leading political scientists warn that democracy is at risk (Macedo et al. 2005; Putnam 2000). These scholars maintain that social and civic engagement is weakening, intolerance is spreading, and people are becoming skeptical about politicians, parties, and political institutions. They claim that contemporary democracies are facing a malaise of the spirit that arises from their own citizens and erodes the very foundations of the democratic process. Others criticize the structures and institutions of democracies and their inability to match their democratic ideals (Zakaria 2003; Wolfe 2006).

How can we be living in the best of times—and the worst of times—at the same time? The previous four editions of this book have discussed the ebb and flow in analysts' evaluations of the democratic process. The two contrasting perspectives are both real. Democracy is a dynamic system that changes to succeed and advance, and each generation seems willing to carry on the debate over its vitality. Democracy's dynamism causes tensions and strains, but if successful it deepens and enriches the democratic process. The contemporary debate about democracy arises from the tremendous social changes that the established democracies experienced in the last half of the twentieth century. The political world is changing, and our task is to understand how and why, and the implications of these changes.

This book focuses on the citizen's role within the democratic process, how this role has changed over time, and how these changes are altering the nature of democracy. Because we focus on citizens, we do not explain the role of elites, interest groups, and other political actors. We also do not presume that the public is all-knowing or all-powerful. Indeed, we could point to many examples of the public's ignorance or error on policy issues (as well as examples of elite errors and many instances in which policymakers disregard the public's preferences). The democratic process, like all human activities, is imperfect, but its strength lies in the premise that people are the best judges of their own destiny. The success of democracy is largely measured by the public's participation in the process, the respect for citizen rights, and the responsiveness of the system to popular demands. As Adlai Stevenson once said, in a democracy the people get the kind of government they deserve (for better or worse).

Before proceeding, we must acknowledge the complexity of studying the citizen's role in democracy. It is difficult to make simple generalizations about public opinion because the public is not homogeneous. It is not a single entity. The public in any nation consists of millions of individuals, each with his or her view of the world and of the citizen's role in politics. Members of the public are liberal, moderate, conservative, socialist, reactionary, communist, or none of the above. They hold all manner of opinions on contemporary political issues, which is why the issues are controversial and eventually require a political decision. Some people favor strict environmental laws; others see environmental standards as excessive. Some favor international trade; others are skeptical of its claimed benefits. All of these differences are revealed by sampling the public through opinion polls.

People also differ in the interests and experiences they bring to politics. A few are full-time political activists, but most of us have modest political interests and ambitions. On some issues, a broad spectrum of society may be involved; other issues are greeted with apathy. Public opinion generally defines the acceptable bounds of politics, within which political elites resolve controversies. When elites exceed these bounds, or when the issues immediately affect people's lives, the potential for political action is great. The difficulty is to understand and predict which course of action the public will choose.

In short, social scientists deal with the most complex problem in nature: to understand and predict human behavior. Yet the task is not hopeless. Scientific public opinion surveys provide valuable tools for researchers. From a sample of a few thousand precisely selected individuals, we can make reliable statements about the distribution of attitudes and opinions (Asher 2007). The survey interview allows us to observe behavior and to study the motivations and expectations guiding behavior. Furthermore, we can divide a survey into subgroups to examine the diversity in individual opinions.

This book relies heavily on public opinion surveys. I do not claim that all we know about the public is found in the statistics and percentages of public opinion surveys. Some of the most insightful writings about political behavior are qualitative studies of the topic. And yet, even insightful political analysts may make contradictory claims about the public. The value of the empirical method is that it provides a specific standard to evaluate contrasting descriptions of public opinion or behavior. Surveys enable people to describe their political views in their own words, and therefore survey data are a tremendously valuable research tool for social scientists.

To assist readers with the interpretation of the relationships and statistics presented here, we have added a new statistical primer (appendix A) to this book. The primer gives guidance in interpreting tables and figures. In addition, it a reference guide for using correlation statistics to understand the relationship between two traits, such as summarizing educational differences in voting turnout.

Drawing on an extensive collection of opinion surveys, this book examines public opinion in several advanced industrial democracies.[1] We describe how people view politics, how they participate in the process, what opinions they hold, and how they choose their leaders through competitive elections. These findings should help us to understand the role of the public in the political process in contemporary democracies.

THE COMPARATIVE STUDY OF PUBLIC OPINION

If you have ever traveled to a foreign country, you have already learned the first lesson of this book: human beings not only differ in many ways but also share some common values and beliefs. Furthermore, we realize what is distinctive to a nation only by making these comparisons.

The comparative study of public opinion in Western democracies has several advantages. A common historical and cultural tradition unites Europe and North America. Although the countries differ in the specifics of their government and party systems, they share broad similarities in the functioning of the democratic process and the role of the citizen in the process. A comparative approach therefore provides a basis for studying those aspects of political behavior that should be valid across nations. General theories of why people participate in democratic politics should apply to citizens regardless of their nationality. Theories to explain party preferences should hold for Americans and Europeans if the theories represent basic features of human nature.

In most instances, we expect similar patterns of behavior in different democracies. If our theories do not function similarly across nations, however, then we have learned something new and important. The physical sciences often progress by finding exceptions to general theory, which necessitates further theoretical work. The same applies to social science.

Comparative analysis also demonstrates the effects of political structures on citizens' political behavior. For example, does the nature of a nation's electoral system affect the public's voting behavior? Or, does the structure of political institutions affect the patterns of political participation? Each nation represents a "natural experiment" wherein general theories of political behavior can be tested in a different political context.

Finally, even if we are interested in just one nation, comparative research is still very valuable. An old Hebrew riddle expresses this idea: *"Question: Who first discovered water? Answer:* I don't know, but it wasn't a fish." Immersing oneself in a single environment makes the defining characteristics of that environment unobtrusive and unnoticed. It is difficult to understand what is unique and distinctive about American political behavior by studying only American politics. Indeed, many students of American politics may be surprised to learn that the United States is often the atypical case in cross-national comparisons. American public opinion and political processes are unique in many ways, but we perceive this only by rising above the waters.

CHOOSING NATIONS TO COMPARE

To balance our needs for comparison and attention to national differences, we focus on citizen politics in four nations: the United States, Great Britain, the Federal Republic of Germany, and France.[2] We used several criteria to choose these nations. By many standards, they are the major powers among the Western democracies. Their population, size, economy, military strength, and political influence earn them leadership positions in international circles. The actions of any one of these nations can have significant consequences for all the others.

These four countries also highlight many of the significant variations in the structure of democratic politics. Table 1.1 summarizes some of the most important differences, such as government structure. Great Britain has a pure parliamentary system of government. The popularly elected House of Commons selects the prime minister to head the executive branch. This system produces a fusion of legislative and executive power, because the same party and the same group of elites direct both branches of government. In contrast, American government has a presidential system, with extensive checks and balances to maintain a separation of legislative and executive power. French politics functions within a modified presidential system. The public directly elects both the president and the National Assembly, which selects the premier to head the administration of government. Germany has a parliamentary system, with the popularly elected Bundestag selecting the chancellor as head of the executive branch. Germany, however, also has a strong federal structure and a separation of powers that is uncommon for a parliamentary government. These contrasting institutional forms should influence the nature of citizen politics in each nation (Powell 2000; Lijphart 1999).

TABLE 1.1 Comparison of Political Systems

National characteristic	United States	Great Britain	France	Germany
Population (in millions)	301.1	60.7	60.8	82.4
Gross domestic product/capita	$44,000	$31,800	$31,100	$31,900
Political regime established	1789	Seventeenth century	1958	1949
State form	Republic	Constitutional monarchy	Republic	Republic
Government structure	Presidential	Parliamentary	Modified presidential	Modified parliamentary
Chief executive	President	Prime minister	President	Chancellor
Method of selection	Direct election	Elected by parliament	Direct election	Elected by parliament
Legislature	Bicameral	Bicameral	Bicameral	Bicameral
Lower house	House of Representatives	House of Commons	National Assembly	Bundestag
Upper house	Senate	House of Lords	Senate	Bundesrat
Power of upper house	Equal	Weaker	Weaker	Equal on state issues
Electoral system				
Lower house	Single-member districts	Single-member districts	Single-member districts	Proportional representation and single-member districts
Upper house	Statewide elections	Inheritance and appointment	Appointed by communes	Appointed by states
Major parties	Democrats Republicans	Labour Liberal Democrats Conservatives	Communists Socialists Greens UDF Gaullists (UPM) National Front	Democratic Socialist (PDS) Greens Social Democrats Free Democrats Christian Democrats (CDU/CSU)

SOURCE: Compiled by the author; population and GDP statistics are from the CIA *World Factbook*, 2007.

Electoral systems are equally diverse. Great Britain and the United States select the members of their national legislatures from single-member districts, where a plurality is sufficient for election. Germany uses a hybrid system for Bundestag elections: half the deputies are elected from single-member districts, and half are selected from party lists. The French electoral system is based on deputies winning a majority in single-member districts, with a second ballot (*tour*) if no candidate receives a majority on the first ballot. Several studies have shown how such institutional arrangements can affect electoral outcomes (Powell 2000; Taagepera and Shugart 1989).

The party systems of the four nations also vary. Party competition in the United States is usually limited to the Democratic and Republican Parties. Both are broad "catchall" parties that combine diverse political groups into weakly structured electoral coalitions. In contrast, most European political parties are hierarchically organized and firmly controlled by the party leadership. Candidates are elected primarily because of their party label and not because of their personal attributes; most party members vote as a bloc in the legislature. Party options are also more diverse in Europe. British voters can select from at least three major parties; Germans have five major parties in the Bundestag. French party politics is synonymous with diversity and political polarization. Dozens of parties run in elections, and a large number of their members win seats in parliament. France, a nation of perpetual political effervescence, provides the spice of comparative politics.

The contrasts across nations take on an added dimension because of German unification. Western Germans developed the characteristics of a stable, advanced industrial democracy. In contrast, the residents of the former East Germany, like most of the rest of Eastern Europe, are still learning about the democratic process. When possible, we broaden our cross-national comparisons to include a range other advanced industrial democracies.

A NEW STYLE OF CITIZEN POLITICS

To understand the findings of this book, we ask you to put yourself back in time. If you are a student, think back to what politics must have been like in the mid-twentieth century—when your grandparents were your age. The Constitution has been amended six times since 1951, but the changes left the institutions of government basically the same. Democrats and Republicans still contend in elections. But, as we argue in this book, the people and politics have changed—and this has transformed the democratic process.

The changing nature of citizen political behavior derives from the socioeconomic transformation of the Western societies after World War II. These nations are developing a set of characteristics that collectively represent a new form of *advanced industrial* or *postindustrial* society (Bell 1973; Inglehart 1977, 1990). The most dramatic changes involve economic conditions. An unprecedented expansion of economic well-being occurred in the second half of the twentieth century. The economies of Western Europe and North

America grew at phenomenal rates in the post–World War II decades. Analysts describe the astonishing expansion of the West German economy as the *Wirtschaftswunder* (Economic Miracle). Average income levels in our four nations are several times greater than at any time in prewar history. By most economic standards, these four nations rank among the most affluent of the world—and the most affluent in human history.

A restructured labor force is another major social change. The number of people employed in agriculture has fallen dramatically in most Western nations, and industrial employment has remained stable or declined. At the same time, employment in the service sector has increased markedly. In addition, because of the expansion of national and local governments, public employment now constitutes a significant share of the labor force. Richard Florida (2003) argues that a new creative class—individuals who create and utilize knowledge—are a vanguard for social and cultural change. Only a minority of jobs in today's economy existed in your grandparents' time. Moreover, social mobility and different career experiences change individual values and their outlooks on life. The life experience of a blue-collar industrial worker on an assembly line is much different from a computer programmer's—and the differences should affect their values.

Advanced industrialism also changes the context of the workplace and the residential neighborhood. Urbanization alters life expectations and lifestyles. It brings an increasing separation of the home from the workplace, a greater diversity of occupations and interests, an expanded range of career opportunities, and more geographic and social mobility. With these trends come changes in social interaction, as communal forms of organization are replaced by voluntary associations, which are less institutionalized and more spontaneous organizations. Communities are becoming less bounded; individuals are involved in increasingly complex and competing social networks that divide their loyalties; and institutional ties are becoming more fluid.

Educational opportunities also have expanded. If your grandparents went to school before 1945, they probably ended their studies with a high school education or less. Access to education steadily has increased as minimal education standards were raised and university enrollments skyrocketed. By 2008 more than three-quarters of American youth and about half of college-age Europeans had some form of postsecondary schooling. This trend has fundamentally changed the educational composition of contemporary mass publics.

Citizen access to political information has also increased dramatically. The electronic media, especially television, have experienced exceptional growth, as has the availability of other information sources, such as books and magazines. Even more revolutionary is the rapid development of electronic information processing: computers, the Internet, podcasts, and related technologies. It seems as if any piece of information is only a Google away. The information environment of today and the 1950s almost defies comparison. Information is no longer a scarce commodity. Indeed, the contemporary information problem is how to adapt to life in cyberspace, managing an ever-growing volume of sophisticated knowledge.

Another major change in Western democracies is the extent to which governments are responsible for protecting and managing society and the economy. Many European societies have extensive welfare programs that protect the individual against economic or medical hardship. Unemployment, illness, and similar problems still occur, but under the social welfare state, their consequences are less dire than they once were. In addition, people now see the government as responsible for protecting the environment, ensuring social rights, enabling lifestyle choices, and for shouldering a host of other new obligations.

Many political analysts doubt whether these development trends can continue. Everywhere, it seems, are signs of retrenchment in government social programs. Increased international economic competition in a globalized economy has created new economic strains within these nations. Elation about the end of the cold war and the democratization of Eastern Europe is tempered by worries not only about financial burdens, but also growing nationalism, international terrorism, and ethnic conflict. Some established democracies fear that economic problems will revive reactionary political groups.

Admittedly, the miraculous economic growth rates of the post–World War II period now seem like distant history. Yet, the transformation of advanced industrial democracies involves more than the politics of affluence. Changes in occupational and social structures continue and bring with them alterations in life conditions and lifestyles. Expanded educational opportunities represent an enduring trait of modern societies. The information revolution continues and grows at an amazing rate. Advanced industrial societies are dramatically different from their predecessors of the 1950s, and I expect change to persist in the decades ahead, even if the pace slows somewhat.

This book maintains that one result of these social trends is the development of a new style of citizen politics. My premise is that as the socioeconomic characteristics of these nations change, so do the characteristics of the public. Greater educational opportunities mean a growth in political skills and resources, producing the most sophisticated publics in the history of democracies. Changing economic conditions redefine citizens' issue interests. The weakening of social networks and institutional loyalties is associated with the decline of traditional political alignments and voting patterns. Contemporary publics and contemporary democratic politics have been dramatically transformed over the past several decades (Dalton 2007a, ch. 1).

The parts of this new style of citizen politics are not always, or necessarily, linked together. Some parts may be transitory; others may be coincidental. Nevertheless, several traits coexist for the present, defining a new pattern of citizen political behavior. My goal in this book is to systematically describe this new pattern of political thought and action.

One aspect of the new citizen politics is political participation (chapters 2–4). Greater participation in political and economic decision making is an important social goal. Participation in elections is the most common form of political action—but it is declining in most nations. At the same time, protest, citizen action groups, boycotts, and contentious participation are increasing. Citizens are less likely to be passive subjects and more likely to demand a say in the decisions affecting their lives. The new style of citizen politics reflects a more active participation in the democratic process.

Another broad area of change involves the values and attitudes of the public (chapters 5–6). Industrial societies aim to provide affluence and economic security, and the success of advanced industrialism fulfills many basic economic needs for a sizable sector of society. Therefore, some people are shifting their concerns to new political goals (Inglehart 1990, 1997). Several of these new issues are common to advanced industrial democracies: social equality, environmental protection, the dangers of nuclear energy, gender equality, and human rights. In some countries, historic conditions focus these general concerns on specific national problems, such as racial equality in the United States or regional conflicts in Britain and France. Many of these issues are now loosely connected into an alternative political agenda that is another element of the new style of citizen politics.

The nature of partisan politics is also changing (chapters 7–11). Comparative party research used to emphasize the stability of democratic party systems. This situation has changed, and instead we find more fragmentation and volatility in most Western party systems. Declining class differences in voting behavior reflect the general erosion in the social bases of voting. Studies in most of these nations document a decline in the public's identification with political parties and growing disenchantment with parties in general. Such patterns indicate a partial *dealignment* of contemporary party systems (Dalton and Wattenberg 2000).

These trends result in part from the addition of new issues to the political agenda and political parties' struggle to respond to them. New parties have arisen across Europe—ranging from New Left green parties to nationalistic New Right parties—while new political movements seek access to the Democratic and Republican Parties in the United States. The changing characteristics of contemporary publics also increase party volatility. Unsophisticated voters once relied on social-group cues and partisan cues to make their political decisions. But with the spread of education and information sources, more people can now deal with the complexities of politics and make their own political decisions. As the influence of traditional group and party allegiances wanes, issues and other short-term factors become a more important basis of voting behavior. The new style of citizen politics therefore features an issue-oriented and candidate-oriented electorate.

Finally, public orientations toward government represent a new paradox for democracy (chapter 12). New issues have joined the agenda, the democratic process has become more inclusive, and the government has generally improved the quality of life, even as people have become more critical of government. The conflict over new issues and new participation patterns may offer a partial explanation for these trends. In addition, emerging value priorities that stress self-actualization and autonomy produce skepticism of elite-controlled hierarchical organizations, such as bureaucracies, political parties, and large interest groups.

One thing a student of political science quickly learns is that serious researchers can reach different conclusions based on similar evidence. Many other writers question this book's basic premise of political change. In reviewing European public opinion trends, for example, Dieter Fuchs and Hans-Dieter Klingemann conclude: "The hypotheses we tested are based on the premise that a fundamental change had taken place in the relationship between citizens and the state, provoking a challenge to representative democracy . . . [but] the postulated fundamental change in the citizens' relationship with the state largely did *not* occur" (1995, 429). Begin your reading from this skeptical position, and then see if the evidence supports it.

My own sense is that this is an exciting time to study what people are thinking, feeling, and doing in politics because so much is changing. The puzzle for researchers, students, and other citizens is to understand how democracy functions in its new context. The development of a new style of citizen politics creates new strains for the political systems of advanced industrial democracies. Protests, social movements, partisan volatility, and political skepticism are disrupting the traditional political order. Adjustment to new issue concerns and new patterns of citizen participation may be a difficult process. More people now take democratic ideals seriously, and they expect political systems to live up to those ideals. I believe that democracy is not an end state, but an evolutionary process. I see the new style of citizen politics as a sign of vitality and an opportunity for these societies to make further progress toward their democratic goals.

SUGGESTED READINGS

Baker, Wayne. *America's Crisis of Values: Reality and Perception.* Princeton: Princeton University Press, 2004.

Dalton, Russell, and Hans-Dieter Klingemann, eds. *Oxford Handbook of Political Behavior.* Oxford: Oxford University Press, 2007.

Florida, Richard. *The Rise of the Creative Class: And How It's Transforming Work, Leisure, Community, and Everyday Life.* New York: Basic Books, 2003.

NOTES

1. See appendix B for information on the major public opinion surveys used in this book. Neither these archives nor the original collectors of the surveys bear responsibility for the analyses presented here.
2. For a brief review of these nations, see Almond, Powell, Dalton, and Strom (2007). More detailed national studies are found in Norton (2000) for Britain, Conradt (2004) for Germany, and Safran (2002) for France.

PART ONE

POLITICS AND THE PUBLIC

CHAPTER 2

The Nature of Mass Beliefs

The Los Angeles Times recently ran an article about a public opinion survey testing Americans' knowledge of pop culture versus politics.[1] The survey found that more people could name two of Snow White's seven dwarfs than could name two members of the U.S. Supreme Court. More Americans knew the name of the British author of the Harry Potter books than the name of Britain's prime minister. More people knew the names of the Three Stooges than the names of the three branches of the U.S. government.

This article and many more like it illustrate a continuing debate about the political abilities of democratic publics—their level of knowledge, understanding, and interest in politics. For voters to make meaningful decisions, they must know something about the issues and understand the available options. Citizens also need sufficient knowledge of the workings of the political system if they want to influence the actions of their representatives. In short, for democratic politics to be purposeful, the citizens must have at least a basic level of political skills.

Learning about the public's level of sophistication also improves our understanding of the public opinion data presented in this book. With what depth of knowledge and conviction are opinions held? Do responses to public opinion surveys represent reasoned assessments of the issues or the snap judgments of individuals faced by an interviewer on their doorstep? It is common to hear the public labeled as uninformed, especially when public opinion conflicts with the speaker's own views; conversely, the public cannot be wiser than when it supports one's position. Can we judge the merits of either position based on the empirical evidence from public opinion surveys?

Debates about the public's political abilities are one of the major controversies in political behavior research. This controversy involves normative assumptions about what level of sophistication is required for democracies to fulfill their political ideals, as well as differences in evaluating the evidence of whether the public fulfills these assumptions.

THE SUPERCITIZEN

Political theorists have long maintained that democracy is workable only when the public has a high degree of political information and sophistication. John Stuart Mill, John Locke, Alexis de Tocqueville, and other writers saw these public traits as requirements for a successful democratic system. Most theorists also claimed that the public should support the political system and share a deep commitment to democratic ideals such as pluralism, free

---

Internet Resource

Visit the Virtual Library on Democracy for links to various sources on public opinion, political parties, and democracy:

http://www.democ.uci.edu/resources/guide.php

---

expression, and minority rights (see chapter 12). Otherwise, misguided or unscrupulous elites might manipulate an uninformed and unsophisticated electorate. In a sense, these theorists posited a supercitizen model: for democracy to survive, the public must be a paragon of civic virtue.

This ideal of the democratic supercitizen is often illustrated by examples drawn from a popular lore about the sophistication of Americans.[2] Tocqueville (1966) praised the social and community involvement of Americans when he described the United States in the nineteenth century. Voters in early America supposedly yearned for the stimulating political debates of election campaigns and flocked to political rallies in great numbers. New England town hall meetings became a legendary example of the American political spirit. Even on the frontier, it was claimed, conversations around the general store's cracker barrel displayed a deep interest in political matters.

History painted a less positive picture of the citizenry in many European nations. In contrast to America, the right to vote came late to most Europeans, often delayed until the beginning of the twentieth century. The aristocratic institutions and deferential traditions of British politics limited public participation beyond the act of voting and severely restricted the size of the eligible electorate. In France, the excesses of the French Revolution raised doubts about the principle of mass participation. The instability of the French political system supposedly produced a sense of "incivism" (lack of civic engagement), and people avoided political discussions and political involvement.

Germany was the most graphic example of what might follow when the public lacks democratic norms. Under the authoritarian governments that ruled during the Second Empire (1871–1918), people were taught to be seen and not heard. The democratic Weimar Republic (1919–1933) was a brief and turbulent interlude in Germany's nondemocratic history, but the frailty of democratic norms contributed to that system's demise and the rise of Hitler's Third Reich. But because a strong democratic culture eventually developed in the postwar Federal Republic, German democracy has flourished. These historical experiences strengthened the belief that a sophisticated, involved, and democratic public is necessary for democracy to succeed.

THE UNSOPHISTICATED CITIZEN

The start of scientific public opinion surveying in the 1950s and 1960s provided the first opportunity to move beyond the insights of theorists and social commentators. It was finally possible to test the lofty images of the democratic citizen against reality. The public itself was directly consulted.

In contrast to the classic images celebrated in democratic theory, public opinion surveys presented an unflattering picture of the American public. Political sophistication seemed to fall far short of the supercitizen model. Most people's political interest and involvement barely extended beyond casting an occasional vote in elections. Furthermore, Americans apparently brought little understanding to their participation in politics. It was not clear that people based their voting decisions on rational evaluations of the candidates and their issue positions. Instead, voting seemed conditioned by habitual group loyalties and personalistic considerations. The seminal work in the area summarized these findings as follows:

> Our data reveal that certain requirements commonly assumed for the successful operation of democracy are not met by the behavior of the "average" citizen. . . . Many vote without real involvement in the election. . . . The citizen is not highly informed on the details of the campaign. . . . In any rigorous or narrow sense, the voters are not highly rational. (Berelson, Lazarsfeld, and McPhee 1954, 307–310)

The landmark study, *The American Voter,* (Campbell et al. 1960) supported these early findings by documenting a lack of political sophistication and ideological understanding by the American electorate.

In an influential essay on mass belief systems, Philip Converse (1964) spelled out the criteria for measuring political sophistication. As modeled in figure 2.1, Converse said there should be a basic *structure* at the core of

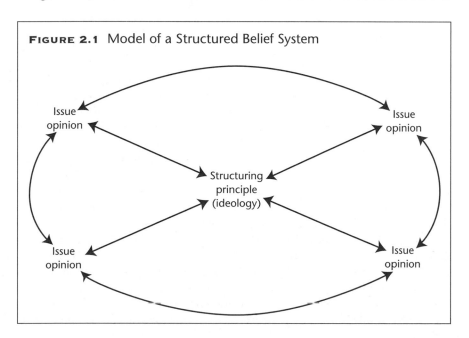

FIGURE 2.1 Model of a Structured Belief System

individual political beliefs. An ideological framework such as liberalism or conservatism presumably provides this structure, at least at higher levels of sophistication. In addition, there should be *constraint* between individual issue positions. Constraint is measured by the strength of the linkage between specific issue positions and core beliefs and by the interrelationship among issues. A person who is liberal on one issue is expected to be liberal on others, and opinions on one issue should be ideologically (or at least logically) consistent with other beliefs. Finally, Converse said that issue opinions should be relatively *stable* over time so that voters held enduring beliefs that guided their behavior. The overall result should be a tightly structured system of beliefs like that depicted in the figure.

In testing this model, Converse maintained that most Americans fell short on these criteria. First, most people did not judge political phenomena in ideological terms, such as liberalism/conservatism or capitalism/socialism. Barely a tenth of the American public appeared to use ideological concepts to structure their belief system, and most were unfamiliar with concepts such as liberal or conservative. Second, Converse found only a weak relationship between issues that seemingly were connected. For example, people who felt taxes were too high nevertheless favored increased spending for many specific government programs. Third, issue beliefs were not stable over time. Interviewing the same group of individuals across three elections showed that many people seemed to change their opinions randomly. The lack of structure, constraint, and stability led Converse (1970) to conclude that public opinion researchers are often studying "nonattitudes"—that is, many people apparently do not have informed opinions even on issues of long-standing political concern.

In the *The American Voter,* Angus Campbell and his colleagues declared that the electorate "is almost completely unable to judge the rationality of government actions; knowing little of the particular policies and what has led to them, the mass electorate is not able either to appraise its goals or the appropriateness of the means chosen to secure these goals" (Campbell et al. 1960, 543). Other studies soon showed that many people could not name their elected representatives, were unfamiliar with the institutions of government, and did not understand the mechanics of the political process.

The image of the American voter had fallen to a new low, and later research claims that little has changed (e.g., Caplan 2007; Bartels 2003). Several studies maintain that political information has not improved over time and may be decreasing because young people are becoming less interested and informed about politics (Delli Carpini and Keeter 1996; Wattenberg 2006). The *Los Angeles Times* article mentioned at the beginning of this chapter typifies this evidence.

The image of the unsophisticated citizen seemed equally applicable to West Europeans. Looking beyond election turnout, political involvement in Europe was often lower than in the United States (Almond and Verba 1963; Verba, Nie, and Kim 1978). Europeans also lacked well-formed opinions on the pressing issues of the day (Converse and Pierce 1986, ch. 7; Butler and Stokes 1969). Sixty percent of Britons did not recognize the terms *Left* and *Right* as they applied to politics. And the telltale signs of nonattitudes—weak linkages between opinions on related issues and high opinion instability over time—were apparent.

Other research raised doubts about the public's commitment in our four democracies to political tolerance and other values underlying the democratic process (Stouffer 1955; McClosky and Brill 1983; Barnum and Sullivan 1989). The public supported democratic ideals in the abstract, but not when applied to real political groups and movements, such as Communists, Nazis, atheists, and political nonconformists. Again, the empirical reality apparently fell short of the democratic ideal.

ELITIST THEORY OF DEMOCRACY

Having found that most people apparently fail to meet the requirements of classic democratic theory, political scientists faced a paradox: most individuals are not "good" democratic citizens, and yet democracies such as the United States and Great Britain have existed for generations. Gradually, scholars developed an *elitist theory of democracy* to interpret these survey findings in a positive light (Berelson, Lazarsfeld, and McPhee 1954, 313–323; Almond and Verba 1963, ch. 15).

This elitist theory turned the supposed limitations of the public into a strength of democracy politics. It held that politics might prove unworkable if every person were active on every issue at all times. Images of the centrifugal forces that destroyed the Weimar Republic were still fresh and generated concerns about the possible effects of excessive participation. These authors suggest that the model citizen "is not the active citizen; he is the potentially active citizen" (Almond and Verba 1963, 347). In other words, people must believe that they can influence the government and become active if the issue is sufficiently important. Few will realize this potential, however. The balance between action and potential action presumably ensures that political elites have enough freedom to make necessary decisions, while keeping the public interest in mind.

Another element of this elitist theory stresses the heterogeneity of the public. "Some people are and should be highly interested in politics, but not everyone is or needs to be" (Berelson, Lazarsfeld, and McPhee 1954, 315). From this perspective, the responsiveness of the political system is secured by a core of active citizens and political elites, leaving the rest of the public blissfully uninformed and uninvolved. The mix between involved and indifferent voters supposedly ensures both the stability and flexibility of democratic systems.

The elitist theory of democracy is drawn from the realities of political life—or at least from the hard evidence of survey research. It is, however, a very undemocratic theory of democracy. The theory maintains that "the democratic citizen ... must be active, yet passive; involved, yet not too involved; influential, yet deferential" (Almond and Verba 1963, 478–479). The values and goals of democracy are at least partially obscured by a mountain of survey data.

Accepting this new creed, some analysts advocated an extreme version of this model, implying that citizen activism is undemocratic and politically destabilizing (Dye and Ziegler 1970; Crozier, Huntington, and Watanuki 1975). As Thomas Dye and Harmon Ziegler (1970, 328) bluntly claimed,

> The survival of democracy depends upon the commitment of elites to democratic ideals rather than upon broad support for democracy by the masses. Political apathy and nonparticipation among the masses contribute to the survival of democracy. Fortunately for democracy, the antidemocratic masses are generally more apathetic than elites.

If a supportive and quiescent public ensures a smoothly functioning political system, then it is virtually the duty of the individual to remain uninvolved. When the public began to challenge political elites during the turbulent 1960s and 1970s, these political scientists cautioned that democracy required a public of followers who would not question political elites too extensively. They argued that too much democracy could threaten the democratic process. Even today, some writers argue that we suffer from too much democracy (Zakaria 2003).

I believe that the elitist theory overlooks the complexities of the democratic process and takes an unsophisticated view of the evidence. For example, this theory ignores the inconsistencies that also exist among political elites. Members of the U.S. Congress routinely endorse formal budget limits and then act to circumvent these same limits in the next piece of legislation; in one vote they endorse strict measures to control crime, in the next they refuse to ban assault weapons.[3] Such inconsistencies in elite behavior are treated as examples of the complexity of politics, but the same patterns in public opinion are cited as signs of a lack of sophistication. In addition, the elitist critique of the public's abilities has been challenged on both normative and empirical grounds.[4] The picture of the public's abilities is not nearly as bleak as that painted by the elitist theory of democracy. As our scientific knowledge has increased, so too has our understanding of how citizens actually make political decisions.

POLITICAL SOPHISTICATION RECONSIDERED

We base our challenge to past descriptions of an unsophisticated public on several points. Profound social and political changes in the advanced industrial democracies have increased the public's political abilities. In addition, research has enriched our understanding of how people actually think about political matters. Each point deserves attention.

Cognitive Mobilization

Even if the public of the 1950s (and earlier) had limited political skills and resources—contemporary publics are different. A process of "cognitive mobilization" has raised the public's overall level of political sophistication (Dalton 2007a; Inglehart 1990). This process has two separate parts: the ability to acquire political information and ability to process political information.

At one time, the average citizen might have had difficulty acquiring political information. In the past, one could read newspapers or magazines, but this task is time-consuming, especially for a public with limited education. Particularly in Europe, the printed press was of uneven quality, and many mass newspapers were little more than scandal sheets. Today, the supply and variety of political news is nearly unlimited, and this is a relatively recent development.

The expansion of the mass media, especially television, is the clearest example of the change (Norris 2000; Prior 2007). In the early 1950s television was still a novelty for most Americans and a luxury for most Europeans. Television sets were in only half of American homes, in less than 10 percent of homes in Great Britain and France, and in less than 5 percent of those in West Germany. The expansion of television ownership over the next two decades produced a growing reliance on television as a source of political information. In the 1952 U.S. elections, 51 percent of the electorate used television news as an information source; by 1960 the number had risen to a plateau of about 90 percent. In 1961 only 50 percent of the West German public depended on television for political information, but by 1974 the Germans had also reached the 90 percent level. British and French trends present similar patterns.

As television viewership increased, so too did the amount of political information provided by the medium. The now-standard American nightly half-hour national news program began only in 1963. Since then, technology and viewer interest have increased the proportion of television programming devoted to news and political affairs, and today, news reporting is instantaneous and done on a worldwide scale. Most Americans have access to news on a 24/7 basis: CNN, MSNBC, C-SPAN, and other cable channels create a rich media environment. Markus Prior (2007) shows that the expansion of media choice has raised the total consumption of political information, but also has increased the inequality in political information between the most and least interested. Those who are interested can find 24-hour news; those who are not interested watch *The Simpsons* during the news hour.

In addition to information from television, many Americans read newspapers and magazines, hear news on the radio, use the Internet, join online discussion groups, or learn about politics from their friends. Although many political scientists are critical of "soft news" programs, such as talk shows or Jon Stewart and *The Daily Show,* these programs also can be valuable sources of information (Baum and Jamison 2005). People have access to an array of information that would have been unimaginable a generation ago. The growth in the quantity and quality of political information provided by the media should improve political awareness.

Similar trends exist in other advanced industrial democracies. The electronic media typically devoted time to political information because the

TABLE 2.1 Most Important Source of Political Information (in percentages)

	United States	Great Britain	France	Germany
Television	76	54	66	75
Newspapers	46	44	40	59
Magazines, other print	4	16	23	24
Personal discussion	—	18	25	20
Radio	15	28	36	38
Internet	11	18	15	14
Other	1	33	29	14
Total	153	211	234	244

SOURCES: United States, Pew Center for People and the Press, November 5–8, 2004, survey, in which only two responses were possible; other nations, Eurobarometer 60 (spring 2003), in which multiple responses were possible.

government managed the media. Today, cable and satellite channels are expanding the available channels, ranging from the national networks, to those of neighboring nations, to a host of news and government information channels. The media's political role has also grown. Until the 1964 election the British government prohibited the BBC from carrying election news during the campaign period. Now television coverage is a central part of most modern campaigns (Norris et al. 1999; Semetko and Schoenbach 1994). And other new media add to this mix.

Most people now cite television as their most frequently used source of political information (see table 2.1).[5] Political scientists are divided on whether the expansion of television as a news source is a boon or a curse for the democratic process (e.g., Prior 2007; Norris 2000; Patterson 1993; Swanson and Mancini 1996). Some scholars argue that television tends to trivialize information, emphasizing entertainment and drama over substance and creating a negative climate of opinion. Others have an idyllic image of a former age and lament the decrease in newspaper readers. Some of these concerns are wellfounded. I believe, however, that the benefits of the new media age outweigh the limits. Television can create a better sense of the political process by allowing all of us to watch legislative deliberations, to see candidates as they campaign, and to experience history firsthand. Observing an important parliamentary debate on television or watching the presidential inauguration live puts citizens in direct contact with their government and gives them a better understanding of how democracy works. Television and other contemporary information sources have great positive and negative potential, and the objective of democratic polities should be to maximize the positive benefits and minimize the negatives (Norris 2000; Prior 2007).

A provocative sign of the change in the information climate comes from a study of opinion-holding on foreign policy matters. Matthew Baum (2003) found more public attentiveness and opinion-holding about the 1991 Persian

Gulf War than either Vietnam or Korea at a similar stage of these conflicts. Many people learn about politics from traditional sources, such as newspapers and network television news, but others also learn from "soft news" programs, from the Internet, from their friends, or other sources. This is the new information age in which we live.

In addition to the media, a good deal of politically relevant information is available from our daily life experiences. Governments now exercise a large role in society, and how well or poorly they perform provides important political information. For example, contemporary governments can strongly influence economic conditions. If the economy is doing well, voters are apt to support the incumbents. Similarly, government runs most schools, sets health standards, administers family and social programs, protects the environment, and provides for our transportation needs. When commuters note that highways are deteriorating (or being improved) or parents note improvements (or deterioration) in their children's schools, they are gathering significant political facts. We live in an information-rich environment, and politically relevant information is easily available.

A second aspect of cognitive mobilization is the public's ability to process political information. Cognitive mobilization means that more citizens now have the political resources and skills necessary to deal with the complexities of politics and to reach their own political decisions. Expanded access to political information provides an opportunity to the citizenry, but the abundance of news may be only a noisy cacophony unless one can process the information. Therefore, it is also necessary for the public's political skills to develop.

The most visible change in political skills is the public's level of education. Advanced industrial societies require a more educated and technically sophisticated electorate, and modern affluence has expanded educational opportunities (see chapter 1). The change in education levels from the 1950s to contemporary publics is amazing. In 1952 almost two-thirds of the American public had less than a high school degree, and only a tenth had some college education. In 2008 roughly two-thirds of the public has some college education. Parallel changes are transforming European publics. In postwar West Germany the number of citizens with only primary schooling exceeded those with a secondary school diploma (*Mittlere Reife*) by about five to one. Today, the number of better-educated Germans is twice as large as the lesser-educated.

The relationship between years of schooling and political sophistication is not one-to-one, but research shows that education is linked to a citizen's level of political knowledge, interest, and sophistication (Nie, Junn, and Stehlik-Barry 1996; Sniderman, Brody and Tetlock 1991). Samuel Popkin (1991, 36) suggested that rising education levels increase the breadth of citizens' political interests, even if they do not raise overall levels of political knowledge or issue constraint by the same amount. A doubling of the public's education level may not double the level of political sophistication, but some increase

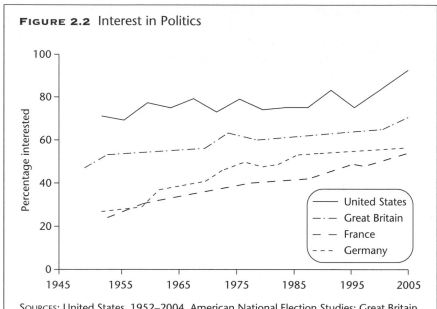

FIGURE 2.2 Interest in Politics

SOURCES: United States, 1952–2004, American National Election Studies; Great Britain, 1949–1953, Gallup (1976a), 1963–1979, 2001–2005 British Election Studies; France, 1953 and 1978, Charlot (1980), 1962, Gallup (1976b), 1978–2002, French Election Studies; and Germany, 1952–2002, surveys of the Institut für Demoskopie, Allensbach.

should occur. In the long history of democracies, contemporary electorates are clearly the most educated, which should contribute toward making a more sophisticated electorate and a new style of citizen politics.

Philip Converse (1972, 1990) maintained that political attention is a more important indicator of the public's political skills than education. Reflecting and reinforcing the general trend of cognitive mobilization, political interest has increased in our four core nations (see figure 2.2).[6] Campaign interest may vary from election to election, but has generally trended upward. Political interest has grown most steadily in the Federal Republic of Germany, partly because of cognitive mobilization and partly because of the nation's resocialization to democracy. Similar trends of expanding interest exist in Great Britain, France, and most Western democracies (Dalton and Wattenberg 2000, ch. 3). Americans' interest in campaigns has erratically followed a slight upward trend, with a sharp upward spike in the contentious Bush-Kerry campaign in 2004. Clearly, contemporary publics are more interested in politics than earlier generations.

Rational Choice versus Reasonable Choice

In the decades since the first public opinion surveys generated their negative images of the public, we have learned a great deal about how people actually process information and make political (and nonpolitical) decisions. This research has stripped away the idealized standards of classic democratic theory and the rationalizations of elitist democratic theory.

Instead of expecting fully informed, sophisticated *rational choices,* which probably seldom occur for most aspects of our lives, researchers focused on how people make *reasonable choices* when full information is lacking. People make political choices on a regular basis, whether the decisions involve voting in an election, donating funds to a political group, or participating in a political discussion. Few people meet the ideal expectations of democratic theorists in rationally evaluating all the information that might go into such choices, but people are nevertheless making real political choices. Shaun Bowler and Todd Donovan (1998, 30) suggest that this finding leads to a different way to think about the citizens' role: "Voters, to use an analogy, may know very little about the workings of the internal combustion engine, but they do know how to drive. And while we might say that early voting studies focused on voter ignorance of the engine, the newer studies pay more attention to the ability to drive."

Cognitive research has described how people actually make choices in their lives, and this research begins with a different view of political information. There is too much information in the world for people to retain all they experience. *The Economist* recently reported that an average person reads around 10 megabytes (MB) worth of material a day; hears 400 MB a day, and sees 1 MB of information every second! Human memory is limited, and most information—about our lives, our community, politics, and other life experiences—is not retained. So, just as political scientists decry the public's limited knowledge about politics, economists say people need to know more about economics, natural scientists lament our limited knowledge of science, and geographers point to voids in our knowledge of the world.[7] But, to acquire "full information" is a daunting task, especially for political activities, which are often secondary to immediate life concerns.[8] Almost all decisions in life are based on partial information, and so research on human behavior should focus on how people make reasonable choices with incomplete information.

Cognitive research highlights three main methods that citizens may use to make reasonable choices with incomplete information. First, instead of following all issues, people concentrate their attention on a few topics of personal interest. The total electorate is divided into several partially overlapping *issue publics* (Converse 1964). Being part of an issue public implies that people devote prior attention to the issue and have firm beliefs. Farmers may closely monitor government agricultural policy while paying scant attention to urban renewal programs. Parents of school-age children may be interested in education policy. The elderly are interested in Social Security. The largest issue publics generally exist for topics of broad concern, such as economic policy, taxes, and basic social programs. At the other extreme, only a few people regularly follow issues of foreign aid, international trade, or agriculture policy abroad. Very few citizens are interested in every issue, but most citizens are members of at least one issue public. To paraphrase Will Rogers, "Everybody is sophisticated, only on different subjects."

The concept of issue publics influences how we think about political sophistication. When people define politics according to their own interests, a surprising level of political sophistication often appears. David RePass (1971) documented a high level of rational issue voting when citizens identified their own issue interests. Similarly, research demonstrates that members of an issue public are more likely to follow media coverage of their issue, gather information on it, hold stable preferences, and use these preferences as a basis of voting choice (Hutchings 2003; Krosnick 1990; Feldman 1989). Therefore, low issue constraint and stability in public opinion surveys do not mean that the electorate is unsophisticated; the alternative explanation is that not all citizens are interested in and informed about all issues.

Some political scientists view issue publics as a negative feature of politics because a proliferation of issue publics works against policymaking based on a broad, coherent ideological framework. The reason is that policy interests in one area are not judged against interests in other policy areas. Policy fragmentation is potentially problematic, but such criticism may be overstated. If people limit their issue interests, it does not mean that they fail to judge these issues using a broad political framework; different clusters of issue interests still may emanate from a common underlying set of values. In addition, Robert Lane (1973; 1962) pointed out the potential negative consequences of an overly structured belief system—for example, dogmatism and intolerance. In a slightly different context, Robert Dahl (1971) restated the Madisonian principle that the existence of competing political groups, with overlapping and cross-cutting memberships and shifting political alignments, contributes to pluralist democracy. In some instances, therefore, issue publics may benefit the democratic process.

Second, the reasonable choice approach argues that belief systems are structured differently than previously assumed. Instead of viewing belief systems as closely interconnecting a diverse range of political attitudes, as Converse originally proposed, we see a vertical structure (or network) of beliefs within specific political domains, as illustrated in figure 2.3. An individual's basic values are linked to general political orientations; specific issue opinions are derived from one or more of these general orientations (Conover and Feldman 1984). For example, attitudes toward government programs assisting minorities might reflect orientations toward the role of government *and* attitudes toward minorities (Sniderman, Brody, and Tetlock 1991). At the same time, even if opinions on specific issues are strongly linked to broader political orientations, the relationships between specific issue opinions can be weak because issues may not be directly linked together. This model therefore lacks the direct linkage between opinions on different issues that is posited in the *American Voter* model (see figure 2.1).

Furthermore, the specific values and political attitudes included within these structures may vary across individuals. Some voters' beliefs will include

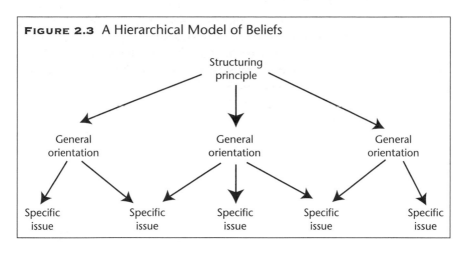

FIGURE 2.3 A Hierarchical Model of Beliefs

only a narrow part of the structure of figure 2.3, such as the issues on the left of the figure. Other voters' structures might include other subsets of issues and general orientations. Thus, this literature often identifies specific cognitive structures that are relevant for subsets of issues, such as foreign policy, racial policies, or candidate evaluations.[9] So, even if citizens are not sophisticated on all political topics, they may have logical and structured beliefs within specific domains that enable them to manage political decision making.

A third aspect of reasonable choice is that people use "shortcuts" or "heuristics" to simplify decision making (Sniderman, Brody and Tetlock 1991; Lupia and McCubbins 1998; Barker and Hansen 2005; Lau and Redlawsk 2006). Samuel Popkin (1991, 218) writes that "the use of information shortcuts is . . . an inescapable fact of life, and will occur no matter how educated we are, how much information we have, and how much thinking we do." The heuristic provides political cues about how people like oneself might view political issues or a party at election time and is a shortcut to collecting and processing information.

People can turn to a wide variety of heuristics or cue-givers. Social groups are one common source of political cues (see chapter 8). Many policy issues involve conflicts between class, religious, ethnic, or other social groupings. One's ties or feelings toward a social group can be a guidepost in dealing with policy questions. French steelworkers might prefer larger social welfare programs because the labor union suggests it will benefit workers like themselves, and they vote for a Leftist party that the union endorses (and which presumably represents the workers' interests). In contrast, a Bavarian Catholic might follow her pastor's advice to support government aid for religious schools and vote for the Christian Social Union candidate. Group references are also a common basis of party evaluation (see table 2.2, p. 27). For many less-educated citizens, group cues may reflect political orientations that they have difficulty explaining in the words that would classify them as sophisticated ideologues. When social conflicts are salient, and the parties take clear positions on these conflicts, then social characteristics can provide people with effective cues for orienting themselves to politics. These individuals may not explain their policy preferences with sophisticated ideological arguments or reference to specific legislative proposals, but overall they still are making reasonable political choices.

Partisanship is an even more powerful heuristic than social-group cues (see chapter 9). Many people develop an enduring attachment to a political party that they feel best represents their views. Parties are central participants in democratic politics, so most political phenomena can be judged within a partisan framework. Because most elections involve a choice between parties, party attachments obviously can simplify voting choices. In Western Europe, where parties act as cohesive units, party voting is an effective and efficient method of decision making. The heterogeneity of American parties lessens the policy value of party voting, but the complexity of American elections makes party a valuable voting cue when one must decide on a long list of federal, state, and local candidates. Partisanship can also shape evaluations of political leaders and new political issues. If voters are unsure about an issue, party cues can suggest where their interests lie. An issue supported by one's party is more likely to benefit oneself, while the policies of the opposition party are suspect. In sum, because of its heuristic value, party identification frequently is viewed as the central thread connecting the citizen and the political process.

Left/Right (or liberal/conservative) orientations are another potential source of political cues. Most people do not express sophisticated ideological views, but they still can locate themselves within a broad ideological family, or *tendance* (Fuchs and Klingemann 1989; Jacoby 1991). A Left/Right orientation provides a framework for evaluating political objects. When someone describes a candidate as too liberal or another as too conservative, he or she is using a shortcut to learning about the candidates' views on specific issues and evaluating them on this basis.

Some people may rely on the media for cues on how to vote. Newspapers list their editorial endorsements before elections and give editorial advice on the issues of the day. Similarly, the endorsements of social groups, political groups, and respected elected officials can be an effective heuristic. If one is an environmentalist, and the Sierra Club endorses an issue, this provides valuable cues about the content of the issue. Other people turn to their family or friends for political advice, or they learn about political choices from coworkers. Indeed, the world is full of political cues that individuals may choose. Experiments by Arthur Lupia and Mathew McCubbins (1998) demonstrate that when individuals gain information from a trusted political source, they can make reasonable choices that reflect their rational self-interest.

Table 2.2 illustrates some of the diverse criteria that people use in making political judgments. People in several nations were asked to describe the good and bad points of two major political parties in their nation. Only a small percentage actively employed ideological concepts in judging the parties. This does not mean, however, that the remaining individuals are devoid of politi-

TABLE 2.2 Bases of Party Evaluations (in percentages)

Criteria based on	United States	Great Britain	West Germany
Ideological concepts	21	21	34
Social groups	40	41	45
Party organizations and competence	49	35	66
Policy concepts	45	46	53
Nature of the times	64	59	86
Political figures	40	18	38
Intrinsic values	46	65	49
No content	14	18	6
Total	319	303	377

SOURCE: Political Action Study, 1974–1975.

NOTE: Totals exceed 100 percent because multiple responses were possible.

cal judgments. About 40 percent of the American, British, and German electorates evaluated the parties according to social-group alignments. Even more people judged the parties by their organization and political competence. Nearly half of the survey responses mentioned policy criteria. Even the broadest and most frequently used criteria—judging parties by the nature of the times—can be a meaningful basis of evaluation. But these data are more than three decades old; we expect new evidence would find that cognitive mobilization is shifting the criteria toward information-based factors. In short, far from suggesting that citizens are uninformed and unsophisticated, these data display a diversity and complexity of public opinion that often is overlooked.

Some researchers remain skeptical of the ability of heuristics to match the standards of "rational" decision making. Michael Delli Carpini and Scott Keeter (1996), for example, note that heuristics can sometimes give incorrect guidance and are subject to elite manipulation (also see Kuklinski and Quirk 2000; Kuklinski and Peyton 2007). In contrast, experiments by Richard Lau and David Redlawsk (2006) and Lupia and McCubbins (1998) are much more positive about the value of heuristics in reaching desired outcomes. So the debate continues. The reasonable choice perspective argues that pretty good choices—not perfect choices—are the foundation of democracy.

The Wisdom of Democratic Choice

Are pretty good choices enough for democracy to be successful? We should be skeptical about setting our democratic expectations too low. Other features of democracy, however, tend to lessen the potential problem of making only reasonable choices.

Although skeptics might cite an individual election result as an example of the failures of mass publics, democracy is an ongoing process. Sometimes electorates do make poor choices or make choices based on what turns out to be mistaken impressions. But all human activity is subject to this imperfection. One of the counterbalancing forces in democracy is that decisions are not permanent. If a politician does not perform, he or she can be voted out at the next election. If parties demonstrate that they are not trustworthy to follow their election promises, their support may fade in future elections. Indeed, experimental research shows that repeated experience playing a game improves the decisions that individuals make (Lupia and McCubbins 1998) and increases the reliance on heuristics (Lau and Redlawsk 2006, 242–244). Democracy succeeds not because it does not make mistakes, but because it is a dynamic system that has the ability to correct mistakes. Some might even say that voters display a greater ability to make such retrospective judgments and change their vote choice than do elected politicians who typically persist in their views.

Perhaps even more important, elections are a *collective decision* of the entire electorate, and we should judge democracy by its collective outcomes rather than the individual choices that make up these outcomes. The collective decisions that come from elections are often better than the individual judgments of any single individual because they cumulate the information and the knowledge of the whole community. Some voters might be biased in one direction, some in the opposite direction; some evaluate one political issue, others use completely different criteria. When cumulated together, however, the total information brought to the collective decision improves the outcome over any single individual, even a fully "rational" individual. James Surowiecki's *The Wisdom of Crowds* (2004) is full of fascinating examples of how collective decisions are better than those of the individuals who contributed to the decision—ranging from guesses about how many jelly beans are in a jar to who should be president. Other studies demonstrate a close fit between the collective preferences of the public and subsequent changes in public policy (Page and Shapiro 1992; Wlezien 2004; Erikson, MacKuen, and Stimson 2002). This aspect of democratic decision making is another explanation for why democracies can be effective even when based on a public in which some members have limited information and engagement.

POLITICS AND THE PUBLIC

We began by asking what democracy expects of its citizens and whether contemporary publics meet these expectations. Classic theorists and democratic elitists set a very high expectation: people should be fully informed in order to make rationally calculated political decisions. Democratic electorates will never meet this expectation, which leads to claims that their shortfall undermines the democratic process.

But democracy has endured for more than two centuries, and a democratization wave has spread across the world since the early 1990s. It therefore makes little sense to argue that democracy requires an ideal that is never met (see Mueller 1999). This conclusion does not mean we have given up on democratic publics by lowering our expectations. Instead, it recognizes that individuals bring their life experiences and knowledge to their political decisions, but in different ways than we initially presumed. Even Thomas Jefferson, who was a sophisticated political thinker, valued the basic abilities of the common citizen:

> State a moral case to a ploughman and a professor. The former will decide it as well and often better than the latter because he has not been led astray by artificial rules.[10]

If Jefferson thought a ploughman could make decisions as well as a professor, then perhaps democracy is not at risk (a good topic to debate with a professor).

Think of this problem in personal terms. When you buy a car or a new flat panel television or make a political decision, you seldom have the full information of an expert in automobiles, electronics, or politics. In addition, even experts will disagree on which is the best car, TV, or candidate. A minority of consumers will follow a rational choice model of conscious and detailed evaluation of the alternatives. They will read *Consumer Reports* and do research as if they were preparing for a bar exam. But most of us will find other means of balancing the costs and benefits of decision making to yield a reasonable choice based on our needs.

How do people make reasonable choices when it comes to politics? This chapter maintains that people can rely on various methods to make their decisions. Many people focus their attention on a few issues of particular interest, rather than devoting equal attention to all issues. The electorate, therefore, is composed of overlapping issue publics, each judging government action on different policies.

The sources of information and the bases of evaluation also vary within the public. Some citizens, but only a minority of them, judge politics by a broad ideological framework. Many more people use political cues, such as social-reference groups or party attachments, to guide their behavior. By limiting their issue interests and relying on decision-making shortcuts, the average voter can balance the costs and benefits of political involvement and still make reasonable political decisions. Perhaps the best description comes from Jon Krosnick (1990, 82), who argues that people are inevitably "cognitive misers" who find shortcuts or heuristics to make "satisficing" political choices, rather than seeking a complete array of relevant information.[11]

Several studies illustrate the diversity of decision-making processes within the public. Paul Sniderman, Richard Brody, and Philip Tetlock (1991), for example, demonstrated that better-educated individuals more often use ideological criteria in making political choices; the less-educated more often use group references or other political cues to make their decisions; in both cases the decisions may broadly reflect the individuals' interests. Similarly, Arthur Lupia's (1994) research on voting on insurance initiatives in California found that a small attentive public was well informed on the initiatives and made choices appropriate for their expressed interests. In addition, many voters used group cues—such as which proposals were supported by Ralph Nader and which by the insurance industry—that also led to rational voting choices. This is pluralistic decision making in practice.

This pluralistic model has several implications for our study of public opinion. We should not interpret unstable or inconsistent issue opinions as evidence that voters lack any attitudes. Survey questions are imprecise; the public's issue interests are specialized; and a complex mix of beliefs may be related to a single issue. In addition, we must be sensitive to the diversity and complexity of mass politics. Simple models of political behavior that assume a homogeneous electorate may be theoretically elegant and empirically parsimonious—yet also unrealistic. Recognizing that people function based on diverse criteria and motivations, we should try to model this diversity, instead of adopting overly generalized theories of citizen politics. Finally, we must not underestimate the potential for change. As this chapter documents, the publics of the four nations examined in this book have fundamentally changed during the postwar period. Public opinion reflects a dynamic process, and we should avoid static views of an unchanging (or unchangeable) public.

On the other hand, we should not be guilty of overestimating the sophistication of the citizenry. At times the public holds ill-advised or ill-informed opinions, and some citizens will remain ignorant of all political matters. Such is the imperfect nature of human behavior. Few individuals deserve the rating of fully sophisticated ideologues. The important lesson is not to ignore or belittle the varied criteria citizens actually use in dealing with politics. Moreover, when voters make a poor decision, or conditions change, they can make new choices at the next election.

The ultimate question, then, is not whether the public meets the maximum ideological standards of classic democratic theory, but whether the public has a sufficient basis for rational political action. Phrased in these terms, and based on the evidence presented in this chapter, we can be optimistic about the political abilities of contemporary publics.

SUGGESTED READINGS

Bishop, George F. *The Illusion of Public Opinion: Fact and Artifact in American Public Opinion Polls.* Lanham, Md.: Rowman and Littlefield, 2004.

Converse, Philip. "The Nature of Belief Systems in Mass Publics." In *Ideology and Discontent,* edited by David Apter. New York: Free Press, 1964.

Delli Carpini, Michael, and Scott Keeter. *What Americans Know about Politics and Why It Matters.* New Haven: Yale University Press, 1996.

Norris, Pippa. *Virtuous Circle: Political Communications in Postindustrial Societies.* Cambridge: Cambridge University Press, 2000.

Popkin, Samuel. *The Reasoning Voter.* 2nd ed. Chicago: University of Chicago Press, 1994.

Prior, Markus. *Post-Broadcast Democracy: How Media Choice Increases Inequality in Political Involvement and Polarizes Elections.* New York: Cambridge University Press, 2007.

Sniderman, Paul, Richard Brody, and Philip Tetlock. *Reasoning and Choice*. New York: Cambridge University Press, 1991.

Surowiecki, James. *The Wisdom of Crowds*. New York: Doubleday, 2004.

NOTES

1. "We Know Bart, but Homer is Greek to Us," *Los Angeles Times*, August 15, 2006, A14.
2. There were, of course, dissenting voices. Walter Bagehot (1978), Joseph Schumpeter (1943), and Walter Lippmann (1922) were highly critical of the average citizen, claiming people fell far short of the theoretical ideal.
3. A candidate in the 2006 Texas gubernatorial election pointed out that the Texas legislature once unanimously passed a motion honoring the Boston strangler; a member sponsored the bill to demonstrate that his colleagues voted on bills without reading them. For other examples of elite inconsistencies, see Arnold (1990).
4. One part of the debate has been methodological, focusing on how sophistication is measured. For a discussion of these points, see Kuklinski and Peyton (2007). Other research has questioned the evidence that elites are more politically tolerant than the general public (Jackman 1972; Sniderman et al. 1991).
5. The differences between the Unites States and Europe are partially a function of different question texts and the response options provided to respondents. The European nations asked about sources of information on the European Union. The question in the United States asked about the use of information sources for news about what is going on in the world today.
6. The British, German, and French questions measure general interest in politics, and the questions differ across nations. The American question asked about interest in campaigns. Because of the differences in question wordings, the absolute levels of political interest should not be compared across nations; for such comparisons, see Jennings and van Deth (1989). For trends in political interest in additional nations, see Dalton and Wattenberg (2000, ch. 3).
7. Critics of the public's level of knowledge often ignore parallel findings among elite groups. For example, Michael Zimmerman (1990, 1991) found that newspaper editors and elected politicians displayed limited knowledge about historical and scientific facts.
8. To the surprise of some political science professors, politics is only one part of people's lives. When the 1999 World Values Survey asked Americans what was very important in their lives, politics came at the end of the list: family (95 percent), friends (64 percent), religion (58 percent), work (54 percent), leisure (43 percent), and politics (16 percent).
9. This literature is quite diverse in its applications (e.g., Hurwitz and Peffley 1987; Peffley and Hurwitz 1985; Sniderman, Brody, and Kuklinski 1984; Miller, Wattenberg, and Malanchuk 1986).
10. Quoted in Surowiecki (2004), p. 267.
11. The public's reliance on various decision-making shortcuts—satisficing behavior—is common to decision makers in business and government (Cyert and March 1963). Nevertheless, democratic elitists denigrate the public when they adopt this model for political choices.

CHAPTER 3

How We Participate

Democracy should be a celebration by an involved public. Citizens should be active because it is through public discussion, deliberation, and involvement that societal goals should be defined and carried out. Without public involvement in the process, democracy loses both its legitimacy and its guiding force. When Germans take the time to cast informed votes, British electors canvass their neighbors, the French protest, or Americans write their president, the democratic process is at work. The global spread of democratization has brought these freedoms to millions of people. The jubilation that accompanied the first democratic elections in Eastern Europe and the expansion of democracy across the globe attests to the value that people place on these freedoms.

In the established democracies, however, observers are now making alarming claims that citizens are becoming apathetic about their democratic rights. The socioeconomic growth and cognitive mobilization in these nations should stimulate political participation. Instead, turnout in elections is trending downward in the United States and many other democracies. Moreover, Robert Putnam (2000) has warned that civic engagement is decreasing to dangerously low levels in America. John Hibbing and Elizabeth Theiss-Morse (2002, 1–2) go a step further and claim, "The last thing people want is to be more involved in political decision making: They do not want to make political decisions themselves; they do not want to provide much input to those who are assigned to make these decisions; and they would rather not know all the details of the decision-making process." (Also see Patterson 2003; Wattenberg 2002.) A recent report by the American Political Science Association sees an ominous problem in these developments:

> American democracy is at risk. The risk comes not from some external threat but from disturbing internal trends: an erosion of the activities and capacities of citizenship. Americans have turned away from politics and the public sphere in large numbers, leaving our civic life impoverished. Citizens participate in public affairs less frequently, with less knowledge and enthusiasm, in fewer venues, and less equally than is healthy for a vibrant democratic polity. (Macedo et al. 2005, 1)

Can the situation really be this bad? Is decreasing participation placing democracy at risk?

A related debate involves the question of how we participate. Some researchers maintain that participation is shifting from elections to new, nonelectoral forms of action (Dalton 2007a; Zukin et al. 2006). Ronald Ingle-

> # Internet Resource
>
> The International Institute for Democracy and Electoral Assistance (IDEA) has data on election turnout around the globe:
>
> http://www.idea.int/vt/index.cfm

hart (1997, 307) says, "One frequently hears references to growing apathy on the part of the public. . . . These allegations of apathy are misleading: mass publics *are* deserting the old-line oligarchical political organizations that mobilized them in the modernization era—but they are becoming more active in a wide range of elite-challenging forms of political action." These new forms of direct action include participation in public interests groups, direct contacting of politicians, and contentious activities.

This chapter studies these questions by looking at political action in its various forms: voting, campaigns, direct contacting, group activities, and protest and other forms of contentious action. Chapter 4 then examines the factors influencing political involvement and how they differ across various forms of action.

MODES OF PARTICIPATION

Democracy means popular rule. So how do you rule? Think for a moment about what you would do if you wanted to influence the government on a policy that was important to you. We often equate political participation with the act of voting. But if you consider political influence from the citizen's perspective, you will see that participation is not limited to voting, nor is voting necessarily the most effective means of affecting public policy. Instead of waiting several years until the next election offers a chance to vote for a candidate who supports your position—if there is such a candidate—you might contact government officials, work with others who share your interests, or find other ways to advocate your cause now. In short, democratic participation can take many forms.

Sidney Verba and his colleagues, Norman Nie, and Jae-on Kim (Verba and Nie 1972; Verba, Nie, and Kim 1978) identified four general types of political action (and we added the last two):

- voting,
- campaign activity,
- contacting officials directly,

- communal activity (working with a group in the community),
- protest and other forms of contentious politics, and
- Internet activism (visiting Web sites, sending e-mails, forwarding e-petitions).

Verba and Nie found that people do not use these activities interchangeably, as analysts once assumed. Instead, people tend to focus on activities that match their motivations and goals. Specific kinds of activities frequently cluster together; and a person who performs one act from a particular cluster is likely to perform other acts from the same cluster but not necessarily activities from another cluster. Verba and Nie labeled these clusters of activities *modes of democratic participation.*

These participation modes place different requirements on participants and differ in the nature of their influence (table 3.1). Verba, Nie, and Kim (1978) classified the modes in terms of several criteria, such as: (1) whether the act conveys information about the individual's political preferences and/or applies pressure for compliance; (2) the potential degree of conflict involved in the activity; (3) the amount of effort required; and (4) the amount of cooperation with others required by the act.

Voting, for example, is a high-pressure activity because it selects government officials, but its policy focus is uncertain because an election involves many issues. Voting also is a reasonably simple act that requires little initiative or cooperation with others. By comparison, campaign activity makes greater demands on a person's time and motivation. Campaign work can also be more policy-focused than the simple act of voting because individuals can choose which candidates to support. Or, an individual may contact the government directly by writing a letter, speaking with a government official, or sending an e-mail. Sometimes contacting is for a particular reason—to have a pothole fixed or request other government services—and other times it can concern broad policy questions. Participation in community groups, or communal activity, may require even more effort by the individual, and it produces a qualitatively different form of citizen input. Citizen groups can control both the methods of action and the policy focus of their activities. Contentious politics, or protest politics, not only expands the repertoire of participation; it also represents a style of action that differs from electoral politics and other forms of activity. Protest can focus on specific issues or policy goals—from protecting whales to challenging the policies of a local government—and can convey a high level of political information with real political force. Internet activism is still developing and can take many forms. It is used to organize and share information with like-minded people, much like communal activity. It is also a form of contacting or even protest. *The point is that the different forms of political participation are not equal:* they involve different groups of individuals and exert different kinds of influence on the political process.

What do Americans say they would do to influence policy? A typical survey question asks what the respondent would do if an unjust or unfair law

TABLE 3.1 Modes of Political Activity and Their Characteristics

Mode of activity	Type of influence	Conflict	Effort required	Cooperation with others
Voting	High pressure/low information	Partisan conflict	Little	Little
Campaign activity	High pressure/low to high information	Partisan conflict	Some	Some or much
Direct contacting	Low pressure/high information	Varies	Very high	Little
Communal activity	Low to high pressure/ high information	Varies	Some or much	Some or much
Protest	High pressure/high information	Very conflictual	Some or much	Some or much

SOURCE: Verba, Nie, and Kim (1978, 55), with modifications.

were being passed by Congress and he or she wanted to do something to stop it (Jennings and van Deth 1989). Nearly four-fifths say that they would contact their representatives directly; more than three-quarters would work with a group of like-minded others to influence the government, and about a sixth mention voting or protest. People try to influence by politics through multiple means.

Cross-national participation studies generally describe modes that are very similar to those Verba and his colleagues found in the United States.[1] This chapter discusses each of these participation modes: their characteristics, the level of activity, and how participation patterns are changing over time.

VOTING

Modern democracies have experienced an almost ever-expanding citizen eligibility to vote in elections. In most democracies, the ability to vote initially was restricted to property owners, often with long residency requirements. The United States was one of the first nations to begin liberalizing suffrage laws; by 1850 virtually the entire white adult male population in the United States was enfranchised. Voting rights expanded more slowly in Western Europe, which lacked the populist tradition of the United States. European social groups were more sharply polarized than in the United States, and European conservatives were hesitant to enfranchise a working class that might vote them out of office. A socialist movement pressed for the political equality of the working class, but mass suffrage often was delayed until war or revolution disrupted the conservative political order. French adult males gained voting rights with the formation of the Third Republic in 1870. Britain limited its election rolls until early in the 1900s through residency and financial restrictions on voting and by allowing multiple votes by business owners and university graduates. (You got two votes if you had a university degree!) Electoral reforms following World War I granted equal voting rights to virtually all British males. In Germany, true democratic elections with universal mass suffrage began with the creation of the Weimar Republic in 1919.

During the twentieth century, governments gradually extended suffrage to the rest of the adult population. Government first acknowledged women's right to vote in Britain (1918), followed by Germany (1919) and the United States (1920). France lagged behind most of Western Europe, enfranchising women only in 1944. The Voting Rights Act of 1965 removed most of the remaining formal restrictions on the voting participation of American blacks. Finally, in the 1970s all four nations lowered the voting age to eighteen.

The right to vote now extends to virtually the entire adult population in the established democracies. There are, however, distinct national differences in the rates of voting. Table 3.2 displays voting turnout rates for twenty-two established democracies from the 1950s to the early 2000s. To compensate for different registration rules across nations, turnout is calculated as a percentage of the eligible voting age public, rather than of registered voters. The

TABLE 3.2 Levels of Turnout from the 1950s to the 2000s (in percentages)

	1950s	1960s	1970s	1980s	1990s	2000s
Australia	83	84	85	83	82	81
Austria	89	90	88	87	77	76
Belgium	88	87	88	89	84	85
Canada	70	72	68	67	60	55
Denmark	78	87	86	85	82	83
Finland	76	85	82	79	70	63
France	71	67	67	64	61	52
Germany (West)	84	83	86	79	74	70
Great Britain	79	74	74	73	72	58
Greece	—	—	83	86	85	86
Iceland	91	89	89	90	87	88
Ireland	74	74	82	76	70	63
Italy	93	94	94	93	90	86
Japan	74	71	72	71	67	65
Netherlands	88	90	85	81	73	77
New Zealand	91	84	83	86	79	75
Norway	78	83	80	83	76	74
Portugal	—	—	87	81	75	72
Spain	—	—	76	76	79	77
Sweden	77	83	87	86	81	76
Switzerland	61	53	61	40	36	37
United States	59	62	54	52	53	53
19-nation average	79	80	80	77	72	69

SOURCE: Institute for Democracy and Electoral Assistance, http://www.idea.int.

NOTE: Turnout figures are based on voting-age public (VAP) in parliamentary elections; for the United States, turnout is for presidential elections. Results for the 2000s are estimates in some cases because VAP turnout is not yet available for all elections. Australia and Belgium have strict enforcement of compulsory voting. Greece, Portugal, and Spain are not included in the 19-nation average.

table shows large cross-national differences in the levels of turnout. In the United States and Switzerland, half of the voting age population (or less) votes in national elections. Voting rates are consistently higher in most European nations, especially in Germany, where typically close to 80 percent of the public casts a ballot in Bundestag elections. Turnout is also relatively high in British House of Commons and French National Assembly elections.

The other significant pattern in table 3.2 is the trend in turnout rates over time. A comparison of the two end points for the nineteen nations with a complete time series shows that seventeen have experienced turnout declines of more than 2 percent (including Britain, France, Germany, and the United States), and two had a turnout increase of more than 2 percent. A closer inspection shows that voting rates peaked in the 1960s and have since declined, especially in the 1990s (Franklin 2004; Wattenberg 2002; Bromley and Curtice 2003). The first elections of the twenty-first century have generated a mixed pattern in specific elections, but a general continuation of the downward trend. Turnout in Britain plummeted from 69 percent of the voting age public in 1997 to 58 percent in 2001 with a slight rebound in 2005 (60 percent). Turnout in the 2004 U.S. elections increased by about 5 percent, but together with the 2000 elections the average is still below the 1950s and 1960s.

Several factors apparently contributed to the decline in voting turnout. Researchers argue that younger generations are disengaged from electoral politics and that lowering the voting age has therefore diminished participation rates (Franklin 2004; Wattenberg 2002). The erosion of both trust in government and attachment to political parties has undoubtedly contributed to these trends as well (see chapter 9 and figure 4.1, p. 60). It is ironic that as the number of voting opportunities has increased in most nations, the average turnout in elections has decreased (Dalton and Gray 2003). Citizens complain about "voter fatigue," even though the opportunities to vote remain quite limited in most nations.

Another set of factors explains cross-national differences in turnout levels. Table 3.2 shows that turnout in the United States is significantly lower than in most other nations, especially since the 1970s. Some analysts cite these statistics as evidence of the American electorate's limited political involvement (and, by implication, limited political abilities). A more complex set of factors—including voter registration systems and other electoral procedures—explain transatlantic differences in turnout. (Wattenberg 2002; Franklin 2004; Blais 2000). Most Europeans are automatically enrolled on the roster of registered voters, which the government updates. In contrast, Americans must take the initiative to register themselves, and many eligible citizens fail to do so.[2] By many estimates, participation in American elections would increase by several percentage points if the United States adopted the European system of registration (Blais 2000). The scheduling of most European elections on weekends also encourages turnout, because more voters can find the time to visit the polls. In addition, most European electoral systems are based on proportional representation rather than on plurality-based single-member districts, as in the United States. Proportional representation stimulates turnout because any party, large or small, can receive representation in the legislature as a direct function of its share of the popular vote. (In plurality systems such as those of the United States and Britain, the margin of victory in a district does not matter.) Some nations, including Australia and Belgium, require that people vote or face government fines. Political competition and sharp ideological cleavages between parties also encourages turnout. When European voters go to the polls, they are deciding whether their country will be run by parties with socialist, green, conservative, ethnic, or even religious programs. These sharp party differences encourage higher voting rates. The number of party choices, the competitiveness of elections, and the structure of legislative power in a system all affect turnout (Powell 1986; Jackman 1987; Franklin 2004).

The United States also differs from most other democracies because citizens vote on a very large number of choices. The typical European voter may have only three or four elections in a four-year period, but many Americans face a dozen or more separate elections over the same time span. Furthermore, Americans face choices for a much wider range of political offices at each election. Only one house of the bicameral national legislature is directly elected in Britain, Germany, and France; the French president is one of the few directly elected European heads of state. Local, regional, and even national elections in Europe normally consist of casting a single ballot for a single office. The extensive list of elected offices and long ballots common to American elections are unknown in West Europe. Finally, Britain, France, and Germany use the referendum and initiative only sparingly.

Instead of counting the total number of people who vote in national elections, an alternative measure of participation is the *amount of electing* being done by the public. When the context of American elections is considered, the amount of electing is actually quite high:

> No country can approach the United States in the frequency and variety of elections, and thus in the amount of electing. No other country elects its lower house as often as every two years, or its president as frequently as every four years. No other country popularly elects its state governors and town mayors, or has as wide a variety of nonrepresentative offices (judges, sheriffs, attorneys general, city treasurers, and so on) subject to election. Only one other country (Switzerland) can compete in the number and variety of local referendums, and only two (Belgium and Turkey) hold party "primaries" in most parts of the country. Even if differences in turnout rates are taken into account, American citizens do not necessarily vote less often than other nationalities; most probably, they do more voting. (Crewe 1981, 262)

A simple comparison of the experiences of a typical European and American voter highlights this difference in the amount of electing: between 2004 and 2008, a resident of Oxford, England, could have voted four times, while a resident of Irvine, California, could have cast about forty votes in 2004 alone.[3]

Turnout rates in national elections are therefore a poor measure of the public's overall political involvement because the structure of institutions and the electoral rules strongly influence turnout. Instead, the simple quantity of voting must be judged by the quality of this activity. Verba, Nie, and Kim (1978, ch. 3) describe voting as a high-pressure activity because government officials are being chosen. Election results, however, can produce only limited information on the public's specific policy preferences because elections involve a diverse range of issues. Did a party win because of a specific policy it advocated or despite its policy position? In addition, if you are dissatisfied with a government policy, you normally must wait years until the next election when you can vote your opinions. Therefore, the infrequent opportunity of most Europeans to cast a single vote for a prepackaged party is a limited tool of political influence. Such influence may increase when elections include a wide range of political offices and include referendums. Still, it is difficult to treat elections as mandates on specific policies because they judge broad programs and not specific policies. Consequently, many people vote because of a sense of civic duty or as an expression of partisan support, rather than as a major means to influence policy.

The limited policy content of voting led some critics to claim that by focusing mass participation on voting alone, parties and political elites are actually trying to limit citizen influence in order to protect their privileged position in the policy process (Piven and Cloward 2000). Even if this skepticism is deserved, voting remains an important aspect of democratic politics, as much for its symbolic value as for its instrumental influence on policy. Voting is one activity that binds the individual to the political system and legitimizes the rest of the democratic process. It is a good way to start participation, but it should not end there. Even so, the decline in voting turnout seems to confirm the claim that participation is waning in contemporary democracies.

CAMPAIGN ACTIVITY

Political campaigns are often described as "retail politics." The campaign gives candidates and their supporters the opportunity to "sell" their programs to the voters. Supporters may go door-to-door to talk to prospective voters and leave campaign materials. They may also contribute to a favorite party or candidate, staff a phone bank, or attend campaign meetings. Sometimes people try to persuade a spouse, friend, or coworker on how they should vote.

Volunteering for a campaign is an extension of electoral participation beyond the act of voting. Fewer people routinely participate in campaigns because this level of activity is more demanding than merely casting a vote. Campaign work requires more initiative, and there is greater need to coordinate participation with others (see table 3.1). Along with the additional effort, however, campaign activity can give a citizen more political influence and convey more policy information than voting. Campaign work is important to parties and candidates, and candidates generally are more sensitive to, and aware of, the policy interests of their activists (Verba and Nie 1972, chs. 17–19).

Campaign activities can take many forms, depending on the context of electioneering in the nation. In the United States, campaigns are now largely media events, and popular involvement in organized campaign activities is modest (see figure 3.1). Few Americans work for a party or candidate, attend party or campaign meetings, or display a campaign button or sticker. (One might note that the top panel of table 3.4, p. 43, shows that U.S. levels of campaign activity are higher than the other nations.)[4] The rates of campaign activities has ebbed and flowed since the 1950s, but without a strong trend. Some studies, however, claim that campaign activity is also steadily eroding (Putnam 2000, ch. 2; Macedo et al. 2005).[5] Today, the most frequent cam-

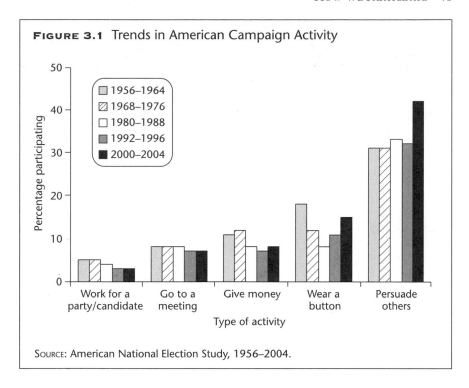

FIGURE 3.1 Trends in American Campaign Activity

Source: American National Election Study, 1956–2004.

paign activities involve individualistic forms of participation: giving money to a campaign, displaying a button, or trying to persuade others how to vote.

British elections differ from American elections in several ways. British elections do not follow a regular time schedule; instead, the prime minister may dissolve Parliament and call for new elections at almost any time during a legislative term. Therefore, elections are often quickly organized, and the campaigns are brief, averaging little more than a month. In addition, British parties depend on a pool of formal party members for much of the campaign work; they attend political rallies, canvass the constituency during the campaign, and contact potential voters on election day (Whiteley and Seyd 2002). Beyond the core of party members, participation in most campaign activities is limited (see table 3.3). The decline in party membership contributes to a general decrease in organized campaign activity over time.

Germany's democratic development after World War II increased citizen involvement in campaigns and most other aspects of politics. Membership in the political parties grew from the 1950s until the 1980s, and participation in campaigns also grew. Eleven percent of the public attended a campaign meeting in the 1961 election; by 1976 this figure had nearly doubled (20 percent). Beginning in the 1970s popular displays of party support also became a visible aspect of campaigns. Since the 1980s, however, campaign participation has dropped off, much as it has in the rest of Europe (Koch, Wasmer, and Schmidt 2001). Formal party membership has also decreased.

TABLE 3.3 Trends in British Campaign Activity (in percentages)

	1964	1966	1970	1974	1979	1983	1987	1997	2001	2005
Canvassed	3	2	1	2	2	2	2	2	—	—
Worked for party or candidate	8	2	2	2	2	2	2	—	3	3
Attended meeting (indoors)	8	7	5	5	4	3	4	4	1	2
Attended meeting (outdoors)	8	3	6	4	2	—	—	7		
Displayed poster	—	—	10	9	8	12	10	9	—	—
Visited a party's Web site	—	—	—	—	—	—	—	—	2	4
Was party member	14	—	10	—	—	7	9	4	4	4
Read electoral address	46	49	53	51	56	49	49	62	69	—

SOURCES: 1964–1974, 1983–1997, British Gallup Poll; 2001–2005, MORI poll; participation data for 1979; and party membership data for all years, British Election Studies.

Still, many Germans are engaged in campaigns, and we have noted that their turnout is much higher than in the United States.[6] In the 2002 Bundestag election, almost a third tried to convince another person how to vote, and a modest number were otherwise involved in the campaign (table 3.4).

Table 3.4 shows that party and campaign activity is generally less extensive in France than in the other three countries. Formal party membership has declined since the 1990s. Attendance at campaign meetings, public displays of party support, and other campaign activities probably have decreased during the past two decades, although the evidence is limited (Boy and Mayer 1993). Participation in the 2002 election was at or above levels of German participation in 2002, but the reason may be that France was voting for a president, not members of parliament, as in Britain and Germany, and a right-wing extremist was in a runoff for the presidency.

Evidence from a larger set of nations suggests that campaign activity is generally decreasing in the established democracies (Dalton and Wattenberg 2000, ch. 3). Fewer people now attend political rallies, work for a party or candidate, or actively participate in election campaigns. The media's expanding electoral role may decrease campaign activity because it lessens the importance of party-organized rallies and canvassing designed to inform the

TABLE 3.4 Participation in Different Modes of Activity (in percentages)

	United States	Great Britain	France	Germany
Active in national campaign				
Tried to persuade others	44	44	28	29
Participated in campaign	30	25	7	7
Contacted by party/candidate	47	26	13	7
Contacting				
Contacted government official in past five years	28	34	12	13
Communal activity				
Worked with others in community in past five years	35	23	20	26
Protesting				
Signed a petition in past year*	35	34	21	35
Boycotted a product in past year*	24	23	29	34
Attended protest in past five years	6	12	24	12
Participated in a demonstration in past year*	6	2	17	6
Internet				
Joined Internet forum*	6	2	4	2

SOURCES: Comparative Study of Electoral Systems for national elections (2004 in United States, 2005 in Great Britain, 2002 in France and Germany). Items marked with an asterisk are from the 2004 the International Social Survey Program.

public. The media's reporting style also encourages the spread of a new type of electioneering. Candidates orchestrate "walkabouts" to generate stories for the evening television news; campaigns focus more attention on candidate personalities; and televised preelection debates are becoming common. Campaigns now devote less time to mass rallies and the in-person contact of past campaigns.

Thus, campaigning seems to provide more evidence of the spreading disengagement of contemporary publics. Because elected officials and party leaders focus on elections (and information on turnout is widely available), it is not surprising that they see decreasing electoral participation as evidence of a general disengagement from politics. Many individuals are still drawn to the excitement and competition of elections, but campaign participation now is more often individualistic, involving activities such as a display of party support or discussing the elections with friends. Meanwhile, the party-organized activities that once marked election campaigns are now less frequent. In short, the *level* of campaign activity may be changing as well as the *nature* of the public's involvement.

DIRECT CONTACTING

Janelly Fourtou is a member of the European Parliament, representing the Liberal Democrats from France. One day she got a package from a public interest group in Austria. The Parliament was debating new copyright and Internet usage laws for Europe, and public and business interest in this legislation was running high. Receiving a package was not unusual because politicians regularly get mail from their constituents. The contents, however, were unusual—the package contained two pig ears, artistically carved from a dead pig and mounted in a frame suitable for display. The ears were part of the Big Brother Award that the Austrian group gave to Fourtou as the "worst" MEP on copyright and intellectual property issues. The pig ears generated press coverage for the interest group and their cause and focused attention on Fourtou's voting record.

One of the most direct ways for people to express support or opposition to new legislation is to e-mail their representatives or write to them, preferably without pig ears enclosed. Or one can go to a city council or school board meeting, talk to a representative in person, or write a letter to the local newspaper. About a fifth of the American public directly contacted government officials in the 1960s. This number almost doubled by the end of the 1980s, and it has increased since then (Verba, Scholzman, and Brady 1995, ch. 3; Dalton 2007a, ch. 4). Moreover, the advent of e-mail has made contacting politicians even easier and made it simpler for political groups to mobilize their supporters to write. Congressional mail statistics show a sharp increase in communications from constituents.

Contacting has also become more common in Britain and in Germany (Pattie, Seyd, and Whiteley 2004, ch. 3; Koch, Wasmer, and Schmidt 2001). The level of contacting now rivals campaign activity (except voting). The second panel of Table 3.4 shows the percentage of the public who had contacted a politician or government official in person or in writing during the previous five years. A full 34 percent of Britons, 28 percent of Americans, 13 percent of Germans, and 12 percent of the French answered affirmatively.

The level of direct contacting is important for several reasons. Contacting can expand the potential influence of the public, perhaps even more than campaign activity. Contacting can occur when, where, and how the citizen thinks it will be most effective—rather than waiting several years for the next election. This high information activity allows citizens to clearly signal their policy preferences. Direct contacting also appears to be increasing in frequency, which contrasts with the decline in electoral participation. Finally, direct contacting requires a significant level of political skill and motivation by the individual, so this implies an engaged citizenry. It is therefore a sign that citizens are still involved in politics, but may be changing how they participate.

COMMUNAL ACTIVITY

The essence of grassroots democracy is communal activity, in which people get together to collectively address their needs. Community activity often involves group efforts to deal with social or community problems, ranging from school issues to improving the roads to protecting the local environment. From the PTA to local neighborhood committees, this is democracy in action. Such autonomous group action defines the civil society that theorists from Jefferson to the present have considered a foundation of democracy. Tocqueville, for example, saw such group activity as a distinctive feature of American democracy:

> The political activity that pervades the United States must be seen to be understood. No sooner do you set foot upon American ground than you are stunned by a kind of tumult; . . . here the people of one quarter of a town are meeting to decide upon the building of a church; there the election of a representative is going on; a little farther, the delegates of a district are hastening to the town in order to consult upon some local improvements; in another place, the laborers of a village quit their plows to deliberate upon a project of a road or a public school. . . . To take a hand in the regulation of society and to discuss it is [the] biggest concern and, so to speak, the only pleasure an American knows. (Tocqueville 1966, 249–250)

This mode is distinct from campaigns because communal participation occurs largely outside of the regularized, institutional setting of elections and lacks a partisan focus. In addition, a relatively high level of political sophistication and initiative is required of communal activists (see table 3.1, p. 35). Citizens define their own issue interests, the methods of influencing policymakers, and the timing of influence. The issue may be as broad as aid to Africa or as narrow as the policies of the local school district—and citizens, not elites, decide. Control over the framework of participation means that communal activities can convey more information and exert more political pressure than the public's restricted participation in campaigns. In short, group activity shifts control of participation to the public and thereby increases their political influence.

Political scientists are intensely debating whether participation in citizen groups is following the same downward spiral as election turnout. In a provocative series of analyses, Robert Putnam (2000) claims that today people are "bowling alone." Tracking the decline of traditional American social and civic associations across the second half of the twentieth century, he finds that participation in groups ranging from the Elks and the PTA to bowling leagues has dropped off markedly since the 1970s. Putnam notes that such groups taught skills and norms that spurred democratic political involvement, and he argues that with the decline of such associations, political involvement has stagnated. He documents a fall off in the number of Americans who attend a public meeting on town or school affairs, who belong to a "better government" group, or who serve on a committee for a local organization. Instead, too many of us are sitting at home in front of our television sets or computer monitors.

Putnam's critics maintain that he is studying the "old" forms of group activity—that contemporary publics are not joining social clubs but participating in self-help groups, neighborhood associations, and issue-oriented organizations such as environmental groups and the women's movement (Skocpol and Fiorina 1999). In fact, Putnam gives examples of these new forms of action when he lists the range of social activities held in one California church:

> [T]he weekly calendar of the Crystal Cathedral . . . included sessions devoted to Women in the Marketplace, Conquering Compulsive Behaviors, Career Builders' Workshop, Stretch and Walk Time for Women, Cancer Conquerors, Positive Christian Singles, Gamblers Anonymous, Women Who Love Too Much, Overeaters Anonymous, and Friday Night Live. (Putnam 2000, 66)

These new forms of social organization are not tapped by membership in the traditional social institutions. In addition, group participation can include the new style of public interest groups, such as environmental advocacy, women's issues, human rights groups, or consumer protection.

The unstructured nature of communal activities makes it difficult to measure participation levels accurately or to compare levels across nations. Still, citizens in all four nations in our study are engaged in communal activities to a significant degree. Group-based participation has long been a distinctive aspect of American political culture, where membership in social groups often exceeds that in other democracies. Sidney Verba, Kay Schlozman, and Henry Brady (1995, 72) found that American participation in community groups grew from 30 percent in 1967 to 34 percent in 1987, and by 2000 participation had increased to 38 percent.[7] The World Values Survey found that American membership in civic associations, environmental groups, women's groups, or peace groups increased from 6 percent in 1980, to 18 percent in 1990, and 33 percent in 1999 (figure 3.2).

European political norms traditionally placed less emphasis on group activities, and the structure of European political systems did not encourage direct citizen contact with government officials. But communal participation has apparently grown in these democracies as well. British participation in social groups and other forms of nonelectoral participation has grown (Curtice and Seyd 2002; Hall 2002), and the World Values Survey finds a general upward trend in civic association membership from 1980 to 1999 (figure 3.2). Communal activity also has increased in Germany (Offe and Fuchs 2002). Voluntary civic associations were an innovation for German politics in the 1970s, but now these groups are a regular aspect of politics. The World Values Survey found that 3 percent of Germans claimed to belong to a civic association or political group in 1980s; this figure bumped up to 12 percent in 1990, and was still 7 percent in 1999. By most accounts, communal activity is more limited in France. Tocqueville, for example, contrasted American

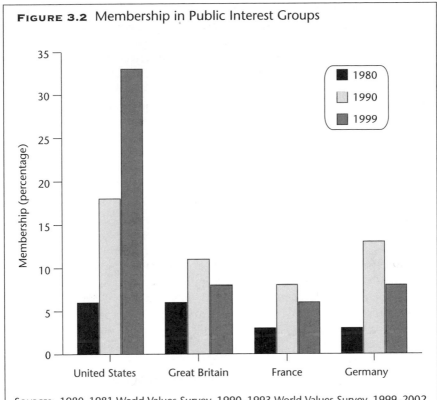

FIGURE 3.2 Membership in Public Interest Groups

SOURCES: 1980–1981 World Values Survey, 1990–1993 World Values Survey, 1999–2002 World Values Survey/European Values Survey.

NOTE: Figure entries are the percentages who belong to a civic association, environmental group, women's group, or peace group in each nation.

social cooperation with the individualism of the French political culture. But even in France the World Values Survey tracks an increase in civic group membership over time.

The third panel in table 3.4 compares the level of community activity across nations. Working together on community issues can obviously take a variety of forms—from working with the PTA to a local environmental group—but this is the nature of communal activity. Collective action is highest in the United States, where 35 percent participated in community activities; 20 percent to 26 percent of the three European publics had worked with others. In fact, communal activity is generally more common than working on an election campaign.

Putnam has identified important changes in the American political process, but I am not convinced that his findings mean that political involvement of all sorts is declining, or that the patterns he described for the United States apply to other democracies. Especially within the three European nations we examine, participation in social and civic groups has increased, introducing more direct citizen involvement in the political process. (Furthermore, many of the factors that Putnam uses to explain the American trends have also occurred in Europe, but apparently without the same effects; see Putnam 2002.) Even if Americans are less likely to participate in electoral politics, engagement in informal groups, social movements, and community initiatives has grown (Dalton 2007a, ch. 4). In summary, communal political involvement reinforces the view that political participation is continuing in contemporary democracies.

PROTEST AND CONTENTIOUS ACTION

Historically, protest and contentious actions arose from feelings of frustration and deprivation. Concentrated among the socially disadvantaged, repressed minorities, or groups alienated from the established political order, protest was an outlet for those who lacked access through conventional channels. A graphic illustration of this form of protest was the democratic revolution that spread through Eastern Europe, East Asia, South Africa, and other democratizing nations in the late 1980s and early 1990s. Immigrant rights protests in the United States and France in recent years are another example of where discontent leads to collective action. When citizens are blocked from exercising political influence through legitimate participation channels, protest is another option.

The nature of protest is, however, changing in advanced industrial democracies. Protest has broadened from the disadvantaged to include a wider spectrum of society: gray Panthers protest for senior citizen rights; consumers actively monitor industry; environmentalists call attention to ecological problems. And citizen groups of all types are proliferating. In the past, protests often challenged the basic legitimacy of political institutions. The new forms of protest in advanced industrial democracies are seldom directed at overthrowing the established political order; after all, the affluent and well-educated participants are some of the primary beneficiaries of this order. Instead, reformism has replaced revolutionary fervor. Modern protest is typically a planned and organized activity in which political groups consciously orchestrate their activities to occur when the timing will most benefit their cause. For many individuals and groups, protest has become simply another political resource for mobilizing public opinion and influencing policymakers. Protest was once considered distinct from conventional forms of democratic political participation, but it now appears to be an extension of conventional participation by other means.

Table 3.5 describes the levels of protest activity across nations. The column on the left ranks nations according to the percentage who have signed a petition—a modest and common form of protest, and, by democratic standards, a conventional part of politics. The column on the right ranks nations by public involvement in any of four more challenging types of protest: at-

TABLE 3.5 Cross-National Levels of Protest Activity (in percentages)

Signed a petition		Participated in a challenging act	
New Zealand	91	Greece	55
Sweden	87	Sweden	48
United States	**81**	Denmark	46
Great Britain	**79**	**France**	**43**
Australia	78	Netherlands	40
Canada	73	Belgium	39
France	**68**	Italy	37
Belgium	68	**United States**	**36**
Norway	65	Norway	34
Switzerland	64	**Germany**	**30**
Japan	63	Australia	30
Ireland	60	Canada	30
Netherlands	59	Spain	29
Denmark	57	New Zealand	28
Austria	57	**Great Britain**	**25**
Italy	53	Ireland	25
Germany	**51**	Finland	22
Finland	50	Switzerland	22
Greece	50	Austria	21
Spain	28	Portugal	17
Portugal	22	Japan	14

SOURCE: 1999–2002 European Values Survey/World Values Survey.

NOTE: Entries in the second column are the percentages who have engaged in at least one of the following challenging acts: a lawful demonstration, a boycott, an unofficial strike, or occupying a building.

tending a lawful demonstration, joining in boycotts, participating in unofficial strikes, or occupying buildings.

The act of signing a petition is routine for a large share of the public in most established democracies. The petition has a long and venerable heritage in British and American politics, and political groups of every orientation use it. One can hardly enter a Wal-Mart in the United States or a Marks & Spencer in Britain without being asked to sign a petition. Most Americans (81 percent) and Britons (79 percent) have signed a petition, and this form of action is commonplace in most other nations as well.

A more telling test of the public's willingness to transcend conventional political bounds is participation in the four challenging acts represented in the right-hand column of table 3.5. The French engage in relatively high levels of protest activity, exceeded by only a few other established democracies. More than two-fifths of the French have participated in at least one of the four protest activities. This finding verifies our earlier description of the French as avoiding conventional politics and relishing protest. William Kornhauser (1959) argued that the very weakness of social groups and conventional participation channels in France encourages support for protest.

Indeed, the French do not rank so highly in the signing of petitions, a political activity that requires face-to-face contact. To this personal aloofness is added a cultural tradition that enshrines France's revolutionary history. In just the single year following the 1999 French survey, truckers opposed to fuel increases blockaded gas stations, citizens demonstrated in support of a sheep farmer who had ransacked a McDonalds restaurant, bus and subway workers disrupted transportation systems in a dispute over shorter workweeks, scientists staged mass resignations in opposition to cuts in government funding, farmers protested the potential introduction of genetically modified crops, non-Christian religious groups demanded greater tolerance of minorities, and prostitutes demonstrated before government offices against unfair competition from immigrants. French protest knows few social bounds.

Most other nations display a modest level of protest, involving 20 percent to 30 percent of the public in at least one of these activities. Many western Germans have participated in one of these activities, as protest is an accepted form of action by groups ranging from neighborhood associations to advocates for the environment. Protest lags behind in the former East Germany, where people are still learning their roles as democratic citizens. Mediterranean and Scandinavian nations are at the top of this ranking, while the Japanese show a marked aversion to protest activities. It is notable that Britain and the United States rank lower in challenging activities than in signing petitions. We return to this point below.

One caveat: protest activity in table 3.5 appears very common because the question asked whether the respondent had "ever done" the activity. By comparison, the fourth panel in table 3.4 presents contentious actions over specific time periods. Still, nearly a third of these publics said they had signed a petition in the last year, and a significant minority had attended a protest or demonstration. The increase in contentious politics is greater if we expand the definition of protest to include political consumerism: buying or boycotting a product for a political reason. This form of protest is often missing from earlier participation studies (Stolle et al. 2005). The International Social Survey found that roughly a quarter of American, British, and French respondents said they had boycotted a product for political reasons in the previous twelve months, and this number rises to a third among Germans (table 3.4). Other studies find that *buy*cotting—purchasing a product for political reasons—is even more common.

Thus, most people in established democracies participate in some form of contentious action, if only by signing a petition. Participation in stronger forms of protest—such as participating in a lawful demonstration or joining a boycott—actually rivals the levels of campaign activity.

Still, some researchers claim that protest participation is declining in the United States along with other forms of action. Certainly the media seem to find protest less newsworthy than a decade or two ago. But because the use of protest politics has spread within society, the overall level of protest has generally risen. Table 3.6 tracks the development of protest activity over time

TABLE 3.6 Protest Participation over Time (in percentages)

	United States					Great Britain					France				West Germany				
	1975	1981	1990	1999	2007	1974	1981	1990	1999	2006	1981	1990	1999	2006	1974	1981	1990	1999	2006
Signed a petition	58	61	70	81	62	22	63	75	81	66	44	51	68	67	30	46	55	47	49
Participated in lawful demonstrations	11	12	15	21	17	6	10	13	13	16	26	31	39	44	9	14	25	22	30
Joined in boycott	14	14	17	25	22	5	7	14	17	16	11	11	13	16	4	7	9	10	9
Participated in unofficial strike	2	3	4	6	—	5	7	8	9	—	10	9	12	—	1	2	2	2	—
Occupied building	2	2	2	4	—	1	2	2	2	—	7	7	9	—	*	1	1	1	—
Damaged property	1	1	—	—	—	1	2	—	—	—	1	1	—	—	*	1	—	—	—
Engaged in personal violence	1	2	—	—	—	*	1	—	—	—	1	1	—	—	*	1	—	—	—

SOURCES: 1974–1975 Political Action Study; 1981–1983, 1990–1993, 1999–2002 World Values Surveys; 1999–2002 European Values Survey; 2006–2008 World Values Survey.

NOTE: Table entries are the percentages who say they have done the activity. An asterisk denotes less than 1 percent; a dash indicates that the question was not asked in this study.

for our four core nations. Because the surveys start with 1974, they do not show the initial growth of protest activity that occurred during the 1960s. It is still clear that protest grew in most established democracies over the last quarter of the twentieth century (Inglehart 1997, ch. 8; Norris 2002, ch. 10). If we use participation in lawful demonstrations as one example, in the thirty plus years since the first survey, this activity increased by 6 percent in the United States, 10 percent in Britain, 18 percent in France, and 21 percent in Germany. Although the rate of increase has slowed in recent years, this form of protest is still higher than other forms of political action.

The growth of contentious actions probably reflects a general increase in small demonstrations over schools, neighborhood issues, and other specific concerns, rather than a just few large-scale movements (such as antiwar protests or immigrant rights protests). In addition, the creation of citizen lobbies, environmental groups, consumer advocacy groups, and other NGOs provides an institutional basis for organizing protests. These new opposition groups may be permanently changing the style of citizen politics. Protest is becoming a common political activity, and the era of protest politics is not passing.

These time trends may also explain why the United States ranks relatively low in recent cross-national comparisons (see table 3.5) despite its reputation for a high level of protest activity. Americans exhibited high levels of protest in the first systematic cross-national studies done in the 1970s (Barnes, Kaase, et al. 1979), and participation has gradually increased since that time. But protest has grown even more rapidly in Great Britain, France, Germany, and other established democracies. Americans' participation in demonstrations grew by the smallest margin of any nation. By 2006 participation in lawful demonstrations in France and Germany exceeded those in the United States. American participation has not declined, but protest has grown at a faster rate in other democracies and is overtaking U.S. activity levels.

Although we have generally spoken about protest in positive terms, the dark side of protest occurs when people engage in violent behavior. Abortion clinic bombings, the 2006 riots and car burnings in Paris suburbs, and the violent activities of terrorists in America and Europe are fundamentally different from protest behavior and go far beyond the tolerable bounds of politics. The early surveys in Table 3.5 show that although protest is widely accepted, the number participating in violent activities is minimal. In 1981, for example, 44 percent of the French public had signed a petition and 26 percent had participated in a lawful demonstration, but only 1 percent had damaged property or engaged in personal violence. Democratic citizens want to protest the actions of their government, not destroy it.

WIRED ACTIVISM

The Internet has created a new way for people to carry on traditional political activities: to connect with others, to gather and share information, and to attempt to influence the political process (Bimber 2003; Bimber and Davis 2003). E-mails are now the most common and rapidly growing form of communications from constituents to members of the U.S. Congress. Web sites were unheard of in the 1992 campaign, but today they are a standard and expanding feature of electoral politics. A wide range of political groups, parties, and interest groups use the Internet to disseminate information. A 2005 survey found that 17 percent of Americans had visited a political Web site in the previous year to find political information.[8] The blogosphere is a still newer source of political information and commentary that potentially empowers individuals as rivals to the established media. The Internet can also be a source of political activism that occurs electronically. The same 2005 survey finds that 13 percent of Americans had forwarded a political e-mail to friends, and other studies indicate that significant numbers have signed e-petitions. Some governments are even experimenting with Internet voting (Alvarez and Hall 2004).

In addition, the Internet is creating political opportunities that had not previously existed. MoveOn.org became an important tool during the 2004 Democratic primaries. Howard Dean used this Web site to connect like-minded individuals who shared an interest in his candidacy, were willing to contribute to his campaign via the Internet, and attend local in-person meetings. MoveOn.org now boasts more than 3 million members and a long list of other political efforts organized through the Web site. The Internet is becoming an important method of political communication and mobilization. The networking potential of the Internet is illustrated on the Facebook.com Web site, where young adults communicate and can link themselves to affinity groups that reflect their values as a way to meet other like-minded individuals. In fall 2006 the top ten advocacy groups on Facebook included nearly half a million members.[9]

The 2004 International Social Survey Program found that Internet activism in joining a political forum was most common among Americans (6 percent), and this activity is now spreading to other established democracies (see table 3.4). Broader measures of Internet activism (including circulating e-petitions and forwarding e-mails) suggest that these activities match or exceed the percentage who had donated money to any political group, worked for a party or candidate, or protested over the same time period. The numbers are still modest, and the uses are still growing, but the Internet is adding to the tools of political activism, especially among the young.

CHANGING PUBLICS AND POLITICAL PARTICIPATION

We began our analysis of political participation with a paradox: the rising levels of education, increased media consumption, and the other aspects of social modernization we described in chapter 1 should increase political participation. Despite these trends, turnout in elections, and possibly campaign activity, has declined in almost all advanced industrial democracies. Richard

Brody (1978) referred to this situation as "the puzzle of political participation." Why is electoral participation decreasing, if the public's political skills and resources are increasing? Several scholars view the decline in participation as an ominous sign for the vitality of democracy.

This is a paradox with many possible explanations. Steven Rosenstone and John Hansen (1993) suggested that declining turnout in the United States is due to political organizations' weakening ability to mobilize individuals into action. In most established democracies, the political parties are now less active in bringing individuals to the polls and getting the public involved in campaigns. Growing social isolation and the decline of community are other explanations (Putnam 2000; Teixeira 1992, ch. 2). Although these arguments carry some weight, they are partially circular in their logic: people are less active in partisan politics because fewer people (and organizations) are mobilizing them to be involved. Moreover, if electoral activity is generally decreasing across nations, this observation leads us to ask why political organizations are generally less engaging.

To understand the trends in participation we must recognize the full impact of social modernization and other social and technological developments on contemporary politics. Greater political sophistication does not necessarily imply a growth in all forms of political activism; instead, rising sophistication levels may change the *nature* of participation. For example, elites and political organizations traditionally can mobilize even disinterested citizens to cast a ballot. High turnout levels often reflect the efforts and skills of political groups to get out the vote rather than the public's concern about the election. Moreover, citizen input through voting is limited by the institutionalized structure of elections, which narrows (and blurs) the choice of policy options and limits the frequency of public input. A French environmental group bluntly stated its disdain for elections with a slogan borrowed from the May Revolts of 1968: *Élections—piège à cons* (Elections—trap for idiots). When citizens can cast only a handful of votes over a four- or five-year period, as in most European democracies, the ballot box is not a channel for active policy engagement. A sophisticated and cognitively mobilized public places less dependence on voting and campaign activity as the primary means of influencing the government.

The public's growing political skills, resources, and cognitive mobilization have increased participation in activities that are citizen-initiated, less constrained, more policy-oriented, and directly linked to government. The self-mobilized individual favors referendums over elections and communal activity over campaign work. Participation in citizen lobbies, single-issue groups, and citizen-action movements is rising in nearly all advanced industrial democracies. Issue-based contacting of political elites has significantly increased among Americans and most European publics. New forms of political consumerism are further expanding the boundaries of political action. Indeed, the range of different activities in table 3.4 is impressive evidence of the diversity of contemporary political activism, and even this list is incomplete (see Zukin et al. 2006). Some scholars have missed this pattern because they focused their attention on electoral participation instead of the full range of possible political activities. Instead of disengagement, *more people are now involved in more forms of political action.*

A second lesson is that our findings should bring an end to the myth of Americans' disengagement from politics. Voting turnout is lower in the United States, and all European nations have higher voting rates than Americans. This is a truism we all recognize. But Americans are highly active in campaigns, contacting, communal activity, and contentious politics. Europeans frequently vote in national elections, but they generally participate less in nonelectoral forms of political action. If we look beyond the electoral arena, we see that America remains a participatory society.

In summary, contemporary democracies are experiencing changes in the style of political action, not just changes in the level of participation. The new style of citizen politics seeks to place more control over political activity in the hands of the citizenry. These nonelectoral forms of participation make greater demands on the participants, and, at the same time, increase public pressure on political elites. Citizen participation is becoming linked to citizen influence.

SUGGESTED READINGS

Blais, André. *To Vote or Not to Vote? The Merits and Limits of Rational Choice Theory.* Pittsburgh: University of Pittsburgh Press, 2000.

Norris, Pippa. *Democratic Phoenix: Reinventing Political Activism.* Cambridge: Cambridge University Press, 2002.

Pattie, Charles, Patrick Seyd, and Paul Whiteley. *Citizenship in Britain: Values, Participation and Democracy.* New York: Cambridge University Press, 2004.

Putnam, Robert. *Bowling Alone: The Collapse and Renewal of American Community.* New York: Simon and Schuster, 2000.

———. *Democracies in Flux: The Evolution of Social Capital in Contemporary Society.* Oxford: Oxford University Press, 2002.

Wattenberg, Martin. *Where Have All the Voters Gone?* Cambridge: Harvard University Press, 2002.

———. *Is Voting for Young People?* New York: Longman, 2006.

Zukin, Cliff, et al. *A New Engagement? Political Participation, Civic Life, and the Changing American Citizen.* New York: Oxford University Press, 2006.

NOTES

1. Geraint Parry, George Moyser, and Neil Day (1992) show that contentious participation forms another mode of British participation; Charles Pattie, Patrick Seyd, and Paul Whiteley (2004) found three dimensions of individual actions: consumerism, contributing, and elections; contacting; and protest. Jan Teorell, Mariano Torcal, and José Ramon Montero (2007) identified five modes in their recent study of participation in Europe. Also see William Claggett and Philip Pollack (2006).

2. Michael McDonald and Samuel Popkin (2001) show that a growing percentage of noneligible adults (noncitizens or those with criminal records) has artificially lowered estimates of U.S. voting rates. This gap has also increased over time. Turnout in 2004, for example, was about 5 percent higher if these noneligibles are excluded.

3. The British voting opportunities included local council and county elections, the 2005 House of Commons election, and the 2004 European Parliament election. The American voter's opportunities included primary and general elections: three votes in the primary for federal offices and two for state offices (these five offices were filled in the general election), three votes for the junior college school district, two for the local school district board, three for city government, one for the water district, and nineteen initiatives and referendums.

4. The highly polarized nature of the 2004 presidential election in the United States increased involvement in this campaign, but even the 2000 U.S. election would rank relatively high compared to electoral participation in European nations. This reflects the decentralized structure of American elections, and the long list of candidates and campaign issues that appear on the ballot, each of which may mobilize supporters. In 1997, for example, the U.S. Census Bureau estimated that there were more than 500,000 elected officials in the United States, each of whom called on friends, neighbors, and donors to support their candidacy at election time (and the same for the losing candidates). In contrast, we estimate that there are only about 25,000 elected officials in Britain.

5. These researchers use Roper and other commercial polls in the United States, which show general declines in participation. Because the academic surveys of political participation have better sampling and interviewing methods, we emphasize the findings from these surveys (Dalton 2007a, ch. 4).

6. Comparisons between eastern and western Germany suggest that easterners lag a bit behind on measures of party and campaign involvement, but display comparable levels of political interest and discussion (Dalton 2007b; van Deth 2001).

7. Information on the 2000 Social Capital Survey is available at http://www.cfsv.org/communitysurvey/index.html.

8. The Center for Democracy and the Third Sector at Georgetown University conducted the "Citizenship, Involvement, Democracy Survey," http://www8.georgetown.edu/centers/cdacs/cid.

9. The top ten groups reflect a mix of youthful ambitions, aspirations, and contradictions: (1) Reduce the drinking age to 18!; (2) legalize same-sex marriages; (3) Americans for alternative energy; (4) support a woman's right to choose; (5) support stem cell research; (6) abolish abstinence-only sex education; (7) government + religion = disaster; (8) AIDS/HIV research; (9) pro-life; and (10) equal rights for gays (downloaded November 1, 2006).

CHAPTER 4

Who Participates?

Political participants come in many shapes and sizes. Virginia R. has been a poll worker in Lawrence, Kansas, at every U.S. election since 1952 (except for the 2006 primary that she missed while having triple bypass heart surgery). Alex W. is a sixteen-year-old living in Northern California. She is too young to vote, but she switched shampoos over animal testing, will not buy clothes produced by child labor, and yells at people who litter. Klaus R. is a long-term member of the German Christian Democrats and has staffed the party's election booth in his hometown square. Sophie C. is twenty-one, a film student, and she marched with thousands of other French students in 2006 to protest a new labor law on youth employment.

The question of who participates in politics is as important as the question of how many people participate. First, if participation influences policy results, then the pattern of who participates determines which citizens are communicating with policymakers and which interests are not being represented. Second, the characteristics of participants partially define the meaning of political activism. Are people who are dissatisfied with the status quo more active in politics or do they withdraw from politics? Whether the dissatisfied or satisfied participate more casts a different light on how we interpret participation. Finally, comparing the correlates of action across nations and modes shows how the political process in each nation shapes citizen choices on how to participate.

THE CIVIC VOLUNTARISM MODEL

Is it rational to be politically active? According to rational choice theorists, the decision to participate is irrational in most cases (Downs 1957). Political participation takes time and resources. For example, voting requires not just the time to cast the ballot but also the time to follow the campaign and make one's voting choices. But then, our single vote is diluted by the votes of thousands or millions of others. Rational actor theory would suggest that we should all stay home, because participation takes more effort than the likely impact of our individual effort. In addition, even if participation does have an effect, people could be "free riders" and reap the benefits of cleaner air, safer highways, or better schools by relying on the efforts of others who are active. Fortunately, most citizens look beyond narrow self-interested calculations and participate because of their desire to be active and influence the policies that affect their lives. Political participation is a social and psychological decision as much as a rational actor calculation.

Internet Resource

Visit the Initiative & Referendum Institute for information on the use of referendums in the United States and other democracies:

http://www.iandrinstitute.org

Sidney Verba, Kay Schlozman, and Henry Brady (1995) summarized previous social-psychological theories of why people participate in terms of the "civic voluntarism model." In their logic, *people participate because they can, they want to, or someone asked them.* This means that three main factors influence the decision to participate:

- the personal resources used to participate,
- political attitudes that encourage participation, and
- connections to groups or people who ask one to participate.

Under the first heading, political scientists maintain that social status (e.g., education and income) provides the resources that facilitate political action. Higher-status individuals, especially the better educated, are more likely to have the time, the money, the access to political information, and the ability to become politically involved. So widespread is this notion that social status is sometimes described as the "standard model" of political participation (Verba and Nie 1972, ch. 8).

We can add a few other personal characteristics to this list. Participation patterns also vary by age. For many young people, politics is a remote world compared to the immediate issues of school, dating, and beginning a career. As individuals age, however, they take on social and economic responsibilities that increase their motivation to follow politics: they become taxpayers and homeowners; their own children enter public schools; and eventually they may draw benefits from government programs. Different generational experiences also affect participation, and political engagement typically increases with age (Campbell 2006; Dalton 2007a). In addition, men are often more politically active than women (Norris 2002; Schlozman, Burns, and Verba 1994). Differences in political resources, such as education level, income, and employment patterns, explain a large part of this gender gap. In addition, society traditionally socialized women to be less politically engaged, but gender may be changing as predictor of participation.

A second set of potential predictors includes attitudes and policy preferences that motivate people to participate. Beliefs about the citizen's role and the nature of political action may influence participation patterns (Dalton 2007a, ch. 4; Pattie, Seyd, and Whiteley 2004). People often vote because they believe this is a duty of citizenship, even if their vote is intermixed with millions of others. A sense of political efficacy—the feeling that one's actions can affect the political process—also may stimulate participation. Conversely, political cynicism may lead to political apathy and withdrawal: if one cannot affect the political process, why bother to try? Researchers also debate the causal role of political dissatisfaction. On the one hand, policy satisfaction may increase support for the political process and encourage political participation. On the other hand, dissatisfaction may stimulate activity to change public policy. Although scholars disagree on the causal direction of policy dissatisfaction, they agree that it is an important factor to consider.

Partisanship or ideology also may influence participation patterns. Do Democrats participate as much as Republicans, or do they participate in different ways? Do members of the British Conservative Party participate as much as Labourites? If participation influences policymakers and the government, then whether activists are drawn equally across political camps has important implications for the representativeness of the democratic process. Political participation that is heavily concentrated among ideological extremists may distort the policy process.

The third set of potential predictors is group-based forces. Some group influences may be psychological, such as attachment to one's preferred political party. Because campaigns and elections are largely partisan contests, party attachments can stimulate individuals into action. A sense of party identification motivates people to vote or participate in campaigns as a display of party support. Conversely, people with weak or nonexistent party bonds are less concerned with election results and are less likely to participate.

Participation in social groups can also increase political action (Verba, Schlozman, and Brady 1995; Putnam 2000; Armingeon 2007; Gray and Caul 2000). Experience in a social club or volunteer organization develops skills and orientations that carry over to politics, and certain groups actively encourage their members to be politically active. Even running the bingo game or bake sale at church teaches skills that can be applied to political activism. Social groups also provide a useful touchstone for judging whether participation is a worthwhile activity (Uhlaner 1989). Therefore, participation in nonpolitical groups may stimulate political involvement.

WHO VOTES?

Voting is the most common political activity, and so we begin by considering which factors influence who is likely to vote. We also use the example of voting to introduce some of the variables in the civic voluntarism model. Because resources provide the "standard model" of participation, we begin with this category. Education is a personal resource that is strongly related to turnout. The better educated are typically more likely to vote because they have a stronger sense of civic duty and possess the resources to follow political campaigns and to be politically active. Figure 4.1 displays the levels of turnout as a function of education in our four core nations.

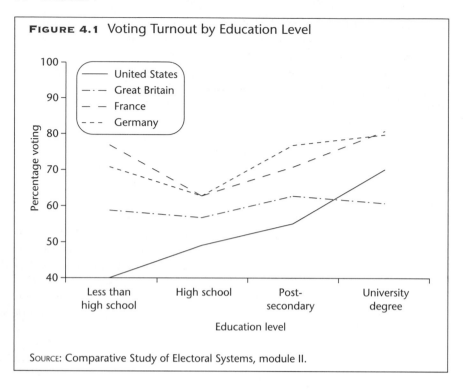

FIGURE 4.1   Voting Turnout by Education Level

SOURCE: Comparative Study of Electoral Systems, module II.

In all four democracies the trend is toward higher turnout among the better educated.[1] Education-based differences in turnout are more pronounced among Americans than Europeans because the complexity of the U.S. registration and electoral system means that educational skills and resources make voting easier. The impact of education is weaker in European nations, often because Labour/Social Democratic Parties target less-educated working class voters, which may explain the uptick in turnout among the least-educated group in Germany and France. In addition, the hurdles to voting are lower in these European democracies because of the registration system and the nature of elections (see chapter 3).

Age also affects voting rates. As a starting point, we expect greater political involvement as people age, assume family and career responsibilities, and become integrated into their communities. This is generally known as the "life cycle model" of participation (Verba and Nie 1972). Several scholars, however, claim that the decreasing electoral engagement among the young continues as they age and produces a downward generational shift in electoral participation (Wattenberg 2006; Franklin 2004; Putnam 2000). William Damon (2001, 123) is pessimistic about youth in contemporary democracies: "Young people across the world have been disengaging from civic and political activities to a degree unimaginable a mere generation ago. The lack of interest is greatest in mature democracies, but it is evident even in many emerg-

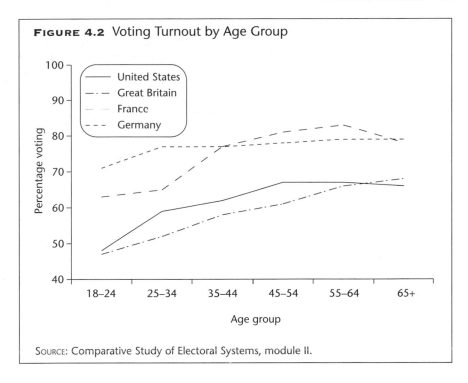

FIGURE 4.2 Voting Turnout by Age Group

Legend:
— United States
—·— Great Britain
— — France
- - - Germany

Y-axis: Percentage voting (40, 50, 60, 70, 80, 90, 100)
X-axis: Age group (18–24, 25–34, 35–44, 45–54, 55–64, 65+)

SOURCE: Comparative Study of Electoral Systems, module II.

ing or troubled ones. Today there are no leaders, no causes, no legacy of past trials or accomplishments that inspire much more than apathy or cynicism from the young." Frankly, I am skeptical of this blanket indictment of the young. Although it is clear that young people vote less often than in the past, we might withhold a final judgment until we compare voting with participation in other types of activity.

Figure 4.2 describes the levels of turnout by age in our four nations and shows that turnout increases significantly with age. Indeed, researchers find that the age gap in turnout has widened (Wattenberg 2006; Franklin 2004). Less than half of Americans under age twenty-four voted in the 2004 election, but turnout averaged more than two-thirds among those over age forty-five. The three European electorates show a similar age gradient. If elections influence politics, then the differential turnout by age has significant implications. As one example, if American youth—with their greater preference for the Democratic Party—had voted at rates equal to their elders in the 2000 and 2004 elections, the Democratic presidential candidate would have won both elections. In addition, when older citizens vote, their participation makes politicians more sensitive to their needs and less responsive to the issue interests of young people who are less likely to vote. In short, who votes makes a difference in electoral outcomes and the content of politics.

We have separately described education and age patterns in turnout, but these variables are only two in the civic voluntarism model. We could examine each factor by itself, but many of them are interrelated. For example, education levels are related to political norms and social group activity, and age groups systematically differ in their education levels and presumably in their norms and values.

Therefore, to determine the separate influence of each variable and the explanatory power of the civic voluntarism model, we combined six different variables into a statistical analysis predicting political participation:

- education;
- age;
- gender;
- political efficacy;
- Left/Right attitudes;
- political party attachments; and
- membership in union or business group.

The first three variables tap the resources and social characteristics described by the model. The next two—political efficacy and Left/Right position—represent the attitudinal elements of the model. The last two variables—party attachments and group membership—indicate possible group influences on participation.

Figure 4.3 shows the influence of each predictor on the decision to vote; this methodology is described in appendix A.[2] The coefficients from the statistical analysis show the importance of each variable, while controlling for the other variables. For example, do gender differences still appear after controlling for educational and attitudinal differences between men and women? The heavier the arrow in the figure, the stronger the influence of the variable.

As we have just seen, education is strongly related to turnout. In all three European nations, the better educated are more likely to vote. Differences in education level are more pronounced in the United States (coefficient $\beta = .13$) because of the complexity of the registration and electoral systems.

Our second category of predictors is political motivations. Feelings of political efficacy exert a modest impact in each nation. Those who feel that voting can influence politics are more likely to participate, and the differences in turnout between Left and Right voters are negligible. In this most common of political activities, the ideological bias in participation is minimal because both sides mobilize their supporters to vote, which is how it should be.

The third category of causes is group effects. Because elections are partisan contests, those who identify strongly with a party are more likely to show up at the polls (and presumably cast a ballot for their own party). The strength of partisan ties therefore should be a significant predictor of turnout. Partisans are like sports fans, and those who feel a strong identity with the team are most likely to show up on game day (see chapter 9). Another organizational influence, group membership, shows a weak influence on turnout, perhaps because the question in the survey is too blunt.[3]

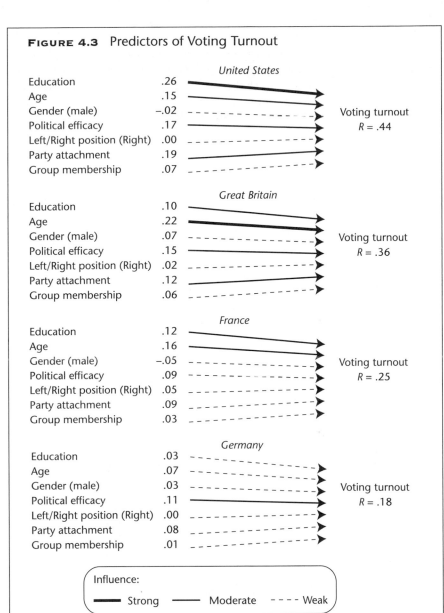

FIGURE 4.3 Predictors of Voting Turnout

United States

Education	.26
Age	.15
Gender (male)	−.02
Political efficacy	.17
Left/Right position (Right)	.00
Party attachment	.19
Group membership	.07

Voting turnout
R = .44

Great Britain

Education	.10
Age	.22
Gender (male)	.07
Political efficacy	.15
Left/Right position (Right)	.02
Party attachment	.12
Group membership	.06

Voting turnout
R = .36

France

Education	.12
Age	.16
Gender (male)	−.05
Political efficacy	.09
Left/Right position (Right)	.05
Party attachment	.09
Group membership	.03

Voting turnout
R = .25

Germany

Education	.03
Age	.07
Gender (male)	.03
Political efficacy	.11
Left/Right position (Right)	.00
Party attachment	.08
Group membership	.01

Voting turnout
R = .18

Influence: ▬▬ Strong ——— Moderate - - - - Weak

SOURCES: Comparative Study of Electoral Systems, module II.

NOTE: Figure entries are standardized coefficients from multiple regression analyses. See endnote 2 for a description of how to interpret regression coeffients.

CAMPAIGN ACTIVITY

Because the characteristics of campaign activity differ from the simple act of voting, we expect that the types of people who participate in campaign activity also differ. As discussed in chapter 3, campaign activity requires greater individual initiative and is a more partisan activity than voting. The patterns of campaign activity should reflect these differences.

We combined two measures of campaign activism into a single index.[4] Then we used our standard set of predictors to explain campaign activism. Table 4.1 presents statistical analyses similar to those in figure 4.3, but in tabular form. Because campaign work is an intensely partisan activity, partisan ties exert an even stronger force on this mode than on voting turnout. Most of the partisanship coefficients in table 4.1 are more than double their effects for vote turnout. These differences are quite large: 72 percent of strong partisans in the United States did at least one campaign activity in 2004, compared to only 31 percent of nonpartisans.

Older citizens tend to be more involved in campaigns, even while holding constant the other variables in the model. These differences are smaller than for voting and in the United States were actually reversed in 2004. And surprisingly, education differences are smaller than for voting turnout, even though campaign activity is a more demanding form of action.

Is there a gender gap? For both voting and campaign activity, gender differences in participation are small. For campaign activity, women show a sys-

TABLE 4.1 Predictors of Campaign Activity

Predictors	United States	Great Britain	France	Germany
Resources				
Education	.09	.06	−.02	.09
Age	−.11*	.08	.00	.10*
Gender (male)	.02	.10	.07	.13*
Motivations				
Political efficacy	.11*	.10*	.09	.11*
Left/Right position (Right)	−.05	−.01	−.08	.01
Group factors				
Party attachment	.27*	.34*	.18*	.24*
Group membership	.07	.04	.10*	.09
R	.37	.44	.29	.37

SOURCE: Comparative Study of Electoral Systems, module II.

NOTE: Table entries are standardized coefficients from multiple regression analyses. Statistically significant effects ($p < .05$) are denoted by an asterisk. See endnote 2 and appendix A, the statistical primer, for a description of how to interpret regression coefficients.

tematic tendency to be more active once other factors are controlled. These small differences are actually a positive sign: changing gender norms are reducing the differences in participation between men and women.

Finally, political efficacy is consistently related to campaign activism. People who feel their input makes a difference are more likely to become active in a campaign. And, because both sides actively mobilize their supporters, the ideological differences in who participates in campaigns are small and unsystematic.

DIRECT CONTACTING

Direct contact is the most diverse form of political action, because it can range from the taxpayer writing city hall about garbage collection to calling the office of a member of Congress to protest federal policy. It can be done as an individual or as a collective effort of individuals working together. In all of these instances, contacting requires substantial individual initiative and significant political skills to identify the appropriate government official and cogently state one's case.

Consequently, resources are important for contacting (table 4.2). Education has some of its strongest effects in predicting contacting. The coefficient for the United States, for example, is the strongest across all the different types of activity we compare (β = .26). Contacting is also more common

TABLE 4.2 Predictors of Direct Contacting

Predictors	United States	Great Britain	France	Germany
Resources				
Education	.26*	.12*	.07*	.15*
Age	.14*	.16*	.08	.06
Gender (male)	.05	.00	.12*	.07
Motivations				
Political efficacy	.06	.03	.03	.02
Left/Right position (Right)	−.03	−.04	.05	.00
Group factors				
Party attachment	.10*	.14*	.07	.16*
Group membership	.02	.09*	.10*	.11*
R	.33	.28	.22	.28

SOURCE: Comparative Study of Electoral Systems, module II.

NOTE: Table entries are standardized coefficients from multiple regression analyses. Statistically significant effects (p < .05) are denoted by an asterisk. See endnote 2 and appendix A, the statistical primer, for a description of how to interpret regression coefficients.

among older citizens, presumably because they have greater needs and more experience in working with government.

As we move away from electoral politics, however, the impact of partisanship weakens. Partisans are politically engaged and therefore more likely to contact politicians, but these effects are weaker than for voting or campaign activity.

Because social groups can organize contacting—through chain letters, e-mail campaigns, or newsletters encouraging members to act—there are modest group influences on contacting—an illustration of Verba, Schlozman, and Brady's dictum that people often participate because they have been asked.

COMMUNAL ACTIVITY

Chapter 3 demonstrated that participation in citizen groups is a central part of democratic politics in America and is growing in importance in European democracies. This is Tocqueville's politics of citizens getting together to address common problems. But when these groups assemble, who is in the room?

Group activity often requires considerable initiative and sophistication from the participant. Table 4.3 shows that the better educated are significantly more likely to participate in communal activities in three of the four nations.

Equally interesting is a nonrelationship in the table. Although the young are systematically less involved in voting, we find no systematic age pattern in communal activity. In fact, in the United States the young are slightly more active once one controls for the other possible predictors. Young people may not be engaged in electoral politics, but they find ways to participate through other venues, such as group activity.

Working with a group is distinct from voting and campaign activity because communal participation is generally not a partisan activity. Participants may be drawn to group efforts precisely because they are distinct from party politics. Table 4.3 shows that partisanship has less impact on communal participation than on voting or campaign activities. Social group membership helps to mobilize individuals to participate in collective efforts, and this variable has its strongest effect for communal activity.

WHO PROTESTS?

Why do citizens protest? If you have attended a protest, why did you go? Every protester has an individual explanation for his or her action. A commitment to an issue stimulates some people to act. General opposition to the government leads other protestors into action. Still others are caught up in the excitement and sense of comradeship that protests produce, or they simply accompany a friend who invites them to come. Social scientists have tried to systematize these individual motivations to explain the general sources of protest activity.

TABLE 4.3 Predictors of Communal Activity

Predictors	United States	Great Britain	France	Germany
Resources				
Education	.16*	.10*	−.02	.05
Age	−.04	.02	−.01	.05
Gender (male)	−.05	.02	.09*	.06
Motivations				
Political efficacy	.01	.04	.10	.04
Left/Right position (Right)	.01	−.05	−.15	−.01
Group factors				
Party attachment	.09*	.17*	.08	.14*
Group membership	.04	.14*	.15*	.12*
R	.21	.29	.29	.25

SOURCE: Comparative Study of Electoral Systems, module II.

NOTE: Table entries are standardized coefficients from multiple regression analyses. Statistically significant effects ($p < .05$) are denoted by an asterisk. See endnote 2 and appendix A, the statistical primer, for a description of how to interpret regression coefficients.

In contrast to other forms of political participation, protest is often described as an "unconventional" form of action that can be stimulated by feelings of frustration and political alienation. Political analysts from Aristotle to Marx have seen personal dissatisfaction and the striving for better conditions as the root cause of protests and political violence. Modern social scientists have echoed and quantified these themes. The seminal study is the work of Ted Robert Gurr, who said, "The primary causal sequence in political violence is first the development of discontent, second the politicization of discontent, and finally its actualization in violent political action against political objects and actors" (1970, 12–13). This view implies that political dissatisfaction should predict protest activity. Indirectly, the theory suggests that protest should be more common among lower-status individuals, minorities, and other groups who feel deprived or dissatisfied.

In contrast, other researchers argue that protest in contemporary democracies has become an extension of conventional politics by other means (Norris 2002; Inglehart 1990). Protest is another political tactic (like voting, campaign activity, or communal activity) that individuals may use in pursuing their goals (see chapter 3). From this perspective, certain elements of the civic voluntarism model may also apply to protest. The civic voluntarism model implies that protest should be higher among the better educated and politically sophisticated—those who have the political skills and resources to engage in these activities. This idea is opposite to the deprivation explanation. Involvement in social groups may also provide resources and experiences that

TABLE 4.4 Predictors of Protest Activity

Predictors	United States	Great Britain	France	Germany
Resources				
Education	.14*	.08	.03	.14*
Age	−.05	−.06	−.16*	−.08
Gender (male)	−.03	.00	.04	.00
Motivations				
Dissatisfied with government performance	.08	.08	.16*	.11*
Political efficacy	.03	.02	.05	.04
Left/Right position (Right)	−.10*	−.17*	−.20*	−.13*
Group factors				
Party attachment	.05	.12*	.11*	.11*
Group membership	.11*	.15*	.04	.05
R	.26	.28	.37	.28

SOURCE: Comparative Study of Electoral Systems, module II.

NOTE: Table entries are standardized coefficients from multiple regression analyses. Statistically significant effects ($p < .05$) are denoted by an asterisk. See endnote 2 and appendix A, the statistical primer, for a description of how to interpret regression coefficients.

encourage contentious activities such as signing a petition, protesting, or joining a boycott. Research routinely shows that the young are more likely to protest; and protest more often involves men, although this pattern may be changing with a narrowing of gender roles.

Often seen as a tool for liberals who want to challenge the political establishment, protest has broadened across the political spectrum and may no longer be the primary domain of the Left. Feelings of political efficacy may also encourage protest activity. And last, if protest is becoming a planned, organized activity, social groups and their members may be more active protesters.

Consequently, we used the six predictors of participation from the other models in this chapter and added a question on satisfaction with government performance to test the dissatisfaction thesis. Table 4.4 presents these analyses of the correlates of protest activity.[5]

Dissatisfaction with the government encourages protest in all four nations, but the effects are modest in the United States and negligible in France and Germany.[6] Furthermore, the pattern of other predictors undercuts the dissatisfaction explanation. For example, the willingness to protest is more common among the better educated, even though less-educated and lower-income citizens are generally more dissatisfied. We also find a consistent, albeit weak, tendency for protest to be more common among those who feel efficacious about politics.

In short, protest is not simply an outlet for the alienated and deprived; often, it is just the opposite. Protest more often follows the expectations from the civic voluntarism model. Protesters are people who have the ability to organize and participate in political activities of all forms, including protest. The clearest evidence of this finding is the tendency in all four nations for the better educated to engage in protest.

In one important area, the correlates of protest differ from conventional electoral activity. Voting and campaign participation routinely increase with age, as family and social responsibilities heighten the relevance of politics. In contrast, protest is the domain of the young. In the United States, 11 percent of those under age twenty-five reported participation in a protest in the previous five years, compared to only 3 percent among those over age sixty-five.

Political scientists differ in their interpretations of this age relationship. On the one hand, the pattern may reflect life-cycle differences in protest. Youth is a period of enthusiasm and rebellion, which may encourage participation in protests and other such activities. Young people also may have more opportunities to protest because of their free time and concentration in university settings. This explanation would predict that an individual's protest activity should decline with age. On the other hand, these differences may represent a generational pattern of changing participation styles. That is, today's young people protest, not because of their youth, but because their generation has adopted a new style of action. Higher levels of education and political sophistication and the changing citizenship norms of younger generations produce support for direct-action techniques. If this assertion is true, age differences in protest represent a generational change in participation patterns. Moreover, protest is but one example of a general pattern of greater use of contentious politics, direct action, and new styles of internet activism among the young (Dalton 2007a, ch. 4; Zukin et al. 2006).

Although groups on the Left and Right both use protest, the willingness to engage in these activities is more common among Leftists. These effects are stronger than the ideological biases in conventional forms of political action, and they are consistent even though two nations—Great Britain and Germany—were headed by leftist governments at the time of the surveys. Protest politics is still disproportionately the domain of the Left.

INTERNET ACTIVISM

The Internet offers a new means of political access and activity that can span many of the distinct modes of participation (see chapter 3). Individuals can contact government officials or the media through e-mail. They can forward Internet petitions and use the Internet to support unconventional forms of action. In addition, the Internet has special potential in bringing together like-minded individuals in a community, or in a virtual community.

The 2005 Citizens, Involvement, and Democracy survey asked about three types of Internet activism that we described in chapter 3: visiting political

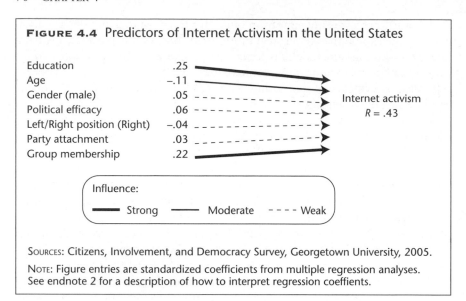

FIGURE 4.4 Predictors of Internet Activism in the United States

Education	.25
Age	–.11
Gender (male)	.05
Political efficacy	.06
Left/Right position (Right)	–.04
Party attachment	.03
Group membership	.22

Internet activism
R = .43

Influence:
———— Strong ——— Moderate - - - - Weak

SOURCES: Citizens, Involvement, and Democracy Survey, Georgetown University, 2005.

NOTE: Figure entries are standardized coefficients from multiple regression analyses. See endnote 2 for a description of how to interpret regression coeffients.

Web sites, forwarding political e-mails, or participating in political activities over the Internet.[7] A fifth of the American public had done at least one of these activities in the previous year.

What results should we expect from a survey of Internet activism? Figure 4.4 shows that—no surprise—Internet activism is more common among the young than older people. In addition, there are strong signs that Internet activism builds on the general civic voluntarism model. The strongest predictor of wired activism is higher levels of education, and those who belong to more social groups are also more likely to use the Internet as a political tool. Similarly, those who believe that politicians care what they think are more likely to participate in Internet-based political activity. These results are only from the United States, but I suspect similar patterns would appear in other established democracies. The Internet seems to broaden the repertoire of political action for the young, but it also provides an additional form of action for those who are already likely to participate.

COMPARING THE CORRELATES OF DIFFERENT ACTIVITIES

At the beginning of this chapter, we stated that who participates does matter because it shows which parts of society are expressing their political views and therefore what interests are influencing public policymaking. In addition, who votes (and does not vote) in elections can affect the outcome.

We also pointed out the concern over the political engagement—or disengagement—of the young. Many well-respected political scientists argue that the young are dropping out of politics and that democracy is at risk as a result (Macedo et al. 2005; Wattenberg 2006; Franklin 2004). Robert Putnam

(2000), for example, holds that the slow, steady, and ineluctable replacement of older civic generations by Generations X and Y is a central reason for the erosion of social engagement in America. An even stronger statement comes from a 2006 study of civic life in America: "Each year, the grim reaper steals away one of the most civic slices of America—the last members of the 'Greatest Generation.' This is a cold generational calculus that we cannot reverse until younger Americans become as engaged as their grandparents" (National Conference on Citizenship 2006, 8). What a cold-hearted description of American youth! But is it accurate?

The broader view of political participation in this chapter suggests that these indictments of the young are overstated. Young people in Western democracies are not dropping out of politics; rather, they are changing their style of action. Their participation in electoral politics is declining, but age groups participate almost equally in communal activities, and the young are more active in direct action methods such as protest, political consumerism, voluntarism, and Internet activism (Dalton 2007a; Wuthrow 2002). Cliff Zukin and his colleagues recently examined the full repertoire of political action among the young, and they also rejected the general claim of youth disengagement: "First and foremost, simple claims that today's youth . . . are apathetic and disengaged from civic life are simply wrong (Zukin et al. 2006, 189). In summary, it is too simple to claim that the young are systematically less politically active—they are active, but not in the same ways as their parents or grandparents. Moreover, we would expect the activism of today's youth to further increase through the life cycle and perhaps change in form.

Our analyses also show the importance of individual resources in spurring political activity. The growing complexity and technical nature of contemporary issues require that citizens are sophisticated enough to cope with the world of politics. Participation in virtually all forms of action is higher among the better educated. An unexpected consequence of the changing patterns of political activism may be an increase in the participation gap between lower-status and higher-status individuals. Working class parties may mobilize the less educated to vote, but it is harder to mobilize these same individuals to write a letter to their representative or participate in other forms of action. Democracies may be experiencing a growing social-status bias in citizen participation and influence, which runs counter to democratic ideals (see, e.g., Hall 2002). The solution to this inequality problem is to find means to raise the participation levels of lower-status groups, not to limit the activity of the better educated. Political leaders must facilitate participation by a broader spectrum of the public and lower the remaining barriers to participation.

Disparities in education levels are often greater in the United States than in the other nations. Educational disparities in U.S. electoral turnout ($\beta = .26$) are far greater than in Britain ($\beta = .10$), France ($\beta = .12$), or Germany ($\beta = .03$). The same pattern occurs for other forms of political action. Too large a gap in participation rates between social strata means that certain groups in America are not participating in the democratic process. This gap is smaller in most European democracies. The weakness of labor unions and the absences of a working-class party to mobilize participation, when coupled with the restrictive registration requirements of the American electoral system, creates a serious participation gap between social groups in the United States. The size of the participation gap shows the need to find a way to equalize the involvement of all social groups in American politics.

Political attitudes also systematically vary in their influence. Political efficacy is important in motivating electoral participation, but seems less important for other forms of political action. For protest, both Leftist attitudes and dissatisfaction with government spur participation—but protest is more common among those with the resources to be active. Left/Right ideology has minimal impact on other forms of action, including Internet-based activism.

Finally, group ties are an important influence on participation. Feelings of party attachments are most important for electoral participation, but this is where partisans can come out to support "their team." Partisan effects are significant, but weaker, for contacting and communal activity. In addition, group membership generally encourages all forms of political action, especially communal activity where the focus of participation is through a group. The characteristics of each mode of action are apparent in the factors that shape who participates.

PARTICIPATION AND CONTEMPORARY DEMOCRACIES

Several scholars argue that citizen involvement in society and politics is waning, and that this trend has serious and dangerous consequences for democracy (Putnam 2000; Macedo et al. 2005; Wolfe 2006). The evidence presented in chapters 3 and 4 questions this conclusion. Overall, political involvement is not generally decreasing in advanced industrial societies. Instead, *the forms of political action are changing.* The old forms of political participation—voting, party work, and campaign activity—are in decline, while participation in citizen-initiated and policy-oriented forms of activity is rising. This trend is even more apparent if we add new forms of action to the mix, such as political consumerism and Internet activism. In the United States the total amount of political activity may have grown by as much as a third since the benchmarks surveys in the late 1960s.

Increases in nonelectoral activities are especially significant because they place greater control over the locus and focus of participation in the hands of the citizenry. Political input is not limited to the issues and institutionalized channels determined by elites; instead, a single individual, or a group of citizens, can organize around a specific issue and select the timing and method of influencing policymakers. These direct-action techniques also are high-information and high-pressure activities. They therefore serve some of the participation demands of an increasingly educated and politically sophisticated public, far more so than voting and campaign activities (Cain, Dalton, and Scarrow 2003, ch. 12).

A major goal of democratic societies is to expand citizen participation in the political process and thereby increase popular control of government. Therefore, increases in communal participation, protest, and other citizen-initiated activities should be generally welcomed. This changing pattern of political action is an important element of the new style of citizen politics in advanced industrial democracies. At the same time, it presents new challenges to contemporary democracies, such as the growing social status bias in who is politically active.

In addition, the new forms of political action such as contacting and even citizen interest groups tend to be more individualistic, replacing the collective actions of election and party work (Pattie, Seyd, and Whiteley 2004). Atomistic participation may decrease attention to the collective needs of society and make it more difficult to balance individual interests and societal interests. Many individuals (and groups) will participate to maximize their own specific interests while downplaying their collective responsibilities. The solution is to construct new methods of aggregating political interests to balance the expansion of interest articulation that has already occurred.

Direct-action methods pose another challenge to contemporary democracies. By their very nature, direct-action techniques disrupt the status quo. These activities occasionally challenge the established institutions and procedures of contemporary democracies. The potential for disruption has led some critics to ask whether rapidly expanding citizen participation, especially in protest activities, is placing too many demands on political systems (Zakaria 2003; Huntington 1981). Policy cannot be made in the streets, they argue. Efficient and effective policymaking requires a deliberative process, where government officials have some latitude in their decisions. A politicized public with intense policy-focused minorities lobbying for their special interests would strain the political consensus that is a requisite of democratic politics. Indeed, just as citizen demands for influence are rising, a survey of Washington political elites suggests that those who make and implement policy doubt the abilities of the American public.[8]

Some writers therefore argue that it is possible to have too much of a good thing—political participation. Some even cite the evidence accompanying the elitist theory of democracy as a basis for this position (see chapter 2). Citizen activism must be balanced against the needs for government efficiency and rational policy planning, they contend, and the expansion of participation in recent years may have upset this balance, leading to problems of governability in Western democracies. These arguments were commonplace in the 1980s, and I believe that even after the democratization wave of the 1990s, there are still too many who would limit the rights of others.

Those who caution about an excess of participation display a disregard for the democratic goals they profess to defend; they seem to have more in common with the former regimes of Eastern Europe than with real democratic principles. The associate editor of *The Economist* noted the irony of worrying about the excesses of democracy as we simultaneously celebrated the fall of communism:

> The democracies must therefore apply to themselves the argument they used to direct against the communists. As people get richer and better educated, a democrat would admonishingly tell a communist, they will no longer be willing to let a handful of men in the Politburo take all the decisions that govern a country's life. The same must now be said, with adjustment for scale, about the workings of democracy. As the old differences of wealth, education and social condition blur, it will be increasingly hard to go on persuading people that most of them are fit only to put a tick on a ballot paper every few years, and that the handful of men and women they thereby send to parliament must be left to take all the other decisions. (Beedham 1993, 6)

Contemporary calls for direct citizen action are not antidemocratic behavior. Typically, they are attempts by ordinary citizens to pressure the political system to become more democratic and responsive to public opinion. Furthermore, very few people subscribe to the extreme forms of violent political action that might actually threaten a democratic system.

I favor a Jeffersonian view of the democratic process. The logic of democratic politics is that expanding political involvement also can expand citizens' understanding of the political process. Citizens learn about the responsibilities of governing and the choices facing society by becoming involved—and that makes them better citizens. And research shows that participation increases the public's knowledge about politics (Parry, Moyser, and Day 1992: ch. 13; Pierce et al. 1992). In the long run, involving the public can make better citizens and better politics.

Ironically, active citizens also may become more critical of politicians and the political process (Parry, Moyser, and Day 1992, ch. 13). The educational aspects of participation can lead to further challenges to the political status quo. But one hopes that a responsive political system could build positive experiences with the democratic process and make progress by addressing the demands of a critical public.

Contemporary democracies clearly face important challenges, and their future depends on the nature of the response. That response should not be to push back the clock in an attempt to re-create images of politics in a bygone age—a politics that probably never existed. Democracies must adapt to survive, ideally by maximizing the advantages of greater citizen participation while minimizing the disadvantages. The experience of the past several years suggests that we are following this course. Institutions are changing to encourage citizen access (Cain, Dalton, and Scarrow 2003), and politicians and bureaucrats are becoming more comfortable with an expanded form of democracy. Democracy is most threatened when we fail to take the democratic creed literally and deal creatively with the challenges posed by the new style of citizen politics.

SUGGESTED READINGS

Burns, Nancy, Kay L. Schlozman, and Sidney Verba. *The Private Roots of Public Action*, Cambridge: Harvard University Press, 2001.

Cain, Bruce, Russell Dalton, and Susan Scarrow, eds. *Democracy Transformed? Expanding Political Access in Advanced Industrial Democracies*. Oxford: Oxford University Press, 2003.

Conway, M. Margaret. *Political Participation in the United States*. 3rd ed. Washington, D.C.: CQ Press, 2000.

Dalton, Russell. *The Good Citizen: How Young People Are Reshaping American Politics*. Washington, D.C.: CQ Press, 2007.

van Deth, Jan, José Ramón Montero, and Anders Westholm, eds. *Citizenship and Involvement in European Democracies: A Comparative Analysis*. London: Routledge, 2007.

Verba, Sidney, and Norman Nie. *Participation in America*. New York: Harper and Row, 1972.

Verba, Sidney, Kay Schlozman, and Henry Brady. *Voice and Equality: Civic Voluntarism in American Politics*. Cambridge: Harvard University Press, 1995.

Zukin, Cliff, et al. *A New Engagement? Political Participation, Civic Life, and the Changing American Citizen*. New York: Oxford University Press, 2006.

NOTES

1. Surveys typically overestimate the percentage of the public that votes. Part of the reason is self-selection among those who agree to be interviewed, and part is that some nonvoters claim to have voted. Therefore, we weighted the turnout percentages so the aggregate total in the survey matches the reported turnout among the voting age population in the election. Figures 4.1 and 4.2 are based on these weighted statistics.

2. Appendix A is a statistical primer that provides a guide for interpreting regression results and other statistics in this book. The results in Figure 4.1 are from multiple regression analyses; the entries are standardized regression coefficients (β). The (β) coefficients measure the impact of each variable, while statistically controlling for the effects of the other variables in the model. We interpret coefficients of .10 or less as a weak relationship, .10–.20 as a modest relationship, and .20 or larger as a strong relationship.

   We use the Comparative Study of Electoral Systems to estimate the factors influencing voting in each nation (and other modes of participation later in this chapter). The CSES includes the 2004 U.S. elections, the 2005 British elections, the 2002 German elections, and the 2002 French presidential elections.

3. The Comparative Study of Electoral Systems asked about membership in unions, business association, farmer associations, and professional association. It did not include other forms of group activity, and it did not assess whether respondents were passive or active members.

4. Campaign activity combines whether the respondent worked for a party/candidate in the campaign and whether they tried to persuade others how to vote.

5. The survey asked whether the respondent had participated in the activity in the past five years.

6. We used the question of whether the respondent was satisfied with the government's performance on the most important issue facing the nation. We find essentially the same results if we use satisfaction with the working of the democratic process.

7. This survey conducted in-person interviews with a random sample of Americans in 2005. The three Internet-related items are discussed in greater detail in chapter 3. Figure 4.4 attempts to replicate the analyses of other participation modes with as similar questions as are available in the U.S. Citizenship, Involvement, Democracy survey. The largest difference is that the index of group membership includes potential membership in almost two dozen different types of social groups, which is likely to increase the weight of this variable in comparison to the Comparative Study of Electoral Systems result. The survey and other reports are available from the project Web site: http://www.uscidsurvey.org.

8. The Pew Research Center (1998b) surveyed members of Congress, top presidential appointees, and members of the Senior Executive Service to find out how leaders view the public. Among members of Congress, just 31 percent think Americans know enough about issues to make wise decisions about public policy. Even fewer presidential appointees (13 percent) and senior civil servants (14 percent) feel this way.

PART TWO

POLITICAL ORIENTATIONS

CHAPTER 5

Values in Change

I n October 2006 the Eurobarometer survey of the European Union asked citizens in the twenty-five member states what values were most important to them. This is a profound question because it asks people to identify the values that presumably shape the essence of their lives, their attitudes, and behaviors. You might think for a minute about what you would say. Our values tell us what is important to us and society. They provide the reference standard for making our decisions. We structure our lives and make our choices based on what we value, whether it is a career, a marriage partner, or something as trivial as a movie on Saturday night.

Politics often involves human values. When they answered the Eurobarometer survey, Europeans listed peace, respect for human life, and human rights as the most important values to them personally. Values identify what people feel are—or should be—the goals of society and the political system. Shared values help define the norms of a political and social system, while the clash between alternative values creates a basis for political competition over which values should shape public policy. Should welfare programs stress economic efficiency or empathy for the families in need? Should attitudes toward stem-cell research reflect moral views about when life begins or concern for those suffering from disease? In a real sense, politics regularly involves conflicts over values.

The new style of citizen politics occurs in part because a growing number of people are changing their basic political values. Compared to a generation ago, contemporary societies display strong evidence of changing social norms: hierarchical relationships and deference to authority are giving way to decentralization, self-expression, and a desire to participate in the decisions affecting one's life. We have already described how participatory norms are stimulating greater political involvement, but the consequences of value change are much broader. The new values affect attitudes toward work, lifestyles, and the individual's role in society.

The definition of societal goals and the meaning of "success" are also changing. Until recently, many Americans and Europeans measured success almost solely in economic terms: a large house, two cars in the garage, and other signs of affluence. The late Malcolm Forbes once said that life was a contest, and the winner was the person who accumulated the most possessions before he or she died. In other industrial democracies, the threshold for economic success might have been lower, but material concerns were equally important.

Internet Resource

Visit the World Values Survey Web site for information on this global survey of values:

http://www.worldvaluessurvey.org

Once affluence became widespread, however, many people realized that bigger is not necessarily better. The desire for economic growth is now tempered by a concern for improving the quality of life. A new interest in protecting the environment has spread throughout advanced industrial societies. Instead of just income, careers are measured by the feeling of accomplishment and the freedom they offer. Social relations and acceptance of diversity are additional examples of values in change. Progress on racial, sexual, and religious equalities are transforming American and European societies.

Evidence of value change is all around us, if we but look. We think in the present, however, and so the magnitude of these changes is not always appreciated. One can get a sense of these changes by comparing contemporary American lifestyles to the images of American life depicted on vintage television reruns from the 1950s and 1960s. TV series such as *Leave It to Beaver, Ozzie and Harriet,* and *Father Knows Best* reflect the values of a bygone era. How well would the Cleavers or the Nelsons adjust to a world transformed by gender equality, the new sexual morality, racial desegregation, rap music, and alternative lifestyles? Imagine June Cleaver hanging out with the *Desperate Housewives.*

This chapter first examines the evidence that values are systematically changing in advanced industrial societies and then turns to the implications of value change for democratic politics.

THE NATURE OF VALUE CHANGE

Citizen values provide the standards that guide their attitudes and behaviors. Some people may place a high priority on freedom, equality, and social harmony and favor policies that strengthen these values. Others may stress independence, social recognition, and ambition in guiding their actions.

Many personal and political decisions involve making choices between valued goals that lie on opposite sides of a given situation. One situation may create a choice between independence and obedience or between polite evasiveness and blunt sincerity. A national policy may present conflicts between the goals of world peace and national security or between economic growth and protecting nature.

People develop a general framework for making these decisions by arranging values in terms of their importance to themselves. Citizen behavior may appear inconsistent and illogical (see chapter 2) unless we consider the values of each person and how they apply these values in specific situations. To one citizen, the issue of immigration reform taps values of social equality and human rights; to another, it concerns obeying the law and protecting his or her livelihood. Both perspectives are reasonable, and attitudes toward immigration are determined by how people weigh these conflicting values.

Value systems should include the salient goals that guide human behavior. Milton Rokeach (1973) developed an inventory of eighteen instrumental values dealing with the methods of achieving desired goals and eighteen terminal values defining preferred end-state goals. A complete list of important human goals, which should be even longer than Rokeach's, would be necessary to explain individual behavior fully. As the evidence of the public's shifting values became apparent, social scientists have offered several theories of how contemporary values are changing (e.g., Flanagan and Lee 2003; Schwartz and Bardi 2001; Nevitte 1996).

The most influential research is Ronald Inglehart's theory of value change in advanced industrial societies (Inglehart 1977; 1981; 1990; Abramson and Inglehart 1995). Inglehart bases his value change theory on two premises. First, he suggests a *scarcity hypothesis:* individuals "place the greatest value on those things that are in relatively short supply" (1981, 881). When a valued object is difficult to obtain, its worth is magnified. If the supply increases to meet the demand, then the object is taken for granted and attention shifts to things that are still scarce. Water is a precious commodity during a drought, but when normal rains return, the concern over water evaporates. The modern concern for clean water arose when pollution became widespread and the availability of clean water became uncertain. This general argument can be applied to other items valued by society.

Second, Inglehart presents a *socialization hypothesis:* "to a large extent, one's value priorities reflect the conditions that prevailed during one's preadult years" (1981, 881). These formative conditions include both the situation in one's family and broader political and socioeconomic conditions. Value change may continue after this formative period as people move through the life cycle or are exposed to new experiences. But Inglehart assumes that later learning must overcome the inertia of preexisting orientations.

The combination of both hypotheses—scarcity and socialization—produces a general model of value change. Individuals initially form their basic value priorities early in life and emphasize the desired goals that are in short supply during this formative period. Once these values priorities develop, they generally endure through later changes in personal and social conditions.

Chapter 1 described how advanced industrial societies are now experiencing unprecedented affluence, higher levels of education, expanding information opportunities, extensive social welfare systems, and other related attributes that changed dramatically during the later twentieth century. We have linked these trends to the growing sophistication, cognitive mobilization, and participation of modern publics. In addition, Inglehart maintains that these social forces are changing the public's basic value priorities. As the relative scarcity of valued objects changes, this trend produces parallel changes in what the public values most.

To generalize the scarcity hypothesis into a broader theoretical model, Inglehart drew on the work of Abraham Maslow (1954), who produced a hierarchical ordering of human goals.[1] Maslow suggested that people are first driven to fulfill basic subsistence needs—water, food, and shelter. When these needs are met, they continue searching until enough material goods are acquired to attain a comfortable margin of economic security. Having accomplished this goal, people may turn to higher-order needs, such as the need for belonging, self-esteem, participation, self-actualization, and the fulfillment of aesthetic and intellectual potential. Thus, social conditions generally predict the broad values emphasized by the public.

The CBS television show *Survivor* presents the Maslovian value hierarchy in practice. Once the group of relatively affluent Americans reaches the island, the quality-of-life concerns they may have emphasized at home are overtaken by the need to survive. Their priorities shift toward subsistence needs: finding water, ensuring that they have enough rice for the day, and maybe even hunting rats for additional protein. This is Maslow as Robinson Caruso.

Inglehart applies the logic of Maslow's value hierarchy to political issues (see figure 5.1). Many political issues, such as economic security, law and order, and national defense, tap sustenance and safety needs. Inglehart describes these goals as *material* values. In a time of depression or civil unrest, for example, security and sustenance needs necessarily receive maximum attention. If a society can make significant progress in addressing these needs, attention can then shift toward higher-order values, reflected in issues such as individual freedom, self-expression, and participation. Inglehart labels these goals *postmaterial* values.

Inglehart contends that a material/postmaterial continuum represents the primary value changes now occurring in advanced industrial democracies. In his more recent writings, Inglehart describes this development as the shift from survival values to self-expressive values (Inglehart 1997; Inglehart and Welzel 2005). In another book, I described a similar shift in citizenship norms among the American public and the impact of these changing norms on political behavior (Dalton 2007a).[2] The broad nature of these value changes leads others to describe the process as a transition from "Old Politics" values of economic growth, security, and traditional lifestyles to "New Politics" values of individual freedom, social equality, and the quality of life. One sign of the significance of this concept is the large number of studies that examine the postmaterial phenomenon (see the extensive literature cited in van Deth and Scarbrough 1995).

The major challenges to Inglehart's theory of value change focus on two themes. First, several studies have questioned whether socioeconomic conditions are linked to citizen values as Inglehart predicts. Harold Clarke and

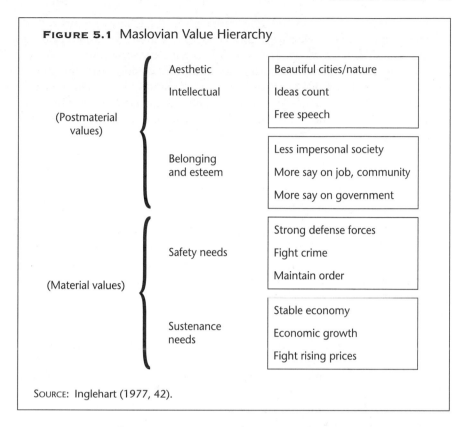

FIGURE 5.1 Maslovian Value Hierarchy

(Postmaterial values)
- Aesthetic — Beautiful cities/nature
- Intellectual — Ideas count
- Free speech
- Belonging and esteem — Less impersonal society / More say on job, community / More say on government

(Material values)
- Safety needs — Strong defense forces / Fight crime / Maintain order
- Sustenance needs — Stable economy / Economic growth / Fight rising prices

SOURCE: Inglehart (1977, 42).

Nitish Dutt (1991; Clarke et al. 1999) demonstrated that Inglehart's simple value index is closely related to the ebb and flow of economic conditions, instead of consistently reflecting the conditions of earlier formative environments. Raymond Duch and Michael Taylor (1993, 1994) questioned whether formative conditions are the principal determinants of values (also see Inglehart's response, in Abramson and Inglehart 1995). In large part, I see these as methodological questions about the measurement of values, such as whether one's level of education primarily represents formative conditions or present social position. This critique does, however, highlight the point that values are dependent on formative conditions *and* present circumstances.

A second critique asks about the content of changing values. Scott Flanagan (1982, 1987; Flanagan and Lee 2003) has argued that values are shifting along at least two dimensions: one that involves a shift from material to noneconomic values, and a second that involves a shift from authoritarian to libertarian values. Valerie Braithwaite, Toni Makkai, and Yvonne Pittelkow (1996) suggested that advanced industrial societies are shifting from security-based values toward harmony-based values. And recently, Shalom Schwartz described human values in terms of dimensions of social change and self/self-transcendent values (Schwartz and Bardi 2001).

In his latest work on global value comparisons, Inglehart presents a more differentiated view of changing values (Inglehart and Welzel 2005). He distinguishes between a dimension of survival to self-expressive values and a dimension of traditional to secular/rational values. Societies are changing in multiple ways that tap different parts of people's value systems. This is clearly an area where further research is warranted. But Inglehart's framework generally overlaps with the value dimensions that other researchers have suggested. And regardless of how we conceptualize this process, there is general agreement that the value priorities of modern publics are changing in important ways.

THE DISTRIBUTION OF VALUES

Most people attach positive worth to material *and* postmaterial goals. The average person favors economic growth *and* a clean environment, social stability *and* individual freedom. Politics, however, often involves a conflict between these goals. Therefore, rather than study one set of values in isolation from another, research asks which goals take priority in the public's mind when values come in conflict.

Surveys use a variety of methods to measure values. Because values are relatively pure feelings and deeply held, they are difficult to tap with a simple opinion survey question. In addition, researchers debate whether we should measure values in terms of personal life conditions or phrased as political goals that are linked to political behaviors.

Following Inglehart's model of the Maslovian value hierarchy, the 2005–2008 World Values Survey (WVS) assessed value priorities by asking respondents to rank the importance of twelve possible political goals. Because all goals are potentially important, they were allowed to choose only two from each set of four items. Table 5.1 presents the top priorities of American, British, French, and German citizens across these items.

Most citizens on both sides of the Atlantic cited material goals as their first priority. Americans most often emphasized economic growth, a stable economy, and crime prevention. In a major change since the previous WVS survey, Americans' emphasis on a strong defense increased from 18 percent to 61 percent. The gain appears to stem from Americans' experience on September 11, 2001, and the continuing war on jihadist terrorism. Europeans stress the same top three material goals, but give decidedly less attention to defense.

Using the choices made among these twelve items, we created a single index that scores individuals by the relative weight they attach to postmaterial goals.[3] Materialists place high priority on the six economic and security goals, while postmaterialists stress participation and the other postmaterial goals. Table 5.2 displays the percentages of postmaterialists on this twelve-item index over time.

In the early 1970s postmaterialists were a relatively small minority in every nation. On the twelve-item index, only 13 percent of West Germans

TABLE 5.1 Distribution of Value Priorities (in percentages)

	United States	Great Britain	France	Germany
High level of economic growth (M)	67	66	68	82
A stable economy (M)	67	61	51	72
More say in work/community (PM)	49	71	72	74
Fight against crime (M)	63	69	50	32
Protect free speech (PM)	59	55	49	38
Maintain order in nation (M)	47	58	48	42
More say in government (PM)	54	56	42	57
More humane society (PM)	37	36	60	52
Fight rising prices (M)	36	26	59	57
Make cities/country beautiful (PM)	28	26	36	23
Ideas count more than money (PM)	29	28	37	37
A strong defense (M)	61	28	18	10

SOURCE: 2005–2008 World Values Survey.

NOTE: Table entries are the percentage of respondents listing the item as first or second choice among items presented in sets of four. Missing data were included in the calculation of percentages. M = material value; PM = postmaterial value.

and 18 percent of Britons scored high on the postmaterial scale. The proportion of materialists was even more pronounced with Inglehart's four-item index (1977; 1990). The larger number of materialists was not surprising because the conditions fostering postmaterial value change were still developing. In historical perspective, the development of advanced industrialism is a relatively recent phenomenon.

By the 1990s the proportion of postmaterialists had increased in each nation where long-term trends are available. More time points are available for the four-item postmaterial index. These trend data show a general shift toward postmaterial values for a large set of advanced industrial societies (Abramson and Inglehart 1995; Inglehart and Welzel 2005, ch. 4). Data from 2006–2007 for our four core nations show a clear increase in the percentage of postmaterialists since 1973. The average percentage of postmaterialists increased by half in Britain, France, and western Germany over this timespan.

Even if the debate over how to measure these values leads to uncertainty about the exact proportion of postmaterialists, the trend toward postmaterialism is clear. Larger proportions of the public in advanced industrial societies—often a third—now give priority to postmaterial goals. Because many other individuals favor both kinds of values, the number of people exclusively preferring material goals is also a minority in most nations. The value priorities in these societies are now characterized by a mix of material and postmaterial objectives.

Since the mid-1970s critics have claimed that postmaterialism is a "sunshine" issue that will fade with the next economic downturn or period of political uncertainty. In the 1970s the OPEC increases in oil prices stimulated

TABLE 5.2 Shift in Postmaterial Values over Time (in percentages)

Country	1973	1990	1999	2007
Belgium	38	38	—	—
Canada	—	29	30	—
Denmark	19	32	—	—
France	33	27	—	35
Germany (West)	13	36	43	30
Great Britain	18	19	—	25
Ireland	15	23	—	—
Italy	16	33	—	—
Japan	—	31	28	—
Netherlands	35	39	—	—
Norway	—	17	20	26
Spain	—	37	29	—
Sweden	—	31	29	—
United States	—	21	23	—

SOURCES: 1973 European Communities Study; for first U.S. time point: 1974 Political Action Study; 1990–1991 World Values Survey; 1998–2002 World Values Survey; for 1999 German time point: 1995–1998 World Values Survey; 2005–2008 World Values Survey.

NOTE: Figure entries are the percentages placing a higher priority on postmaterial goals, using the twelve-item values index in table 5.1, p. 85. See endnote 3 on scale construction. Dashes indicate the question was not asked.

global recessions that some claimed would end the liberalism of the 1960s. The 1980s were heralded as the "me" decade. The 1990s were years of economic strains in Germany, Japan, and many other nations. Despite these potential countertrends, public opinion surveys document the growth of postmaterial values over time. We expect that value change will continue in the future, albeit at a slower pace because the rate of social change has also slowed. For example, education levels are increasing, but not as dramatically as in the past. Nevertheless, this evolutionary change in values has transformed the nature of citizen politics.

THE PROCESS OF VALUE CHANGE

How do we know that support for postmaterial goals really reflects the social modernization of advanced industrial societies? At first, the evidence was tentative. With time, however, the evidence of postmaterial value change has grown. The trends cited in Table 5.2 provide one sort of evidence.

The most telling evidence supporting the postmaterial thesis comes by testing the two hypotheses of Inglehart's theory. The scarcity hypothesis predicts that the socioeconomic conditions of a nation are related to the priorities of its citizens. The socialization hypothesis predicts that values become crystallized early in life. Therefore, the overall values of a society reflect the conditions decades or more earlier, when values were being formed.

FIGURE 5.2 Formative Economic Conditions and Postmateral Values

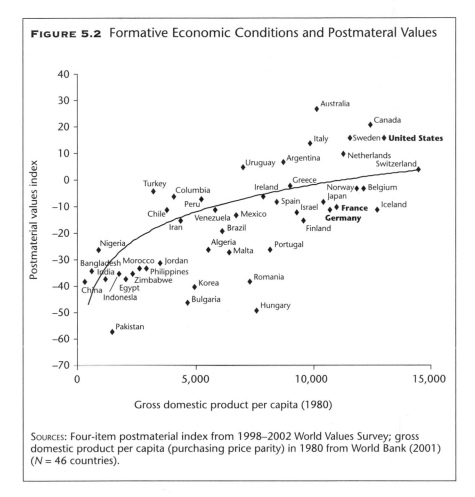

Sources: Four-item postmaterial index from 1998–2002 World Values Survey; gross domestic product per capita (purchasing price parity) in 1980 from World Bank (2001) (*N* = 46 countries).

We can test the first hypothesis by comparing national levels of postmaterial values to the socioeconomic conditions of each nation. If scarcity breeds a concern for material values, then these concerns should be more common in nations with lower living standards. Conversely, the affluence of advanced industrial societies should increase support for postmaterial goals, and, according to the socialization hypothesis, these effects should occur with a time lag. So the best predictor of values should be national conditions a generation earlier, when values were forming.

Figure 5.2 shows a clear relationship between national affluence (GDP per capita in 1980) and the distribution of material/postmaterial values in 1998–2002 for forty-five nations where we have both measures.[4] Postmaterialists are generally most common in nations (including the core nations in this book) that had relatively high living standards during the formative years of the average adult surveyed in 2000. In contrast, we find fewer postmaterialists in poor nations, such as Nigeria, India, China, Pakistan. One should note that these relationships exist even ignoring economic changes—for the better or the worse—in the two decades between measuring GDP and surveying citizen value priorities. As further evidence in support of Inglehart's theory, this measure of GDP in 1980 is slightly more related to postmaterialism than GDP/capita in the year of the survey.[5]

The figure also describes a curved relationship between economic conditions and value change. The greatest value shift occurs during the transition from a subsistence economy to an advanced industrial society, such as that found in postwar Western Europe. Once this level of affluence is achieved, further improvements in living standards produce progressively smaller changes in values, which implies that value change will continue at a slower rate in the future.

Another test of the postmaterial theory involves the socialization hypothesis. Older generations, reared in the years before World War II, grew up in a period of widespread uncertainty. These individuals suffered through the Great Depression of the 1930s and endured two world wars and the social and economic traumas that accompanied these events. Given these conditions, older generations in most Western democracies should have been socialized into a greater concern with material goals: economic growth, economic security, domestic order, and social and military security. These values should also persist over time, even if social conditions have improved dramatically.

Conversely, younger generations in Europe and North America grew up in a period of unprecedented affluence and security. Present-day living standards are often several times higher than those experienced before World War II. The expansion of the welfare state now protects most people from even major economic risks. Postwar generations also have a broader worldview, reflecting their higher educational levels, greater exposure to political information, and more diverse cultural experiences. Furthermore, the end of the cold war capped one of the longest periods of international peace in modern European history. Under these conditions, the material concerns that preoccupied prewar generations should diminish in urgency, and younger generations should shift their attention toward postmaterial goals.

Furthermore, Inglehart's socialization hypothesis predicts that values formed during adolescence should persist through the life span. That is, different age groups should retain the mark of their formative generational experiences even if family or societal conditions change. Older Europeans should still stress security concerns even if their present lifestyles reflect a high level of affluence. Generations socialized in the conditions of the postwar Economic Miracle should retain their greater concern for postmaterial values even as they age and assume greater family and economic responsibilities.

A crucial test of the value-change thesis tracks the value priorities of generations over time. Figure 5.3 describes the values of several European generations from 1974 until 2005, using Inglehart's four-item value index.[6] The oldest generation—those born between 1885 and 1909 (who were ages sixty-five to eighty-eight in 1974)—is located near the bottom of the figure. In 1974

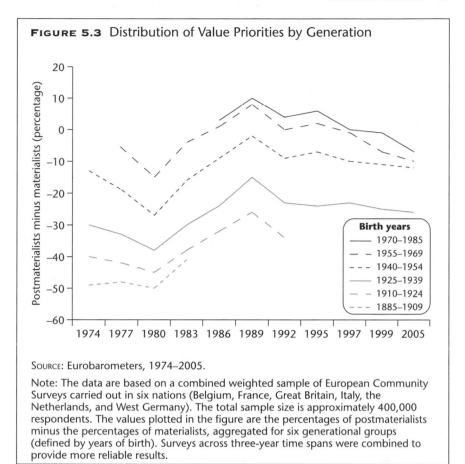

FIGURE 5.3 Distribution of Value Priorities by Generation

SOURCE: Eurobarometers, 1974–2005.

Note: The data are based on a combined weighted sample of European Community Surveys carried out in six nations (Belgium, France, Great Britain, Italy, the Netherlands, and West Germany). The total sample size is approximately 400,000 respondents. The values plotted in the figure are the percentages of postmaterialists minus the percentages of materialists, aggregated for six generational groups (defined by years of birth). Surveys across three-year time spans were combined to provide more reliable results.

the proportion of materialists in this generation outweighs postmaterialists by nearly 50 percent. In contrast, in 1974 the youngest generation—those born between 1940 and 1954—is almost evenly balanced between material and postmaterial values.

Not only is the relative ranking of generations important evidence in support of Inglehart's theory, but so is the persistence of this pattern. The level of values fluctuates over time in response to random sampling variation and the sensitivity of the four-item values index to inflation levels (which I consider a methodological imperfection in the four-item measure).[7] Most important, the generational gaps in value orientations remain fairly constant over time—as seen in the parallel movement of each generation—although all cohorts are moving through the life cycle. The youngest age group from 1974 has reached middle age by the mid-1990s, but their average level of material/postmaterial values does not change significantly between 1974 and 2005. Life-cycle experiences normally modify, but do not replace, the early learning of value priorities.

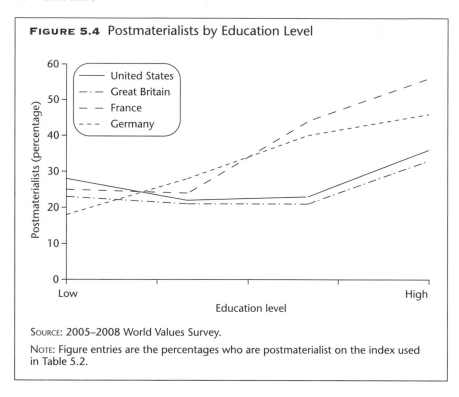

FIGURE 5.4 Postmaterialists by Education Level

SOURCE: 2005–2008 World Values Survey.

NOTE: Figure entries are the percentages who are postmaterialist on the index used in Table 5.2.

The size of the generational differences in values across nations provides further support for the value-change thesis. West Germany, for example, experienced tremendous socioeconomic change during the twentieth century. Consequently, the value differences between the youngest and oldest German cohorts are larger than for many other nations. In nations that experienced less socioeconomic change during the same period, age groups should display smaller differences in their values. Abramson and Inglehart (1995, 134) demonstrated that there is a strong relationship between rates of economic growth and the size of the age gap in value priorities. Large social changes produce large changes in values.[8]

Education is another indirect measure of an individual's economic conditions during the formative years of adolescence because access to higher education often reflects the family's social status.[9] In addition, education may affect values because of the content of learning. Contemporary Western educational systems generally stress the values of participation, self-expression, intellectual understanding, and other postmaterial goals. The liberal orientation of the modern university milieu may encourage a broadening of social perspectives. And finally, the effects of education overlap with those of generation; the young are better educated than the old.

Figure 5.4 presents the differences across levels of education in the percentages of respondents expressing postmaterial values in the most recent

World Values Survey. In each nation, there is a positive relationship between level of education and support for postmaterial goals. In France only 25 percent of those with less education are postmaterialists, compared to 56 percent of those with at least some university education. One could argue that the U.S. system of education is the most egalitarian of those portrayed in the figure, and so the link between education level and early life conditions is weaker than in Britain and Germany—consequently, the relationship between education and values is also weaker.

The concentration of postmaterial values among the young and better educated gives added significance to these orientations. If Inglehart's theory is correct, the percentage of postmaterialists should gradually increase over time, as older materialist generations are replaced by younger, more postmaterialist generations.[10] And, if overall education levels continue to increase, support for postmaterial values should continue to grow. This point is important because postmaterialists are more active in politics than materialists, and the political influence of postmaterialists is greater than their numbers imply. Indeed, among the group of future elites—university-educated youth—postmaterial values predominate.[11] As these individuals succeed into positions of economic, social, and political leadership, the impact of changing values should strengthen. Value change appears to be an ongoing process.

THE CONSEQUENCES OF VALUE CHANGE

Postmaterialists are only a minority of the population in most advanced industrial democracies, but their impact is already apparent, extending beyond politics to all aspects of society. Indeed, one of the most impressive aspects of Inglehart's 1990 book, *Culture Shift in Advanced Industrial Society*, is the range of phenomena he links to postmaterialism. In the workplace these new value orientations fuel demands for a flexible work environment that better accommodates individual needs. Rigid, hierarchical, assembly-line systems of production are being challenged by worker participation (codetermination), quality circles, and flexible working hours. The 1999 European Values Survey found that materialists list good pay and job security as important characteristics of a job, while postmaterialists emphasize goals such as having the opportunity to use initiative, holding a job that is useful to society, and working with pleasant people. Many business analysts bemoan the decline of the work ethic, but it is more accurate to say that the work ethic is shifting to a new set of goals.

These new values are also changing social relations. Neil Nevitte (1996) shows that deference to all types of authority is waning: bosses, army officers, university professors, and political leaders all decry the decline in deference to their authority. The postmaterial credo is that an individual earns authority, rather than having it bestowed by a position. Parents today, especially the postmaterialists, are stressing greater independence as they educate their children. The public's behavior in many aspects of social and political life is becoming more self-directed. This increasing independence is reflected in the declining brand-name loyalty among consumers and in the decline of political party loyalty among voters. In short, contemporary lifestyles reflect a demand for greater freedom and individuality, which appears in fashion, consumer tastes, social behavior, and interpersonal relations. The process of value change includes religious values and sexual mores (Inglehart 1997; Nevitte 1996). In addition to their concern with economic security, materialists are more likely to hold restrictive attitudes on sex-related issues, such as extramarital sex, abortion, and homosexuality.

Postmaterialists champion a new set of political issues—environmental quality, anti-nuclear energy, gender equality, and limited consumerism—that the political establishment had often overlooked. Debates in Washington about global warming, the safety of nuclear plants, and gender equality have close parallels in the capitals of Europe. Proponents of these issues have similar characteristics: they are young, better educated, and postmaterialist.

Value change also affects political participation. Postmaterial values stimulate direct participation in the decisions affecting one's life—whether at school, in the workplace, or in the political process. Postmaterialists are more interested in politics than are materialists and more likely to translate this interest into political action. In all three European nations in the 2005–2008 WVS, postmaterialists generally were more likely than materialists to be interested in politics and say that politics is important in their lives.

The activist orientation of postmaterialists adds to the puzzle of participation noted in chapter 2: If postmaterialism stimulates political action, why are voting and some other forms of participation declining? Our answer reinforces the argument that the style of political action is changing in advanced industrial democracies. The participatory orientation of postmaterialists does not affect all participation modes equally. Postmaterial values do not necessarily stimulate voting or campaign activity; in some nations, voting turnout is often lower among postmaterialists.[12] One reason is that most established parties have not embraced postmaterial issues. In addition, postmaterialists are skeptical of formal hierarchical procedures and organizations, such as elections and most political parties.

Instead, postmaterial values stimulate participation in citizen initiatives, protests, and other forms of direct action. The 2005–2008 WVS found that postmaterialists are much more likely than materialists to participate in protest (see figure 5.5). These nonpartisan participation opportunities provide postmaterialists with a more direct influence on politics, which matches their value orientations. Most postmaterialists also possess the political skills to carry out these more demanding forms of political action. As noted in chapters 3 and 4, along with increasing levels of citizen involvement has come a change in the form of political participation.

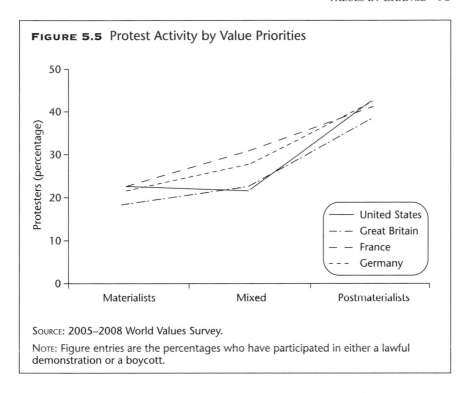

FIGURE 5.5 Protest Activity by Value Priorities

SOURCE: 2005–2008 World Values Survey.

NOTE: Figure entries are the percentages who have participated in either a lawful demonstration or a boycott.

VALUE CHANGE AND VALUE STABILITY

The values of Western publics are changing, but it might be more accurate to stress the growing diversity of the public's value priorities. More people still give primary attention to material goals, and the socioeconomic issues deriving from these values will continue to dominate political debate for decades to come. The persistence of material values should not be overlooked.

At the same time, postmaterial values are becoming more common. A sizable proportion of the public is willing to sacrifice further economic growth for a clean environment. Many people value the opportunity to participate in the decisions affecting their lives more than they value procedures that ensure stability and order at the possible cost of citizen input. Public values are changing.

The current mix of values sometimes makes it difficult for political analysts and politicians to know what the public wants. For nearly every example of the persistence of traditional material value patterns, a counterexample reflects postmaterial values. For almost every citizen lobbying a local town council to stimulate the economy, another worries that growth will mean a loss of green space or a diminution in the quality of life. The diversity of values marks a major change in the nature of citizen politics: political debates again involve the definition of goals and not just the means to reach consensual goals.

The mix of values also makes it difficult for journalists to discern the public's priorities. During the 1960s media reports made it seem that every young person was joining the counterculture. In the 1980s images of the yuppie in pursuit of an MBA and a BMW were equally pervasive. Now, GenXers are defined, in part, by the lack of either identity. The strength of empirical research is that we can track the values of the public in a more scientific manner. And what we find is a slow evolution toward postmaterial goals.

This process of value change has several consequences for contemporary politics. The issues of political debate are shifting. Concerns about environmental protection, individual freedom, social equality, participation, and the quality of life have been *added* to the traditional political agenda of economic and security issues. Some of the most telling evidence comes from a study of legislation in the U.S. Congress by Jeffrey Berry, who found that a majority of the congressional agenda was concerned with material issues in 1963, but by 1991 the emphasis had shifted to a predominately postmaterial agenda (Berry 1999, ch. 4–5). Inglehart (1997) tracked a sharp increase in the attention that political parties devote to environmental and other New Politics issues over time. At present and for the foreseeable future, politics in most advanced industrial societies will address a mix of material and postmaterial issues.

As noted above, value change also reshapes the patterns of political participation. Postmaterialists are less likely to embrace the structured electoral politics of representative democracy. Instead, they are advocates for direct participation and new forms of direct democracy, which adds to an active civil society with a diverse range of public interest groups. Such groups have proliferated both in the United States and in Europe (Meyer and Tarrow 1998). The public's participatory demands have prompted reforms within established political parties to enlarge the role of members, such as the convention reforms of the U.S. Democratic Party and the activities of constituency associations in the British Labour Party. As we discuss in chapters 7 and 8, such reforms inject the material/postmaterial debate into partisan politics.

Inevitably, changes in value priorities carry over to the institutions of the political process. Postmaterialists advocate a greater use of initiative and referendum, the opening up of administrative processes, and the expansion of the legal rights of citizen groups (Cain, Dalton, and Scarrow 2003). In summary, postmaterialists favor expanding the democratic process and more directly involving citizens in the political process.

Only a few skeptics still doubt that value priorities are changing among Western publics; the evidence of change is obvious. It is more difficult to anticipate the many consequences of these new values. By monitoring these trends, however, we may get a preview of the nature of citizen politics in advanced industrial democracies.

SUGGESTED READINGS

Clark, Terry Nichols, and Vincent Hoffmann-Martinot, eds. *The New Political Culture*. Boulder: Westview, 1998.

Dalton, Russell. *The Good Citizen: How the Young Are Reshaping American Politics*. Washington, D.C.: CQ Press, 2008.

Inglehart, Ronald. *Culture Shift in Advanced Industrial Society*. Princeton: Princeton University Press, 1990.

Inglehart, Ronald, and Christian Welzel. *Modernization, Cultural Change, and Democracy: The Human Development Sequence*. New York: Cambridge University Press, 2005.

Nevitte, Neil. *The Decline of Deference*. Petersborough, Canada: Broadview, 1996.

van Deth, Jan, and Elinor Scarbrough, eds. *The Impact of Values*. New York: Oxford University Press, 1995.

NOTES

1. Inglehart's early work was closely linked to the Maslovian value hierarchy, but Maslow figures in less prominently in Inglehart's recent research. As Inglehart has broadened his research beyond advanced industrial societies, he has examined how cultural forces and local conditions can shape what values are considered scarce and are therefore valued by the public.

2. For those who use the data supplement (appendix C) to do research, I expect that "engaged citizenship" (V014) is strongly related to postmaterial values. The engaged citizen questions, however, have not been asked in the same survey as the postmaterial values questions.

3. We counted the emphasis placed on the six material goals and the six postmaterial goals in table 5.1; entries are the percentages in each nation who place a higher priority on postmaterial goals. This table uses a different method from Inglehart's standard twelve-item index so that we can begin the trend with the 1970s surveys that used a different question format. Inglehart's twelve-item index is a count of postmaterial items, excluding the beautiful cities item.

   Several of the analyses in this chapter use a four-item subset of the twelve items to construct a single index of material/postmaterial values (Inglehart 1990, ch. 2; 1977). The disadvantage of the four-item index is that it yields a narrow basis for tapping human values. In some surveys, however, it is the only index available.

4. We use 1980 GDP/capita (purchasing price parity) to approximate the period when values were being formed for many of the adults surveyed in 2000. See earlier editions of this text for comparable analyses for earlier time periods.

5. There is a strong relationship ($r = .72$) between GDP/capita in 1980 and values in 2000, and this correlation is stronger than if GDP/capita in 2000 is used ($r = .66$). Also see Abramson and Inglehart (1995).

6. Figure 5.3 is based on the combined results of samples from six nations: Great Britain, West Germany, France, Italy, Belgium, and the Netherlands. The results were combined to produce age-group samples large enough to estimate values precisely. For additional discussion of generational effects, see Abramson and Inglehart (1995) and Inglehart and Welzel (2005).

7. One weakness of the Inglehart index is that it attempts to measure basic values using specific political issues. It is therefore not surprising that the four-item index is sensitive to inflation rates because one of the items taps concern about

rising prices (Clarke and Dutt 1991; Clarke et al. 1999). A broader measure of values, such as Inglehart's twelve-item index or the social priorities question of Flanagan (1982), would be less susceptible to these measurement problems.

8. These patterns also imply that age differences in postmaterial values will narrow in more recent surveys, because the older pre-WWII generations are leaving the electorate and they were most distinct in holding materialist priorities. Contemporary publics are increasingly composed of those raised in advanced industrial societies.

9. Raymond Duch and Michael Taylor (1993) used multivariate analysis to argue that formative conditions do not influence current value priorities. Paul Abramson and Ronald Inglehart (1995) challenged this interpretation, arguing that Duch and Taylor had distorted the results by their selection of timepoints and had misinterpreted the meaning of education effects (also see Duch and Taylor 1994). I believe that the evidence of generational change is predominant, and that educational effects are another measure of formative life conditions, especially in Europe.

10. Even during this relatively brief time span, generational turnover has contributed to a postmaterial trend (Abramson and Inglehart 1995). In 1970 the pre–World War I generation constituted about 16 percent of the West German public; by 1980 this group constituted about 5 percent. By 1990 the WWI generation had essentially left the electorate, and young Germans, socialized in the affluent post–World War II era, had replaced them.

11. Ronald Inglehart (1981) finds that European political elites (candidates for the European Parliament) are nearly three times more postmaterialist than the total public. Postmaterialists are also more common among younger elites.

12. Markus Crepaz (1990) shows that the presence of a green or New Left party increases voting rates, presumably by encouraging postmaterialists to turn out at the polls.

CHAPTER 6

Issues and Ideological Orientations

I ssues are the everyday currency of politics. Issue opinions identify the public's preferences for government action and their expectations for the political process. Political parties are distinguished by their issue positions, and elections provide a means for the public to select between the competing issue programs they offer. As citizens become more sophisticated and involved in politics, issue opinions have a stronger influence on voting choice and the policy process. The public's issue preferences should directly influence policy outcomes in democratic systems. Indeed, issues are what politics is about.

Issue opinions also represent the translation of broad value orientations into specific political concerns. Issues are determined in part by the values examined in the last chapter, as well as by other factors: cues from political elites, the flow of political events, and the contexts of specific situations. A person may favor the principle of equal rights for all citizens, but her own mix of values and practical concerns may determine her attitudes toward legislation on voting rights, job discrimination, school busing, and open housing. Consequently, issue opinions are more changeable and varied than broad value orientations.

Another important characteristic of issues is that people focus their attention on a few areas—they are members of one or several "issue publics" (see chapter 2). Some people are especially concerned with education policy; others are interested in foreign affairs, civil rights, environmental protection, or immigration. In general, most Americans belong to at least one interest group, although no single interest group includes a majority of the public. Members of an issue public are relatively well informed about their issue and generally follow the actions of politicians and the political parties on that issue. The salient issue for an individual has a strong impact on his or her voting behavior.

Issue opinions are a dynamic aspect of politics, and the theme of changing popular values also applies to the study of issues. In some areas, contemporary publics are obviously more liberal than their predecessors. The issues of women's rights, environmental protection, social equality, and individual lifestyles were unknown or highly divisive two or three decades ago, but a fairly solid consensus now exists on these issues. In other areas, people remain divided on the goals of government. Support for tax revolts, neoconservative revival, "family values," and supply-side economics suggests that conservative values have not lost their appeal for many people. This chapter

---

Internet Resource

Visit the International Social Survey Program (ISSP) Web site for additional information on these surveys:

www.issp.org

---

describes the present issue opinions of Western publics and highlights, where possible, the trends in these opinions.

DOMESTIC POLICY OPINIONS

At one time, domestic policy was synonymous with economic matters, and economic issues still rank at the top of the public's political agenda for most elections. But the number of salient domestic issues has proliferated, and many people are now concerned with noneconomic issues such as social equality, environmental protection, and immigration. This section provides an overview of the wide range of domestic policy concerns.

Socioeconomic Issues and the State

For most of the twentieth century, the political conflicts that emerged from industrialization and the Great Depression dominated politics in democratic party systems. This debate revolved around the question of the government's role in society and the economy, especially the provision of basic social needs.

A prime example of this policy area is the set of government-backed social insurance programs that most governments administer (such as Social Security in the United States or government health care programs in Europe). European social programs protect individuals from economic calamities caused by illness, unemployment, disability, or other hardships. In some nations, the government's involvement in the economy also includes public ownership of major industries and active efforts to manage the economy.

Labor unions favor the extension of government social policy as a way to improve the life chances of the average person. Business leaders and members of the middle class frequently oppose these policies as an unnecessary government intrusion into private affairs. At stake is not only the question of government involvement in society but also the desirability of certain social goals and the distribution of political influence between labor and business. To a large extent, the terms *liberal* and *conservative* have been synonymous with one's position on these questions. Attitudes toward these issues provide a major source of political competition in most elections.

Despite expanding government policy efforts in these areas, or perhaps because of them, new questions about the scope of government activity arose in the 1980s. Conservative politicians on both sides of the Atlantic championed a populist revolt against big government. Margaret Thatcher, Ronald Reagan, and Helmut Kohl attempted to turn back the growth of government, privatizing government-owned businesses or government-run programs and reducing government social programs. Political observers interpreted their electoral successes as evidence of a new conservative trend in public attitudes toward government.

Evidence suggests that support for the principle of big government has waned: between 1964 and 1980 the number of Americans who believed that the federal government was too powerful rose from 30 percent to 49 percent (although it declined to 39 percent in 2000). The American public became more critical of taxation levels and the use of their tax money. The Gallup surveys show that in the 1950s less than half of the American public felt they were paying an unfair amount of taxes; since the late 1970s, however, more than three-quarters believe their share of taxes is too high. These opinions fueled popular opposition to tax policy among Americans, and the Republican Party has successfully appealed to these antitax sentiments as a basis of its electoral support.

Some signs of a growing cynicism about big government also appear among Europeans. British public opinion surveys showed an increasing criticism of big government beginning in the late 1970s (Heath and McMahon 1992). British desires for the denationalization of some industries grew during the early Thatcher years, paralleling the government's privatization of several government-owned enterprises and a general attempt to reduce the scope of government.[1] Germany attempted to reduce the scope of its government in similar ways, and in the late 1980s the French government also began a retrenchment in its programs. The policy debate about the proper scope of government has continued to the present day on both sides of the Atlantic. Currently the Grand Coalition of the Christian Democratic and Social Democratic Parties in Germany struggles to reach agreement on these issues, and Nicolas Sarkozy has charted a new economic reform program in France.

Despite the promotion of conservative policies, public opinion surveys show that many people still believe that government is responsible for promoting individual well-being and guaranteeing the quality of life for its citizens (Borre and Scarbrough 1995). Table 6.1 displays the percentages of citizens who think the government is "definitely responsible" for dealing with specific social problems. The British and the French have very high expectations of government: more than half believe the government is definitely responsible for providing health care, ensuring a decent standard of living for the elderly, and maintaining strict environmental laws. Survey data reveal strong support for government action on price controls, public housing, and even aid to college students. Many Germans believe that government is responsible in these policy areas—and the percentages are even higher among the residents of the former East Germany.[2] Data from other European nations show that support for government action to resolve social needs is a core element of the European political culture (Taylor-Gooby 1998).

TABLE 6.1 Government Responsibility for Dealing with Policy Areas (in percentages)

	United States	Great Britain	France	Germany
Provide health care for the sick	39	82	53	55
Provide decent living standard for the elderly	38	73	51	52
Pass strict environmental laws	46	63	67	62
Give aid to needy college students	35	38	59	31
Keep prices under control	25	44	42	28
Provide job for everyone who wants one	14	29	40	36
Reduce income differences between rich and poor	17	36	49	31
Provide housing for those who need it	20	37	44	25
Provide a decent living standard for the unemployed	13	29	34	22
Provide industry with help	17	41	36	20
Average	26	47	48	36

SOURCE: 1996 International Social Survey Program.

NOTE: Table entries are the percentages who say that each area should definitely be government's responsibility. Missing data were excluded from the calculation of percentages.

In comparison to most Europeans, Americans are more hesitant about government action. Even in areas where government is a primary actor, such as care of the elderly and assistance to the unemployed, only a minority of Americans views these problems as definite government responsibilities (table 6.1). The United States is a major exception among Western democracies in its limited support for activist government. The state has never attempted to own a significant portion of industry, and most Americans oppose nationalization on even a limited scale. Popular support for basic social programs remains low by European standards. These conservative socioeconomic attitudes are often explained by the individualist nature of American society and the absence of a socialist working-class party.

Another measure of citizens' expectations of their government involves preferences for government spending. One of the great contradictions in public opinion is that even as people are critical of taxes and the overall size of government, support for increased spending on specific policy programs remains widespread. Table 6.2 displays the percentages of Americans who favor more government spending in a policy area minus those who want to

TABLE 6.2 Budget Priorities of the American Public over Time (in percentage difference scores)

Priority	1973	1976	1980	1984	1988	1991	1996	2000	2002	2006
Halting rising crime rate	60	57	63	62	64	59	61	55	50	52
Protecting the nation's health	56	55	47	51	63	66	60	69	71	70
Dealing with drug addiction	59	51	52	57	64	50	48	53	49	55
Protecting the environment	53	45	32	54	60	63	50	55	53	62
Improving the educational system	40	41	42	59	60	62	65	67	69	68
Solving problems of big cities	36	23	19	31	36	35	45	40	30	36
Improving the condition of blacks	11	2	0	19	19	20	13	21	15	22
The military and defense	−27	−3	45	−21	−22	−13	−15	−2	9	−15
Welfare	−31	−46	−43	−16	−19	−15	−43	−19	−20	−11
Space exploration program	−51	−51	−21	−27	−16	−26	−32	−29	−26	−24
Foreign aid	−66	−72	−64	−65	−63	−68	−69	−52	−59	−52
Average	13	9	16	19	22	21	16	23	22	24

SOURCE: National Opinion Research Center General Social Survey, various dates.

NOTE: Table entries are the percentages saying "too little" being spent on the problem minus the percentages saying "too much."

spend less. These data describe a long-term consensus in favor of increased government spending on education, crime prevention, health care, preventing drug addiction, and environmental protection. Only welfare, the space program, and foreign aid are consistently identified as candidates for budget cuts. Moreover, although specific spending priorities change over time, the average preference for increased government spending listed across the bottom of the table has varied surprisingly little across seven administrations.

Americans' priorities for spending on specific programs do, however, respond to changes in the federal budget and the political context in a manner consistent with Benjamin Page and Robert Shapiro's (1992) description of a rational public. The perceived military weakness of the Carter administration stimulated calls for greater defense spending; in spring 1980, 56 percent of Americans thought the government was spending too little on defense (11 percent said too much was being spent), and these attitudes supported the large defense expenditures early in the Reagan administration. Then, as examples of Pentagon waste became commonplace—the $500 hammers and $7,000 coffeepots—popular support for defense spending was replaced by endorsement of the status quo or even a cut in defense budgets. Similarly, the Reagan administration's cuts in social spending exceeded the wishes of many Americans. Between 1980 and 1991 support grew for *more* spending in the areas of health care, environmental protection, education, urban problems, and minority aid. Even while the George W. Bush administration was attempting to cut government spending, the American public wanted more money spent on these programs in 2002. In fact, support for greater government spending hit a high point in 2006!

Cross-national opinion polls show that support for higher spending on specific policy programs such as health care, environmental protection, education, housing, and social services is widespread among Europeans (table 6.3). The British favor increased spending in most areas, especially on policies identified with the welfare state. Germans display modest support for higher spending, but this attitude must be seen in the context of already large public expenditures and the economic uncertainties accompanying German unification. The other European nations in the survey generally support greater government spending (Kaase and Newton 1998). Americans also favor increased government spending on various government programs, despite their general reservations about the scope of government.

The contrast between the general skepticism about government and the endorsement of higher spending on specific areas reflects a common contradiction in public opinion. The motto for government is clear: tax less and spend more. Seymour Martin Lipset and Everett Ladd (1980) described this paradox as the combination of "ideological conservatism" and "programmatic liberalism." Americans and Europeans continue to demonstrate an ambiguous mix of support for and opposition to government action.

The most accurate description of popular attitudes toward government might be that citizens are now critical of "big" government, but they also are

TABLE 6.3 Cross-National Comparison of Citizen Budget Priorities (in percentage difference scores)

Priority	United States	Great Britain	France	Germany
Education	72	84	56	48
Health	61	91	36	52
Police and law enforcement	51	72	26	56
Old-age pensions	41	79	23	51
Environment	36	39	37	53
Unemployment benefits	5	16	−12	21
Culture and arts	−31	−59	−21	−19
Military and defense	−12	−14	−59	−61
Average	28	39	11	25

SOURCE: 1996 International Social Survey Program.

NOTE: Table entries are the percentages saying "too little" being spent on the problem minus the percentages saying "too much." Missing data were excluded from the calculation of percentages.

accustomed to, and depend on, the policies of the modern state. When people confront the choice between cutting taxes and maintaining government services, many surveys find that a plurality prefer the services option even in the midst of the so-called tax revolt. The mix of opinions limits initiatives for dramatic increases in public spending, but the massive tax reduction introduced by the Bush administration has stimulated public worries that this policy will reduce benefits in many desired government programs.

Race and Equality

The world is getting smaller, and Western democracies are becoming more racially and ethnically diverse. After generations of dormancy, the demand for civil rights and racial equality inflamed U.S. politics in the mid-1960s. For most of the next two decades, the civil rights issue preoccupied the attention of many Americans and became a major source of political conflict. Race and ethnicity continue to be central in American politics, for the success of the civil rights movement among African Americans has encouraged similar activity among Hispanics, Asian Americans, and other minorities.

Europe also has begun to confront issues of racial tolerance and civil rights as immigration has increased the diversity of these societies. Decolonialization by Great Britain and France created a steady inflow of minority immigrants from former colonies (Hollifield 1993). Labor-force shortages led the West Germans to invite "guestworkers" from less developed Mediterranean

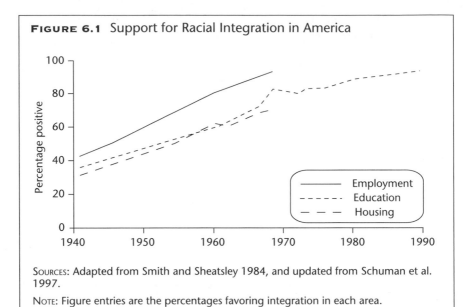

FIGURE 6.1 Support for Racial Integration in America

SOURCES: Adapted from Smith and Sheatsley 1984, and updated from Schuman et al. 1997.

NOTE: Figure entries are the percentages favoring integration in each area.

countries to work in German factories. And the number of immigrants and asylum-seekers increased dramatically during the 1990s. Nonwhites now account for 5 percent to 10 percent of the population in these three nations, and as much as a quarter of the workforce in some cities. Moreover, the recent wave of immigrants has introduced greater cultural differences and greater political tensions, as these newcomers often differ from the indigenous populations in race, religion, and social status.

Despite Western democracies' efforts to address these issues, backlashes against minorities persist. Tensions between French and North Africans have occasionally erupted into violence in southern France, and the National Front Party espouses antiforeigner policies. Immigrants and minority groups staged massive urban protests and violence in France in 2005 and 2006. German unification produced a surge of violence against foreigners, the emergence of the xenophobic Republikaner Party, and eventually a tightening of German immigration and asylum laws. Perhaps the most dramatic example was the emergence of the List Pim Fortuyn in the Netherlands, headed by an otherwise liberal gay activist who was extremely critical of the presence of Muslim fundamentalists in Dutch society.

Although racial and ethnic conflicts are still part of contemporary politics, the trends in racial attitudes document a massive change in the beliefs of Americans. In the 1940s a majority of white Americans openly endorsed racial segregation of education, housing, transportation, and employment (see figure 6.1). The values of freedom, equality, and justice that constitute the American creed did not apply to blacks. A phenomenal growth in support for racial integration occurred over the next four decades, however, as integration of housing, education, and employment won widespread endorsement. A dramatic sign of how things have changed is Barack Obama's strong campaign for the Democratic presidential nomination in 2008.

In a provocative book on public attitudes toward racial issues, Paul Sniderman and Thomas Piazza (1993) showed that as racial integration became accepted, the politics of race broadened to include a new set of issues—affirmative action, government social programs, and equity principles—that now divide the American public. Some actions aimed at redressing racial inequality—affirmative action policies (such as school busing and preferential treatment) and racial quotas—are opposed by most Americans (Schuman et al. 1997). Many political analysts claim that these divided opinions are signs of a new racism in America. Based on an innovative set of survey experiments, Sniderman and Piazza concluded that although a minority of Americans still harbor racial prejudice, the contemporary clash over racial policies is more attributable to broader ideological conflicts over the scope of government, beliefs about equality, and other political values.

European attitudes toward racial and ethnic minorities seem to reflect a similar mix of two factors (Sniderman et al. 2001; Sniderman and Hagendoorn 2007). One factor is simple prejudice toward individuals of a different race or religion—although such sentiments appear among only a minority of Europeans. The other factor is a clash of interests or goals that is analogous to class, regional, or other social interests. For example, middle-class individuals can disagree with policies to benefit the working class, without being prejudiced against the working class. Genuine prejudice is difficult to address or correct, but differences in interests are open to reconciliation and compromise. The mix of factors is important in judging the potential resolution of these issues.

Perhaps the best way to compare opinions across nations is to focus on attitudes toward immigrants (McCrone and Surridge 1998; Alba, Schmidt, and Wasmer 2003). Table 6.4 shows that citizens in all four nations are concerned about issues of immigrant and minority relations. Other surveys routinely find that most people say that immigration is a major problem in their nation and that the levels of immigration should be reduced (also see table 6.8, p. 114). The first item in the table shows that the majority of Europeans favor limits on immigration and that Americans, despite their immigrant heritage, are only slightly more open. Europeans also favor an assimilation policy, whereby immigrants assume the values of their new country rather than maintaining their culture and customs. Indeed, these differences in values contribute to contemporary culture clashes in Europe (and the United States).

At the same time, tolerance toward immigrants is apparent in other survey items in the lower half of the table. Majorities in each of these European nations feel a moral duty to help immigrants, and nearly equal proportions say they feel a sense of sympathy for immigrants. But worries about the impact of immigrants on jobs, crime, and society are commonplace. Most people still favor giving a priority to native workers over immigrants if jobs are scarce

TABLE 6.4 Cross-National Comparison of Attitudes toward Immigrants
(in percentages)

	United States	Great Britain	France	Germany
Attitudes toward immigration				
Anyone can come	12	4	6	5
Come if there are jobs	45	34	34	33
Strict limits	39	49	50	56
Prohibit immigration	4	13	10	7
Multicultural vs. assimilation of immigrants				
Can maintain customs	—	45	27	24
Should assimilate	—	55	73	76
Attitudes toward immigrants				
Moral duty to help immigrants	—	59	62	60
Feel sympathy for immigrants	—	63	53	67
If jobs are short, priority to native population	49	58	54	59
Immigrants bad for nation	43	50	50	60

SOURCES: 1999–2002 European Values Survey/World Values Survey; final item, Pew (2003).

NOTE: Table entries are the percentages agreeing with each statement. Missing data were excluded from the calculation of percentages.

(although Europeans are more liberal on this view than respondents in other regions in the World Values Survey). It is the juxtaposition of abstract support for the principles of equality and tolerance and the fears over concrete problems in the clash between different cultures that makes this issue so difficult for Americans and Europeans.

Although the climate of opinion now accepts more racial and ethnic diversity, one must be careful not to overlook the real racial problems that persist. Support for the principle of equality coexists with the remnants of segregation in the United States; and racial conflict can still flare up in Brixton, Marseilles, or Berlin. Problems of housing segregation, unequal education, and job discrimination are real. Public opinion alone is not sufficient to resolve these problems, and some survey respondents undoubtedly overstate their tolerance level. Still, the shift of social norms toward support of racial equality makes these problems easier to address than when discrimination was openly practiced.

Gender Issues

Another social dimension concerns equality between men and women. Throughout history, traditional gender roles were deeply entrenched on both sides of the Atlantic. American women faced limited career opportunities,

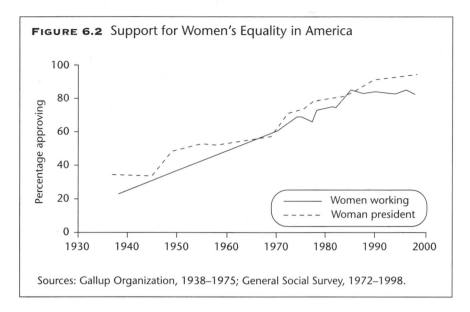

FIGURE 6.2 Support for Women's Equality in America

Sources: Gallup Organization, 1938–1975; General Social Survey, 1972–1998.

and German housewives were expected to devote their efforts to *Kinder, Kirche, und Küche* (children, church, and kitchen). The status of women in Great Britain, France, and other advanced industrial societies was equally constrained.

These attitudes underwent a profound transformation in the latter half of the twentieth century. The women's movement grew most rapidly in the United States, and women's groups also expanded in Europe (Lovenduski and Norris 1996). These groups, along with individual women, raised society's consciousness about the different treatment of men and women. As political action led to legislation equalizing the rights of both sexes, the public at large became more sensitive to gender issues, and social norms gradually changed.

Most Americans now express belief in equal opportunities for men and women. One survey question asks about approval of a married woman working if she has a husband to support her, by implication condoning the norm that married women belong at home (see figure 6.2). In 1938, when this question was first asked, only 22 percent of Americans approved of a woman working in these circumstances; this figure had increased to 80 percent or more by the end of the 1990s. Gallup data show that in 1936 only 31 percent of Americans said they would vote for a woman as president; by the 1990s this figure had risen above 80 percent. Indeed, the political advance of women in a single generation has been amazing. Margaret Thatcher was Britain's first woman prime minister in 1979, Angela Merkel became Germany's first woman chancellor in 2005, and the political successes of Hillary Clinton in the United States and Ségolène Royal in France mark just how much has changed.

Table 6.5 provides further evidence on how Americans and Europeans think about gender-related issues (also see Inglehart and Norris 2003; Scott,

TABLE 6.5 Attitudes toward Gender Equality (in percentages)

	United States	Great Britain	France	Germany
Situation of women has improved	70	68	60	68
Women's role				
Working/nonworking mothers can establish same relationship with children	79*	73	77*	67*
Men have more right to a job (disagree)	85*	76	74	63*
University education more important for boy (disagree)	92*	93*	93*	81*
Being a housewife is fulfilling	51	68	53	—
Action				
Member of women's group	14	2	>1	4
Volunteer work for a women's group	8	1	>1	2
Political/economic role				
Men better political leaders (disagree)	73	80*	79*	76
Men better business executives (disagree)	86*	83*	86*	78*

SOURCES: 1999–2002 and 2005–2008 World Values Survey; first item: European Community, "European Men and Women Study 1995."

NOTE: Table entries are the percentages who agree (or disagree) with each statement. Asterisks denote women's role items on which there are substantial differences between genders (Tau-b greater than .10).

Braun, and Alwin 1998). The items focused on the role of women are a good example of these changing attitudes. Most people believe that a working woman can establish close ties with her children. Large majorities now disagree with the proposition that men have first right to employment or to a university education. At the same time, small minorities agree that being a housewife can be fulfilling.

Another panel in the table focuses on political action. Americans are more likely to be members of women's group and to participate in voluntary activities for these groups. The data reflect Americans' stronger participatory norms, as well as the earlier origins of the women's movement in the United States.

One striking pattern involves images of whether politics or business are predominately male roles. Large majorities reject the idea that men are better than women in politics or business, which is quite a shift from public opinion a generation or two ago. Although women remain underrepresented in the top stratum of political officials, old stereotypes of politics as an exclusively male domain have eroded. Even if these expressed opinions are not fully matched by the reality of actions, the changes in political norms are having real effects on the status of women and encouraging further policy change.

In one sense, it is amazing that gender roles developed over millennia have shifted so rapidly. At the same time, this transformation has been incomplete. Evidence from European surveys shows that most men still feel that women are primarily responsible for housework and a man has more right to a job (Scott, Braun, and Alwin 1998). Other survey data find that many working women feel their situation is worse that men's in regard to job opportunities, wages, promotion prospects, and job security. Ultimately, the legacy of the women's movement may be the creation of a choice for women—both work and family are now accepted options—instead of limitation to a single role.

Environmental Protection

Environmental quality is one of the new issue concerns of advanced industrial democracies. Environmentalism was initially stimulated by a few very visible ecological crises, after which these concerns persisted and expanded. Separate issues were linked together into environmental programs; citizen groups mobilized in support of environmental issues; and new green parties formed in several nations (Rootes 1999). Gradually, these societies developed an awareness of how human activity and economic development could harm the natural environment, reduce the quality of life, and threaten the sustainability of human progress.

The broadest sign of public concern is interest in the host of environmental issues that have reached public consciousness (Dalton and Rohrschneider 1998). Issues of global warming, the ozone hole, and biodiversity have become global concerns. Interest in environmental issues translates into support for environmental protection; contemporary publics broadly support government actions to protect the environment (see table 6.6).

Many political analysts discount these environmental opinions because these views can easily be expressed in a survey without concern for the actual costs of a policy. But when people are asked to balance their environmental beliefs against the potential economic costs of environmental protection, the support is still considerable. The data in the middle panel of table 6.6 show that roughly half of the public (except in Germany) would give up part of their income or pay higher taxes to prevent pollution. A clear majority of Americans favors protection of the environment even if it risks holding back economic growth, and most Europeans agree (Dalton and Rohrschneider 1998).

Participation in the environmental movement is further evidence of public support for environmental reform. The bottom panel in table 6.6 demonstrates that membership in environmental groups is relatively high in the United States. In addition, the movement involves a small but vocal minority in most European nations. Other less demanding examples of consumer

TABLE 6.6 Environmental Attitudes (in percentages)

	United States	Great Britain	France	Germany
Policy support				
Government should reduce pollution	57	77	84	68
Trade-off questions				
Would give up part of income to prevent pollution	69	49	46	33
Would pay more taxes to prevent pollution	61	50	37	29
Action				
Member of environmental group	20	2	2	3
Volunteer work for an environmental group	9	8	1	2

SOURCES: 1999–2002 European Values Survey/World Values Survey.

NOTE: Table entries are the percentages who agree with each statement. Missing data were excluded from the calculation of percentages.

behavior demonstrate even broader levels of environmental activism among European publics.[3]

People are now interested in new political issues, such as environmentalism, that tap the noneconomic concerns typical of postmaterial values. Today, many people say they are willing to sacrifice financially to improve the environment. These concerns reflect more than just a growing awareness of the hidden health and economic costs of pollution. In a broad cross-national study of attitudes toward the environment, Ronald Inglehart (1995) notes that the citizens of prosperous countries with relatively cleaner environments are the most willing to make sacrifices for the environment. Environmental group membership is also more common in advanced industrial democracies. Material success allows the citizens in these nations to shift attention to the quality of their lives. Similarly, support for environmental protection is more common among the young, the better educated, and postmaterialists. Environmentalism reflects the processes of value change that are part of the new style of citizen politics.

Social and Moral Issues

Many contemporary democracies are experiencing a turbulent debate over social and moral norms associated with interpersonal relations and life choices. In the late 1960s and early 1970s, young people began to question traditional values by making symbolic statements, such as the use of drugs or the choice of hairstyles, clothing, and music. This movement tested the extent of individual freedom on matters such as abortion, divorce, homosexuality,

TABLE 6.7 Attitudes on Social and Moral Issues (in percentages)

	United States	Great Britain	France	Germany
Divorce is sometimes justified	88	93	91	95
Homosexuality is sometimes justified	65	80	85	91
Abortion is sometimes justified	61	80	86	85
Prostitution is sometimes justified	45	70	59	83
Euthanasia is sometimes justified	76	79	88	72
Abortion attitudes				
Abortion is not wrong:				
If child may have birth defect	47	63	81	49
If parents are poor	31	34	53	22
Religious attitudes				
Am religious person	80	49	38	54
God is important in my life	85	51	47	49
Religious attitudes average	83	50	43	52

SOURCES: 2005–2008 World Values Survey; abortion items: 1998 International Social Survey Program.

NOTE: Table entries are the percentages who agree with each statement. Missing data were excluded from the calculation of percentages.

and pornography. These issues entered the political debate in a variety of ways, often spawning countermovements from conservative members of society. Pro-choice groups stimulated pro-life replies; advocates of gay rights evoked a conservative backlash.

These issues are often linked to the values of the New Politics, but they also tap traditional Old Politics concerns because of their moral content. Social issues such as abortion or homosexuality address basic moral principles of right and wrong. Religious/secular values are typically an important influence on these opinions. People often find it is difficult to compromise on social issues because their moral views are bound up in who they are. The issue publics for social policy questions often are larger than might otherwise be expected. The active interest groups on social issues are religious organizations and Christian Democratic parties, not labor unions and business groups.

Table 6.7 presents public opinion data on several social and moral issues. In the past, traditional value orientations led many people to be highly critical of divorce; scandal, dishonor, and religious isolation often accompanied the divorce decree. The data in table 6.7 present a different picture: large majorities in our four countries now believe that divorce is sometimes justified. As attitudes toward divorce have become more tolerant, nearly all Western democracies have changed their laws to remove the stigma of divorce and provisions discriminating against women.

Perhaps even more striking is the broad tolerance of homosexuality, which was once seen as a form of social deviance. Few gay individuals felt they could openly acknowledge their sexual orientation. Longitudinal data from the World Values Survey and trends from the American General Social Survey show that opinions are becoming more tolerant over time (Dalton 2007a, ch. 5). As another sign of changing values, even the emotionally charged issue of euthanasia finds a majority in each nation that sees circumstances in which it is justifiable.

Proponents and opponents of abortion are intense in their beliefs and oriented toward political action. Abortion has periodically been the subject of major legislative or judicial action in all four nations. Most people today believe that abortion is sometimes justified, as when the health of the mother is at risk. Fewer people approve of abortion when it is based on economic factors. Despite the dramatic ebbs and flows in public events on abortion, there does not appear to be a strong trend either upward or downward in these attitudes over time.

These findings lead to two broad conclusions. First, Americans are generally more conservative than Europeans on social and moral issues. This pattern is likely the result of national differences in religious feelings, as seen in the bottom panel in the table. Despite the affluence, high mobility rates, and social diversity of its citizens, the United States is among the most religious of Western societies. American church attendance and religious feelings are among the highest in the world. A full 80 percent of Americans say they consider themselves religious, and 85 percent say God is important in their lives. Barely half of Europeans share these same opinions.[4]

Second, public opinion has generally become more tolerant on most social issues as the processes of modernization and secularization have transformed Western societies. Long-term opinion series for the United States and Germany show a gradual liberalization of attitudes toward sexual relations and homosexuality. Data presented in the earlier editions of this book document a growth in tolerant attitudes across the waves of the World Values Survey.

A decline of religious attachments and values underlies these changes in opinion on social/moral issues. Church attendance has decreased, and religious attachments have weakened (see chapter 8). Fewer Americans and Europeans now attend church on a regular basis.[5] Furthermore, there has been a shift in norms even within many churches, depicting a greater tolerance for individual choice. Because we attribute these trends to the general process of social modernization in advanced industrial societies, we expect these trends to continue.

The change in values has mixed effects on politics. The decline in religiosity may prompt greater tolerance of abortion and homosexuality. At the same time, weakening religious attachments are probably linked to declining respect for and acceptance of authority, as well an erosion in moral and ethical standards. A more secular public sees humankind in a different light.

FOREIGN POLICY OPINIONS

Foreign policy tends to be an area of shifting issue opinions (Eichenberg 2007). After decades of silent conflict during the cold war, the collapse of the Soviet Union dramatically reshaped the international order. The democratic revolution that spread throughout Eastern Europe altered the international distribution of power and values in a fundamental way. Then, just as a new stability was emerging, the world was shocked by the horrific terrorist attacks on the World Trade Center and the Pentagon in September 2001. The war to liberate Afghanistan was followed by the American overthrow of the Iraqi regime of Saddam Hussein and the continuing sectarian war in Iraq. The world is changing rapidly, and governments and people are unsure about what lies ahead and what policies governments should follow. This section describes contemporary foreign policy opinions in several areas.

Conflict

Although the cold war is over, the world can still be a brutish place. Regional and local conflicts—such as those in Sudan—threaten individual and international security. The end of the cold war has transformed peace and conflict issues in the current world. Potential conflict between the United States and Russia is no longer the central theme of international relations, and public attention has shifted toward other sources of international conflict.

A German Marshall Fund (GMF) survey in 2007 found that Americans displayed a greater concern than Europeans about a range of potential international threats in the next ten years (table 6.8). Worry about energy dependence topped the list, but substantial numbers of Americans thought that international terrorism, Iran's acquiring nuclear weapons, and a large influx of immigrants/refugees were very likely threats.

Although Americans generally reported higher threat perceptions, Europeans concerns have been growing since 2005 (German Marshall Fund 2007). Perceptions of threats from international terrorism, Islamic fundamentalism, and global warming rose substantially among Europeans. Even the Germans, who stayed out of the conflict in Iraq, now see that their nation is also a target of international terrorists. Other items (not shown in the table) demonstrate popular concern with political developments in Russia and China. American and European perceptions of the potential threats in the future are converging.

These publics are also willing to send national troops to a variety of international conflicts. There is broad support for using troops to provide humanitarian assistance in Darfur, reconstruct Afghanistan, and maintain peace in the Balkans, but many fewer Europeans are willing to use troops to combat the Taliban in Afghanistan. A host of other polling data document Europeans' broad criticism of U.S. actions in Iraq. The GMF surveys found that Europeans' approval of President Bush dropped from 38 percent in 2002 to 17 percent in 2007. And approval of the United States playing an

TABLE 6.8 Attitudes on Foreign Policy Issues (in percentages)

	United States	Great Britain	France	Germany
Concerned about international threats				
Energy dependence	88	69	88	76
Global warming	70	89	83	80
International terrorism	74	70	70	48
Increase in immigrants/refugees	72	53	74	68
Iran acquiring nuclear weapons	72	63	63	58
Islamic fundamentalism	59	61	58	50
Global disease	57	49	52	57
International cooperation				
Confidence in UN	57	60	54	52
Confidence in NATO	53	59	—	51
Confidence in European Union	—	26	49	37
Globalization				
Global trade has positive impact	78	87	88	91
International organizations have positive influence on nation	60	67	66	66
Multinational corporations have positive influence on nation	55	61	50	57
Antiglobal protestors have positive influence on nation	30	39	44	34

SOURCES: Top panel, German Marshall Fund 2007 Transatlantic Trends Survey; other data, Pew (2002, 2003).

NOTE: Table entries are the percentages agreeing with each item.

international role in world affairs dropped from 64 percent to 36 percent over this same time period.

Cooperation

Another new element of foreign policy opinion is the positive sentiment toward international organizations. Data from the Pew Surveys (2002, 2003) in the second panel of table 6.8 show that most people express confidence in the United Nations; this is true even in the United States, where conservative politicians have long denounced the UN. The majorities in the table may seem modest, but the citizens of all four nations place more confidence in the UN than in their own national parliaments! In contrast to the criticism the UN has received from some prominent American politicians in the past, this support may be an indicator of a new spirit of international cooperation—although the potential for such a development is being tested by the Iraq conflict. Support for the North Atlantic Treaty Organization (NATO) is also high in the three member-states. Trends from the GMF surveys, however, suggest that support for NATO has slipped since the early 2000s These data and other survey evidence indicate that support for internationalism is now common among Western democracies, reflecting part of a new world order.

Another example of international cooperation is the process of globalization, which involves trade and other international exchanges. Despite the active, organized opposition to globalization, especially among liberals in the Western democracies, the citizens of the four nations we are studying do not share this opinion. Very large majorities say that global trade has had a positive impact on their nation. People are generally favorable to international organizations that are the vehicles for globalization and to multinational corporations, despite often unfavorable treatment in the press. The antiglobalization protestors, in contrast, garner much less support. Certainly globalization represents new economic, social, and cultural challenges to Western democracies, but most people appear to believe that the positives outweigh the negatives.

We are living in a period in which international relations are in flux, and new threats to world order have appeared. Although it is too early to discern the exact shape that foreign policy opinions will take in this new context, it appears that Western publics are broadening their perspectives and thinking about foreign policy in more cooperative and international terms.

LEFT/RIGHT ORIENTATIONS

Despite the extent of change in the public's opinions on equality issues and social programs, we cannot use specific issue opinions to make sweeping generalizations about any country's political orientations. Citizens are now interested in a wider range of issues than just socioeconomic concerns, and so a general assessment of overall political tendencies must weigh several different issues. The rate of social change across various issues is uneven: support for environmental protection has grown rapidly over time, while attitudes toward abortion have been more stable. In addition, the ongoing political controversies change over time. In the United States the intense racial issues of the 1960s—school desegregation, open housing, and public accommodations—now register overwhelmingly liberal responses, but new racial issues—quotas and affirmative action programs—divide the public. This change represents progress in the development of racial tolerance, but racial policy remains politically contentious. One of the major points we have (re)learned from recent political trends is that new issues of conflict inevitably replace old resolved issues.

One way we can generalize about the overall political orientations of Western publics is to examine broad ideological orientations that extend beyond specific issues. Political scientists frequently measure broad orientations in terms of Left/Right attitudes (Fuchs and Klingemann 1989). Political issues are often discussed or summarized in terms of Left/Right or liberal/conservative

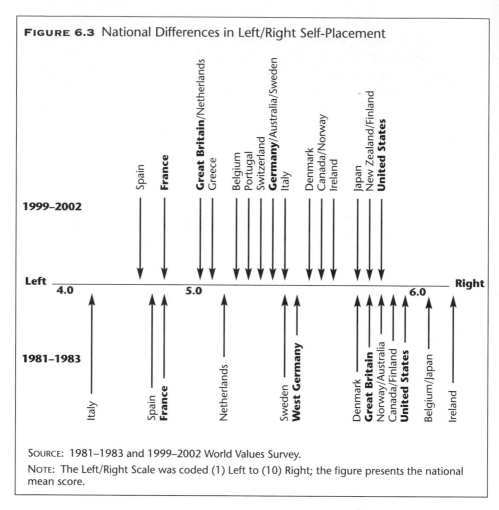

FIGURE 6.3 National Differences in Left/Right Self-Placement

SOURCE: 1981–1983 and 1999–2002 World Values Survey.

NOTE: The Left/Right Scale was coded (1) Left to (10) Right; the figure presents the national mean score.

philosophies. Republicans attack what they call the "loony Left," while Democrats rail against the "reactionary Right." These labels provide reference points that help voters interpret and evaluate political activities.

Citizens' ability to identify themselves in Left/Right terms does not imply that they possess a sophisticated conceptual framework or theoretical dogma. For many individuals, Left/Right attitudes summarize their positions on the political issues of greatest concern. These issues can vary with and across nations. So Left/Right is a sort of "super-issue" that summarizes these differing political orientations.

Figure 6.3 presents the distribution of Left/Right orientations across several nations in the early 1980s (lower figure) and at the end of the 1990s (upper figure). The survey asked respondents to place themselves on a 10-point scale, extending from "Left" to "Right." The figure plots the average Left/Right self-placement of these electorates.

The United States is one of the more conservative nations in overall Left/Right terms; in fact, few advanced industrial democracies are farther to the right (for additional nations, see Inglehart 1997). This placement on the political scale reaffirms the impression derived from many of the specific issue areas examined in this chapter. Germany and most other advanced industrial democracies are clustered around the midpoint of the scale. At the liberal pole are Mediterranean nations—France and Spain—that have significant leftist traditions.

Some evidence suggests that Left/Right attitudes are moving in a liberal direction over time, although the cross-national pattern is varied. Between 1981 and 1999, Australia, Belgium, Britain, Canada, Ireland, Japan, Norway, and the United States showed a significant leftward shift. Only Italy moved decisively in a conservative direction. Generational comparisons provide even stronger indication of political change: the young are generally more liberal than their elders. This generation gap suggests that democratic publics are gradually becoming more liberal in their overall political orientations.[6] But these data tell only a partial story.

As we suggested above, the content of Left and Right orientations reflects the issues of salience to the public, and this is another source of political change. The meaning of the terms themselves varies across age and political groups (Inglehart 1984; Fuchs and Klingemann 1989). For older citizens, these terms are linked to attitudes on socioeconomic issues: *Left* shows support for social programs, working-class interests, and the influence of labor unions; *Right* is identified with limited government, support for middle-class interests, and the influence of the business sector. Among the young, the New Politics issues of environmental protection, social equality, and lifestyle freedoms are added to socioeconomic interests. For the young, the term *Left* can mean opposition to nuclear energy, support for sexual equality, internationalism, or endorsement of social programs.

It is therefore difficult to speak in simple terms about whether contemporary publics are becoming more liberal or conservative in an overall sense. Indeed, the best longitudinal evidence from the United States suggests that these broad orientations shift in both directions, depending on the issues of controversy and the political currents of the time. James Stimson (1999) shows that the 1960s were a period of liberal ascendance, while the 1980s were a decade of conservative swing. Underlying these overall trends, however, it appears that the Left/Right placement of young citizens differs from their elders, and the meaning of *Left* and *Right* in political discourse is also changing.

PUBLIC OPINION AND POLITICAL CHANGE

A significant feature of contemporary issue opinions is that more people are interested in more issues. Opinions on socioeconomic issues were once the predominant concern of voters and political elites; one could realistically describe political competition in terms of a single overarching policy area, such as the New Deal in the United States or capitalist/socialist conflicts in Europe. Now the public's issue interests have diversified. Socioeconomic matters still attract widespread attention, but issues of social equality, environmental protection, social morals, and foreign policy also capture the interest of a growing number of citizens.

The expansion of the boundaries of politics to include these new issues has several implications for the nature of contemporary politics. Governments have increased the scope of their activity and must worry not only about economic policy but also whether the environment is clean and whether personal life choices are tolerated. The expansion of the government's role has rekindled ongoing debates about the appropriate scope of government, although the policy content of the current debate is much different from earlier debates about the economic role of the state.

The proliferation of issue publics also changes the structure of political representation and decision making. Issue publics focus their efforts to maximize representation on their issues, but the proliferation of such focused interests probably increases the complexity of the governing process. A majority of (differing) voters wants government to spend more on (differing) specific programs; a majority also wants government to tax them less. Policymakers get mixed signals from the public and have no method (or perhaps no motivation) to resolve these conflicts systematically. Government responses to the demands of one issue public may conflict with the demands of another. Policy proliferation can lead to issue-by-issue decisions rather than broad programmatic planning. One of the challenges facing contemporary governments is how to adapt the democratic process to this different pattern of interest representation.

What can we say about the overall political orientations of contemporary publics? Journalists and social commentators frequently refer to a liberal or conservative mood sweeping a nation. The early 1960s and early 1970s supposedly were a time of radical change and liberal ascendance. Similarly, discussions of a new conservative mood in Western democracies became commonplace in the 1980s, exemplified by the electoral strength of Reagan, Thatcher, Kohl, and Jacques Chirac. Bill Clinton's victory in 1992 was called a signal of a new era, but just two years later the Republican midterm victories supposedly marked another new era, which in turn quickly came to an end with Clinton's reelection in 1996. The pundits were then surprised again when George W. Bush took the White House in 2000, with Republicans controlling both houses of Congress (while Blair and Schröder's victories moved Britain and Germany to the left). Bush and Karl Rove planned to create a new Republican majority under Bush's presidency, but then lost both the House and Senate to the Democrats in 2006.

Tested against actual public opinion data, generalizations about shifts from right to left and back again are difficult to substantiate. The counterculture movement of the 1970s was not as widespread as the media suggested, and the conservative revival of the 1980s was equally overdrawn. The visible public actions of political groups can distort our perception of the broader currents of public opinion.[7] Furthermore, there are many issues of potential interest to the public, and not all of them move in a consistent direction over time.

Still, some general trends emerge from our findings. One apparent trend has been the shift toward what might be termed *libertarian attitudes*. Contemporary publics are becoming more tolerant of individual diversity and are interested in protecting individual freedoms. This applies to the rights of minorities and women, as well as to a general acceptance of individual freedom in social relations. These trends appear in attitudes toward social equality, moral issues, and the quality of life. Paralleling these changes is a decline in respect for authority and concern about social order.

The counter evidence is *socioeconomic attitudes*. Uneasiness over the excessive cost and bureaucracy of government is now commonplace (even if people favor greater government spending on a wide variety of programs). The end of socialism and the retrenchment of the welfare state in the West have made it impossible for the Left to attain its traditional goals of state control of the economy and state guarantees of basic social needs. There has been a conservative shift on these aspects of the socioeconomic issue.

In a period of increasing issue proliferation, such conflicting trends are not surprising. A gradual liberalization of political values on social issues can co exist with a conservative tilt on socioeconomic matters. But even this generalization would be difficult to sustain because the meaning of such ideological labels has changed as part of the process of issue proliferation. No longer does liberalism stand for the creation of social programs, the nationalization of industry, and peaceful coexistence with the communist world: it may just as well mean protection of a clean environment or women's rights legislation. No longer does conservatism represent the prohibition of government social programs or the defeat of the Soviet empire: it may instead mean advocacy of term limits or supporting family policies.

The content of contemporary political debate is therefore difficult to compare to the political conflicts of the New Deal era of the 1930s or even those of the Great Society of the 1960s. Perhaps this shift in the content of the political debate is what most directly shows how advanced industrial societies are modernizing and progressing politically in the new millennium.

SUGGESTED READINGS

Alba, Richard, Peter Schmidt, and Martina Wasmer, eds. *Germans or Foreigners? Attitudes toward Ethnic Minorities in Post-reunification Germany.* New York: Palgrave Macmillan, 2003.

Borre, Ole, and Elinor Scarbrough, eds. *The Scope of Government.* New York: Oxford University Press, 1995.

Inglehart, Ronald, and Pippa Norris. *A Rising Tide: Gender Equality and Cultural Change around the World.* New York: Cambridge University Press, 2003.

Jowell, Roger, et al., eds. *British—and European—Social Attitudes: The 15th Report.* Brookfield, Vt.: Ashgate, 1998.

Niedermayer, Oskar, and Richard Sinnott, eds. *Public Opinion and International Governance.* New York: Oxford University Press, 1995.

Norris, Pippa, and Ronald Inglehart. *Sacred and Secular: Religion and Politics Worldwide.* New York: Cambridge University Press, 2004.

Schuman, Howard, et al. *Racial Attitudes in America: Trends and Interpretations.* Rev. ed. Cambridge: Harvard University Press, 1997.

Sniderman, Paul, et al. *The Outsider: Prejudice and Politics in Italy.* Princeton: Princeton University Press, 2000.

Stimson, James. *Public Opinion in America: Moods, Cycles, and Swings.* 2nd ed. Boulder: Westview, 1999.

NOTES

1. As the Conservative government sold off public enterprises, the public responded to the changing political context—support for further privatizations decreased over this same time span (Heath and McMahon 1992, 118–119).
2. For more on East-West contrasts, see Bauer-Kaase (1994).
3. The percentage of green consumers is high in Europe, where waste problems and recycling efforts are more common. The 2000 International Social Survey found that 93 percent of Germans said they sort their trash for recycling, as do 51 percent of Britons and 57 percent of Americans. The same survey showed significant numbers who claim to have signed an environmental petition: 22 percent in the United States, 30 percent in Britain, and 31 percent in Germany; nearly equal numbers say they have contributed to an environmental group: 23 percent in the United States, 24 percent in Britain, and 20 percent in Germany.
4. Opinion differences within Germany reflect the legacy of the two German states. We find that 60 percent of Westerners consider themselves religious, but only 28 percent of Easterners.
5. Most advanced industrial societies have experienced a long-term trend toward secularization. Church enrollment has dropped off in most nations, as have other forms of involvement in the churches (Norris and Inglehart 2004, ch. 4).
6. These generational differences might be due to life-cycle effects, implying that younger people will become more conservative as they age. To evaluate this idea requires data over a longer time period, and the length of the available series is too brief for this purpose. Even if longer-term data were available, the information would not address questions about the changing content of the terms *Left* and *Right*, as discussed later.
7. Elections provide a poor indicator of ideological trends except in a very long-term perspective. Elections measure the positions of parties and candidates relative to the electorate, but not the overall distribution of opinion on any specific issue. A party that moves too far left can lose votes, as can one that moves too far right. Furthermore, the combination of issues in an election makes it difficult to make simple estimations of the voters' intentions on specific policies.

PART THREE

THE ELECTORAL CONNECTION

CHAPTER 7

Elections and Political Parties

Citizens have various methods to affect politics, but the electoral connection through political parties is the primary basis of public influence in representative democracies. Elections are one of the few ways that a society can reach a collective decision based on individual preferences. The choice between (or among) parties aggregates the preferences of individual voters, thereby converting public opinion into specific political decisions. Other forms of citizen participation may influence government policymaking, but they lack this representative quality.

Elections also are important because of what they decide. Electoral outcomes determine who manages the affairs of government and makes public policy. The selection of leaders—along with the ability to "throw the rascals out" at the next election—is the public's penultimate power. Political elites may not always deliver what they promise, but the selection of a government provides a measure of popular control over these elites.

To study elections, one must first understand the political parties that are the foundation of the electoral process. Parties are the primary institutions of representative democracy, especially in Europe. Parties define the choices available to voters. Candidates in most European nations are selected by the parties and elected as party representatives, not as individuals. Open primaries and independent legislators are virtually unknown outside the United States. A large proportion of Europeans (including the Germans) vote directly for party lists rather than for individual candidates.

Political parties also direct the content of election campaigns. Party programs help define the issues that are discussed during a campaign (Klingemann et al. 2006). In many European nations, it is the parties, not individual candidates, that control campaign advertising. Political parties and party leaders therefore exercise a primary role in articulating the public's concerns.

Once in government, parties control the policymaking process. Leadership of the executive branch and the organization of the legislative branch are decided based on party majorities. The parties' control is often absolute, as in the parliamentary systems of Europe, where representatives from the same party vote as a bloc (Bowler, Farrell, and Katz 1999). American parties are less united and less decisive, but even in the United States parties actively structure the legislative process. Because of the centrality of political parties to the democratic process, political scientists describe many European political systems as examples of "responsible party government."

Political parties thus provide the focus for our study of the electoral connection, and ultimately of the workings of democratic representation. A

Internet Resource

Virtually all democratic political parties have Web sites that can be found at:

http://en.wikipedia.org/wiki/User:Electionworld/Electionworld

---

well-known political scientist, E. E. Schattschneider (1942, 1), concluded that "modern democracy is unthinkable save in terms of political parties." British historian James Bryce (1921, 119) said, "Parties are inevitable. No one has shown how representative government could be worked without them." Many contemporary political scientists share these views.

This chapter summarizes the history and social bases of contemporary party systems. We present a framework for understanding the party options available to the voters, as well as the characteristics of the major parties as political organizations and agents of representative democracy.

AN OVERVIEW OF FOUR PARTY SYSTEMS

To introduce the party systems in our four core nations, we first describe the characteristics of the major parties in each nation.[1] Parties vary in size, structure, and governmental experience, as well as in their political orientation.[2]

As table 7.1 shows, the American party system is atypical in many ways. The single-member-district electoral system encourages the development of a two-party system of Democrats and Republicans because seats are awarded only to the candidate who wins the most votes in each district. A party system based on only two parties is unusual; most democracies have more parties competing in elections, and multiparty coalitions are necessary to form a government majority. In the United States, in contrast, power shifts back and forth between the two major parties. The Republicans' dramatic breakthrough in the 1994 congressional elections ended forty years of Democratic rule. Since then, the national electorate has been fairly evenly divided between the parties. The fluctuation in congressional vote totals over time is relatively small, averaging less than a 3 percent vote change between elections.

The results of presidential races are usually more varied than congressional elections. Lyndon Johnson won in a huge Democratic landslide in 1964, and Ronald Reagan won an equally impressive Republican majority in 1984. The presidential elections of 2000 and 2004, however, demonstrated the current parity of party support. Presidential elections are heavily influenced by the candidates' attributes, and voting results can fluctuate sharply with each election. Therefore, our cross-national analyses of voting behavior use American congressional elections rather than presidential contests, because congressional elections are more similar to Western European parliamentary contests.

TABLE 7.1 Party Characteristics

Party	Year founded	Legislative election Vote %	Seats	Party structure	Years in government (1977–2007)
United States (2004)					
Democrats (US Dem)	1832	44.0	201	Decentralized	17
Republicans (US Rep)	1856	55.0	233	Decentralized	13
Great Britain (2005)					
Labour (Lab)	1900	35.2	356	Centralized	19
Liberal Democrats (LibDem)	1987	22.1	62	Decentralized	0
Conservatives (Con)	1830	32.4	198	Mixed	11
Scottish National Party (SNP)	1934	1.5	6		0
Plaid Cymru (PCy)	1925	.6	3		0
Other parties		18.2	16	Mixed	0
France (2007)					
Communist Party (PCF)	1920	4.3	15	Centralized	5
Socialists (PS)	1905	24.7	186	Centralized	13
Greens (Verts)	1978	3.3	4	Decentralized	5
Union for Popular Movement (UPM/RPR)	1947	39.5	313	Mixed	24
New Center (formerly UDF)	1978	2.3	22	Mixed	24
National Front (FN)	1972	4.3	0	Personalistic	0
Other parties		21.6	37		
Germany (2005)					
Linke.PDS	1990	8.7	54	Centralized	0
Social Democrats (SPD)	1863	34.2	222	Centralized	15
Greens (Grüne)	1980	8.1	51	Decentralized	8
Free Democrats (FDP)	1948	9.8	61	Decentralized	21
Christian Democrats (CDU/CSU)	1950	35.2	226	Mixed	18
Republikaner/NPD	1983	2.2	0	Mixed	0

SOURCE: Compiled by the author; election statistics from election world database on Wikipedia.

Another distinctive aspect of the American political system is the decentralized nature of party organizations. Because of the federal system of American government, instead of one Democratic Party (or Republican Party) there are really fifty—one in each state. National party meetings are something like medieval gatherings of feudal states, rather than the conclaves of a unitary organization. The presidential nominating conventions are not controlled and directed by the national party but are taken over every four years by the personnel of the winning candidates. Even in Congress, American legislators are more likely to cross party lines when voting on legislation than are parliamentarians in disciplined party systems, which makes the American party system considerably more diverse and fluid than in Europe. The institutional weakness of the parties is also apparent in their small memberships (see chapter 3).

Great Britain presents a different partisan pattern—often described as a two-and-a-half-party system. The Labour Party is the major force on the left, and the Conservative Party is the representative of the right. Each of these major parties routinely receives between 35 percent and 45 percent of the national vote. The smaller Liberal Democratic Party, located near the center of the political spectrum, garners 15 percent to 20 percent.[3]

The diversity of the British party system has grown since the 1970s. Revived regional movements strengthened the nationalist parties in Scotland (Scottish Nationalist Party) and Wales (Plaid Cymru) in the 1970s, and the development of regional parliaments in the 1990s further strengthened these parties. At the end of the 1980s, the Liberal Party was reformed as the Liberal Democrats, combining traditional conservatism on economic issues with more liberal policies on social issues. Other minor parties have periodically won significant vote shares, especially in the European Parliament elections, which are proportional representation elections. Despite these changes in the party system, the competition between Labour and the Conservatives still structures British electoral competition for the House of Commons.

The British political parties also are more highly organized and centralized than the American political parties. Because Britain, like most other democracies, lacks the system of primaries that select candidates in the United States, the national party organizations work with the formal party members in each constituency in selecting candidates and determining the strategies of election campaigns. Once elected, members of Parliament generally follow party lines in policy debates and in their voting behavior.

Another feature of parliamentary systems is the emphasis on the party rather than on individual politicians. British voters do not cast a vote for the chief executive (the prime minister), as Americans vote for president on the ballot. Under the procedures of its parliamentary system, the party group that controls Parliament elects the prime minister, who heads the executive branch. Even when it comes to electing a local district representative, British voters choose a party, often without knowing much about the candidate who represents the party in the district. The British political system follows a model of strong party government.

The German party system is even more diverse. The electoral system is based on proportional representation: a party's share of the votes ultimately determines its share of the seats in parliament.[4] As a result, Germany has a multiparty system, with two major parties and several smaller parties. The Christian Democrats (CDU/CSU) are the major conservative party, and the

Social Democrats (SPD) are the major leftist party. The CDU/CSU controlled the government for the first two decades of the Federal Republic (1949–1969), and again from 1982 to 1998. The SPD controlled the national government from 1969 until 1982, and held power from 1998 to 2005 in a coalition with the Green Party. Because the 2005 election resulted in a deadlock between the two major parties, they took the unusual step forming a joint government. Their combined votes totaled 69 percent in the election.

Several smaller parties also compete in German elections. The Greens emerged on the partisan stage in the 1980s as representatives of a postmaterial agenda (Poguntke 1993). The Greens advocate a variety of New Politics causes. For example, when they were part of the SPD/Green government they initiated policies to close down nuclear power plants and enact a new green energy tax. The small Free Democratic Party (FDP), which captures between 5 percent and 10 percent of the vote, was a junior coalition partner in earlier governments.

German unification in 1990 further changed the political landscape, adding millions of new voters from the East. The Party of Democratic Socialism (PDS) emerged as a successor to the communist and socialist values of the German Democratic Republic, and the party still attracts the bulk of its support from the East. In 2005 the PDS allied itself with a group of former SPD and leftists in the West to form Linke.PDS. The party won votes away from the SPD and gained fifty-four seats in the parliament. In 2007 the two parties united under the name *Die Linke* (the Left). Germany has several small parties on the extreme right—the Republikaner, NPD, and DVU that advocate nationalist and antiforeigner sentiments. None of them has won seats in the national parliament, but their presence affects the country's political debate.

The German political system emphasizes the role of political parties to a greater degree than does the U.S. system. Parties control the candidate selection process. In Bundestag elections, the voter casts two votes. The first vote (*Erststimme*) is for a district candidate who is nominated by a small group of official party members or by a committee appointed by the membership (not through a primary election). The second vote (*Zweitstimme*) is directly for a party, which leads to the selection of half the Bundestag deputies from lists created by the parties. The government finances election campaigns, and it allocates funding and access to public radio and television to the parties rather than the individual candidates. Government funding for the parties also continues between elections to help them perform their educational functions as prescribed in the Basic Law. With the notable exception of the Greens, the German political parties are highly organized and centralized institutions. Therefore, it is not surprising to hear Germany described as a system of "party government."

France has an even more highly fragmented multiparty system. Instead of one party on the left, there are several: the Communist Party (PC), the Socialist Party (PS), and various smaller extreme leftist parties. Instead of one major party on the right, there are several: the Union for a Popular Movement

(UPM, formerly the Rally for the Republic or RPR), represents the Gaullist tradition, and the Union for French Democracy (UDF) holds a more center-right position. During the 1980s the National Front (FN) emerged as an extreme right-wing party that attracts nationalist voters and those opposed to foreign immigrants. A new environmental party was born in the early 1980s; it reformed in the mid-1980s and again in the early 1990s. Now called the Greens (*Verts*), it attracts some support from young, postmaterial voters. Added to this mix are miscellaneous small centrist or extremist parties. In the 2007 election, nine party groups won representation in the parliament, and many more ran for office.

The electoral history of the Fifth Republic is one of party change and electoral volatility. The Gaullist Party, now UPM, was originally the major party on the right and participated in conservative governments for the first two decades of the Fifth Republic. The tide shifted to the left in the 1980s, especially toward the Socialists, with their broad program of Old Politics and New Politics reforms. The Socialist Party won a majority in the 1981 legislative elections. The conservatives controlled the parliament from 1986 to 1988, and then a leftist majority reestablished itself. The conservatives swept the parliamentary elections of 1993, and then a Socialist/Green/PCF majority formed after the 1997 elections. A conservative majority won legislative control in 2002. In 2007 the Right won both the presidency and a new majority in the parliament. In short, the French party system is exceptionally fluid.

It is difficult to describe the French system in terms of a model of responsible party government. On the one hand, the French party system gives voters greater ideological choice than is available to American, British, or German voters. The parties exert their influence over the political campaigns and the activities of the parliament. On the other hand, the fragmentation of the party system typically requires coalition politics, wherein several parties are forced to negotiate and compromise on their programs. This process weakens the chain of party responsibility that exists in the British or German governments. Moreover, it is often the party leader, rather than the national party organization, who defines a party's goals and strategies. French parties—even a highly centralized party such as the PC—are often highly personalistic. The French party system could be characterized as a party system in constant transition.

THE HISTORY OF PARTY SYSTEMS

Discussions of political parties normally focus on the present: the policy positions and political leaders that define current party images. We often think of each election in terms of the issues of the day. But across elections, parties normally take consistent positions that reflect their historical roots based in either an ideology or a connection with enduring social interests. Many voters repeatedly support the same party across elections for the same reasons. The Democratic tendencies of American Catholics, for example, result from their

TABLE 7.2 Social Cleavages and Voter Alignments

Historic era	Cleavage	Voting groups
National Revolution	Center/periphery Church/state	Region Religious denomination Religious/secular
Industrial Revolution	Land/industry Owners/workers	Urban/rural Middle/working class
Postindustrial Revolution	Cultural values	Material/postmaterial

SOURCE: Compiled by the author.

class position when they first emigrated to America and the manner in which Catholics were integrated into society and politics. The Republican leanings of Cuban Americans reflect their unique historical experiences, which link them to the Republican Party.

Seymour Martin Lipset and Stein Rokkan (1967) described modern party systems in terms of the historical patterns of national and socioeconomic development. Table 7.2 summarizes their analyses and outlines the voting implications of this framework. Lipset and Rokkan held that two successive revolutions in the modernization of Western societies—the *National Revolution* and the *Industrial Revolution*—created divisions among certain social groups that still structure partisan competition today. Although their discussion dealt primarily with Western Europe, the approach is relevant to other Western democracies, including the United States.

The National Revolution involved the process of building unified national states in Europe during the eighteenth and nineteenth centuries. The National Revolution spawned two sets of competing social groups (social cleavages) that are represented in the middle column of table 7.2. The *center/periphery* cleavage pitted the dominant national culture against ethnic, linguistic, or religious minorities in the peripheral regions. For example, were Alsatians to become Germans or French; was Scotland a separate nation or a region within Britain? The diverse state histories within the United States generated similar tensions between regional cultures, eventually leading to a civil war. This cleavage is visible today in persistent regional differences in political orientation: between the English and the Welsh and the English and the Scots; between Bretons and the Parisian center; between the "Free State of Bavaria" and the Federal Republic of Germany; between the old Federal Republic and the new German states in the East; and between the distinct regional cultures in the United States.

The National Revolution also formalized *church/state* conflict, which cast the centralizing, standardizing, and mobilizing forces of the national government against the traditional values of the Catholic Church. In the face of a growing secular government, the church often tried to protect its privileges by resisting the new national government or creating political groups to represent religious interests. Protestants often allied themselves with nationalist forces in the struggle for national autonomy. Contemporary divisions between religious denominations and between secular and religious groups continue these earlier social divisions.

The Industrial Revolution in the nineteenth century generated two additional social cleavages (table 7.2). The *land/industry* cleavage pitted rural and agrarian interests against the economic concerns of a rising class of industrial entrepreneurs. The barons of industry challenged the landed gentry of Britain and agrarian interests in the United States; the Ruhr industrialists challenged the power of the Prussian Junkers. This cleavage continues in contemporary conflicts between rural and urban interests.

As industrialization progressed, a second cleavage developed between *owners and workers* within the industrial sector. This cleavage reflected class conflict between the working class and the middle class composed of business owners and the self-employed. The struggle for the legitimization and representation of the working-class movement often generated intense political conflict in the late nineteenth and early twentieth centuries. Today, this cleavage appears in the competition between labor unions and business associations and more generally between members of the working class and the middle class.

These historical events may seem very distant from contemporary party systems, but Lipset and Rokkan (1967) claimed that a connection exists. These four cleavages define major sources of social conflict existing within most democracies. As social groups related to these cleavages developed—such as farmer associations or labor unions—they participated in the political process even before the extension of the voting franchise. When mass voting rights were granted to most Europeans around the turn of the twentieth century, this structure of group competition was already in place. New voters tended to support the parties that already were politically active and entered the electorate with preexisting partisan tendencies. The Conservative Party in Britain, for example, was the representative of the middle-class establishment, while the Labour Party catered to the interests of the working class. The working class in France and Germany supported the Communist and Socialist Parties. The American party system developed more gradually because the voting franchise was granted earlier and social groups were less polarized. But the modern party system continues to reflect cleavages from the Civil War and the Great Depression. The Democratic Party, for example, still draws upon the New Deal coalition that formed its base in the 1930s.

The formation of mass political parties thus institutionalized the existing group alignments, creating the framework for modern party systems. Once voters formed party loyalties, and interest groups established party ties, these relationships became self-perpetuating. At each election, parties turned to the same social groups for their core support, and most voters in these groups habitually supported the same party. In one of the most often cited conclusions of comparative politics, Lipset and Rokkan stated that "the party systems of the 1960s reflect, with but few significant exceptions, the cleavage structures of the 1920s" (1967, 50).

Early electoral research substantiated Lipset and Rokkan's claims. Regional voting patterns from the early twentieth century appear in recent election returns. Survey research found that social cleavages, especially class and religious differences, exerted a potent effect on voting. For example, Richard Rose's (1969) comparative study of voting patterns in the 1960s found that voting choices were clearly related to the cleavages that Lipset and Rokkan described.

Just as this theme of partisan stability was becoming the conventional wisdom, dramatic changes began to affect these party systems starting in the 1970s. The established parties faced new demands and challenges, and evidence of partisan change mounted (Dalton, Flanagan, and Beck 1984).[5] New parties emerged to compete in elections, and some of the established parties fragmented. The evidence of more fluid and dynamic party politics has grown over the subsequent decades.

At the root of this development is a weakening relationship between traditional social cleavages and partisan choice. In their comparative study of Western democracies, Mark Franklin, Tom Mackie, and Henry Valen (1992) found that traditional social divisions were losing their ability to predict voting choices (also see chapter 8). Because of this erosion in traditional social group–based politics, voting choices became more fluid. Partisan volatility increased at the aggregate and individual levels. Popular attachments to political parties weakened (see chapter 9). The major research question changed from explaining the persistence of historical patterns in contemporary party systems to explaining their growing instability.

Several unique national circumstances contributed to this instability: the Vietnam War and racial desegregation in the United States, regional and economic tensions in Britain, and the student movement in France and Germany. The party systems of Europe and North America also experienced their normal share of political crises and economic problems that often rocked the incumbent parties.

In addition, the Postindustrial Revolution brought new postmaterial issues onto the political stage (see table 7.2 and chapter 5). The established parties confronted a different set of issues: environmental protection, social equality, nuclear energy, gender equality, and alternative lifestyles. Some voters demanded more opportunities for participation in the decisions affecting their lives and pressed for a further democratization of society. Once these trends began, they provoked a conservative response that opposed the liberalization of social norms and other postmaterial issues. Sometimes this backlash has led to a reassertion of traditional value conflicts based on religion or other historic social cleavages. These new postmaterial conflicts are now an important aspect of contemporary politics.

The initial failure of the major parties to respond fully to what the public demanded was a major factor in the destabilization of modern party systems. As a result, new parties formed specifically to represent the new political perspectives. The first wave included environmental parties, such as the Green parties in France and Germany or Left-libertarian parties (Richardson and Rootes 1995). This was followed by a counterwave of New Right parties, such as the National Front in France and the Republikaner in Germany (Ignazi 2003). It is unclear whether these parties reflect temporary responses to modern issues or a more permanent realignment of political conflict. American history is full of third-party movements that were eventually incorporated into the established parties. The present partisan instability in advanced industrial democracies could be just another case of this recurring pattern.

Party systems are in a state of flux, and it is difficult to determine how fundamental and long-lasting these changes will be. It is clear, however, that the new political conflicts of advanced industrial societies have contributed to this fluidity. While we wait for history to determine the significance of these trends, we can look more closely at the political alignments that now exist in the United States, Britain, France, and Germany.

THE STRUCTURE OF POLITICAL ALIGNMENTS

Most parties and party systems are still oriented primarily toward the traditional political alignments that Lipset and Rokkan described. We refer to them as the Old Politics cleavage; it pits the Old Left coalition against the Old Right. Lipset and Rokkan considered social class to be the primary factor of the Old Politics cleavage because class issues were highly salient when the franchise expanded. The Old Left identifies itself with the working class and labor unions, as well as with secular groups and urban interests. The Old Right is synonymous with business interests and the middle class. When political issues tap the concerns of the Old Politics cleavage—for example, wage settlements, employment programs, or social security programs—class characteristics are strongly related to voting preferences.

A second element of the Old Politics is conflict over religious or moral issues. Many Western democracies still face conflicts over the relationship between church and state. Sometimes this cleavage separates Catholics and Protestants who have different views on these matters. At other times, the cleavage divides secular and religious voters. Indeed, several European party systems feature Christian or Christian Democratic parties as major forces on the right.

Most advanced industrial societies now contain a new dimension of postmaterial cleavage (see chapter 5). The New Politics dimension involves conflict over issues such as environmental quality, alternative lifestyles, minority rights, social equality, and other postmaterial issues. This dimension represents the cleavage between proponents of these issues, the New Left, and citizens who feel threatened by these issues, the New Right.

The Old Politics cleavage is likely to remain the primary basis of partisan conflict in most advanced industrial democracies for the near future. The New Politics dimension is significantly affecting these party systems, however, because it can cut across the established Old Politics cleavage. Despite their economic differences, labor unions and business interests often join forces to support nuclear energy. Farmers and students sometimes become allies to oppose industrial development projects that may threaten the environment. Fundamentalist blue-collar and white-collar workers unite to oppose challenges to their moral code. The emergence of New Left and New Right interests may restructure social group alignments and party coalitions in new and contrasting ways. In sum, the simple dichotomy between Old Left and Old Right no longer adequately describes patterns of political competition. The contemporary political space is now better described by at least two dimensions (or more).[6]

We can illustrate the separation of the Old Politics and New Politics cleavages with examples drawn from the United States. For much of the past century, the Old Politics cleavages structured party competition in the U.S. party system. The New Deal coalition created in the 1930s in response to the Great Depression determined the social bases of party support: the Democratic Party and its working-class supporters against the Republicans and big business. The formal separation of church and state muted religious differences in America.

Beginning in the 1960s and 1970s student protesters, the women's movement, and the alternative lifestyles movement challenged the symbols of the political establishment. Herbert Weisberg and Jerold Rusk (1970) described how this cultural conflict generated a new cleavage, as represented by dissident Democratic candidates such as George McGovern and Gary Hart. These researchers found, however, that Democrats and Republicans were not clearly aligned on New Politics issues, which divided parties internally rather than separating them politically (also see Inglehart 1984).[7]

The policies of the Reagan and first Bush administrations (1981–1993) stimulated a convergence of Old Politics and New Politics alignments. The Reagan administration's taxing and spending priorities sharply favored business and the more affluent sectors of society, which reinforced ties between business interests and the Republican Party. Furthermore, the Reagan administration pursued a conservative social agenda and developed political links to religious groups such as the Moral Majority and other fundamentalist organizations, bringing religion into partisan politics to an extent atypical of modern American politics.

The Reagan-Bush administrations also clarified party positions on the New Politics agenda. The Republican Party previously had supported some environmental issues; for example, Richard Nixon created the Environmental Protection Agency and introduced a variety of environmental legislation. But the Reagan and Bush administrations were openly hostile toward the environmental movement and thwarted further environmental reform. In addition, these two Republican administrations were openly antagonistic toward feminist organizations. The abortion issue became a litmus test of Republican values in the appointment of federal judges and the selection of candidates.

As the Republicans grew more critical of the New Politics agenda, the Democrats became advocates of these same causes. The Democrats supported environmental reform and stronger environmental protection standards. Bill Clinton (1993–2001) and his "New Democrats" coalition attempted to unite the old constituency of labor unions and the new constituency of environmentalists and feminists. Al Gore focused on environmental issues both in his bid for the presidency in 2000 and since then as an advocate for environmental reform.

Meanwhile, the Republican Party united its traditional middle class and business supporters with its new voters among cultural conservatives. George W. Bush moved even further to strengthen the conservative identity of the Republican Party. Since 1980 the American party system has experienced a clear polarization of the political parties.

We can illustrate the current social and partisan alignments with data from the 2004 American National Election Study. The survey asked respondents whether they felt close or distant to a set of sociopolitical groups and the political parties.[8] We used a statistical analysis method to represent the interrelationship of group perceptions in graphic terms.[9] This technique maps the political space as perceived by Americans. When there is a strong similarity in how two groups are evaluated, they are located near each other in the space. When groups are evaluated in dissimilar terms, they are positioned a distance apart. This figure charts the political map that voters use to place themselves in relation to social groups and political parties.

Figure 7.1 depicts the American sociopolitical space in 2004. The traditional Left/Right cleavage of the Old Politics is quite evident as the horizontal dimension in the figure. John Kerry is located at the left, along with the Democratic candidate for the House of Representatives in the survey respondent's district (Dem. House), and both politicians are seen as close to the labor unions. In contrast, George W. Bush is located at the opposite end of the continuum, and the nearest groups are business, the Christian Coalition, and the Republican candidate for the House.

The figure also shows the position of other political groups in this political space. New Left groups, including feminists and environmentalists, are seen as close to Kerry and the Democrats in 2004—a closer proximity because of Kerry held more leftist politics than either Bill Clinton or Al Gore. The positioning of these New Left groups near the Democrats, and the Christian Coalition near the Republicans, may indicate the integration of cultural issues into American party politics, at least with the candidate choices in 2004. Another part of the political space is occupied by minority groups—blacks, Hispanics, and the poor—who are perceived as closer to the Democratic Party, but distinct from either Old Left or New Left groups.

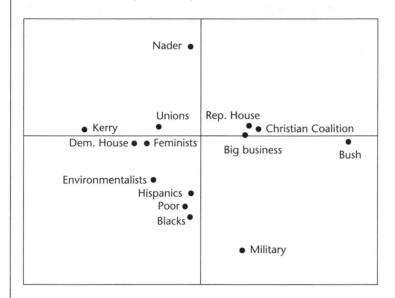

FIGURE 7.1   Sociopolitical Space in the United States

SOURCE: 2004 American National Election Study.

NOTE: The figure presents a mapping of groups in the political space; similarly evaluated groups are located near each other, and dissimilar groups are at a greater distance in the space. The map is based on a multidimensional scaling of thermometer scores (see endnote 9).

The opposite ends of the vertical dimensions are represented by Ralph Nader, the former Green Party candidate who ran as an antiestablishment independent in 2004, and the military, which Americans see as the group most opposite to Nader. This contrast between Nader and the military also suggests that an establishment/antiestablishment dimension also frames the American political space.[10]

Comparable current data on the sociopolitical space in Britain, Germany, and France are not available, but we can describe the relative positions of political parties with a different method. Kenneth Benoit and Michael Laver (2006) asked political experts in each nation to position the parties on a set of policy dimensions. We can use these expert opinions to compare how parties are perceived on different policy dimensions, and how parties compare across nations.

Figure 7.2 presents party positions on two policies: maintaining social spending versus tax cuts as a measure of the socioeconomic issues of the Old Politics, and environmental protection versus economic growth as a measure of New Politics issues. The dots in the figure represent individual parties in

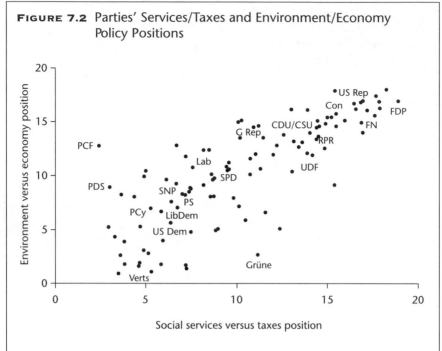

FIGURE 7.2 Parties' Services/Taxes and Environment/Economy Policy Positions

SOURCE: Party positions from Benoit and Laver (2006); parties from eighteen advanced industrial democracies are included in the figure.

NOTE: The figure presents the position of political parties on both policy dimensions determined by a panel of experts. Party abbreviations are listed in Table 7.1.

each of the eighteen established democracies in the Benoit/Laver study.[11] The major parties in our four nations are denoted by the parties' initials in the figure (see table 7.1).

The horizontal axis in the figure locates parties on the social spending versus tax cut issue.[12] We see the traditional Left/Right party alignment. The farthest left parties are the French Communist Party (PCF) and the post-Communist PDS in Germany, which strongly favor raising taxes to increase social services. At the opposite end of the Old Politics dimension are conservative parties that favor reducing social services to cut taxes.

The vertical dimension represents a party's position on protecting the environment versus supporting economic growth even at the cost of the environment—a postmaterial/material cleavage. The French Greens (*Verts*) and German Greens (*Grünen*) are strong advocates of the former position.

By identifying the parties in a specific nation in the figure, one can also see the diversity of party choice in each system. The French party system offers a wide spread of parties along the left/right diagonal, from the Verts to the Front National (FN), with a range of parties along this axis. The PCF offers a distinct mix of leftist policies on the Old Politics dimension and a conservative position on the New Politics dimension. The German party system also covers a wide span of this political space, from the PDS to the FDP, with the Greens advocating a distinct environmental option. The fluidity of contemporary party systems is perhaps best illustrated by the British parties. Tony Blair and Gordon Brown consciously moved the Labour Party to the ideological center to attract greater voter support, and their efforts are apparent by the party's location in the figure. Now the Labour Party is outflanked on both the Old Left and New Left by the Liberal Democrats, as well as the Scottish National Party (SNP) and Plaid Cymru (PCy). A generation ago, the British party system would have displayed sharp polarization along the social spending/tax cut dimension, with Labourites at one pole, Conservatives at the other, and Liberals in the middle.

The two American parties display a wide separation in this political space. Experts position the Democrats as favoring more social services and more strongly supporting the environment than the major leftist parties in Britain, France, and Germany. Conversely, the Republicans are perceived as one of the most conservative parties on both dimensions, and are located at the upper right of the figure. I suspect this polarization is an overstatement, reflecting the growth in party differentiation over the preceding decade and heightened political tensions between parties during the George W. Bush administration. With only two parties, the tendency is strong to locate one at one pole and the other at the opposite end. American political parties have become more distinct, but perhaps not as much as suggested by the figure.[13]

Economic and environmental policies are important sources of party competition, but social or moral issues also divide parties. These issues reflect the persistence influence of religion on politics that are often expressed in terms of gender rights and life style choices. Therefore, we also mapped party positions with services/tax cut on the horizontal axis and positions on social policies on the vertical axis (figure 7.3). The social policy dimension taps support for conservative positions on issues such as abortion, homosexuality, and euthanasia.[14] Parties have the same position on the social services/tax cut dimension as in figure 7.2, but now one sees a different alignment on the social policy dimension. Parties of the economic left also hold fairly liberal positions on social issues, clustering at the bottom left of the figure. In contrast, social issues create divisions within economically conservative parties. For example, the German FDP is strongly conservative on the economic dimension, but distinctly liberal on social policy issues. So-called New Right parties, such as the German Republikaner and French National Front hold distinctly conservative views on the social issues, even to the right of the German Christian Democrats. So just as environmentalism causes divisions among the economic Left, social policy issues cause divisions within the economic Right.

In the United States, the experts again see a stark policy separation between Democrats and Republicans. The Democrats are seen as taking a liberal position on social issues, leading to frequent claims that support for reproductive

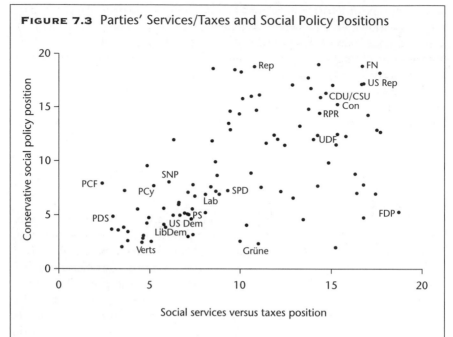

FIGURE 7.3 Parties' Services/Taxes and Social Policy Positions

SOURCE: Party positions from Benoit and Laver (2006); parties from eighteen advanced industrial democracies are included in the figure.

NOTE: The figure presents the position of political parties on both policy dimensions determined by a panel of experts. Party abbreviations are listed in Table 7.1.

rights and homosexual rights have become a litmus test for Democratic Party candidates. Conversely, the Republicans have become more conservative on social issues since the 1980s, and especially during the George W. Bush administration. This party cleavage also appears in Figure 7.1, in which the public locates the Christian Coalition as Bush's close political ally. In the United States, the alignment of the two parties is now similar on both Old Politics and New Politics dimensions.

If Old Politics issues, such as government social spending, were the only source of electoral competition, then Lipset and Rokkan would still be correct in describing contemporary party systems in terms of the cleavages of the 1920s. The class-based Left/Right party alignment that historically structured partisan politics remains clearly visible in political experts' positioning of the contemporary parties on the social services versus tax cut dimension.

The content of the political agenda, however, now includes more than Old Politics economic concerns. As the New Politics has introduced postmaterial interests into the political debate, these issues have led to a different alignment of parties. For example, the German Green Party is a strong advocate for environmental causes and is located at the far left end of this continuum (see figure 7.2). The Social Democrats are closer to the conservative CDU/CSU on the environmental dimension than they are to the Greens. The environmental dimension separates the Greens and other New Left parties from *all* the other parties.

In addition, social issues, such as homosexual rights, and controversies over immigration and international issues, such as globalization, international trade, or conflict in the Middle East, introduce more variability into party alignments (Benoit and Laver 2006). Instead of a single Old Politics cleavage to structure electoral competition, parties are asked to take positions on a set of potentially contradictory political dimensions, which introduces greater complexity and fluidity to contemporary electoral politics. The mix of these old and new dimensions fuels the current processes of electoral change in these nations.

CONTEMPORARY PARTY SYSTEMS

This chapter has described broad similarities in the ideological structure of contemporary party systems. Most political parties are still oriented to the Old Politics divisions of class and religion. Even if these cleavages have become less salient, the political ties between social groups and political parties perpetuate this framework. Parties are, after all, still turning to the same interest groups and associations for the core of their support. Contemporary publics see rightist parties as linked to business interests (and sometimes church groups) and leftist parties as allied with the labor unions.

Major party differences exist on the Old Politics dimension, but we see signs that the New Politics cleavage is taking on greater importance. Chapters 5 and 6 showed that people are developing postmaterial values that lead to new policy interests. These new issues initially were represented outside the established parties through public interest groups, but they are now gaining representation within partisan politics, which places new demands on the established parties.

We can see signs of partisan change along the New Politics dimension in several nations. New parties, such as the German and French Greens, have emerged to represent New Politics concerns. These small parties draw their support from the young, the better educated, and postmaterialists—the groups that define the New Politics cleavage. Similarly, New Right parties have emerged in many Western party systems, typically advocating conservative social values, social order, and often a criticism of immigration and minority politics.

Some established parties are trying to combine Old Left and New Left issue appeals into a single program, although such a coalition is difficult to maintain because of widely contrasting interests. Unions that would be pleased with a socialist party's position on social services might be displeased by pro-environmental policies that would threaten employment. Similarly, some conservative parties have attempted to appeal to both Old Right groups on economic issues and New Right groups on social issues and have experienced the same tensions in pulling this coalition together. Consequently, many established parties have been hesitant to formalize close ties to these new issue groups, especially in Western Europe, where the Old Politics ties remain strong. Parties are naturally cautious about taking clear stands on a new dimension of conflict before the costs and benefits are clear.

The 2008 U.S. presidential primaries illustrated these multiple dimensions of electoral competition within and between the parties. Mitt Romney began the campaign with close ties to the fiscal conservatives in the Republican Party, but alienated many social conservatives. Mike Huckabee drew strong support from Republican social conservatives, but not from fiscal conservatives. Rudi Giuliani appealed to defense conservatives, but not to social conservatives. Other divisions existed within the Democratic primaries. John Edwards and Hillary Clinton had strong ties to labor, and Clinton drew support from women's groups such as EMILY's List. Barack Obama appealed to younger postmaterial voters, minorities, and a politically cynical middle class. Electoral politics has fragmented into a fluid, multidimensional issue space. Because of this uncertainty, few experts correctly predicted the course of the primaries even as 2008 began.

Because of the uncertainties facing the parties and the difficulties in integrating new political cleavages into the existing party systems, future partisan change is likely in most established democracies. Continuing changes in citizen values and issue interests mean that the potential for further partisan change is real.

SUGGESTED READINGS

Abramson, Paul, John Aldrich, and David Rohde. *Change and Continuity in the 2004 Elections.* Washington, D.C.: CQ Press, 2005.

Benoit, Kenneth, and Michael Laver. 2006. *Party Policy in Modern Democracies.* New York: Routledge.

Clarke, Harold, et al. *Political Choice in Britain.* Oxford: Oxford University Press, 2004.

Evans, Geoffrey, and Pippa Norris, eds. *Critical Elections: British Parties and Voters in Long-Term Perspective.* Thousand Oaks, Calif.: Sage, 1999.

Langenbacher, Eric, ed. "The 2005 Bundestag Election." Special issue, *German Politics and Society* (Spring 2006).

LeDuc, Lawrence, Richard Niemi, and Pippa Norris, eds. *Comparing Democracies: New Challenges in the Study of Elections and Voting.* 2nd ed. Thousand Oaks, Calif.: Sage, 2002.

Lewis-Beck, Michael S., ed. *How France Votes.* New York: Chatham House, 1999.

Luther, Richard, and Ferdinand Mueller Rommel, eds. *Party Change in Europe.* Oxford: Oxford University Press, 2002.

Norris, Pippa. *Electoral Engineering: Voting Rules and Political Behavior.* New York: Cambridge University Press, 2004.

———. ed. *Britain Votes 2001.* Oxford: Oxford University Press, 2001.

Webb, Paul, David Farrell, and Ian Holliday, eds. *Political Parties in Advanced Industrial Democracies.* Oxford: Oxford University Press, 2002.

NOTES

1. There are several good analytic studies of recent U.S. elections (Abramson, Aldrich, and Rohde 2005), British elections (Clarke et al. 2004, 2008; Norris 2001), German elections (Langenbacher 2006; Rohrschneider and Dalton 2003), and French elections (Lewis-Beck 1999).
2. We calculated vote share based on the most recent national election: United States (2004), Britain (2005), Germany (2005), and France (2007). The computation of years in government is complicated by the separation of powers in the United States and France. We decided to count the number of years a party was part of the legislative majority between 1977 and 2007 as the most comparable cross-national statistic.
3. Because of the single-member-district electoral system, the Liberal Democrats are routinely disadvantaged in winning seats in Parliament. In 2005, for example, the party won 22 percent of the popular vote nationwide but received less than 10 percent of the seats in the House of Commons.
4. German electoral law requires that a party win 5 percent of the national vote on the second ballot, or three district seats, in order to share in the proportional distribution of Bundestag seats.
5. Stefano Bartolini and Peter Mair (1990) forcefully argue that earlier historical periods were also marked by high levels of partisan volatility. But their methodology underestimates the degree of the current levels of partisan change (Dalton and Wattenberg 2000, ch. 3).
6. Although this chapter presents new alignments in terms of the two dimensions of the Old Politics and New Politics, it is more accurate to describe party systems as moving from simple structures of one or two dimensions to a fragmented structure of many dimensions.
7. The 1984 Democratic primaries featured a confrontation between Old Left and New Left Democrats. Walter Mondale, who was identified with the traditional New Deal policies of the Democratic Party, won early endorsements from labor unions and the party establishment. Gary Hart explicitly claimed that he was the New Politics candidate, the representative of new ideas and a new generation. Hart's core voters were the Yuppies—young, urban, upwardly mobile professionals—one of the groups linked to the New Politics cleavage.
8. These are the so-called feeling thermometer questions that measure positive and negative feelings toward each object. Respondents are given a thermometer-like scale to measure their "warmth" or "coldness" toward each group.
9. The feeling thermometers were analyzed using a multidimensional scaling program, and the solution was then rotated so the Kerry-Bush dimension was aligned horizontally in the scale. For earlier analyses of similar sociopolitical spaces, see Barnes, Kaase, et al. (1979); Inglehart (1984); and previous editions of this text.
10. Ideally, what is needed is a tracking of sociopolitical alignments over time to see if there has been a systematic change in the Democrats' and Republicans' electoral alliances.

11. The figure includes parties from Australia, Austria, Belgium, Britain, Canada, Denmark, Finland, France, Germany, Ireland, Italy, Japan, Netherlands, New Zealand, Norway, Spain, Sweden, and the United States.
12. The services/taxes dimension ranges from (1) promotes raising taxes to increase public services, to (20) promotes cutting public services to cut taxes. The environment dimension ranges from (1) supports protection of the environment, even at the cost of economic growth, to (20) supports economic growth, even at the cost of damage to the environment.
13. See the voters' own left/right placement of the parties in chapter 10 (figure 10.2).
14. The social dimension ranges from (1) favors liberal policies on matters such as abortion, homosexuality, and euthanasia, to (20) opposes liberal policies on matters such as abortion, homosexuality, and euthanasia.

CHAPTER 8

The Social Bases of Party Support

A central political activity of a citizen in a democracy is to vote in elections. As we noted in chapter 7, elections provide the foundation of democratic governance by selecting the officials who hold public office. Elections are also an exceptional political event in which candidates, the media, political analysts, and citizens discuss the issues facing the nation and what should be done in the future.

Elections also attract attention from political scientists for other reasons. Elections involve most of the public, so we can study how most people make political decisions. Voting also provides an opportunity to determine how political attitudes influence actual behavior—the casting of a ballot. Because people make a specific voting decision, voting choices are likely to be relatively well thought out, intelligible, and predictable. The electoral connection therefore offers a good setting for studying political thoughts and behavior beyond a simple response to a public opinion survey. If there is one political act that provides a window into the minds of citizens, it is voting.

In addition, voting behavior reflects the changing patterns of citizen politics described in this book. A different calculus of voting existed in the 1950s and 1960s, when most elections began with the outcomes already decided for most voters. The majority of voters relied on long-term predispositions derived from their social position or partisan loyalties. This chapter and the next describe these predispositions. We also describe how these factors are weakening as an influence on voting choice. In the new style of citizen politics, more voters make their decisions during campaigns based on their views of the candidates and issues of the day.

This chapter examines voting behavior by studying the group bases of voting that evolve from the social alignments described in chapter 7. We track group voting patterns over time and across nations. We highlight both stability and change in group-based voting.

THE SOCIAL GROUP MODEL OF VOTING

The setting in Marienplatz, Munich's central town square, is always the same the weekend before the national elections. The various political parties set up information booths and try to convince people to vote for their party. Labor union members and their families typically staff the booth for the Social Democratic Party. Members from Catholic auxiliary groups participate at the Christian Social Union booth. Young professionals or older businesspeople help out at the Free Democratic Party's booth. And the Greens typically have

---

Internet Resource

Visit the Web sites of the American National Election Studies (ANES) and
the British Election Study (BES):

ANES: www.electionstudies.org
BES: www.essex.ac.uk/bes

---

shaggy-haired college students handing out information on the party. The
linkage between social groups and political parties is a common feature of
democratic party systems and elections.

From its beginnings, electoral research has stressed social group attachments as an important influence on voting behavior. Social groups represent
the distinct social interests—such as between different class or religious
groups—we discussed in chapter 7, and elections are a means of resolving
these different interests. One of the first empirical studies of American voting
focused on the social bases of partisanship (Lazarsfeld, Berelson, and Gaudet
1948). This study found that an *index of political predispositions* based on
social class, religion, and rural/urban residence was strongly related to voting
choice. Social stratification is greater in Europe than in the United States, producing sharper group differences in voting patterns. A common cliché notes
that social class is the basis of British politics, and all else is just embellish-
ment and detail. In Germany and France, class and religion are strong correlates of voting.

Social characteristics such as class and religion can influence a voter's electoral choice in several possible ways. First, one's social position often indicates
his or her values and political beliefs. A French steelworker is more likely than
a shopkeeper, for example, to favor an expansion of social services or government regulation of business. Opposition to liberal abortion laws is more
likely among devout Catholics than among the nonreligious. Social characteristics indirectly reflect the attitudinal differences between groups of voters
and their perceptions of which party best represents their policy positions.

Second, social characteristics indicate some of the political cues to which
an individual is exposed. A British mineworker may hear about politics from
his coworkers or other working-class neighbors and friends, and he receives
political information from the union representative at work and from union
publications at home. His working-class milieu provides repeated cues on
which policies will benefit people like him and which party best represents his
interests; these cues inevitably convey a strong Labour Party bias. A Bavarian
Catholic hears about political issues at weekly church services, from Catholic
social groups, and from predominately conservative Catholic friends; this information generally encourages a favorable opinion of the Christian Social
Union and its program.

Third, social groups can be important reference points in orienting voters to political issues and providing information about politics. Even if they are not members of a labor union or regular churchgoers, the knowledge that unions favor one party and the Catholic Church another can help voters locate themselves in relation to the parties. The cues provided by social networks and group party associations help to guide many citizens' political orientations and voting behavior.

Reliance on social group cues illustrates the "satisficing" decision-making model described in chapter 2. Social cues can narrow voters' choices to parties that are consistent with their social position. Voters therefore face an election favoring the party (or parties) that historically supports the class or religious groups to which they belong, while excluding parties with unsupportive records. Political parties nurture such ties, communicating their group loyalties to the voters by calling themselves "Labour" or "Christian Democrats."

Many voters decide between competing parties based on the cues that social groups provide—the endorsements of labor unions, business associations, religious groups, and the like—as well as the group appeals of the parties themselves. In most cases, such decision making produces reasonable voting choices, even if the voter is not fully informed on all the relevant issues. When British industrial workers cast their votes for Labour because the party represents people like themselves, they are making a reasonable electoral choice.

Reliance on social characteristics is a shortcut in making voting decisions. A citizen who is knowledgeable about all the issues and all the candidates is well prepared to make an informed voting choice and to justify this decision in issue-oriented and ideological terms. Social characteristics provide a simpler, although less certain, method of choosing which party represents one's interests. Still, when strong social group identities are matched by clear party positions on these social cleavages, as in most European nations, social characteristics can provide a meaningful guide for voting choice.

SOCIAL CLASS AND THE VOTE

Class politics taps the essence of what we have described as the Old Politics—an economic conflict between the haves and the have-nots. The class cleavage reflects the problems industrial societies face in reaching their economic and material goals: improving standards of living, providing economic security, and ensuring a just distribution of economic rewards. Issues such as unemployment, inflation, social services, tax policies, and government management of the economy reinforce class divisions.

Social scientists have probably devoted more attention to the relationship between social class and voting than to any other social characteristic. In theory, the class cleavage involves some of the most basic questions of power and politics that evolve from Marxist and capitalist views of societal development. Historically, one's position in the class structure has been a strong predictor of voting choice. Seymour Martin Lipset's early cross-national study of electoral politics described the class cleavage as one of the most pervasive bases of party support:

> Even though many parties renounce the principle of class conflict or loyalty, an analysis of their appeals and their support suggests that they do represent the interests of different classes. On a world scale, the principal generalization that can be made is that parties are primarily based on either the lower classes or the middle and upper classes. (1981, 230)

Research normally defines social class in terms of occupation. Following Karl Marx's writings, occupations are typically classified based on their relationship to the means of production. The bourgeoisie are the self-employed and the owners of capital, and the workers who sell their labor to live are the proletariat. This framework is then generalized to define two large social groupings: the middle class and the working class. Socialist and communist parties emerged to represent the interests of the working class; conservative parties, in turn, defend the interests of the middle class.

This Marxian dichotomy once defined the class cleavage, but the changing nature of advanced industrial societies has reshaped the class structure. The traditional bourgeoisie and proletariat have been joined by a "new" middle class or a "salatariat" that primarily consists of salaried white-collar employees and civil servants (Heath, Jowell, and Curtice 1991). Richard Florida (2003) has described a special subset of the new middle class as "knowledge workers," those who make their livelihood on the creation and use of information and are typically the vanguard for New Politics views. Daniel Bell (1973) defined a "postindustrial" society as one in which most of the labor force holds new middle class positions; by the 1980s, nearly all Western democracies met that definition.

The new middle class is an important addition to the class structure because it lacks a clear position in the traditional class conflicts between the working class and the old middle class. The separation of management from capital ownership, the expansion of the service sector, and the growth of government (or nonprofit) employment creates a social stratum that does not conform to Marxist class analysis. The new middle class does not own capital as the old middle class did, and it differs in lifestyle from the blue-collar workers of the traditional proletariat. Members of the new middle class seem less interested in the economic conflicts of the Old Politics and more attuned to the New Politics issues we examined in chapters 5 and 6. Consequently, the political identity of the new middle class differs from both the bourgeoisie and the proletariat.

Table 8.1 presents the voting preferences of these social classes in the most recent election for which data are available.[1] Historical class alignments persist in each nation. The working class gives disproportionate support to leftist parties, ranging from 43 percent voting for Labour in Britain to 61 percent voting Social Democrats (SPD), Greens, or Linke.PDS in Germany.

TABLE 8.1 Social Class and Party Support (in percentages)

	Working class	New middle class	Old middle class
United States (2004)			
Democrats	56	55	48
Republicans	44	45	52
Total	100	100	100
Great Britain (2005)			
Labour	43	37	36
Liberal Democrats	20	27	24
Conservatives	22	27	35
Other parties	15	9	5
Total	100	100	100
France (2002)			
PC/Far Left	12	7	3
Socialists	43	39	28
Greens	15	14	16
UDF	2	10	11
RPR	22	27	38
National Front	6	3	3
Total	100	100	99
Germany (2005)			
Linke.PDS	12	8	8
Greens	9	9	14
SPD	40	39	17
FDP	9	11	18
CDU/CSU	31	33	43
Total	101	100	100

SOURCES: United States, 2004 American National Election Study (CSES); Great Britain, 2005 British Election Study (CSES); France, 2002 International Social Survey (ISSP); Germany, German Election Study 2005 (CSES).

NOTE: U.S. data are based on vote for Congress; German data are for East and West electorates combined. Social class is based on occupation of the respondent.

At the other extreme, the old middle class is the bastion of support for conservative parties. This traditional proletariat/bourgeoisie cleavage remains strong in each nation—even though less than half of the electorate in each nation now belong to either of these two classes.

The new middle class is now the majority of voters and, more important, holds ambiguous partisan preferences. It is normally located between the working class and the old middle class in its Left/Right voting preferences and gives disproportionate support to parties that represent a New Politics ideology, such as Green or New Left parties. The new middle class is a

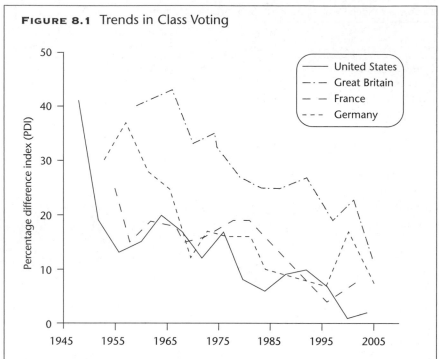

Figure 8.1 Trends in Class Voting

Sources: United States, 1948–2004, American National Election Studies; Great Britain, 1955, Heath et al. (1985); 1959, Civic Culture study; 1964–2005, British Election Studies; France, 1955, MacRae (1967, 257); 1958, Converse and Dupeux survey; 1962, IFOP survey; 1967, Converse and Pierce survey; 1968, Inglehart survey; 1973–1988, Eurobarometer; 1996 and 2002, ISSP; Germany, 1953–2005, German Elections Studies (Western Germany only, 1990–2005).

Note: Figure entries are the Alford Class Voting index, i.e., the percentage of the working class preferring a leftist party minus the percentage of the middle class voting for the Left. U.S. data are based on congressional elections, except for 1948, which is based on presidential vote.

major element in the changing political alignments of advanced industrial democracies.[2]

Although social class can still influence voting choice, class cues carry less weight than they did in the mid-twentieth century (Nieuwbeerta and de Graf 1999; Oskarson 2005; Knutsen 2006). Figure 8.1 presents the long-term pattern using the Alford index of class voting in our four core nations. This index calculates class voting as the simple difference between the percentage of the working class voting for the Left and the percentage of the middle class (old and new) voting for the Left.

The general trend in figure 8.1 is obvious: class differences are declining. The class voting index has decreased dramatically in Britain and Germany during the past fifty years.[3] The gap in Leftist support between the working class and middle class was once 40 percent, but now it barely registers in double digits. Class voting follows an irregular decline in U.S. congressional elections; in the 2000 and 2004 elections, the gap was virtually nonexistent. Paul Abramson, John Aldrich, and David Rohde (2005, ch. 5) show that the erosion of class voting also occurs in U.S. presidential elections. In France, social class had a modest impact on voting during the Fourth Republic (1946–1958), but the turbulent events accompanying the formation of the Fifth Republic—including the creation of a broad-based Gaullist Party—abruptly lowered class voting in 1958. Since then class voting has generally trended downward (Lewis-Beck and Skalaban 1992; Boy and Mayer 1993).

Despite the evidence that class voting differences are narrowing, some researchers argue that emerging class alignments in advanced industrial societies are perpetuating class voting, albeit in new forms (Evans 1999, 2000; Manza and Brooks 1999; Heath, Jowell, and Curtice 1991; Wright 1997). John Goldthorpe (1987) proposed a class categorization that adds notions of job autonomy and authority relationships into traditional class criteria such as income level and manual labor. Others have created class categories that reflect new social contexts, such as the middle-class salatariat or affluent blue-collar workers. Researchers also explore criteria other than employment as potential new bases of socioeconomic cleavage: some suggest that education may form the basis of a political cleavage separating the information-rich, technologically sophisticated voter from the information-poor, unskilled voter. Others maintain that conflicts between the public and private sectors are supplanting traditional class conflicts.

This reconceptualization of social class implies that social cues now function in more complex and differentiated ways than in the past. Still, the empirical reality remains: even these new class frameworks have only a modest value in explaining how citizens vote. Harold Clarke and his colleagues (2004, ch. 3) used three different ways to estimate class voting in Britain from the 1960s to the present, finding that all three trace a very similar downward trend. Paul Nieuwbeerta (1995; Nieuwbeerta and de Graf 1999) showed that alternative statistical measures of class voting do not change these long-term trends across a large set of Western democracies.

Figure 8.2 examines a more elaborate measure of social class and places the current levels of class voting in our four nations in cross-national perspective. We compare the voting preferences of six class groups to allow for greater variation in the composition of the class structure.[4] The Cramer's V correlation measures the size of class voting differences among these class groups (see appendix A). Across five editions of *Citizen Politics,* we have tracked the downward trend in class voting with such analyses. Today, class is only modestly related to vote choice. The greatest class polarization exists in Scandinavian countries, albeit at a lower level than in the past. Even with this more extensive measure of social class that includes multiple middle-class categories, the average level of class differences in these nations is quite modest (average Cramer's V = .14).

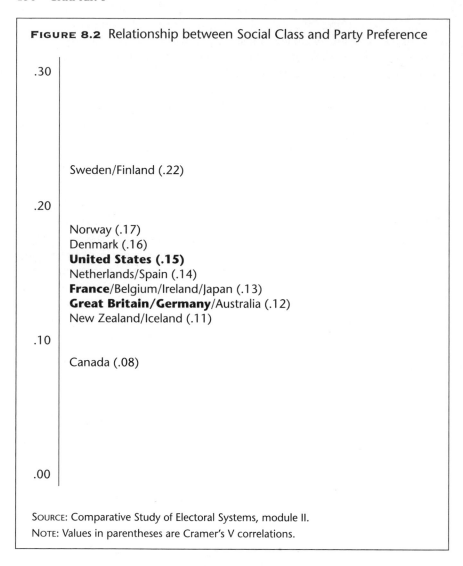

FIGURE 8.2 Relationship between Social Class and Party Preference

.30

Sweden/Finland (.22)

.20

Norway (.17)
Denmark (.16)
United States (.15)
Netherlands/Spain (.14)
France/Belgium/Ireland/Japan (.13)
Great Britain/Germany/Australia (.12)
New Zealand/Iceland (.11)

.10

Canada (.08)

.00

SOURCE: Comparative Study of Electoral Systems, module II.
NOTE: Values in parentheses are Cramer's V correlations.

In terms of our four core nations, British class differences once were fairly large, reflecting the relative importance of class interests in British politics—and the influence of class cues on voting. These differences have clearly moderated over time. Germany and France display modest levels of class voting, less than the cross-national average and smaller than in the past. The United States public was atypically polarized in 2004; the United States normally ranks below Britain, France, and Germany. In most elections the American two-party system blurs the influence of social class on voting choice, as both parties draw substantial parts of their support from across class lines.

WHY IS CLASS VOTING DECREASING?

David Butler and Donald Stokes (1969, 85–87) developed a framework to explain group-based voting that may help to identify the sources of declining class voting. They described group-based voting as a two-step process: voters are first linked to a social group, and then the group is linked to a political party. The combined strength of these two links determines the overall level of group-based voting. Which has changed: the relationship between voters and class groupings or the relationship between class groupings and the political parties?

Their first explanation highlights how the changing class structure of contemporary societies may weaken the link between individuals and class groupings. Members of the traditional social strata—industrial workers, farmers, and the self-employed—often remain integrated into class networks and remain distinct in their voting preferences. But the number of such voters has diminished. The growth of the new middle class reduces the percentage of the public for whom traditional class ties are directly relevant.[5]

A general narrowing in the life conditions of social classes can also weaken the link between individuals and their respective class. On the one hand, spreading affluence leads to the *embourgeoisement* of some sectors of the working class—some workers have incomes and living standards that overlap with those of the middle class. On the other hand, the expanding ranks of low-paid and low-status white-collar employees and the growth of white-collar unions are producing a *proletarianization* of part of the middle class. Few individuals now possess exclusively middle-class or working-class social characteristics, and the amount of class overlap is growing over time. In sum, a convergence of life conditions may contribute to the convergence of class voting patterns.

Increasing social and occupational mobility also may weaken the link between individuals and traditional social classes. Each of the nations in this study saw a decline in the number of farmers and a rise in middle-class employment during the second half of the twentieth century. High levels of social mobility mean that an individual's ultimate social position is often different from that of his or her parents. Many farmers' children moved from a conservative political upbringing into unionized, working-class environments in the cities, just as many working-class children went from urban, leftist backgrounds into white-collar occupations that are traditionally conservative. Some socially mobile adults will change their class identity and voting behavior to conform to their new social contexts; others will not. This mix of social forces blurs traditional class and partisan alignments.

A second explanation for declining class voting is the changing relationship between class groups and the political parties. Over the latter half of the twentieth century, many political parties tried to broaden their electoral appeal to attract new middle-class voters. This outreach led parties to moderate their positions on traditional class-based issues. Socialist parties in Europe shed their Marxist programs and adopted more moderate domestic and foreign policy goals. Conservative parties also tempered their views and accepted the basic social programs proposed by the Left. Socialist parties vied for the votes of the new middle class, and conservative parties sought votes from the working class. Historical analyses of party programs show a general convergence of party positions on socioeconomic issues during this period (Caul and Gray 2000). With smaller class-related differences in the parties' platforms, it seems only natural that class cues would become less important in guiding voting behavior.

Initially at least, this second theory appears to be another plausible explanation for the decline in class voting differences. Various studies, however, show that parties are still politically distinct on many class-related issues. A survey of political experts documented a clear awareness of the continuing party differences on the socioeconomic issues that underlie the class cleavage (Benoit and Laver 2006; also see chapter 7). Furthermore, contemporary publics still clearly perceive the partisan leanings of unions and business associations (chapter 7; Wessels 1994). In short, it does not appear that people are unaware of the class voting cues that parties provide; instead, these cues are simply less relevant to today's voters.

In summary, the decline in class voting patterns is important for several reasons. First, it signals a change in the nature of political conflict, away from the class-based issues that once dominated elections (or at least the addition of nonclass issues to the electoral mix). Parties that draw significant support across different social classes are less likely to advocate single-class interests if they enter the government. Second, these trends signal a change in how voters reach their decisions. The bonds linking voters to social classes are apparently weakening, even while the political cues provided by traditional class groups (and parties) persist. Union members may understand that labor leaders want them to vote for leftist parties, but they are now more likely to make their own decisions because other factors influence voting decisions. Third, social modernization implies that the long-term decline in class voting should continue.

RELIGION AND THE VOTE

Religion is another possible basis of social division in contemporary societies. The relationship between religion and parties arises from a centuries-old interplay of these two forces. As with the class cleavage, disagreements over religion structured elite conflict and defined the political alliances existing in the late nineteenth century. The political parties that formed during this period often allied themselves with specific religious interests: Catholic or Protestant, religious or secular. The party alignments that developed at the start of the twentieth century institutionalized the religious cleavage, and many features of these party systems have endured to the present (Lipset and Rokkan 1967).

Early empirical research on voting behavior underscored the importance of the religious cleavage. Richard Rose and Derek Urwin's examination of the social bases of party support in sixteen Western democracies concluded that "religious divisions, not class, are the main social bases of parties in the Western world today" (1969, 12). Numerous others have found a persisting importance of the religious cleavage. Many contemporary political issues—abortion, homosexual rights, and moral standards—are often linked to religious values. And cultural conflicts and religious fundamentalism are reviving the importance of religion in the political world (Norris and Inglehart 2004; Leege et al. 2002).

Measuring the impact of religious cues on voting behavior is more complex than the study of class voting. The class composition of most industrial democracies is similar, but their religious compositions are varied. Britain is largely Protestant, and nearly two-thirds of the population are nominally Anglicans. In contrast, the large majority of French citizens—about 80 percent—are baptized Catholics, and the Protestant and Muslim minorities are small. Germany has a mixed denominational system, with Lutheran Protestants slightly outnumbering Catholics. The United States lacks a dominant national religion and instead has significant numbers of Catholics, Reformation-era Protestants, Pietist Protestants, other Protestant and Christian groups, Jews, and the nonreligious.

In addition to the different religious composition of nations, the partisan tendencies of religious denominations can also vary. Catholics normally support parties on the right, and Protestants normally support parties on the left, but historical events have sometimes led to different religious alignments. The voting cues provided by religious affiliation may differ across nations in contrast to the consistent working-class/middle-class pattern for social class.

We first describe the relationship between religious denomination and party support in the four core nations. As table 8.2 shows, religious differences in voting are often substantial, but each nation displays a unique pattern. The historical conflict between the Catholic Church and the Liberal/Socialist Parties still appears in Germany. Most Catholics support the CDU/CSU, which defends traditional values and the church's prerogatives. A near majority (47 percent) of Catholics voted CDU/CSU in 2005, and this vote increases to 69 percent among Catholics who attend church weekly. In contrast, Protestants and the nonreligious give greater support to the leftist parties: SPD, Greens, and PDS.

The differences in voting behavior between French Catholics and non-Catholics are sizable. In 2002 only 17 percent of those without a religion favored conservative parties, but 56 percent of the Catholic vote went to these parties. But because the French public is overwhelmingly Catholic, the electoral impact of non-Catholics is modest.

In Britain, religious divisions follow another pattern. The Church of England historically has allied itself with the political establishment, and Anglicans are more likely to vote for the Conservative Party. Catholics lean toward

TABLE 8.2 Religious Denomination and Party Support (in percentages)

United States (2004)	No religion	Jewish	Catholic	Reformation Protestant	Baptist	Other Protestant
Democrats	65	73	52	41	56	51
Republicans	35	27	48	59	44	49
Total	100	100	100	100	100	100

Great Britain (2005)	No religion	Catholic	Presbyterian	Anglican
Labour	37	46	39	36
Liberal Democrats	31	21	22	22
Conservatives	24	25	20	36
Other parties	8	8	19	6
Total	100	100	100	100

France (2002)	No religion	Catholic
PC/Far Left	16	3
Socialists	49	32
Greens	19	9
UDF	3	13
RPR	11	38
National Front	3	5
Total	101	100

Germany (2005)	No religion	Protestant	Catholic
Linke.PDS	18	7	4
Greens	12	11	7
SPD	39	40	29
FDP	11	11	13
CDU/CSU	20	31	47
Total	100	100	100

SOURCES: United States, 2004 American National Election Study (CSES); Great Britain, 2005 British Election Study (CSES); France, 2002 International Social Survey (ISSP); Germany, 2005 German Election Study (CSES).

NOTE: U.S. data are based on vote for Congress; German data are for East and West electorates combined.

the Labour Party because of their minority status and the persistent issue of Irish independence. Presbyterians usually support Labour and the Liberal Democrats.

Religious and moral conflicts are a recurring theme in American history (Wald 2003; Layman 2001; Kohut et al. 2000); yet the formal separation of church and state lessens the impact of religion on partisan politics. Table

8.2 shows that the Reformation-era Protestant denominations (Anglicans, Calvinists, Lutherans, etc.) predominately supported the Republicans in 2004, while Baptists and other Protestant groups leaned toward the Democrats. These differences are modest, however, and may reflect factors other than religion per se. The slight Democratic leanings of American Catholics reflect the historical legacy of ethnic and class influences rather than explicitly religious values. Jewish Americans also historically give disproportionate support to the Democrats, and they continued to do so in 2004.

Figure 8.3 places these religious voting patterns into a cross-national context. The left side of the figure displays the levels of denomination-based voting across fourteen established democracies. Religiously divided societies, such as the Netherlands and Switzerland, often display the starkest religious differences. In a set of Scandinavian nations—Denmark, Finland, and Sweden—the correlation largely results from differences between religious voters (of all denominations) and those without any religious affiliation. The impact of religious denomination on party preferences is slightly greater (average Cramer's V = .18) than the impact of social class. The persisting strength of religious differences is surprising, because in many nations religious matters are not explicitly discussed in elections. Clearly, religion taps value orientations that provide a basis for voting choice.

Another aspect of the religious cleavage is the influence of religiosity, such as church attendance or religious feelings separate from denominational affiliation. In predominately Catholic nations, such as France, this dimension represents a voter's integration into the Catholic culture. In mixed denominational systems, the secularization process has often stimulated an alliance between Protestants and Catholics in a joint defense of religious interests, so denominational differences are replaced by a secular/religious cleavage. In Germany the Christian Democratic Union unites active Catholics and Protestants against secular interests in society. Similar patterns have developed in the United States. When he was campaigning for president, George W. Bush actively sought the votes of religious conservatives of all denominations. The Bush campaign hoped to tap a common concern for the preservation of traditional values and opposition to abortion, even among social and ethnic groups that were traditionally affiliated with the Democratic Party.

Table 8.3 presents the relationship between religious involvement, measured by party preference, and the frequency of attending religious services. The gap between religious and nonreligious citizens is considerable in France and Germany. Only 15 percent of French citizens who attended church weekly preferred the Socialist or Communist Parties in 2002, compared to 58 percent among those who never went to church. Because of the Church of England's relationship to the government, religious conflicts have not been a major factor in British electoral politics since early in the twentieth century.

The role of religion in U.S. elections, especially in the most recent elections, has generated considerable discussion. Many analysts argue that Bush's emphasis on his evangelical beliefs and deliberate appeal for religious

---

FIGURE 8.3 Relationship between Religion and Party Preference

Religious denomination	Church attendance
Netherlands (.30) .30	
Finland (.27)	
	Switzerland (.26)
Switzerland (.25)	
Spain (.24)	
Canada (.21)	
United States (.20) .20	Sweden (.20)
	New Zealand (.19)
	Belgium (.18)
New Zealand (.17)	**Germany (.17)**
Germany/Belgium/Australia (.16)	
	Denmark/Ireland (.15)
Great Britain (.13)	**United States/France (.13)**
France/Ireland (.12)	Australia (.12)
	Japan (.11)
.10	
Japan (.09)	
	Iceland (.08)
	Great Britain (.07)

SOURCE: Comparative Study of Electoral Systems, module II.

NOTE: Values in parentheses are Cramer's V correlations between religious denomination and party preference on the left and church attendance and party preference on the right.

---

voters produced his margin of victory in the 2004 popular vote. Table 8.3 indicates, however, that the impact of church attendance on the presidential election was limited (Cramer's V =.09). And those who actively attend religious services were only slightly more likely to choose the Republican congressional candidate over the Democrat in 2004 (Cramer's V = .13). Because of the multiplicity of denominations and the complexity of religious attachments in America, it is an oversimplification to claim that religious feelings

TABLE 8.3 Church Attendance and Party Support (in percentages)

	Never	Occasionally	Weekly
United States (2004)			
Democrats	57	58	46
Republicans	43	42	54
Total	100	100	100
Great Britain (2005)			
Labour	38	38	37
Liberal Democrats	27	23	25
Conservatives	26	34	27
Other parties	9	5	11
Total	100	100	100
France (2002)			
PC/Far Left	11	5	1
Socialists	47	32	14
Greens	16	12	8
UDF	5	11	21
RPR	17	36	53
National Front	5	4	4
Total	101	100	101
Germany (2005)			
Linke.PDS	15	6	4
Greens	12	10	4
SPD	40	37	23
FDP	11	12	9
CDU/CSU	22	36	60
Total	100	101	100

SOURCES: United States, 2004 American National Election Study (CSES); Great Britain, 2005 British Election Study (CSES); France, 2002 International Social Survey (ISSP); Germany, 2005 German Election Study (CSES).

NOTE: U.S. data are based on vote for Congress; German data are for East and West electorates combined.

exert a clear partisan influence in the United States (e.g., Kohut et al. 2000; Layman 2001).[6]

The cross-national pattern of secular/religious voting displayed on the right-hand side of figure 8.3 shows that the secular/religious divide (average correlation = .15) is a stronger explanation of the vote than social class. Despite the paucity of explicitly religious issues in most campaigns, religious attachments are often a strong predictor of party choice. In Scandinavia, for example, religion reflects continuing controversies over lifestyle issues, such as temperance and moral values. In other nations, the religious/secular cleavage is related to issues such as abortion or other moral questions (see chapter 6). Religion constitutes a hidden agenda of politics, tapping differences in values and moral beliefs that might not be expressed in a campaign but nevertheless influence voter choices. Indeed, a variety of evidence indicates that moral or religious issues continue to divide the parties in many Western democracies.[7]

Our analyses also underscore the diversity of religious voting patterns across the four core nations. Religious denomination and church attendance are both significantly related to partisan preferences in Germany. The religious cleavage in France is based on the voting differences between practicing Catholics and the nonreligious. In Britain we see only modest partisan differences by church attendance. The limited degree of religious voting in the United States illustrates the continued separation of church and state despite the attempts by some candidates to politicize religion.

Despite these relationships between religious values and partisan preferences, we expect the religious cleavage to follow the same pattern of decline as the class cleavage. Social modernization may disrupt religious alignments in the same manner that social class lines have blurred. Changing lifestyles—and changing religious beliefs—have reduced involvement in church activities and diminished the church as a focus of social (and political) activities. Most Western nations display a steady decline in religious involvement over the past fifty years. In the Catholic nations of Europe, frequent church attendance has decreased by nearly half since the 1950s. Predominately Protestant countries, such as the United States and the nations of northern Europe, began with lower levels of church involvement but followed the same downward course. By definition, the trend toward secularization means that fewer voters are integrated into religious networks and exposed to the religious cues that can guide the vote.

We can explore the possible decline in religious voting by observing its pattern over time. Similar to the class voting index, figure 8.4 plots a religious voting index based on the difference in party preferences between the two religious denominations noted for each nation. For instance, the differences in Conservative Party support between Anglicans and nonconformist Protestants in Britain have narrowed since 1959. The gap in leftist voting between German Catholics and Protestants averaged in the 25-point range for the first half of this series. This gap narrowed during the 1980s, and the merger with a secular eastern electorate (two-thirds of whom express no denominational affiliation) has further dampened religious voting differences.

Partisan differences between American Catholics and Protestants vary across elections. The religious cleavage intensified with John Kennedy's candidacy in 1960, while other elections display weak religious voting. In addition, despite the stress on religious voting blocs in recent American elections, there is actually a slight convergence in Protestant/Catholic voting in congressional elections (see Abramson, Aldrich, and Rohde 2005, ch. 5, for evidence on presidential elections).

The long-term trends in voting differences between religious and nonreligious citizens are relatively stable over time (data not shown). Religious involvement in France has a strong and persisting impact on voting preferences,

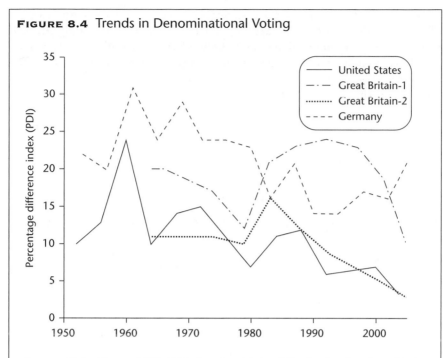

FIGURE 8.4 Trends in Denominational Voting

SOURCES: United States, 1952–2004, American National Election Studies; Great Britain, 1964–2005, British Election Studies; Germany, 1953–2005, German Election Studies (western Germany only, 1990–2005).

NOTE: Comparisons for the United States and Germany are between Protestants and Catholics. Great Britain-1 is a comparison of the Labour Party vote of Anglicans and Catholics; Great Britain-2 is a comparison of the Conservative Party vote of Anglicans and nonconformists.

averaging a greater than 40 percent difference in leftist party support. British party differences on the religious voting index have dropped off markedly in recent elections. The religious cleavage in Germany was relatively stable from the 1960s until 1980, and since then it has fluctuated but with weaker effects. In the United States the Republican Party's attempts to court religious voters has heightened attention to religion—but the gap between religious and non-religious voters remains limited.[8]

In summary, the trends for religious voting do not show the sharp drop-off found for class voting. Denominational differences have narrowed slightly in several nations, but denomination remains a stronger predictor of vote choice than social class. The secular/religious divide is also a strong correlate of voting preferences. This continued pattern of religious voting is even more surprising because advanced industrial societies have become more secular during the past few decades. In addition, many of the societal changes that weakened the class cleavage presumably should have the same effect on religious voting.

Religion is declining as a basis of voting behavior, but the pattern of decline is less obvious than for class voting. Comparisons of the voting patterns of religious denominations appear to be moderating slightly, but these relationships include only those voters with religious attachments. People who attend services regularly remain well integrated into a religious network and maintain distinct voting patterns; however, there are fewer of these individuals today. By definition, secular voters do not turn to religious cues to make their electoral choices. Therefore, as the number of voters who rely on religious cues decreases, the partisan significance of religious characteristics and their overall ability to explain voting outcomes are slowly weakening.

OTHER SOCIAL GROUP DIFFERENCES

The decline of social group–based voting is most apparent for class and religion, but a similar erosion of influence has occurred for other social characteristics.

Regional differences occasionally flare up as basis of party choice. Great Britain, the United States, and now the unified Germany have seen regional interests polarize in recent years. The rhetoric of red and blue states illustrates the persistence of regional differences in the U.S. elections (Fiorina 2005), but they tend to be mild compared to those in Canada, Italy, and Spain. In most nations, region exerts only a minor influence on voting. Similarly, urban/rural residence produces only modest differences in voting patterns. The impact of such social traits on voting has generally weakened as social modernization reduces the gap between urban and rural lifestyles or regional differences.

Some political analysts have stressed the importance of the gender gap in voting. The available empirical evidence, however, suggests that gender is seldom a major explanation of voting patterns. Normally, the difference in voting between men and women averages less than 10 percent. Moreover, in the United States the gender gap traditionally ran in the opposite direction from what we see today; that is, women historically favored parties of the right. As feminism changed the political orientations of some younger women, male/female voting differences narrowed—and then reversed—with more women supporting parties of the left (Studlar, McAllister, and Hayes 1998; Jelen, Thomas, and Wilcox 1994). Even in the 2004 U.S. elections, the gender gap was modest compared to other influences on vote choice. Significant voting differences begin to emerge, however, if one combines gender and life-status measures, such as employment status (Norris 1999a).

Race and ethnicity are possible exceptions to the declining impact of social cleavages. There are sharp racial differences in partisan support within the American electorate, and these differences have widened over time (Abramson, Aldrich, and Rohde 2005). Ninety-two percent of African American voters selected Democratic candidates for Congress in 2004, compared to 71 percent of Hispanics and 44 percent of white Americans. The minority populations in Europe often display significant differences in their party preferences. Ethnicity has the potential to become a highly polarized cleavage because it often involves large differences in social conditions and strong feelings of group identity. Yet most societies remain relatively homogeneous in terms of ethnicity, which limits the impact of race or ethnicity as an overall predictor of vote choice. For example, the Cramer's V correlations for race and vote is significant in the United States (.25), but quite modest in Britain (.12 in 2005), which has a small minority population (Saggar and Heath 1999; Saggar 2007).

All of these analyses lead to one of the most widely repeated findings of modern electoral research: sociological factors have a declining influence on voting behavior. Mark Franklin, Tom Mackie, and Henry Valen (1992) compiled the most comprehensive evidence supporting this conclusion by tracking the impact of social characteristics (including social class, education, income, religiosity, region, and gender) on voting over time. Across fourteen democracies, they found a marked erosion in the impact of social characteristics on voting choice. The rate and timing of this decline varies across nations, but the result is the same. In party systems such as the United States and Canada, where social group–based voting was initially weak, the decline has occurred slowly. In other electoral systems—such as Germany, the Netherlands, and several Scandinavian nations—where sharp social divisions once structured the vote, the decline has been steady and dramatic. Franklin, Mackie, and Valen (1992, 385) conclude with the new "conventional wisdom" of comparative electoral research:

> It is now quite apparent that almost all of the countries we have studied show a decline . . . in the ability of social cleavages to structure individual voting choice.

NEW POLITICS AND THE VOTE

As traditional social group influences decrease in importance, the New Politics (or postmaterial) cleavage may produce a new partisan alignment. The erosion of Old Politics cleavages is at least partly the result of the increasing salience of New Politics issues (Knutsen 1995b). Environmental protection, gender equality, and other social issues are not easily related to traditional class or religious alignments. Furthermore, New Politics issues attract the attention of the same social groups that are weakly integrated into the Old Politics cleavages: the young, the new middle class, the better educated, and the nonreligious.

Developing a new basis of partisan cleavage can be a long and difficult process. Groups must organize to represent New Politics interests and mobilize voter support, but the group bases of these issues are still ill-defined. The environmental and women's movements, for example, have multiple groups representing them, but they seldom speak with a single voice, and the voters' bonds to specific groups are weaker than to class and religious groups. Many established political parties are hesitant to identify themselves with New Politics issues because the stakes are still unclear and the parties are often internally divided on the issues.

Despite these limiting factors, the potential impact of New Politics values on voting has increased. Small green or New Left parties now compete in many European democracies. In response, the established parties are gradually becoming more receptive to the political demands of New Politics groups. The inclusion of green parties in the government coalitions in France (1997) and Germany (1998) and Al Gore's candidacy in the 2000 U.S. elections signal how the established parties are accepting green issues.

Many voters also seem willing to base their choices on New Politics concerns. Harvey Palmer (1995), for example, found that postmaterial values were gradually becoming a better predictor of British party preferences than either income or occupation. Postmaterialism has also exercised a significant impact on German voting preferences, at least until unification created a new set of policy concerns (Fuchs and Rohrschneider 1998). Oddbjorn Knutsen's research (1995a; Knutsen and Kumlin 2005) also points to a growing relationship between postmaterial values and party choice in most European nations. In addition, many Europeans express a willingness to vote for an environmental party—the potential electorate for a green party rivals that of socialist and Christian Democratic parties (Inglehart 1990, 266)!

We used the material/postmaterial values index (chapter 5) to see if these orientations influence voting. Materialists emphasize security, stability, economic well-being, and other Old Politics objectives, while postmaterialists place greater stress on New Politics goals such as participation, social equality, and environmental protection.

Table 8.4 displays the relationship between postmaterial values and party preferences. In every nation, postmaterialists favor the Left, while materialists lean toward the Right. The influence of changing values is especially clear for the New Left environmental parties in France and Germany. For example, 30 percent of French postmaterialists supported the Greens, compared to only 10 percent of materialists.

The overall size of these voting differences is considerable, often exceeding the Alford index scores for class or religious voting. The four-item postmaterialism index tends to understate the impact of these values (compared to the twelve-item index). Still, in Germany and France the gap in Left/Right support is 22 percent. Significant percentage difference scores also appear in Britain (15 percent), while value differences are less pronounced in the United States (5 percent).

Figure 8.5 describes the extent of postmaterial values–based voting across advanced industrial democracies. Postmaterialism has an exceptionally strong influence in Denmark and the Netherlands, where established political parties have responded to these new issue concerns. Postmaterial values–based voting is also significant in Germany and France, exceeding the influence of class-voting differences (compare to figure 8.1). Repeating a pattern we have seen for other cleavages, New Politics values only weakly affect American electoral behavior.

TABLE 8.4 Value Priorities and Party Support (in percentages)

	Materialists	Mixed	Postmaterialists
United States			
Democrats	57	62	62
Republicans	43	38	38
Total	100	100	100
Great Britain			
Labour	43	48	58
Liberal Democrats	19	20	29
Conservatives	38	32	12
Total	100	100	99
France			
PC	4	4	6
Socialists	43	34	37
Other Left	2	2	8
Greens	10	23	30
UDF	11	8	5
RPR/UPM	23	24	11
National Front	7	5	2
Total	100	100	99
Germany			
PDS	3	5	7
Greens	2	6	12
SPD	36	33	44
FDP	1	4	3
CDU/CSU	59	51	35
Total	101	99	101

SOURCES: 1999–2002 World Values Survey/European Values Survey; 1997 British Election Study.

NOTE: Value priorities are measured with the four-item index (see chapter 5).

Previous research found that the extent of values polarization is partly a function of the diversity of choice in a party system; with more parties, it is more likely that one of them will represent these New Politics concerns. In addition, affluence stimulates postmaterial concerns. This is evident in the East/West German comparisons: postmaterial values have a significant influence on the voting choices of many westerners (Cramer's V = .21), but eastern Germans are less likely to have postmaterial values and more likely to be preoccupied with the economic problems that accompanied German union. Postmaterial values have less influence over the voting behavior of easterners (Cramer's V = .14) even though all Germans are voting on the same party

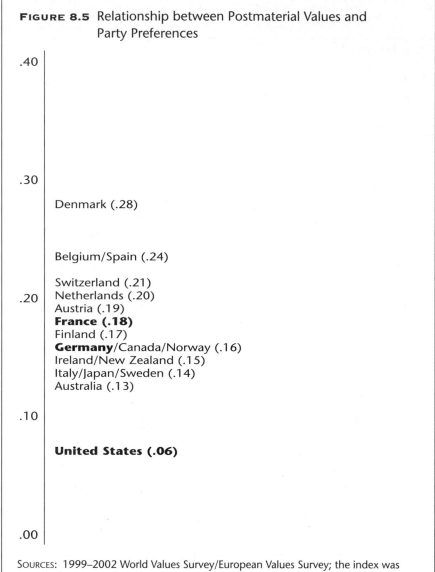

FIGURE 8.5 Relationship between Postmaterial Values and Party Preferences

.40

.30

Denmark (.28)

Belgium/Spain (.24)

Switzerland (.21)
.20   Netherlands (.20)
Austria (.19)
France (.18)
Finland (.17)
Germany/Canada/Norway (.16)
Ireland/New Zealand (.15)
Italy/Japan/Sweden (.14)
Australia (.13)

.10

United States (.06)

.00

SOURCES: 1999–2002 World Values Survey/European Values Survey; the index was not asked in Great Britain.

NOTE: Values in parentheses are Cramer's V correlations between the postmaterial values index and party preferences.

choices. Figure 8.5 also shows that across the advanced industrial democracies, the average weight of postmaterial value priorities (Cramer's V = .17) now exceeds the weight of social class in determining party choice (figure 8.1).

In contrast to the impact of social characteristics that are weakening over time, postmaterial values should have greater influence as these issues enter

FIGURE 8.6 Trends in Postmaterial Values Voting

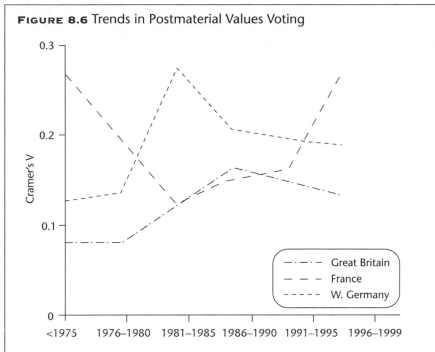

SOURCE: Eurobarometer cumulative file, 1970–1999.

NOTE: Figure entries are the Cramer's V correlations between the four-item postmaterial values index and party preference, cumulated for five-year intervals. Nonpartisans were not included in the calculation of correlations.

the political agenda, and parties respond by offering policy choices on postmaterial concerns. The postmaterial values index is not routinely included in national election study surveys, but we can track the impact across European nations using the Eurobarometer time series. Figure 8.6 presents the correlations between postmaterial values and party preference for Great Britain, France, and West Germany, with the data cumulated for five-year periods to emphasize the broad trends. In contrast to class voting, which is decreasing over time, the impact of postmaterial values is increasing, albeit with some variability in the trends. For example, the voting difference between materialists and postmaterialists in West Germany was modest in the early 1970s, but had increased by the end of the 1990s (with a spike in the early 1980s when the Greens first ran for parliament). The sources of partisan cleavage are changing in advanced industrial democracies: the long-standing Old Politics cleavages are being joined by a new values cleavage.

It would be a mistake to assume that the growing electoral salience of New Politics issues means an inexorable increase in support for leftist parties. The Old Politics cleavages will remain as major forces structuring party competition for some time. Furthermore, the partisan consequences of the New

Politics depend on how parties respond to these issues. Even though American environmentalists normally feel closer to the Democratic Party, it was a Republican president, Teddy Roosevelt, who nurtured the modern environmental movement and another Republican president, Richard Nixon, who created the Environmental Protection Agency. German chancellor Angela Merkel has emphasized the importance of global warming, while the SPD seems tentative on many environmental issues. Environmentalism is not a Left or Right issue in the traditional Old Politics meaning of these terms; rather, the partisan effects of these issues depend on how the parties respond (see Dalton 2008). The major lesson is that public interests and party alignments are changing, and the party systems in advanced industrial democracies are affected by these trends.

THE TRANSFORMATION OF SOCIAL CLEAVAGES

Harold Clarke and his colleagues (2004) began their study of voting choice in the 2001 British election with a vignette that captures the spirit of this chapter:

> Jim Hill voted Labour in the 1955 general election. Jim worked as a welder . . . and made castings for the motor industry. He belonged to the Transport and General Workers' Union. He rented a house . . . from the local council. . . . Jim did not think much about politics—although he paid his union dues and occasionally talked politics with his mates in the local pub. Like most people he knew, Jim had always thought of himself as "Labour."
>
> Jim's granddaughter, Melanie, still lives today in the Midlands town where her grandfather spent his life, although the foundry where he worked closed in the early 1980s. She lives in her own terraced house, which she is buying with her partner, in an area where 40 percent of the population is Asian. After graduating from university in the early 1990s, she became a teacher. She left in 1996, disillusioned with work in the public sector, to become a customer services manager at a nearby airport. . . . In the 1997 general election, Melanie voted Labour. In 2001, she thought about not voting at all, but finally opted for the Liberal Democrats.

The transformation of social conditions between Jim Hill and Melanie Hill—and consequently the political choices of the Hill family across three generations—illustrates the social transformations that have affected all advanced industrial democracies.

Throughout much of the twentieth century, the dominant social cleavage in most democracies separated working-class and middle-class parties. The socioeconomic transformation of these societies, however, is weakening class alignments. Similarly, the number of churchgoers available for mobilization by confessional parties is declining along with the influence of religion on voting behavior. These class and religious trends are often accompanied by a drop in the influence of regional, residential, and other social cleavages.

Because of the tendency to view party systems as representing social group differences, one response to the erosion of group divisions has been to search for possible new social bases of alignment. Political scientists define a *partisan realignment* as a significant shift in the group bases of party coalitions, usually resulting in a shift in the relative size of the parties' vote shares.

Western party systems have undergone many such realignments, in which one system of group cleavages is replaced by another. Realignments have been a regular feature of American electoral politics since the emergence of the first mass-party coalitions around 1800. The 1930s New Deal realignment in the United States can be traced to the entry of large numbers of blue-collar workers, Catholics, and blacks into the Democratic Party coalition. Similar realignments have occurred in European party systems, such as the British Labour Party's rise in the early 1900s and the Gaullist realignment at the beginning of the French Fifth Republic.

Some analysts suggest that New Politics issues may provide the basis of a new partisan alignment. These issues are attractive to voters who are weakly integrated into traditional group alignments. Eventually, these interests may coalesce into political movements that will realign electorates and party systems. The growing partisan polarization along the New Politics value cleavage apparently supports this realignment thesis. Value priorities have become a more important influence on voting choice, and new parties now represent these perspectives.

I am not convinced that it is accurate to think of contemporary partisan politics in the same terms as past partisan realignments. Partisan realignment is normally based on clearly defined and highly cohesive social groups—such as union workers or church members—that can develop institutional ties to the parties and provide clear voting cues to their members.

Today, we find few social groupings comparable to labor unions or churches that might establish the basis of a New Politics realignment. Generational differences in support for New Politics parties might indicate an emerging New Politics cleavage, but age groups provide a transitory basis for mobilizing voters. Other potential group bases of voting cues, such as education or alternative class categorizations, so far remain speculative, without firm evidence of realigning effects.

Postmaterial values are related to partisan preferences, but values per se are unlikely to provide a basis for a new group-party alignment. Values define clusters of like-minded people, but one cannot identify a postmaterialist in the same way that class, religion, or region provides a basis of personal identity and group mobilization. Indeed, postmaterial values are antithetical to traditionally structured organizations such as unions and churches. Instead, a vast array of single-issue groups and causes represents New Politics concerns—from the women's movement to peace organizations to environmental advocates. In general, these groups are loosely organized with ill-defined memberships that wax and wane. Such groups also are hesitant to form the close party ties that characterize traditional social groups.

The lack of a group basis for the New Politics cleavage highlights another aspect of the new style of citizen politics. The kinds of cleavages that divide modern electorates and the kinds of groups they represent are changing. Electoral politics is moving from cleavages defined by identities with fixed social groups to issue/value cleavages that are linked to communities of like-minded individuals. Social groups may still represent some of the political interests of contemporary electorates, but *we are witnessing a transformation from social group cleavages to issue group cleavages.*

Consequently, the bases of political mobilization are becoming more individualized and focused on discrete issue publics. Interest mobilization along any political dimension—Old Politics or New Politics—will be characterized by more complex, overlapping, and crosscutting associational networks; more fluid institutional loyalties; and looser, more egalitarian organizational structures. Fewer citizens will use voting cues from external reference groups such as unions or churches, but economic and moral issues remain important elements of the political agenda. Labor union leaders will still support leftist parties, and labor union members will still perceive these cues, but now rank and file workers are less likely to follow their leaders and support the leftist party. The fact is that fewer individuals are following such external cues, and this independence affects the breadth, effectiveness, and stability of any future partisan alignment.

The new style of citizen politics therefore should include more fluid voting patterns. Political coalitions and voting patterns will lack the permanence of past class and religious cleavages. Without clear social cues, voting decisions will become a more demanding task for each voter and more dependent on the individual beliefs and values of each citizen.

SUGGESTED READINGS

Anderson, Christopher J., and Carsten Zelle, eds. *Stability and Change in German Elections: How Electorates Merge, Converge, or Collide.* Westport, Conn.: Praeger, 1998.

Clark, Terry Nichols, and Seymour Martin Lipset, eds. *The Breakdown of Class Politics: A Debate on Post-industrial Stratification.* Baltimore: Johns Hopkins University Press, 2001.

Clarke, Harold, et al. *Political Choice in Britain.* Oxford: Oxford University Press, 2004.

Evans, Geoffrey, ed. *The End of Class Politics? Class Voting in Comparative Context.* New York: Oxford University Press, 1999.

Franklin, Mark, Tom Mackie, and Henry Valen, eds. *Electoral Change.* New York: Cambridge University Press, 1992.

Judis, John, and Ruy Teixeira. *The Emerging Democratic Majority.* New York: Scribner, 2002.

Knutsen, Oddborn. *Class Voting in Western Europe: A Comparative Longitudinal Study.* Lanham, Md.: Lexington Books, 2006.

Manza, Jeff, and Clem Brooks. *Social Cleavages and Political Change*. New York; Oxford: Oxford University Press, 1999.
Norris, Pippa. *Electoral Change in Britain since 1945*. Cambridge, Mass.: Blackwell, 1997.

NOTES

1. Most American voting studies analyze presidential elections. Because of the importance of candidate image, presidential elections reflect a different set of electoral forces than are normally found in European parliamentary elections. To ensure comparability of American and European results, the U.S. analyses in this chapter use elections for Congress.

   In the United States, we use the percentage voting Democratic in congressional elections; in Britain, the percentage voting Labour; in Germany, the percentage voting SPD of the two-party vote (SPD and CDU/CSU) before 1980, and leftist percentage (SPD, Greens, and PDS) in later elections; in France, the percentage voting for leftist parties (PC, Socialist, and other Left).

2. Generational patterns in class voting also reinforce the argument for the long-term erosion in this cleavage (Franklin, Mackie, and Valen 1992, ch. 19). Research generally finds strong relationships between class and the vote among older generations, and weaker relationships among younger generations.

3. We use only respondents in Western Germany beginning with the 1990 election to be comparable to earlier elections. For a discussion of East/West differences in voting see (Dalton and Bürklin 2003).

4. We measured social class by the occupation of the head of household coded into the following categories: (1) white collar, (2) manual worker, (3) farmer, (4) self-employed, (5) homemaker, and (6) other occupations/no occupation.

5. In support of this interpretation, new middle class voters have been a major source of electoral volatility in the United States (Hout et al. 1995; Abramson, Aldrich, and Rohde 2005) and European democracies (Knutsen 2006; Oskarson 2005).

6. Religion also interacts with racial and class patterns in the United States. African Americans are very strong Democrats, but they also tend to be religious. Therefore, many studies of religious voting examine only white voters, where religious attachments are more likely to lead to Republican Party preferences. We are analyzing the entire U.S. electorate, which displays weaker religious patterns.

7. Kenneth Benoit and Michael Laver (2006) show that political elites in most Western democracies still perceive significant party differences on dimensions such as pro- and anticlerical and the permissiveness of social policy (also see chapter 7). Germans see clear differences in the parties' religious leanings, and these perceptions have grown more distinct over time (Wessels 1994). Finally, chapter 7 found that the American public perceives conservative religious groups as closer to the Republican Party than to the Democratic Party.

8. The gap in party support between those who never attend church and those who attend on a weekly basis was 18 percent in 2000 and only 11 percent in 2004. This is within the range of the level of religious polarization in elections of the 1950s and 1960s, but is still half the level of religious differences in nations such as France and Germany.

CHAPTER 9

Partisanship and Voting

Modern party systems may have emerged from social group divisions, as seen in chapters 7 and 8, but their origins represent only the start of electoral politics. Each election presents voters with choices over policy proposals and candidates for office. Social characteristics and group cues may influence the choices of many voters, but their own political opinions also affect their electoral calculus. And these opinions are often distinct from those derived from group cues.

Consequently, contemporary research emphasizes the opinions and attitudes of voters as pivotal factors in understanding voting choice. Most voters do not regard elections as conflicts over historical cleavage alignments, but as opportunities to deal with more contemporary problems (which may reflect long-term conflicts). People make judgments about which party best represents their interests, and these perceptions guide voting behavior. Attitudes toward the issues and candidates in an election are therefore necessary elements in any realistic model of voting. Attitudes are also changeable, and their incorporation into a voting model helps explain variation in party results across elections.

A SOCIOPSYCHOLOGICAL MODEL OF VOTING

Faced with the limitations of a purely sociological approach to voting, early electoral researchers developed voting models to include psychological factors, such as issues and attitudes, as influences on voting decisions and other political behavior. A team of researchers at the University of Michigan first formalized a model integrating both sociological and psychological influences on voting (Campbell et al. 1960, ch. 2). This sociopsychological model describes the voting process in terms of a *funnel of causality* (figure 9.1). The figure has many elements, but its basic logic is straightforward. At the wide mouth of the funnel on the left side of the figure are the socioeconomic conditions that generate the broad political divisions of society: the economic structure, social divisions such as religion or race, and historical alignments such as the North/South division in the United States. These factors structure the party system (see chapter 7), as represented by the arrows in the figure, but are distant from the actual voting decisions of individual citizens.

As we move through the causal funnel, socioeconomic conditions influence group loyalties and basic value orientations (as signified by the arrows). For example, economic conditions may bond an individual with a social

Internet Resource

Visit the Political Compass Web site to take a short political quiz and locate yourself in a 2-D political space in Great Britain or the United States:

http://www.politicalcompass.org

class, or regional identities may form in reaction to social and political inequalities. Social conditions are translated into attitudes that can directly influence the individual's political behavior.

The causal funnel narrows further as group identities and values influence more explicitly political attitudes. Angus Campbell and his colleagues (1960; 1966) explained individual voting decisions primarily in terms of three attitudes: party attachment, issue opinions, and candidate images. These attitudes are closest to the voting decision and therefore have a direct and very strong impact on the vote. In addition, the events of the campaign—media influence, campaign activity, economic and political conditions—influence the voter's issue opinions and candidate images.

Although the logic of the funnel of causality is simple by contemporary standards of social science, it represented a major conceptual breakthrough

FIGURE 9.1 Funnel of Causality Predicting Vote Choice

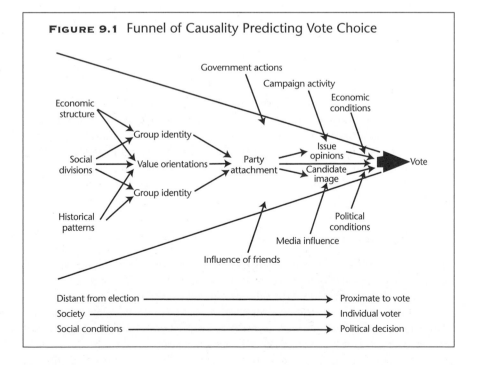

for voting research. The model provides a useful device for organizing the factors that can influence voting choices. To understand voting, one has to recognize the causal relationship between the many factors involved.

- The wide end of the funnel represents broad *social conditions* that structure political conflict; attention shifts to explicitly more *political factors* as we move through the funnel.
- The factors on the left are temporally *distant* from the actual voting decision; the factors on the right are more *proximate* to voting choice.
- The factors on the left are *conditions of society,* and then groups; the factors on the right are considerations made by the *individual voter.*

In summary, the funnel of causality is a framework to connect the various elements—either distant or proximate—that influence voting choices. Social characteristics are an important aspect of the voting process, but their primary influence is in forming broad political orientations and group identities. The impact of social characteristics on voting is mostly mediated by attitudes closer to the actual voting decision. Attitudes, in turn, depend on the group identities and values of the individual, as well as external stimuli such as friends, media, government actions, and the activities of the campaign. Each element of the voting process has a place in the funnel of causality, and we can understand each element in relation to the others.

In addition to the descriptive value of the model, the sociopsychological approach successfully predicts voting choices. Researchers have applied the basic model in a variety of nations. Attitudes toward the parties, issues, and candidates of an election are psychologically close to the actual voting decision and therefore are strongly related to this decision. In fact, the model can predict voting decisions more accurately than individuals can predict their own behavior in the months before the election (Campbell et al. 1960, 74)!

The sociopsychological model guides how we think about elections and how researchers analyze the voting process. This chapter examines partisan attachments as a central concept in the sociopsychological model of voting. We also discuss how party attachments have changed over time. The next chapter examines how specific issue opinions provide another element in this model.

PARTISAN ATTITUDES

The sociopsychological model leads us to focus on the specific issue opinions and candidate evaluations that determine voting choice. Yet, it soon became clear that partisan identities strongly influenced many of the specific political beliefs and behaviors of the citizenry. As one elderly Tallahassee voter once commented to me while we were waiting to vote, "I vote for the candidate and not the party. It just seems like the Democrats always choose the best candidate." Many voters begin each electoral season with partisan predispositions.

These partisan loyalties are a central element in an individual's belief system, serving as a source of political cues for other attitudes and behaviors.

The Michigan researchers described these partisan attachments as a sense of *party identification,* similar to identifications with a social class, religious denomination, or other social group. Party identification is a long-term, affective, psychological identification with one's preferred political party (Campbell et al. 1960, chap. 6).[1] Often these attachments are learned from one's parents long before one is eligible to vote. Party attachments are distinct from voting preferences, which explains why some Americans vote for the presidential candidate of one party while expressing loyalty to another party. Indeed, the conceptual independence of voting and party identification initially gives the latter its significance.[2]

The discovery of party identification is one of the most significant findings of public opinion research. Partisanship often serves as a core value for individual belief systems, as discussed in chapter 2. Partisanship is the ultimate heuristic, because it provides a reference structure for evaluating many new political stimuli—what position does "my" party take on this issue—and making political choices. As seen in chapter 4, partisanship is a stimulus for engagement in campaigns and elections. The developers of the concept emphasized the functional importance of partisanship for many aspects of political behavior:

> Few factors are of greater importance for our national elections than the lasting attachment of tens of millions of Americans to one of the parties. These loyalties establish a basic division of electoral strength within which the competition of particular campaigns takes place. And they are an important factor in ensuring the stability of the party system itself . . . the strength and direction of party identification are of central importance in accounting for attitude and behavior. (Campbell et al. 1960, 121)

Herbert Weisberg and Steve Greene (2003, 115) wrote, "Party identification is the linchpin of our modern understanding of electoral democracy, and it is likely to retain that crucial theoretical position."

After the description of party identification in the United States, the concept was exported to other democratic nations. In several cases, researchers had problems finding an equivalent measure of partisanship in multiparty systems or in nations where the term *partisanship* holds different connotations for the voters (Budge, Crewe, and Farlie 1976). The concept of a partisan "independent" is not as common in other nations as it is in the United States. Because researchers could not simply translate the American party identification question into French or German, they had to find a functional equivalent for measuring partisan attachments.[3] Still, most public opinion specialists agree that voters hold some party allegiances that endure over time and strongly influence other opinions and political behavior. Equivalent measures of party identification are now included in the election studies of virtually all contemporary democracies.

Learning Partisanship

The significance of party identification for political behavior results in part from the early origins of these attachments. Socialization studies find that children develop basic partisan orientations at a very early age, often during the primary school years (Hess and Torney 1967, 90). Children learn party loyalties before they can understand what the party labels stand for—a process similar to the development of many other group ties. These early party attachments then provide a reference structure for future political learning (which often reinforces early partisan biases).

The early life formation of party identities means that parents play a central role in the socialization of these values. The transmission of partisanship within the family can be seen by comparing the party identifications of parents and their children. A cross-national socialization study interviewed parents and their children to compare their opinions directly (table 9.1). This research found relatively high levels of partisan agreement within American, British, and German families.[4] In the United States, 70 percent of Democratic parents have children who were also Democrats, and 54 percent of Republican parents have Republican offspring. Fewer than a sixth of the children actually favor the party in opposition to their parents. These levels of partisan agreement are similar to those found in a larger and more representative study of American adolescents (Jennings and Niemi 1973). British and German studies also show that the party attachments of parents are frequently re-created in the values of their offspring (Zuckerman and Kroh 2006). Parents have a strong formative influence on the partisan values of their children, even before the children become active in the political process.

Parents are successful in transmitting their partisanship to their children because partisan loyalties are formed when parents are the dominant influence in a child's life and exposure to partisan cues from the parent is common. Parties are visible and important institutions in the political process, and virtually all political discussion includes some partisan content: we identify candidates and judge them by their party affiliation, and we evaluate policies by their party sponsor. It does not take long for a child to identify the parents' partisan leanings from their reactions to television news and statements in family discussions. In addition, most parents have party attachments that endure across elections, and children are exposed to relatively consistent and continuous cues on which party their parents prefer. One of my university colleagues was openly proud that he had conditioned his preschool child to groan each time a specific former president appeared on television. Either through explicit reinforcement or subconscious internalization of parental values, many children adopt their parents' partisan preferences.

Once individuals establish party ties, later partisan experiences often follow these early predispositions. Democrats tend to vote for Democratic candidates; Republicans vote for Republicans. Electoral experience normally reinforces initial partisan tendencies because most citizens cast ballots for their

TABLE 9.1 Transmission of Parental Partisanship (in percentages)

	United States		
	Parental party preferences		
	Democrat	Republican	Independent
Child's party preference			
Democrat	70	25	40
Republican	10	54	20
Independent	20	21	40
Total	100	100	100

	Great Britain			
	Parental party preference			
	Labour	Liberal	Conservative	None
Child's party preference				
Labour	51	17	6	29
Liberal	8	39	11	6
Conservative	1	11	50	6
None	40	33	33	59
Total	100	100	100	100

	West Germany			
	Parental party preference			
	SPD	FDP	CDU/CSU	None
Child's party preference				
SPD	53	8	14	19
FDP	4	59	1	3
CDU/CSU	9	—	32	12
None	34	33	53	66
Total	100	100	100	100

SOURCE: Political Action Survey.

preferred party.[5] The accumulated experience of voting for the same party and the political agreement that leads to such partisan regularity tend to strengthen partisan ties. Consequently, partisan loyalties generally strengthen with age—or, more precisely, with continued electoral support of the same party (Converse 1969, 1976).[6]

Figure 9.2 displays the increasing percentage of party identifiers by age.[7] Most people develop a strong sense of party identity by middle age, which

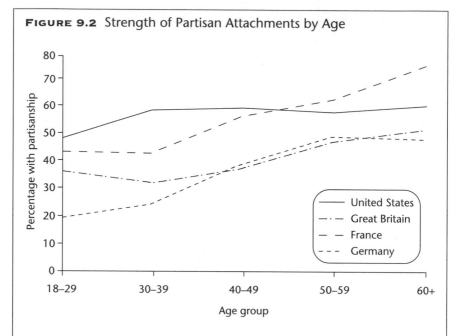

FIGURE 9.2 Strength of Partisan Attachments by Age

SOURCES: Comparative Study of Electoral Systems (CSES): United States (2004); Great Britain (2005); France (2002); Germany (2002).

NOTE: The CSES uses a comparably worded question on partisanship, so direct cross-national comparisons of the level of partisan attachments are appropriate.

continues to strengthen through the rest of the life cycle. Only 43 percent of the youngest French age group said they are partisans, compared to 75 percent among the oldest group. The same general age pattern is evident for Britons and Germans. The weakest relationship seems to be in the United States, but the reason may be that this survey uses a question that does not tap the feeling of partisan identity normally asked in U.S. surveys. Overall, the strength of partisanship shows a similar pattern of intensifying party bonds with age or, more precisely, with accumulated experience of supporting the same party in successive elections.[8]

The partisan ties learned early in life become deeply embedded in a child's belief system and then are reinforced by later partisan experiences. Partisanship may change in reaction to later life experiences, but these attachments are not easily altered once they have formed. Party identification is one of the most stable political attitudes, far exceeding the stability of opinions on long-standing national issues such as race relations, economic programs, and foreign policy (Converse and Markus 1979). Additional evidence of long-term partisan stability comes from a panel study of high school seniors and their parents. M. Kent Jennings and Greg Markus (1984) found that 78 percent of American adults and 58 percent of adolescents held the same partisan ties in

TABLE 9.2 Relative Stability of Party Attachments and Vote (in percentages)

Party identification	United States, 1972–1976	
	Vote	
	Stable	Variable
Stable	71	22
Variable	4	3
N = 539		

Party identification	Great Britain, 1970–1974	
	Vote	
	Stable	Variable
Stable	75	10
Variable	5	10
N = 795		

Party identification	West Germany, 1976	
	Vote	
	Stable	Variable
Stable	71	22
Variable	4	3
N = 707		

SOURCES: LeDuc (1981, 261); Berger (1977, 504)

NOTE: The tables present percentages of the total N based on those who were voters and identified with a political party at each time point. American and British results are based on
changes between two elections; West German data are based on changes during a three-wave
1976 election panel.

1965 and 1973, spanning one of the most turbulent political periods in twentieth century American history (also see Jennings 2007).

Evidence from other nations mirrors this pattern. British party attachments are significantly more stable than other political beliefs (Schickler and
Green 1997). On average, between 80 percent and 90 percent of the British
public retain constant party ties from one election to the next. Longitudinal
studies in Germany also found that partisanship is a very stable political attitude (Zuckerman and Kroh 2006). Even the limited evidence for France
shows considerable continuity in the partisan orientations of the French public, despite the substantial turbulence in the actions of party leaders (Converse and Pierce 1986, ch. 3).

The relative constancy of partisan attachments can also be seen by comparing the stability of partisanship and voting preferences (see table 9.2).
Reinterviews with the same American voters in 1972 and 1976 found that

93 percent had stable party identifications, but only 75 percent had stable congressional voting preferences. Even when voters selected the opposite party (22 percent), only 4 percent changed parties. Party preferences were also more stable than voting preferences in Great Britain and Germany, but this difference was more modest than in the United States (LeDuc 1981; cf. Heath and Pierce 1992). In Europe the tendency for partisanship and vote to go together is greater; when one changes, so does the other (Holmberg 1994). Because of their limited number of voting opportunities, Europeans are less likely to distinguish between long-term partisanship and current voting preferences. Still, partisanship is generally stable over time, even in the face of vote defections.[9]

In sum, partisanship is a central element in an individual's belief system and a basis of political identity. These orientations are formed early in life and may condition later life learning. It is therefore easy to see why researchers give it a central role in a sociopsychological model of voting choice.

THE IMPACT OF PARTISANSHIP

In sports, loyalty to a team helps one know who to root for and which players to admire, and it motivates individuals to actively support their team. People often develop such ties early in life, and they endure through the ups and downs of the franchise. In my case, my attachment to the Dodgers strengthens with repeated trips to cheer on my team, even if it loses.

The same feelings apply to partisan attachment: parties help to make politics "user-friendly." When the political parties take clear and consistent policy positions, the party label provides an information short-cut on how "people like me" should decide. Once voters decide which party generally represents their interests, this single piece of information can act as a perceptual screen—guiding how they view events, issues, and candidates. A policy advocated by one's party is more likely to meet with favor than one advocated by the other team.

Compared to social-group cues such as class and religion, party attachment is a more valuable heuristic. Party cues are relevant to a broader range of political phenomena because parties are so central to democratic politics. Issues and events frequently are presented to the public in partisan terms, as the parties take positions on the political questions of the day or react to the statements of other political actors. People vote for parties or party candidates at elections. Governments are managed by partisan teams. So, reliance on partisanship may be the ultimate example of the "satisficing" model of politics.

The *Washington Post* performed an interesting experiment that illustrates the power of partisanship as a political cue (Morris 1995). The paper included a question on a fictitious government act in one of its opinion surveys. One form of the question referred to either President Bill Clinton's or the Republicans' position on the issue, and another form discussed the act without any partisan cues. They found that the number of people expressing an opinion on the act increased when a partisan cue was given. Moreover, the partisan effects were clear: Democrats were far more likely to oppose the fictitious act when told Clinton wanted repeal, and Republicans disproportionately opposed the act when told the Republicans in Congress wanted repeal.

Another example demonstrates the power of partisanship to shape even nonpartisan opinions. Before the 2000 U.S. elections, the American National Election Study (ANES) survey asked the public to judge whether the national economy would improve or worsen over the next twelve months. With the Democrats in the White House, Democrats were more optimistic about the nation's economic future than Republicans by an 8 percent margin. After the election, with Bush the apparent winner (although the election outcome was still in doubt), Republicans became more positive about the economy by a small margin.

This reversal of the relationship between preelection and postelection surveys illustrates the power of partisanship to shape citizen perceptions of the political world. Partisanship has an even stronger influence on opinions that are more closely linked to the parties, such as evaluations of government performance and candidate images (Abramson, Aldrich, and Rohde 2005, ch. 8; Miller and Shanks 1996). Partisans root for the players (candidates) on their team and save their catcalls for the opponents.

Party ties also mobilize individuals to become politically active (see chapter 4). Just like loyalty to a sports team, attachment to a political party encourages an individual to become active in the political process to support his or her side (chapter 2). The 2004 ANES found that turnout was 32 percent higher among strong partisans than among independents. In addition, strong partisans are more likely to try to influence others, to display campaign materials, to attend a rally, or to give money to a candidate during the campaign. Partisanship functions in a similar way in other established democracies. Strong partisans voted at a higher rate in the 2002 German Bundestag elections, and they were several times more likely to participate in campaign events and twice as likely to try to persuade others how to vote. Eighty-eight percent of strong partisans believed it makes a difference who controls the German government, but only 49 percent of weak partisans and 44 percent of nonpartisans shared this conviction.

The cue-giving function of partisanship clearly affects voting choices. Partisanship means that voters have a predisposition to support their preferred party. Philip Converse (1966) described partisanship as the basis for a "normal vote"—the vote expected when other factors in the election are evenly balanced. If other factors come into play, such as issue positions or candidate images, their influence can be measured by their ability to change preferences from initial partisan leanings. For the unsophisticated voter, a long-term partisan loyalty and repeated experience with one's preferred party provides a clear and low-cost cue for voting. Even for the sophisticated citizen, a candidate's party affiliation normally signifies a policy program that serves as the basis for reasonable electoral choice.

Generally, there is a close relationship between partisanship and voting in parliamentary elections (Holmberg 1994). In the 2001 British elections, only 14 percent of partisans defected to vote for another party. Even with multiple parties to choose from, defection rates were low in the 2002 German Bundestag elections. A full 81 percent of German partisans voted for a district candidate from the party they identified with, and 78 percent cast a party vote on the second ballot even though many strategic voters supported a smaller party to help their own party's coalition chances. The limited voting opportunities in most European nations tend to narrow the separation between partisanship and vote.

The American citizen, in contrast, "has to cope simultaneously with a vast collection of partisan candidates seeking a variety of offices at federal, state, and local levels; it is small wonder that he becomes conscious of a generalized belief about his ties to a party" (Butler and Stokes 1969, 43). The separation between attitudes and behavior is therefore most noticeable in American elections, especially when voters are asked to make a series of choices for local, state, and federal offices (Beck et al. 1992). In highly visible and politicized presidential elections, candidate images and issue appeals have the potential to counteract partisan preferences, and party defections are common in these elections. The success of Republican presidential candidates from Ronald Reagan to George W. Bush occurred because they attracted defectors from the Democratic majority. Even in the highly divisive two-party contest of 2004, 7 percent of American partisans cast presidential votes contrary to their party identification.

A similar situation exists in France. The two-candidate runoff in French presidential elections is decided by the size of the vote the candidates can attract from parties other than their own (Boy and Mayer 1993). In French parliamentary elections, however, voting choice more closely conforms to standing partisan preferences.

Partisanship is the ultimate heuristic because it:

- creates a basis of political identity;
- provides cues for evaluating political events, candidates, and issues;
- mobilizes participation in campaigns and election turnout;
- provides cues on voting preferences; and
- stabilizes voting patterns for the individual and the party system.

Thus, partisan attachments became the cornerstone to our understanding of how citizens manage the complexities of politics and make reasonable decisions on the questions they face at election time.

PARTISAN DEALIGNMENT

Because partisanship is so important for different aspects of citizen political behavior, it came as a surprise when researchers first noted that party ties

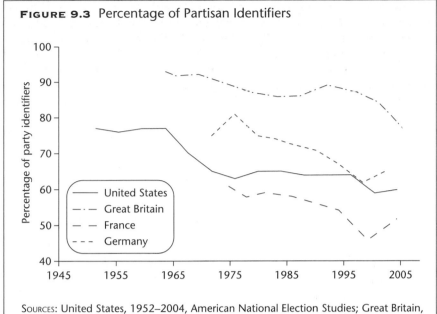

FIGURE 9.3 Percentage of Partisan Identifiers

SOURCES: United States, 1952–2004, American National Election Studies; Great Britain, 1964–2005, British Election Studies; France, Eurobarometer Surveys (1975, 1978, 1981, 1986, 1988) and European Election Studies (1994, 1999, and 2004); Germany, 1972–2002, German Elections Studies (Western Germany only 1990–2002).

were eroding in many advanced industrial democracies. Initial signs of partisanship decline appeared in the rising fluctuations of party outcomes in elections during the 1970s and early 1980s (Crewe and Denver 1985). The erosion of the social-group basis of party support contributed to this trend of increasing party volatility. The frozen group alignments that Seymour Martin Lipset and Stein Rokkan (1967) had described were beginning to thaw (chapter 8). Election surveys in several nations found that partisan identifications were weakening (Dalton, Flanagan, and Beck 1984).

At first, it was difficult to be certain that party bonds were eroding when this trend was intermixed with the normal patterns of partisan change between elections. Partisan change is a regular element of the electoral process, and periods of heightened partisan volatility and fragmentation dot the electoral histories of most democracies. As we argued above, however, relatively few voters change their partisan preferences between adjacent elections.

The weakening of party ties first became apparent in the United States (see figure 9.3). American partisanship was stable from the 1950s to the early 1960s; the percentage of party identifiers remained within the 70 percent to 75 percent range, and less than a quarter of the public claimed to be "independents" without fixed partisan ties. Partisan loyalties began to weaken after the 1964 election, and by the 1980s, more than a third of the electorate were nonpartisans. In the 1990s H. Ross Perot's candidacy pushed the percentage of partisans down still further (Wattenberg 1998). The percentage of partisans reached a new low (59 percent) in the 2000 election survey, and this level continued into the 2004 election, despite the highly politicized and partisan nature of the campaign.

Several American politics experts question the existence and significance of these trends. Bruce Keith and his colleagues (1992) doubted that the decrease in the percentage of party identifiers was a meaningful change. Donald Green, Bradley Palmquist, and Eric Schickler (2002, 31) examined a broad array of partisan behaviors in the ANES time series and concluded, "Partisanship is alive and well, and as far as we can tell, it is as influential for us as it was for our parents and grandparents." Other researchers claimed that the ability of partisan identities to predict presidential vote preferences had not significantly diminished over the five-decade series of the ANES (Miller and Shanks 1996; Bartels 2000). The significance of partisanship is so great that many doubted that these ties were really weakening.

The topic of partisanship is a good example of the value of cumulative research, and especially of comparative analysis. As the body of evidence has grown, adding more nations and more elections, it is now clear that a general pattern of partisan decline is broadly affecting advanced industrial democracies (Dalton and Wattenberg 2000; Fiorina 2002; Webb 2002; Clarke and Stewart 1998). Voters are not simply defecting from their preferred party in one or two elections, or just in the United States. Instead, across a wide set of nations, the evidence shows an erosion in partisan loyalties—the same loyalties that electoral research emphasized as a core element in explaining citizen political behavior.

For example, an almost identical pattern of declining party ties occurred in Great Britain as in the United States (figure 9.3). Because of the traditions of the British party system and the format of the British partisanship questionnaire, fewer Britons claim to be nonpartisans. In the 1964 British election study, 93 percent claimed a standing partisan preference; by the 2005 election the share of partisans had dropped to 77 percent. Responses to questions about the strength of attachments among partisans display an even clearer pattern: more than 40 percent of the British public were strong partisans during the late 1960s, but less than 20 percent claimed to be strong partisans in the most recent elections.

Germany initially deviated from the pattern of partisanship found in other advanced industrial democracies. Partisanship increased between 1961 and 1976, as West Germans developed commitments to the postwar party system (Baker, Dalton, and Hildebrandt 1981, ch. 8). In the late 1970s, however, the trend began moving in the opposite direction. Partisans were 81 percent of the public in 1976; by 2002 they accounted for 65 percent among westerners. Partisanship is even lower among easterners because they lack prior partisan experience and are just beginning to develop party attachments. During the 2002 election, 45 percent of eastern Germans claimed to lack any party ties (Dalton and Bürklin 2003).

The series of comparable French survey data is much shorter and is drawn from the Eurobarometer and European Election Surveys. Beginning in the 1970s, the percentage of partisans slowly decreased, with a marked drop-off at the end of the 1990s (also see Haegel 1993).

This weakening of party ties in our four core nations typifies a pattern occurring in almost all advanced industrial democracies. Among the nineteen advanced industrial democracies for which we have long-term survey data, seventeen show a drop in the percentage of partisans (Dalton 2000; 2004, ch. 2). Furthermore, the *strength* of partisanship has decreased in all nineteen nations. In countries as diverse as Austria, Canada, Japan, New Zealand, and Sweden, the pattern is the same: the partisan attachments of the public weakened during the latter half of the twentieth century.

Other evidence points to growing public doubts about parties as political institutions. Several international surveys find that public confidence in political parties rates at the bottom of a list of diverse social and political institutions. Data from Britain, Canada, Germany, Sweden, and other nations demonstrate that contemporary publics are significantly less trusting of political parties (Dalton and Weldon 2004; Bromley and Curtice 2003; Carty 2002).

Advanced industrial democracies are experiencing a new period of *partisan dealignment,* which means that a significant proportion of the public is not developing party attachments and is often openly critical of political parties. Electoral analysts first thought that partisan dealignment was a temporary phenomenon, as parties and politicians struggled with new problems that temporarily weakened their support among the public (like a sports team on a losing streak). Now, however, it is apparently a continuing feature of contemporary politics. Even today, American partisanship remains below its highpoints in the 1950s and early 1960s. If party identification is the most important attitude in electoral behavior research, then dealignment should have major implications for all these nations.

CONSEQUENCES OF DEALIGNMENT

Does it matter if fewer people now identify with a political party? If our theories about the value of partisanship are correct, It should. Because partisan ties are seen as so central to citizen political behavior, the erosion of these ties should have obvious and predicable effects on citizen politics. Indeed, the evidence of partisan dealignment is visible in a range of different aspects of electoral behavior.

Partisanship binds individual voters to a preferred party. As these ties weaken, so should patterns of partisan-centered voting choice. Indeed, weakened party attachments lead fewer American and German voters to cast straight-party ballots, and the rate of split-ticket voting has risen in recent elections (figure 9.4). In the 1960s less than a sixth of U.S. voters split their ballots between a presidential candidate of one party and a congressional

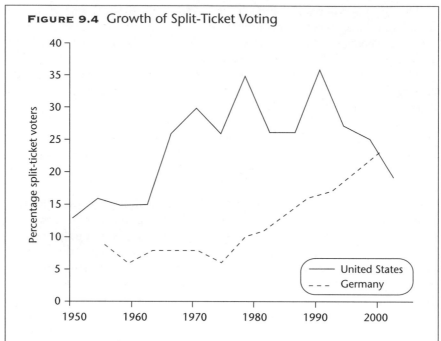

FIGURE 9.4 Growth of Split-Ticket Voting

SOURCES: United States, 1952–2004 American National Election Studies (a vote for third-party presidential candidates counted as split voting); Germany, Dalton and Bürklin (2003, 68); data for 1990–2002 are from western Germany.

candidate of another party; by the 1980s this proportion had risen to a quarter of the electorate. With Perot's third-party candidacy in 1992, 36 percent of Americans split their ballots. Even without Perot, split-ticket voting remained relatively high in the 2000 election, but then dropped off in the polarized 2004 contest. (It is likely to rise again in 2008 with two nonincumbents running.) Split-ticket voting between House and Senate votes has also increased over time (Stanley and Niemi 2000). And we find similar evidence of a rise in split-ticket voting in Germany between first and second ballots (Schoen 2000). Split-ticket voting appears to be a general consequence of the dealignment trend across other nations as well (Dalton and Wattenberg 2000, ch. 3).

Weakened partisanship adds to the fluidity of voting patterns. The number of political parties and the shift in vote shares between elections are generally increasing in advanced industrial democracies, including the four we are studying here (Dalton and Wattenberg 2000, ch. 3). Although most voters continue to support the same party over time, the number of floating voters is rising in these party systems. Partisanship was once a stable guidepost for citizen political behavior, but now fewer individuals are following its guidance.

Because partisanship also mobilizes individuals to participate in politics, it is no surprise that dealignment has been accompanied by a decline in electoral participation (see chapter 3). Voter turnout has fallen in most advanced industrial democracies. Participation in campaign activities—going to meetings, working for candidates, and displaying party support—has also atrophied (Dalton and Wattenberg 2000, ch. 3). If politics is like sports, then the decreasing number of habitual fans means that there are fewer to attend each game and participate in the sport.

Finally, the voting process has changed as a result of the decline in partisanship. As long-term party and social-group cues are losing importance, the decision-making process shifts toward the issues and candidates of specific campaigns. As one indicator of this shift, trend data show a systematic tendency for voters to make their decisions later in the campaign (Dalton and Wattenberg 2000, ch. 3). Campaigns are now more likely to matter more because fewer voters base their choices on standing partisan predispositions—voters are beginning to choose.

CAUSES OF DEALIGNMENT

There are several explanations for the dealignment trend. One explanation focuses on the *performance of political parties*. Initially, researchers linked declining partisanship to political events and crises. In the United States, the dramatic events of the 1970s turned many young people away from political parties. The antipartisan sentiments stirred by the Vietnam War, Watergate, and the civil rights movement kept new voters from developing the early-life partisan attachments that could build over time. The student protests in Europe and an apparently growing number of party scandals may have had a similar effect in these nations.

More generally, poor performance is supposedly perpetuating dealignment (Zelle 1995; Thomassen 2005). On the one hand, contemporary parties are struggling with problems of maintaining social services in the face of mounting government deficits. Some of the economic and welfare issues traditionally associated with the class cleavage have not been fully resolved. On the other hand, the new issues of advanced industrial societies often appear unsuited for mass political parties. Many of these issues, such as nuclear energy, minority rights, or local environmental problems, are too narrow to affect mass partisan alignments on their own. The rise of single-issue interests does not translate well into partisan attachments, because the electoral impact of these issues is uncertain and because it is difficult to accommodate these issues within large political coalitions. In the United States, the lack of connection between issues and parties has led to a proliferation of citizen interest groups and direct-action politics. In Europe, it has spawned similar groups, as well as a variety of small parties on the left and right. Analysts therefore maintain that political parties see their critical programmatic function of aggregating and articulating political interests slipping away. In a creative new study, Frode Berglund and colleagues (2005) show that the extent of distinct policy choices between the parties is related to the strength of partisanship across six European democracies; as the distinction has blurred, partisanship has weakened.

A Functionalist Explanation

The cross-national breadth of dealignment trends, however, suggests that more than a series of coincidental poor performance lies behind these trends. Partisan dealignment also reflects broader patterns of social modernization that is common to advanced industrial democracies. A *functionalist explanation* claims that the declining role of parties as political institutions seems to be a critical part of this process. Other institutions have taken over many of the parties' traditional political functions. A myriad of special-interest groups and single-issue lobbies are expressing the public's issue interests, and political parties have little hope of representing all of them. Party leaders are even losing some control over the selection of elected party representatives. The most advanced example is the United States, where the expansion of open primaries and nonpartisan elections has weakened the parties' hold on recruitment. The British Labour Party has experienced a similar shift in nominating power away from the party in Parliament to party conventions and local constituency groups. These and other developments lessen the importance of parties in the political process and therefore weaken the significance of parties as political reference points.

Changes in the mass media also contribute to dealignment trends. The mass media now perform many of the information activities that political parties once controlled. Instead of learning about an election at a campaign rally or from party canvassers, prospective voters now turn to television and newspapers as the primary sources of campaign information (see chapter 2). Furthermore, the content of the mass media has changed to downplay the importance of political parties. The American media have shifted their campaign focus away from the political parties toward the candidates, and a weaker parallel trend is evident in several parliamentary democracies (Dalton and Wattenberg 2000, ch. 3).

Although these systematic factors are important, their ability to explain the dealignment trend is limited. It is true that some failures in party performance may have initially stimulated a dealignment trend, but this trend did not reverse when a new party won control of the government or when policy failure was replaced by policy success. The research literature in each nation typically points to a unique set of policy failures, but the dealignment trend is a common feature across these diverse experiences. Therefore, we look for general changes affecting advanced industrial societies. Even the emphasis on the changing role of the media overlooks their significance across these nations, because of their different public/private ownership patterns and different journalistic norms. We believe that more fundamental changes in contemporary publics have contributed to partisan dealignment.

Cognitive Mobilization and Apartisans

The cognitive mobilization explanation begins by accepting the importance of partisanship as a heuristic that helps citizens orient themselves to politics (Shively 1979; Borre and Katz 1973). But, because the voters' political awareness and sophistication are growing, more people can deal with the complexities of politics without passive reliance on external cues or heuristics (see chapter 2). In addition, the availability of political information through the media reduces the costs of making informed decisions.

Cognitive mobilization therefore reduces some citizens' need to develop party identifications as a shortcut to help them handle difficult and often confusing political decisions. Indeed, the self-defined political interests of the cognitively mobilized may drive them away from habitual party cues that provide less room for individual choice.

The cognitive mobilization theory also implies that the rising number of independents should be concentrated among a distinct group of citizens: the better educated, the better informed. In contrast, the early literature on partisanship held that nonpartisans were at the margins of the electoral process; they were unsophisticated about politics and uninvolved in elections (Campbell et al. 1960).

We think of party mobilization and cognitive mobilization as two alternative ways that citizens can connect themselves to the political process (Dalton 1984; 2007c). Some voters orient themselves to politics based on their partisan attachments, a potent source of political cues. Cognitive mobilization produces another group of politically interested and well-educated voters who orient themselves to politics on their own. The combination of these traits defines a typology of four types of citizens (figure 9.5). *Apoliticals* are neither attached to a political party nor cognitively mobilized; this group conforms to the independents originally described by Campbell and his colleagues (1960, 143–145). *Ritual partisans* are mobilized into politics primarily by their strong party attachments and are not cognitively mobilized. *Cognitive partisans* are highly ranked on both mobilization dimensions: they have strong party attachments, and they are psychologically involved in politics even when party cues are lacking.

Apartisans are the "new independents." It is essential to distinguish them from traditional independents (apoliticals). Apartisans are cognitively mobilized, which implies high levels of political involvement and sophistication, although these citizens remain unattached to any political party. Apartisans are also concentrated among the young, the better educated, and postmaterialists (Dalton 1984). Other research shows that the development of advanced industrial societies is increasing the proportion of apartisans within contemporary publics, as well as shifting the ratio of ritual and cognitive partisans. Data from the American National Election Studies find that the number of apartisans has more than doubled since 1964—to one-fifth of the

FIGURE 9.5 Patterns of Political Mobilization

Strength of partisanship

		Independent	Party identification
Cognitive mobilization	High	Apartisan	Cognitive partisan
	Low	Apolitical	Ritual partisan

electorate.[10] In addition, the number of cognitive partisans has grown slightly, while the proportion of ritual partisans has decreased by almost half. Ronald Inglehart found that the percentage of apartisans in Europe increased significantly over a single decade (1976–1987) (Inglehart 1990, 366). Inglehart also found sharp differences in the percentage of apartisans across European generations, suggesting that the number of apartisans will continue to rise.

The growth of apartisans has implications for contemporary political behavior (Dalton 2007c). Apartisans have the political resources to follow the complexities of politics, and they are free of affective party ties. These new independents are therefore less consistent in their voting patterns because voting behavior is not dependent on long-standing party predispositions. This group may be expected to inject more issue voting into elections and to demand that candidates be more responsive to public opinion (see figure 10.6, p. 212). Apartisans also may press for an expansion of citizen input beyond the narrow channel of elections and other party-related activities. The political skills of apartisans enable them to organize effective citizen-action groups, citizen lobbies, protest demonstrations, and other unconventional political activities. The nonpartisan, issue-oriented characteristics of these activities make them ideal participation modes for apartisans.

Finally, ongoing processes of socioeconomic change should gradually increase the number of apartisans. The actions of parties in specific elections may hasten or retard this process in the short term, but the evidence suggests a long-term trend toward partisan dealignment in advanced industrial societies.

Politics in a Dealigned Era

Most elections involve a choice among parties or their representatives, and so parties remain the central actors in elections. This chapter maintains that most citizens develop a psychological identification with a preferred political party, and these attachments are a potent guide for political behavior. If one could ask any question to understand the political behavior of an individual, the question should be about partisanship because these attachments influence so many aspects of citizen behavior.

And yet, party ties are eroding in virtually all the advanced industrial democracies, resulting in a new pattern of partisan dealignment. In addition, the new apartisans are concentrated among the better educated and the politically engaged. It is as if the most sophisticated fans of the sport of politics are becoming disengaged with the partisan players they see on the field.

Furthermore, as with the weakening of social group-based voting, the similarity of dealignment trends across various nations is striking. Long-term sources of partisan preference—social characteristics and partisanship—are weakening in most advanced industrial democracies. In a single nation, we might explain such developments by the specific trials and tribulations of the parties. When a pattern appears across a wide variety of nations, however, it suggests that the causes are common to advanced industrial societies. Indeed, linking the process of cognitive mobilization to partisan dealignment seems to represent yet another aspect of the new style of citizen politics. Cognitively mobilized citizens are better able to make their own political decisions—and more interested in doing so—without relying on heuristics or external cues. These new apartisans are producing the dealignment trend.

Partisan dealignment is part of a general process of political change that is transforming the relationship between voters and parties, and it has real consequences for the operation of the political process. The personal connection between parties and voters is being replaced by professional organizations that rely on the media and direct mailing to connect to voters. Instead of depending on party members for staffing, election campaigns have become professionalized activities run by hired specialists. Instead of drawing on membership dues to fund party activities, many party systems are turning to public funding sources. Such changes in organizational style may exacerbate dealignment trends, by further distancing parties from the voters.

Weakened party-line voting also may contribute to split-party control of the federal and state governments in the United States (Brody et al. 1994). Between 1981 and 1986 different parties controlled the House and Senate for the first time since 1916, and this pattern recurred from 1994 to 2000, and again in 2001–2002. Most visible has been the division in partisan control of the presidency and Congress. From 1952 to 2008 the same party controlled the presidency and the House for only twenty-two out of fifty-six years.

The Federal Republic of Germany also has a federal system, and the same pattern is found there. For the first twenty years of the FRG's history, the same party coalition controlled the Bundestag (the directly elected lower house of parliament) and the Bundesrat (which represents the majority of state governments). Between 1976 and 2005, however, federal and state control was divided for more than a third of this period. In Great Britain, one sees a growing regionalization of voting patterns, as local electoral results are less closely tied to national patterns.

One of the strongest signs of dealigned politics is the rise of new political parties that can draw on independents for their initial support. The number of political parties grew during the latter half of the twentieth century in most parliamentary democracies. Ross Perot's candidacy in the 1992 and 1996 U.S. presidential elections and Ralph Nader's 2000 and 2004 campaigns illustrate the potential to appeal to nonpartisans. Perot, a candidate without prior political experience and without the support of a party apparatus, garnered 19 percent of the presidential vote in 1992.[11] The success of "flash parties"—such as List Pim Fortuyn in the Netherlands, Silvio Berlusconi's *Forza Italia!* and Jorg Haider's Freedom Party in Austria—and the general rise of New Left and New Right parties in Europe are additional indicators of the volatility we see in contemporary party systems.

Finally, the eroding influence of long-term sources of partisanship would suggest that factors farther along the funnel of causality can play a larger role in voter choice. Citizens are still voting, even if they are not relying on party cues or early-learned partisanship to the degree they once did. This new independence may encourage the public to judge candidates and parties on their policies and government performance—producing a deliberative public that more closely approximates the classic democratic ideal. But, the lack of longstanding partisan loyalties may also make electorates more vulnerable to manipulation and demagogic appeals (Holmberg 1994, 113–114). Dealignment has the potential to yield both positive and negative consequences for electoral politics, depending on how party systems and voters react in this new context. In the following chapters, we consider how the changing role of issues and candidate images is affecting the calculus of voting.

SUGGESTED READINGS

Dalton, Russell, and Martin Wattenberg, eds. *Parties without Partisans: Political Change in Advanced Industrial Democracies.* New York: Oxford University Press, 2000.

Green, Donald, Bradley Palmquist, and Eric Schickler. *Partisan Hearts and Minds: Political Parties and the Social Identities of Voters.* New Haven: Yale University Press, 2002.

Jennings, M. Kent, and Thomas Mann, eds. *Elections at Home and Abroad.* Ann Arbor: University of Michigan Press, 1994.

Lewis-Beck, Michael, et al. *The American Voter Revisited.* Ann Arbor: University of Michigan Press, 2008.

Rose, Richard, and Ian McAllister. *The Loyalties of Voters: A Lifetime Learning Model.* Newbury Park, Calif.: Sage, 1990.

Thomassen, Jacques, ed. *The European Voter.* Oxford: Oxford University Press, 2005.

Wattenberg, Martin. *The Decline of American Political Parties, 1952–1996.* Cambridge: Harvard University Press, 1998.

NOTES

1. The standard party identification question is one of the most frequently asked items in U.S. public opinion surveys, measuring both the direction of partisanship and the strength of party attachments: "Generally speaking, do you think of yourself as a Republican, a Democrat, an Independent, or what?" For those expressing a party preference: "Would you call yourself a strong Republican/Democrat or a not very strong Republican/Democrat?" For Independents: "Do you think of yourself as closer to the Republican or Democratic Party?"

    The question yields a seven-point measure of partisanship ranging from strong Democratic identifiers to strong Republican identifiers.

2. One of the current debates in the American voting literature is the question of how closely aggregate levels of partisanship track current voting preferences. For the contrasting sides of this debate, see MacKuen, Erikson, and Stimson (1989); Abramson and Ostrom (1991, 1994).

3. For example, the German version of the party identification question specifically cues the respondent that the question is about long-term partisan leanings: "Many people in the Federal Republic lean toward a particular party for a long time, although they may occasionally vote for a different party. How about you?"

4. These data come from the Political Action study, which supplemented its national sample of adults with additional parent-child interviews of families with sixteen- to twenty-year olds living in the parent's home. For additional analyses, see Jennings et al. (1979).

5. Morris Fiorina (1981) describes partisanship as a "running tally" of an individual's accumulated electoral experience. If early partisan leanings are reinforced by later voting experience, party ties strengthen over time. If voting experiences counteract partisanship, then these party loyalties may gradually erode. Also see Niemi and Jennings (1991).

6. Researchers have debated whether age differences in American partisanship represent generational or life-cycle effects (Converse 1976; Abramson 1979). We emphasize the life-cycle (partisan learning) model because the cross-national pattern of age differences seems more consistent with this explanation.

7. Part of these relationships are due to patterns of accumulated partisanship over the life cycle. In addition, the lower levels of partisanship among the young can be traced in part to decreasing initial attachments among younger generations.

8. In the previous editions of this book, the Federal Republic of Germany was an exception to this general pattern. Residents of communist East Germany obviously did not have the same opportunity to develop attachments to democratic parties, so researchers found significantly weaker levels of partisan attachments in the East and little age difference in the strength of partisan ties. As we predicted, as

eastern Germans have gained more experience with democratic electoral politics, the life-cycle pattern of partisan learning is becoming more apparent, and the differences in the level of party attachments between West and East has narrowed.

9. Although we stress the stability of partisanship, we find evidence that this stability has eroded over the past several decades (Dalton and Wattenberg 2000, ch. 3).

10. We define cognitively mobilized citizens as having a combination of interests and skills—that is, being "very interested" in politics and/or having at least some college education. The following table presents the distribution of types using data from the American National Election Studies (also see Dalton 2007c):

	1964–1966	1980–1990	2000–2004
Apartisans	10%	14%	20%
Cognitive partisans	27	29	35
Ritual partisans	47	36	26
Apoliticals	16	21	19

11. The 1992 American National Election Study found that Ross Perot won 10 percent of the vote among Democratic identifiers, 17 percent among Republican identifiers, and 36 percent among independents. This pattern continued in the 1996 election, and in 2000 both Patrick Buchanan and Ralph Nader gained the greatest percentage of their votes from independents.

CHAPTER 10

Attitudes and Electoral Behavior

Election day is approaching, and you have to decide how you will vote. How do you make this decision as a good democratic citizen? The American Voter Revisited (Lewis-Beck et al. 2008) reported on how one American voter thought about this decision in the 2000 presidential election:

> *(What do you like about Al Gore?):* I definitely like his stand on Social Security. He'll keep it and improve it. His strong protection of the environment and stand against drilling oil in Alaska. He is trying to work on the health program, which will be slow going. I love his pro-choice stance and his program for schools.
> *(What do you dislike about Gore?):* His personality bothers me a lot. He does not come across well as a public speaker.
> *(What do you like about George Bush?):* Nothing.
> *(What do you dislike about Bush?):* His whole platform, gun control, the environment, Social Security and health care. He is going to try to eliminate the [Social Security] program and have people invest on their own.

This person seems like a good citizen who has reasoned bases for voting. Most voters are not as articulate in expressing their likes and dislikes about the candidates in specific terms, but we think that most voters have views on the issues that are important to them and views on how the parties and candidates differ on these issues. In addition, factors such as personality and party ties enter into these calculations.

Electoral politics may begin as the competition between rival social groups or party camps as discussed in the previous chapters, but elections should revolve around the issues and candidates of the campaign.[1] Deciding how to vote is complicated. Citizens should judge the parties on their policy positions, whether they agree with one more than the others, and how they view each party's capacity to govern. Issues and candidates give political meaning to the partisan attachments and social divisions we discussed in earlier chapters.

Issue opinions and candidate images also matter because they represent the dynamic aspect of electoral politics. The distribution of partisanship may define the broad parameters of electoral competition, but each campaign is fought over the policies that the contenders advocate, the images of the candidates, or the incumbent government's policy performance. Because the mix of these factors varies across elections, issue beliefs and candidate images explain the ebb and flow of election outcomes. The importance of issue beliefs and candidate images is why the funnel of causality locates them so close to voting choice (see figure 9.1, p. 171). Although partisanship may influence

---

Internet Resource

Visit the Comparative Study of Electoral Systems Web site; the project surveys voters in dozens of nations:

http://www.cses.org

---

these attitudes, the content of a campaign also shapes these attitudes and the ultimate voting decision.

Finally, because the electoral impact of long-term partisan attachments and social cues is waning, many political scientists point to a corresponding increase in the influence of issue opinions and candidate images on voting choice. Martin Wattenberg (1991) has written provocatively about the rise of candidate-centered choices by American voters, and the role of candidate images is now more widely debated in European party systems (Aarts, Blais, and Schmitt 2005).

This chapter examines the role of issues and candidate images in voting choice. We consider how these attitudes might influence the vote, as well as their actual impact in contemporary elections. This evidence enables us to complete our model of voter choice and discuss the implications for the democratic process.

PRINCIPLES OF ISSUE VOTING

The study of issue voting is closely intertwined with the debate on the political sophistication of the public. Scholars consider issue voting as characterizing a sophisticated, rational electorate: the voter evaluates the government and the opposition and then thoughtfully casts a ballot for his or her preferred party. For the skeptics of mass democracy, this theoretical ideal seldom exists in reality. Instead, they see voters as lacking knowledge of the parties' positions, sometimes unsure of their own positions, and often voting based on ill-formed or even incorrect beliefs (see chapter 2).

The early voting studies criticized the electorate's ability to make informed choices. The authors of *The American Voter* maintained that meaningful issue voting is based on three requirements:

- citizens should be interested in the issue;
- they should hold an opinion on the issue; and
- they should know the party or candidate positions on the issue. (Campbell et al. 1960, ch. 8)

The American Voter maintained that on most policy issues, most voters fail to meet these criteria. It classified a third of the public or less as possible issue voters on each of a long list of policy topics. Paul Abramson, John Aldrich, and David Rohde (2005) updated these assessments of potential issue voters and came to similar conclusions. Moreover, researchers claim that these small percentages reflect the conceptual and motivational limits of the electorate—the lack of issue voting is presumably an intrinsic aspect of mass politics (Converse 1990). These political scientists therefore doubt that election results represent the policy choices of the public.

Since the beginning of voting research, however, critics have challenged this negative image of issue voting. V. O. Key showed that citizens were "moved by concern about the central and relevant questions of public policy, of government performance, and of executive personality." In short, Key's unorthodox argument was that "voters are not fools" (1966, 7–8). Key's position has become less unorthodox as our understanding of citizen voting behavior has grown.

That only a minority of the public fulfills the issue voting criteria for each specific issue does not mean that only a third of the total public is capable for any and all issues. Contemporary electorates are composed of overlapping *issue publics,* groups of people interested in a specific issue (see chapter 2). These issue publics vary in size and composition. A large and heterogeneous group of citizens may be interested in basic political issues such as taxes, inflation rates, budget deficits, and the threat of war. On more specific issues— agricultural policy, nuclear energy, transportation policy, or foreign aid—the issue publics normally are smaller and politically distinct.

Most voters are attentive on at least one issue, and many voters belong to several issue publics. Using open-ended questions about the likes and dislikes of the parties and candidates, Amy Gershkoff (2005) classified Americans in terms of their interest in various issues. She found that about a quarter of the public are not members of any issue public, and another quarter mention an interest in only one specific issue. She also found that half of the electorate belongs to two or more issue publics and a seventh belongs to four or more. Gershkoff concluded that voters are information specialists: they focus their attention on a few major issues, follow the news on these issues, and use them as a basis for electoral choice.

When citizens define their own issue interests, they are more likely to fulfill the issue-voting criteria for their issues. David RePass (1971) found that only 5 percent of Americans were interested in medical programs for the elderly, but more than 80 percent of this small group could be classified as potential issue voters. One may assume that this issue public would be mostly older Americans, as few college students follow the Medicare debate. If one asked about environmental sustainability and global warming, the generational patterns might be reversed. Other studies of American voting behavior have expanded this research on issue salience (Krosnick 1990; Anand and Krosnick 2003; Gershkoff 2005), and there is mounting evidence from European electoral research (Clarke et al. 2004; Mayer and Tiberj 2004).

FIGURE 10.1 Classification of Issues

Time frame	Type of issue		
	Position	*Performance*	*Attribute*
Retrospective	Policy appraisal	Performance evaluation	Attribute voting
Prospective	Policy mandate	Anticipatory judgment	

Adopting a diversified view of the electorate—not all citizens must be interested in all issues—therefore strengthens the evidence of issue voting.

The conflicting claims about issue voting also may arise because researchers think of issue voting in different terms or use contrasting evidence to support their claims. Indeed, the literature is full of descriptions of how various types of issues function within the electoral process and why we should distinguish between these types of issues, the demands they place on voters, and their likely impact on voting choices.[2] Issue voting may be more likely for some sorts of issues than for others, and the implications of issue voting also may vary depending on the type of issue.

Figure 10.1 introduces a framework for thinking about issue voting. One important characteristic is the type of issue. *Position issues* involve conflicts over policy goals (Stokes 1963). A typical position issue might concern whether the U.S. government should support stem-cell research, or whether France should support Turkey's entry in the European Union. Discussions of issue voting often focus on position issues.

Performance issues involve judgments on how effectively the candidates or parties pursue widely accepted political goals.[3] Most voters favor a strong economy, but they may differ in how they evaluate a government's success in accomplishing this goal. Conflicting claims about performance judgments often lie at the heart of electoral campaigns.

Voters may also judge the *attributes* of the parties or candidates: Do they possess desired traits or characteristics? A voter might consider a party as trustworthy if its campaign promises are to be believed. As depicted in the figure's framework, these issue characteristics reflect the different types of electoral decisions and each category has different implications for assessing voters' judgments and voting outcomes.

The nature of issue voting also varies by the time frame of the voters' judgments (Fiorina 1981; Abramson, Aldrich, and Rohde 2005, ch. 7). *Retro-*

spective judgments evaluate political actors on their past performance. Evaluating Chancellor Gerhard Schröder in 2005 based on the performance of the economy—something he encouraged German voters to do when he was first elected in 1998—is an example of retrospective voting. *Prospective* judgments are based on expectations of future performance. An evaluation judg of Schröder based on what his administration might do differently in the future would be an example of prospective voting.

Retrospective and prospective judgments have different implications for the nature of voting choice. Retrospective judgments should have a firmer base in the facts because they are based on experience. Such evaluations can be a relatively simple decision-making strategy: praise the incumbents if times have been good; criticize them if times have been bad. But a pure reliance on retrospective judgments limits the scope of citizen evaluations. In an election, voters are selecting a government for the future, and their decisions should include evaluations of a party's promises and its prospects for success. Therefore, voting decisions should include prospective judgments about a government's likely behavior in the future. Prospective judgments are based on a speculative and complex decision-making process. Individuals have the difficult task of making their own forecasts about the expected performance of political actors. How citizens balance retrospective and prospective judgments reflects directly on the nature of voting choice.

These characteristics define a typology of the different types of issue calculations that voters may use in elections. Some issue voting involves a *policy appraisal* that assesses a party's (or candidate's) past position on a policy controversy. The voters who supported George W. Bush in 2004 because they approved of his strong measures against terrorists were making a judgment about the past policies of his administration. Other voters may base their voting decisions on what a party or candidate promises for policies in the future. When Bush wanted voters in 2000 to support his plans to reduce taxes, he was asking for a *policy mandate* from the electorate.

Policy appraisals and policy mandates represent a sophisticated form of issue voting in which citizens are making choices between alternative policy goals for their government. This process places high requirements on the voters: they must inform themselves about the policy issue, settle on a preferred policy, and see meaningful choices between the contenders. Voters might acquire this information directly or through surrogate information sources (Popkin 1991; Lupia 1994).

Performance evaluations involve general judgments about how a political actor (party, candidate, or government) has been doing the job. If the political actor has been successful, voters support its return to office; if it has struggled, voters look for acceptable alternatives to the incumbents. In 1980 Ronald Reagan asked Americans to make a performance evaluation of Jimmy Carter's presidency when he asked: "Are you better off than you were four years ago?" In other instances, voters may make *anticipatory judgments* about the future performance of government. Some analysts claim that the

Labour Party lost in 1992 because enough voters doubted the party's ability to govern effectively, despite favoring many of Labour's policy proposals.

Finally, some aspects of issue voting are based on judgments about candidate or party attributes as a basis of choice. This type of voting often lacks a specific time frame. Voters judge candidates on their personal characteristics, which, although not immediately political in their content, are legitimate factors to consider in selecting a candidate (Kinder et al. 1980). Just as Carter's moral integrity helped him in 1976, Bill Clinton's "slick Willie" image hurt him at the polls in 1992—and both images were politically relevant although they did not involve explicit policy or performance calculations. Similar stylistic considerations can influence voter choices of a political party. Tony Blair's 1997 victory in Britain and Schröder's 1998 victory in Germany are attributed in part to each candidate's ability to project a more dynamic, forward-looking image than his electoral opponents.

Electoral researchers consider attribute voting as an example of limited political sophistication because it does not involve explicit policy criteria. As we discuss later, however, many attributes involve traits that are directly relevant to the task of governing or to providing national leadership. We therefore consider attribute voting as a potentially meaningful basis of electoral choice.

The typology of figure 10.1 thus provides a useful framework for thinking about different types of issue voting. For example, Martin Wattenberg's analysis of support for Reagan provides an especially insightful example of how policy positions and performance evaluations reflect theoretically and empirically distinct aspects of issue voting (Wattenberg 1991, ch. 6). Some candidates win because of their policy promises; others win despite their program. A similar interplay of factors is at work in many elections.

POSITION ISSUES AND THE VOTE

Some political scientists have argued that advanced industrial democracies are resolving the political controversies that had long divided their populations (the controversies of the Old Politics), which would lead to a new politics of affluence and harmony—sort of like life on the Starship *Enterprise* (e.g., Franklin, Mackie, and Valen 1992). This has not occurred.

Instead, policy-based voting is more prevalent in most democracies and involves a greater number of issues. Changes in the nature of electorates (and politics itself) facilitate issue voting. The process of cognitive mobilization increases the number of voters who have the conceptual ability and the political skills necessary to fulfill the issue-voting criteria. The growth of citizen-action groups and new issue-oriented parties on both the Left and Right also stimulate (and reflect) greater issue awareness. In response, political elites have become more conscious of the public's preferences and more sensitive to the results of public opinion polls.

Contemporary issue voting still involves many long-standing Old Politics debates. Economic cycles inevitably stimulate concerns about the government's role in the economy and how it affects the public's economic security. Indeed, economic controversies seem to arise frequently, spawned by the "free market" programs of Reagan, Thatcher, Kohl, and their progeny, and by ebbs and flows in national economies. Political events, such as the latest Supreme Court decisions on affirmative action in the United States or renewed regional tensions in many democratic societies, can revive latent conflicts.

Issue controversies also arise from the changing political context. Foreign policy clearly illustrates this pattern. The United States and other Western democracies are grappling with a new post–cold war international system. The attacks of September 11 signaled the global threat of jihadist terrorism and other international conflicts that challenge peace and stability throughout the world. Today, political controversies include New Politics concerns such as nuclear energy, gender equality, and environmental protection. It was not so long ago that politicians and voters did not even know that problems of global warming and ozone depletion existed. But these new issues can provide a political base for fledgling parties and reorient the voting patterns of the young.

The diversity of issues across elections and electoral systems makes it difficult to compare the impact of issues across time or nations. Indeed, the impact of specific issues should shift across time because they represent a dynamic part of elections. A much richer compendium of information on issue voting exists for each nation separately (Abramson, Aldrich, and Rohde 2005; Clarke et al. 2006; Anderson and Zelle 1998). Research finds that position issues often influence voters' choices, although debate continues about the role of specific issues and how it has changed over time (Aardal and van Wijnen 2005).

We can assess the general impact of policy preferences on voting behavior by examining the relationship between Left/Right attitudes and the vote. Chapter 6 described Left/Right attitudes as a sort of "super issue," a summary of positions on the issues that are most important to each voter. To a French union member, for example, Left/Right attitudes may reflect positions on traditional economic conflicts; to a German university student Left/Right attitudes may reflect positions on New Politics controversies. In some cases, Left/Right attitudes signify a mix of different types of issues. Specific issue interests will vary across individuals or across nations, but Left/Right attitudes can summarize each citizen's overall policy views.[4]

Most citizens can position themselves along a Left/Right scale, and their attitudes are linked to specific policy views, fulfilling the first two criteria of policy voting (see chapter 6; Inglehart 1990, ch. 9). Figure 10.2 shows that people in each nation can also fulfill the third requirement: positioning the major political parties on the Left/Right scale. For each of our four nations, the figure presents the voters' average self-placements and the average scores they assign to the major political parties in their respective nations.

American voters are the most conservative, placing themselves to the right of the British, German, and French publics. Americans perceive modest

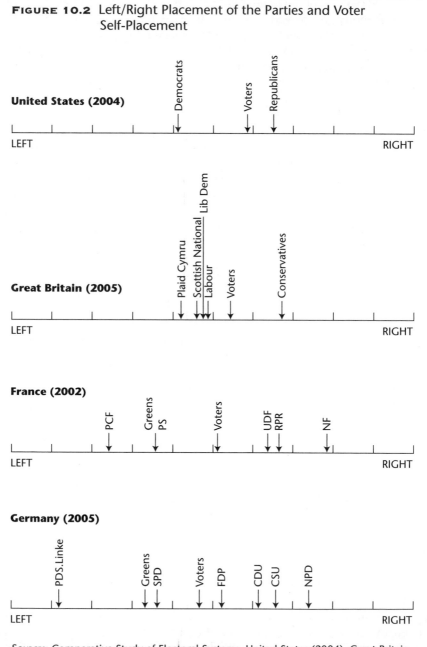

FIGURE 10.2 Left/Right Placement of the Parties and Voter Self-Placement

SOURCES: Comparative Study of Electoral Systems, United States (2004), Great Britain (2005), France (2002), and Germany (2005).

NOTE: Figure entries are public placement of parties on the Left/Right scale (mean scores on a 0–10 scale).

political differences between the Democratic and Republican Parties, and this polarization is greater than between Republican and Democratic voters themselves.[5] This discrepancy suggests that the growing divisions of American political parties at the elite level exceeds the differences within the electorate (Fiorina 2005). Although specific presidential candidates may be seen as relatively more or less ideological, the positions of the parties change relatively little from election to election.

Perceived party differences are typically greater in European party systems. In France the political spectrum runs from the Communist Party at the leftist extreme to the National Front on the far right. By crude estimate, the French voter sees a range of party choices that extends more than twice as far across the political landscape than the span between the major American political parties. The German partisan landscape ranges from the PDS.Linke, the reformed Communist Party, on the far left to the extremist NPD on the far right. In Great Britain the Labour and Conservative Parties assume distinct positions on the Left/Right scale, although the Labour Party moved toward the center under Blair's leadership.[6] Most political observers would agree that these party placements are fairly accurate portrayals of actual party positions.[7] Therefore, in overall terms, citizens fulfill the third issue-voting criterion: knowing the party positions.

Figure 10.3 shows the percentage voting for the party on the right in each country according to the Left/Right attitudes of survey respondents. The impact of Left/Right attitudes is greatest where a large number of parties offer clear policy options. In France only 4 percent of self-identified leftists favored a rightist party (UDF, RPR, or FN) in the 2002 legislative elections, compared to 86 percent among self-identified rightists. Even in the United States, with only two major parties, there is a 61-percentage-point gap in the Republicans' share of the vote as a function of Left/Right attitudes. These voting differences are much larger than the effects of social characteristics noted in chapter 8. The substantial influence of Left/Right attitudes is visible because policy evaluations are located closer to the end of the funnel of causality (figure 9.1, p. 171).

A closer look at the patterns of party support also confirms the relative positions of the parties along the Left/Right continuum. As the most extreme leftist party in France, the PC attracts the greatest share of its vote among the most extreme leftists, while the Socialists do best among more moderate leftists; and this pattern is mirrored in support for the UDF and the RPR on the right. Another significant contrast is between the Greens in Germany and France. The German Greens' strong support from leftists reflects their position along the continuum, while the French Greens typically draw more support from the center.

We can add more detail as to how issue positions affect the vote by studying the relationship between specific policy attitudes and party preferences. Several surveys from the International Social Survey Program include different issue positions across several policy domains (see chapter 6 for additional

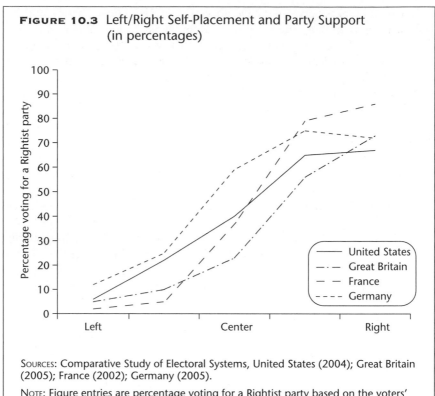

FIGURE 10.3 Left/Right Self-Placement and Party Support (in percentages)

SOURCES: Comparative Study of Electoral Systems, United States (2004); Great Britain (2005); France (2002); Germany (2005).

NOTE: Figure entries are percentage voting for a Rightist party based on the voters' self-placement on the Left/Right scale.

discussion of these items). Table 10.1 describes the relationship between these issue positions and party choices in our four nations (see appendix A on the interpretation of correlations).[8] We should be cautious about over-interpreting these data because the strength of each relationship reflects both the varying size of the relevant issue public and the clarity of party positions. The dynamic, short-term nature of issue beliefs means that either of these factors, and therefore the impact of an issue, may change between elections. These data offer only a snapshot of the relationship between issue opinions and party preferences. Still, snapshots can provide a valuable picture of reality.

The economic issues of the Old Politics—such as support for social services and government measures to reduce income inequality and manage the economy—display strong relationships with party preferences in all four nations. In each nation, the strongest correlation involves an economic issue. This pattern occurs because economic topics have large issue publics, and most political parties have clear policies on the government's role in the economy and related economic policies (see figure 7.2, p. 136). In the United States, for example, the Republican Party has challenged social spending programs as part

TABLE 10.1 Correlation between Issue Opinions and Party Preferences

Issue	United States	Great Britain	France	Germany
Left/Right attitudes	0.39	0.34	0.40	0.27
Socioeconomic issues				
Social services over taxes	0.35	0.22	0.37	0.21
Government reduce inequality	0.19	0.17	—	0.13
Government control wages	0.16	0.17	0.20	0.14
Government control prices	0.15	0.14	0.17	0.14
Environmental issues				
Pay more for environment	0.19	0.19	—	0.15
Government responsible for environmental laws	0.14	0.12	0.16	0.12
Economic growth harms environment	0.07	0.13	—	0.07
GM foods are dangerous	—	0.13	—	0.10
Nuclear power is dangerous	0.11	0.12	—	0.13
Gender issues				
Husbands work/wife at home	0.08	0.12	0.14	0.14
If wife works, family suffers	0.08	0.09	0.12	0.14
If mother works, child suffers	0.08	0.10	0.14	0.16
Foreign policy				
Spend more on defense	0.14	0.15	0.26	0.15

SOURCES: 1996, 1998, 2000, and 2002 International Social Survey Program; Left/Right attitudes correlation, Comparative Study of Electoral Systems and 2001 British Election Study.

NOTE: Table entries are Cramer's V coefficients between issue positions and party vote preference. See endnote 8 and appendix A for a description of how to interpret Cramer's V coefficients.

of the party's core program, and conservatives in Great Britain, France, and Germany typically take conservative economic positions. The conflict over economic issues, social programs, and the role of government remains a central theme in contemporary elections. Moreover, these correlations are based on the full public; if we limited our analysis to only members of the relevant issue public that follows these issues, the correlations would be even stronger.

New Politics issues dealing with the environment have a modest impact on party choice. In Britain the average correlation for socioeconomic issues is .18; for environmental issues, the average is .14. Although many people are interested in environmental protection, the translation of these policy attitudes into party preferences remains secondary to economic concerns. Material, economic issues still attract greater attention, and the established parties often offer less distinct policy choices on environmental and other New Politics issues. The German and French Greens have a distinct profile on environ-mental issues, but the positions of the remaining established parties are more centrist (see figure 7.2, p. 136).

Gender-related issues also often cut across established party lines. In the United States, the party positions are clearly stated, but the parties are inter-nally divided on issues such as the role of women in the family and work-place; therefore, these issues are not strongly related to party preferences. In Europe, the impact of gender issues is somewhat stronger, especially in France and Germany, where large Catholic voter blocs and/or Christian par-ties tend to polarize opinions on these issues. In sum, environmental and gen-der issues tend to cut across traditional party lines.

Foreign policy can influence partisan choice (Anand and Krosnick 2003), but its impact is normally secondary to domestic issues. France is a nation where foreign policy issues often affect partisanship because of continuing conflicts over France's role in the international system, ranging from its rela-tionship to NATO to the policies of European unification. Foreign policy is-sues attract attention from only a small share of the public, except at times of international crisis. Party differences on most foreign policy issues are also smaller than party polarization on many other topics.

The modest impact of each of these issues should not be interpreted as a limited role for issues, because not all issues are salient to all voters. In fact, issue interests have probably increased in diversity over time, and the linkage between issues and political parties has become more complex. A more re-fined analysis of specific issue publics would find that individual voting deci-sions are strongly influenced by each voter's specific issue interests and that these interests vary from person to person (Krosnick 1990; Gershkoff 2005). Correlations based on the total public combine those inside and outside of each issue public, which decreases the overall evidence of issue voting.

In addition, cognitively sophisticated voters are more likely to rely on is-sues as a basis for their electoral choice, further magnifying the importance of issue voting. A simple example can illustrate this effect. If we use Left/Right attitudes in the 2004 American National Election Study as a sum-mary of issue positions, then the correlation between Left/Right and con-gressional vote was .26 for the entire electorate (also see figure 10.3, p. 202). This relationship is, however, strongly conditioned by the voter's level of po-litical knowledge:

- Lowest on political knowledge: correlation is .03.
- Know one knowledge item: correlation is .17.
- Know two knowledge items: correlation is .26.
- Know all three knowledge items: correlation is .39.

Similar patterns exist for the importance of issues for members of the re-spective issue public. Thus, Key's positive assessments of the public's issue voting no longer appear so unorthodox.

PERFORMANCE ISSUES AND THE VOTE

Another form of issue voting involves performance evaluations. Many voters follow Reagan's advice to ask themselves if they are better off than they were four years ago and then vote for or against the incumbents on that basis (Anderson et al. 2005). Morris Fiorina (1981, 5) put it best: Citizens "typically have one comparatively hard bit of data: they know what life has been like during the incumbent's administration. They do not need to know the precise economic or foreign policies of the incumbent administration in order to judge the results of those policies." In other words, performance-based voting offers people a reasonable shortcut for ensuring that unsuccessful policies are dropped and successful policies continued.

This research argues that this process requires only that voters dispense electoral rewards and punishments based on past performance—regardless of whether the policies and the outcomes are connected. Benjamin Page (1978, 222), for example, wrote, "Even if the Great Depression and lack of recovery were not at all [Herbert] Hoover's fault . . . it could make sense to punish him in order to sharpen the incentives to maintain prosperity in the future." Page acknowledged that blame may be placed unfairly, yet "to err on the side of forgiveness would leave voters vulnerable to tricky explanations and rationalizations; but to err on the draconian side would only spur politicians on to greater energy and imagination in problem solving." Performance voting therefore requires that voters have a target for their blame when the government falters in some respect, whether it is economic slowdown or a foreign policy mistake.

Research on performance-based voting often focuses on the importance of economics on voting choices (MacKuen, Erikson, and Stimson 1992; Lewis-Beck 1988; Lewis-Beck and Paldam 2000; Anderson 1995; Norpoth 1992). A simple measure of performance evaluation—such as judgments about the performance of the national economy over the previous year—is significantly related to voting choices. Figure 10.4 displays the relationship between perceptions that the economy is improving/worsening and support for the incumbent party. In each case, negative economic perceptions hurt the incumbents, and positive perceptions benefit them. In the 2005 British election, Blair's Labour Party won 75 percent support among those who thought the economy was getting a lot better, but only 14 percent among those who thought it was getting a lot worse.

We might ask, however, whether these relationships are evidence of causality (Wlezein, Franklin, and Twiggs 1997). As we noted in chapter 9, some people adjust their economic expectations to reflect their general images of the government (see p. 179). Voters who like the incumbent government are more likely to put a favorable spin on economic conditions; those who are critical of government for one aspect of policy may generalize this dissatisfaction to include their economic judgments. Such projections, which are a normal part of incumbent images, likely magnify the relationship between

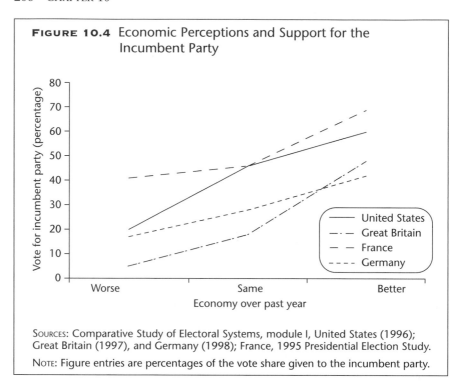

FIGURE 10.4 Economic Perceptions and Support for the Incumbent Party

SOURCES: Comparative Study of Electoral Systems, module I, United States (1996); Great Britain (1997), and Germany (1998); France, 1995 Presidential Election Study.

NOTE: Figure entries are percentages of the vote share given to the incumbent party.

economic perceptions and party preferences. Nevertheless, the underlying relationship is still important. A rising economic tide benefits the incumbents, while a failing economy often spells defeat at the next elections.

Another factor involves the scope of economic evaluations. Researchers have examined whether voters base their political evaluations on their personal economic situation (pocketbook voting) or on the broader national economy (sociotropic voting). Most studies find that voters follow the sociotropic model, which implies that policy outcomes rather than narrow self-interest are the driving force behind performance voting (Nadeau, Niemi, and Yoshinaka 2002; Listaug 2005; Lewis-Beck 1988).

Economics is but one example of the many policy areas that can lead to performance-based voting. But the state of the economy can sometimes be so important that it overrides other policy considerations. Many election analysts claim that incumbent parties are virtually unbeatable during strong economic upturns and extremely vulnerable during recessionary periods. Researchers argue that Americans and Britons elected conservative governments in 1979 and 1980 not for ideological reasons, but because they were voting against incumbent governments that had failed to deliver the economic goods (Crewe and Searing 1988; Wattenberg 1991). Four years after coming to power, both Margaret Thatcher and Ronald Reagan won reelection on the basis of improved economic performance (and the success of the Falklands

War in Thatcher's case)—in spite of continuing policy differences with most of their country's voters (Norpoth 1992). Other studies have documented the role of economic performance in other European states (Anderson 1995).

Although narrow performance voting does not conform to democratic theory's emphasis on policy evaluation, researchers defend performance voting as entirely rational. Does it make sense, they ask, to pay attention to the policy positions of an ineffective administration that seemingly cannot make good on its promises and program? Voting theorists emphasize that the only really effective weapon of popular control in a democratic regime is the electorate's capacity to throw a party out of power.

CANDIDATE IMAGES AND THE VOTE

The interview cited at the opening of this chapter highlighted the issue positions of this American voter. But the responses included comments about Al Gore's personality and communication skills as factors affecting voting choice. Other interviews discussed the features people liked or disliked about George Bush. Candidate images are inevitably part of the calculus of voting.

Democratic theorists describe issue voting in positive terms, but they often view candidate-based voting decisions less positively. Some researchers view personality characteristics as irrational or at least apolitical influences on voting choice (cf. Converse 1964; Page 1978). Candidates' images can be seen as commodities packaged by image-makers who sway the public by emphasizing traits with special appeal to the voters. People's judgments about alternative candidates are, in this view, based on superficial criteria such as a candidate's style or looks. Indeed, many experimental studies demonstrate that it is possible to manipulate a candidate's personal appearance to affect voters' choices.

More recent voting literature emphasizes a different approach to candidate assessments. This view holds that candidate evaluations are not necessarily superficial, emotional, or purely short-term. Voters may focus on the personal qualities of a candidate to gain important information about characteristics relevant to assessing how the individual will perform in office. This approach suggests that people organize their thoughts about candidates into broad categories or "prototypes" that they use in making judgments when other information is limited. Donald Kinder and his colleagues (1980), for example, explored the features that citizens use to define an ideal president. They showed that people choose attributes they believe would make for an ideal president, and they apply these to ratings of the incumbent president.

Arthur Miller, Martin Wattenberg, and Oksana Malanchuk (1986, 536) similarly argued for a rational interpretation of candidate-based voting: "Candidate assessments actually concentrate on instrumental concerns about how a candidate would conduct governmental affairs." They found that the three most important dimensions of candidate image for Americans are integrity, reliability, and competence. Such criteria are hardly irrational, for if a candidate is too incompetent to carry out policy promises or too dishonest for those promises to be trusted, it makes perfect sense for a voter to pay attention to personality as well as policies. David Glass (1985) and Miller, Wattenberg, and Malanchuk (1986) found that college-educated voters are the most likely to judge the candidates by their personal attributes.

The United States is clearly in the lead in developing a pattern of candidate-centered electoral politics (Wattenberg 2000; Funk 1999). Presidents are the focal point of the quadrennial elections, and the large shifts in vote shares between presidential elections often reflect the effects of candidate images. Presidents (and chief executives in state and local governments) are directly elected, and they largely run on personal platforms rather than as representatives of a fixed party position. Candidate image is one of their major electoral resources. A similar personalization of politics occurs in France, where the president functions separately from the legislative majority and even from his own party within the legislature.

Electoral research on parliamentary systems initially suggested that popular images of party leaders had a minor impact on voting choice because citizens did not directly vote for the chief executive. Further research, however, found more varied evidence. Clive Bean and Anthony Mughan (1989) showed that the perceived effectiveness of party leaders was moderately important in the British and Australian elections of the 1980s. German parliamentary elections also showed the voters' greater interest in candidate images (Ohr 2000). French politics has long valued the importance of a strong political leader, institutionalized in the directly elected presidency. The evidence from elections and from internal party politics generally points to the growing importance of candidate images even in parliamentary systems (Aarts, Blais, and Schmitt 2005; Curtice and Holmberg 2005; Poguntke and Webb 2005; McAllister 1996). Anyone who has watched modern parliamentary campaigns, with candidates staging walkabouts for television and hosting discussion sessions with voters (in front of the cameras) must recognize that candidate images are an important part of contemporary electoral campaigns in virtually all advanced industrial democracies.

THE END OF THE CAUSAL FUNNEL

At the end of the causal funnel, when people are ready to vote, it is difficult to come to a precise assessment of the influence of partisanship, issues, and candidate images on voting choices. Candidate images are at the very end of the funnel, indicating that they are strongly related to voting preferences, at least in systems where voters cast a ballot for a specific candidate. At the same time, however, candidate images are themselves the cumulation of prior influences. Long-term partisanship can have a potent effect in cuing voters on which politicians to like or dislike, just as voters' issue preferences can lead them toward a specific candidate.

This overlap between party and candidate likes—and even issue positions—is typical for many voters. In the 2005 German election, among those who voted for the CDU/CSU, 78 percent said they liked Angela Merkel, but only 20 percent liked Gerhard Schröder; among SPD voters the patterns were reversed—84 percent liked Schröder, and 25 percent liked Merkel. Furthermore, in parliamentary systems, partisan and candidate preferences are often closely intertwined because parliamentary candidates normally are more clearly chosen as party representatives; in some nations citizens vote directly for parties. British voters did not elect Blair, and German voters did not elect Merkel—both were selected by the members of their respective parliaments. Only in a system of direct election of candidates who are not selected by the party organization—such as through the primary system in the United States—are we likely to see much separation between party preferences and candidate preferences.

So, with overlapping candidate, party, and issue preferences, it is difficult to assess the independent influence of each. Comparing the weight of several issue and candidate variables can illustrate the mix of factors at play. Figure 10.5 combines Left/Right attitudes, satisfaction with the government's performance, and candidate images to explain voting choices. (We should consider other factors, such as party identification and social group cues, but the figure summarizes the variables at the very end of the causal funnel.) The left side of the figure presents the impact of these factors in predicting vote choices for the legislature. The right side of the figure presents the relationships for presidential vote in the United States and France.

Each of the three factors significantly affects legislative voting in each nation, but the most interesting feature is the relative pattern across nations and election types. Candidate images strongly influence legislative voting in all four nations; in three nations it is the strongest predictor.[9] In the United States, for example, feelings toward George W. Bush and John Kerry strongly influenced congressional voting preferences in 2004. Moreover, candidate images are even more important in presidential elections, where people are voting for the candidate, rather than a party. Therefore, images of the U.S. presidential candidates have a strong impact on congressional voting, but an even stronger influence on presidential vote choice. Similarly, the images of party leaders are more strongly tied to vote choice in the French presidential elections than in National Assembly elections. Although it is difficult to determine the exact impact of candidate images on voter choice, the evidence reaffirms the point that candidate images are an important basis of voting choice in contemporary elections.

Issues—represented in figure 10.5 by Left/Right attitudes and perceptions of the government's performance—generally carry more weight in European parliamentary elections. The figure shows that Left/Right attitudes have a stronger effect on vote choice in all three European democracies than in the United States. Because European parties offer clearer party choices than

FIGURE 10.5 Influence of Issues and Candidate Images on Vote

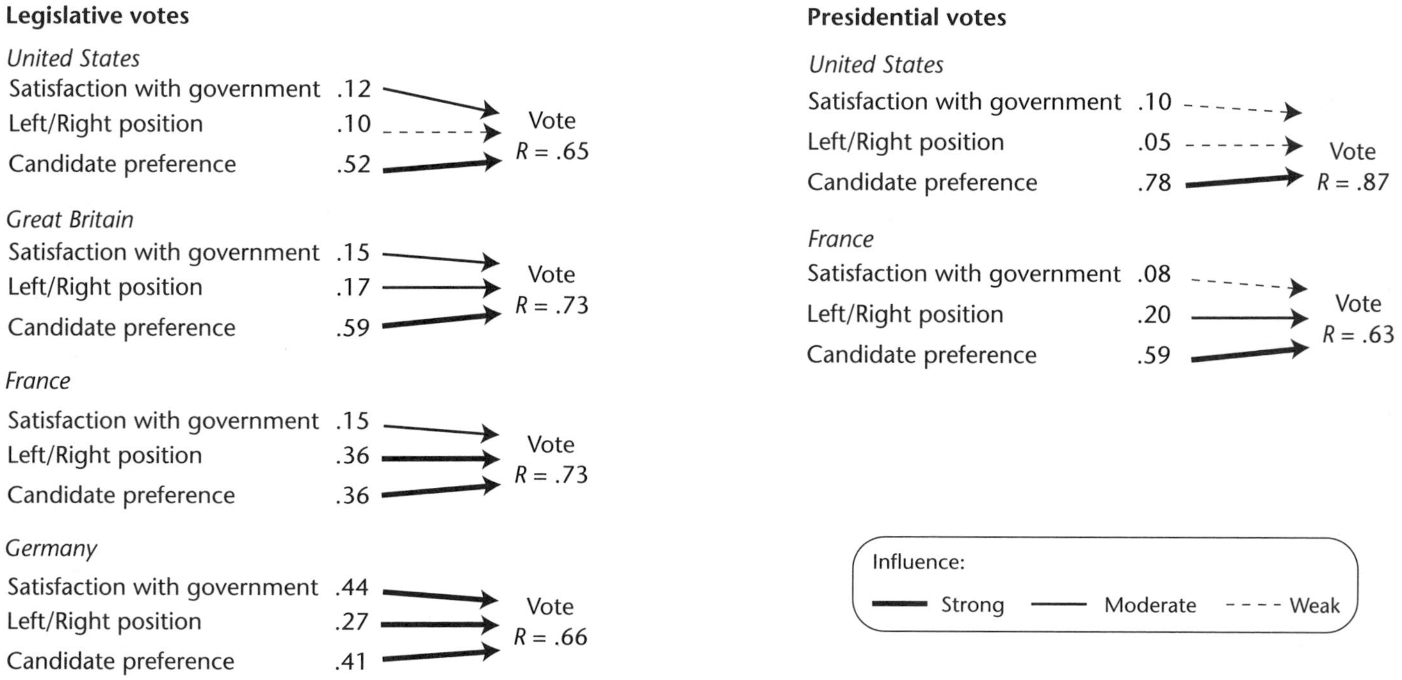

Legislative votes

United States

Satisfaction with government .12
Left/Right position .10
Candidate preference .52
Vote
R = .65

Great Britain

Satisfaction with government .15
Left/Right position .17
Candidate preference .59
Vote
R = .73

France

Satisfaction with government .15
Left/Right position .36
Candidate preference .36
Vote
R = .73

Germany

Satisfaction with government .44
Left/Right position .27
Candidate preference .41
Vote
R = .66

Presidential votes

United States

Satisfaction with government .10
Left/Right position .05
Candidate preference .78
Vote
R = .87

France

Satisfaction with government .08
Left/Right position .20
Candidate preference .59
Vote
R = .63

Influence:
———— Strong   ——— Moderate   - - - - Weak

SOURCES: United States, 2004 American National Election Study (CSES); Britain, 2001 British Election Study; France, 2002 French Election Study (CSES); Germany, 2002 German Election Study (CSES).

American parties do, and Europeans vote for a party more than for a candidate, it is not surprising that the policy images of the parties are a stronger basis of voting in European elections. The specific mix of issue and candidate influences will be highly variable across elections because they are short-term elements of the vote, but these transatlantic differences reflect institutional structures that are likely to endure over time.[10] In contrast, it is striking that in neither U.S. congressional nor presidential elections do liberal/conservative orientations have a strong relationship to vote independent of candidate image.

ONE ELECTORATE OR MANY?

Another characteristic of the new style of citizen politics is an increasing diversity of factors that people use in their voting decisions and the fragmentation of the public into separate electorates that see an election and their voting decisions in different terms. For some individuals, the mere presence of a party label may be sufficient to decide their vote. As the old saying goes, some Americans would vote for a yellow dog, if it were a Democrat. Other voters focus on the candidates, their qualities to govern, or just their likeability. Even greater fragmentation occurs when we consider how the weight of issues might vary across different issue publics.

When we combine all of the electorate in a single correlation—such as the relationship between social class and vote or Left/Right attitudes and vote—we may be combining very different decision-making processes for different voters. The impact of candidate image and Left/Right attitudes in predicting vote in Figure 10.5 does not mean that every voter gives the same weight to the predictors. Some actually base their vote primarily on candidate image, while others judge the election in Left/Right terms. The statistics in this figure and other similar analyses average together the separate processes within distinct subelectorates.

In theory, the number of distinct subelectorates that may exist in any one election is unlimited. Part of the challenge facing researchers is to determine which subelectorates are most important to compare. If we draw upon the idea of issue publics, then we would want to distinguish between the significant issue publics. The existence of issue publics means that some people see the campaign as a referendum on taxes, while others focus on foreign policy or social welfare policies. Single issue voting occurs when some individuals focus on a limited set of issues (or a single issue) to decide their vote.

To illustrate the concept of subelectorates, we return to the political mobilization typology presented in figure 9.5 (p. 188). We described how some people rely on their partisan identities as a political cue, while others have the cognitive skills and resources to reach their own political judgments. And some have both—or neither. These different bases of political mobilization should affect the sources of voting choice. Previous research found that better-educated and politically sophisticated voters place more weight on

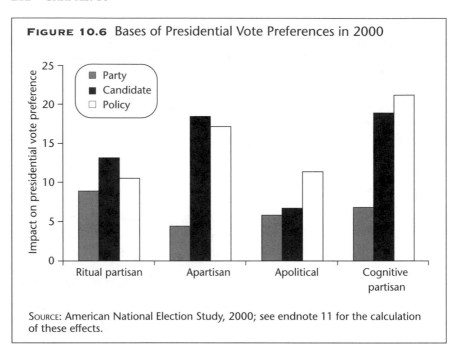

FIGURE 10.6 Bases of Presidential Vote Preferences in 2000

SOURCE: American National Election Study, 2000; see endnote 11 for the calculation of these effects.

issues as a basis for their electoral decision making; less sophisticated voters rely more on partisanship and social cues (Sniderman, Brody, and Tetlock 1991; Stimson 1975). And we would expect partisans to weight party cues more heavily than nonpartisans.

Figure 10.6 estimates the influence of party cues, candidate image, and policy preferences for voter choice in the 2000 U.S. presidential election.[11] The weight of each factor is separately calculated for the four mobilization types of figure 9.5. The figure shows that Ritual Partisans (who rely on their strong party identities but have limited political sophistication) are twice as likely as Apartisans (who are politically sophisticated but lack a party identity) to vote on the basis of party cues. Conversely, candidate image and policy preferences have substantially greater impact among Apartisans. The figure also documents a sharp difference between Apartisans and the unsophisticated Apoliticals who lack both party cues and cognitive sophistication. None of the three predictors exerts much influence on the Apolitical's candidate preferences. Cognitive Partisans present a mixed pattern; the force of party cues nearly matches Ritual Partisans, and the force of issues and candidate images nearly matches that of Apartisans. In summary, each of these groups uses a different decision-making calculus when deciding how to vote. These groups also tend to perceive election campaigns in different terms; some focus on the candidate, and others on the issues.

We could show a similar fragmentation of the electorate if we compared the impact of specific issues across issue publics. We would expect members of an issue public to vote for the candidate who agrees with their views on that issue. For citizens not in that issue public, a candidate's stand on the issue is much less relevant to their electoral calculus. Campaigns are therefore fragmented in this way as well. Combining the variations by cognitive mobilization and issue publics, we might conclude that there is not one election campaign, but many; there is not one electorate, but many.

CITIZEN POLITICS AND VOTING BEHAVIOR

The last several chapters have described changes in the patterns of voting behavior in advanced industrial democracies. Three major changes are intertwined. The first is a *general decline in the long-term determinants* of voting choice. Social class has a decreasing impact on voting choices in virtually all established democracies, along with similar declines in the impact of religion, residence, and other social characteristics (chapter 8). Similarly, dealignment has decreased the effect of party attachments on voting decisions; fewer voters now approach elections with standing party predispositions based on either social characteristics or early-learned partisan ties (chapter 9).

The second change is the *growth in the importance of short-term attitudes,* such as issue opinions and candidate images. The most persuasive cross-national evidence comes from a study of voting behavior in seventeen Western democracies. In reviewing their findings, Mark Franklin, Tom Mackie, and Henry Valen (1992, 400) concluded: "If all the issues of importance to voters had been measured and given their due weight, then the rise of issue voting would have compensated more or less precisely for the decline in cleavage politics."

The trend toward greater issue voting and candidate voting is a self-reinforcing process. Issue voting contributes to, and benefits from, the decline in partisanship-based voting. As party ties weaken, the potential for issues to influence voting choice strengthens. In addition, as issues become more important than party to the voters, this attitude encourages some party defection and erodes the voter's party attachments still further.[12] Thus, the rise of issue voting and the decline of partisanship are interrelated trends.

The shifting balance of long-term and short-term voting influences is another aspect of the new style of citizen politics. As modern electorates have become more sophisticated and politically interested, and as political information has become more available, many citizens can now reach their own voting decisions without relying on broad external cues such as social class or family partisanship. In short, more citizens now have the political resources to follow the complexities of politics; they have the potential to act as the independent issue voters described in classic democratic theory but seldom seen in practice. In addition, the public's rising political sophistication contributes to this pattern of greater issue voting.

The third change is the *fragmentation of voter choice* into separate voting processes. Despite the improvements we have noted, some individuals remain politically disengaged: if they vote at all, they may base their choice on idiosyncratic criteria. Some voters, although fewer and fewer in number, vote on the basis of social group identities such as class or religion. Other voters, whom we have labeled Ritual Partisans, think about politics in terms of their partisan identities and view the campaigns and candidates in these terms. More sophisticated voters may have strong issue beliefs and make their electoral decision on which party or candidate best represents their views. This pattern of issue voting can further fragment the electorate and divide people into separate issue publics. Yet another group of voters might focus on candidate traits or other factors. The most sophisticated voters consider a range of factors spanning issues and candidate characteristics. This diversity of decision making means that there is not one election campaign, but many, as the voters focus on different factors. It also means there is not one voting calculus, but many, as the voters use distinct factors to make their electorate choices.

The impact of economics on the vote illustrates these changes. Traditionally, social divisions defined economic conflicts: the working class versus the middle class, industrial versus agrarian interests. In this situation, one's social position was often a meaningful guide to voting decisions. As social divisions have narrowed, the group bases of political interests have blurred, other issues attract voter attention, and social class has decreased as a source of voting cues. Some people still vote on class or union cues, but they are fewer in number. This decline does not mean that economic issues are unimportant—quite the opposite: contemporary evidence of economic voting is widespread. But today, issue positions are individually based rather than group-derived. The political cues of a union leader or business association must compete with a voter's own opinions on economic policy and party programs. That a continuing concern for economic growth and security has not revived traditional class divisions provides compelling evidence that a new style of citizen politics now affects voting patterns.

This new style of individually based voting decisions may signify a boon or a curse for contemporary democracies. On the positive side, sophisticated voters should inject more issue voting into elections, increasing the policy implications of electoral results. In the long term, greater issue voting may make candidates and parties more responsive to public opinion and move the democratic process closer to the democratic ideal.

On the negative side, many political scientists are concerned that the growth of issue voting and single-issue groups may place excessive demands on contemporary democracies (see chapter 12). Without the issue-aggregating functions performed by party leaders and electoral coalitions, democratic governments may face conflicting issue demands, which they find difficult to satisfy.

Another concern involves the citizens who lack the political skills to meet the requirements of sophisticated issue voting. These people may become atomized voters if traditional political cues (party and social groups) decline in usefulness. Lacking firm political predispositions or a clear understanding of politics, they may decide not to vote or they may be mobilized by demagogic elites or fraudulent party programs. Many political analysts see the rise of New Right parties in Europe, especially those headed by charismatic party leaders, as a negative consequence of a dealigned electorate. Indeed, television facilitates unmediated one-on-one contacts between political elites and voters. Despite its potential for encouraging more sophisticated citizen involvement, this medium also offers the possibility of trivialized electoral politics in which video style outweighs substance in campaigning.

The trends discussed here do not lend themselves to a single prediction of the future of democratic party systems. The future is, however, within our control, depending on how political systems respond to these challenges. The new style of citizen politics is characterized by a greater diversity of voting patterns. A system of frozen social cleavages and stable party alignments is less likely in advanced industrial societies where voters are sophisticated, power is decentralized, and individual choice finds greater latitude. The diversity and individualism of the new style of citizen politics are major departures from the structured partisan politics of the past.

SUGGESTED READINGS

Aarts, Kees, André Blais, and Hermann Schmitt, eds. *Political Leaders and Democratic Elections*. Oxford: Oxford University Press, 2005.

Anderson, Christopher, and Carsten Zelle, eds. *Stability and Change in German Elections: How Electorates Merge, Converge, or Collide*. Westport, Conn.: Praeger, 1998.

Klingemann, Hans-Dieter, ed. *The Comparative Study of Electoral Systems*. Oxford: Oxford University Press, 2008.

Lau, Richard, and David Redlawsk. *How Voters Decide: Information Processing during Election Campaigns*. New York: Cambridge University Press, 2006.

LeDuc, Lawrence, Richard Niemi, and Pippa Norris, eds. *Comparing Democracies: New Challenges in the Study of Elections and Voting*. 2nd ed. Thousand Oaks, Calif.: Sage, 2002.

Niemi, Richard, and Herbert Weisberg, eds. *Controversies in Voting Behavior*. 4th ed. Washington, D.C.: CQ Press, 2001.

Poguntke, Thomas, and Paul Webb, eds. *The Presidentialization of Politics: A Comparative Study of Modern Democracies*. New York: Oxford University Press, 2005.

Wattenberg, Martin. *The Rise of Candidate-centered Voting*. Cambridge: Harvard University Press, 1991.

NOTES

1. I want to acknowledge my collaboration with Martin Wattenberg (Dalton and Wattenberg 1993, 2000), which helped to develop my thinking on many of these issues.

2. Ted Carmines and James Stimson (1980) make a distinction between "hard" issues, which are complex and difficult to evaluate, and "easy" issues, which

present clear and simple choices. Donald Kinder and Rod Kiewiet (1981) stress the distinction between narrow personal issues, such as voting on the basis of economic self-interest, and issues that reflect national policy choices, such as voting on the basis of what will benefit most Americans.

3. Bernard Berelson, Paul Lazarsfeld, and William McPhee (1954) described these as style issues; Donald Stokes (1963) used the term "valence issue." Later research made the further distinction between performance and attributes that we present here (Miller and Wattenberg 1985; Shanks and Miller 1990).

4. Anthony Downs conceived of Left/Right labels as a way to reduce information costs, rather than as fully informed ideological orientations. As he explained, "With this short cut a voter can save himself the cost of being informed upon a wide range of issues." (1957, 98)

5. Americans who voted for the Democratic congressional candidate locate themselves at 4.9 on the Left/Right scale, more toward the center than the average placement of the Democratic Party (4.1). Conversely, voters for the Republican congressional candidate were just as conservative (6.7) as the overall public's placement of the Republican Party (6.7).

6. The Labour Party pursued a conscious effort to moderate its leftist image in 1997 and continued doing so in 2001 and 2005 (Clarke et al. 2008). Moving closer to the voters was a major factor in propelling Labour to victory in these elections.

7. Powerful evidence of the collective wisdom of the electorate comes from comparing the public's Left/Right placement of the parties with the placements made by political science experts in each nation (Benoit and Laver 2006). When we correlated these two Left/Right scores for 107 parties in established democracies with the scores of the party experts, the extremely high correlation ($r = .92$) indicated almost complete agreement.

8. The relationship is described by a Cramer's V correlation statistic: a value of .00 means that issue opinions are unrelated to party preference. A Cramer's V of .20 is normally interpreted as a moderately strong relationship, and .30 is considered a strong relationship.

9. We measured affect toward George W. Bush and John Kerry in the United States, and Tony Blair and William Hague in Britain. For Gerhard Schröder and Edmund Stoiber in Germany, we combined two questions on trust and competence. The French models used Jacques Chirac and Lionel Jospin as the major rival party leaders in the legislative elections, and Chirac and Jean-Marie Le Pen as the candidates in predicting the 2002 presidential runoff in which they were the two candidates. The government performance question asked about how good a job the government had done since the last election.

10. One productive new area of research examines how institutional context systematically affects the correlates of voting. For example, candidate effects are predictably stronger in candidate-based systems than in party-based proportional representation. The ability of the electorate to identify party responsibility also affects the potential for issue voting. See Powell (2000); Anderson (2000); Miller and Niemi (2002); Whitten and Palmer (1999).

11. We first counted the number of times the respondent mentioned party, candidate, or issues in their likes/dislikes about the parties and candidates. Then we calculated the relationship between these three variables and candidate preferences. Last, we computed the force of each factor as the product of the number of items

favoring a candidate and the relationship of this factor with vote choice. For more information, see Dalton (2007c).

12. The conventional wisdom holds that partisanship is often a strong influence on issue opinions, while the reverse causal flow is minimal (figure 9.1, p. 171). As issue voting has increased, however, researchers have found that issues can remold basic party attachments. Studies show that the causal influence of issues in changing partisanship can be quite large (Niemi and Jennings 1991; Fiorina 1981).

CHAPTER 11

Political Representation

If you have ever watched the classic movie *Mr. Smith Goes to Washington,* you have seen the model of representative democracy at its best and worst. An idealistic Jimmy Stewart is appointed to fill a vacancy in the U.S. Senate. He naively proposes the creation of a national boy's camp to aid youth in the midst of the Depression, but his idea created conflict with entrenched interests and corruption in Washington. In the end, the film is about how democracy, freedom, and idealism can triumph over corruption and oppression.[1]

Contemporary democracies owe their existence to the invention of representative democracy in which elected officials act in behalf of their constituents. From the ancient Greeks through the eighteenth century, democracy meant the direct participation of the citizens in the affairs of government. Political theorists believed that democracies must limit either the definition of citizenship or the size of the polity so that the entire public could assemble in a single body to make political decisions. The Greek city-state, the self-governing Swiss canton, and the New England town meeting exemplify this democratic ideal.

The invention of representative government freed democracies from these limits. Instead of directly participating in political decision making, the public selects legislators to represent them in government deliberations. The democratic process therefore depends on the relationship between the representative and the represented.

The case for representative government is largely one of necessity. Democracy requires citizen control over the political process. But in large nations, the town-meeting model is no longer feasible.[2] Proponents of representative government also stress the limited political skills of the average citizen and the need for professional politicians. Citizen control over government occurs through periodic, competitive elections to select these elites. Elections should ensure that government officials are responsive and accountable to the public. By accepting this electoral process, the public gives its consent to be governed by the elites selected.

Many early political philosophers criticized the concept of representative government because they believed it undermined the tenets of democracy by transferring political power from the people to a small group of selected officials. Voters had political power only on the day their ballots were cast, and then they had to wait in political servitude until the next election—four or five years hence—for the opportunity to exercise that power again. Under representative government, citizens may control, but elites rule. Rousseau warned, "The instant a people allows itself to be represented it loses its freedom."

Internet Resource

Visit the Eurobarometer Web site of the European Union for information on the latest citizen and elite surveys:

http://ec.europa.eu/public_opinion/index_en.htm

Contemporary proponents of direct democracy are equally critical of representative government. European green parties criticize the process of representative government while calling for increased citizen influence through referendums, citizen-action groups, and other forms of "basic" democracy. Populist groups in the United States display a similar skepticism of electoral politics in favor of direct citizen participation. Benjamin Barber (1984, 145) expressed these concerns:

> The representative government principle steals from individuals the ultimate responsibility for their values, beliefs, and actions. . . . Representation is incompatible with freedom because it delegates and thus alienates political will at the cost of genuine self-government and autonomy.

Such critics worry that the democratic principle of popular control has been replaced by a commitment to routinized electoral procedures—democracy is defined by its means, not its ends. Moreover, they claim we have not developed other opportunities for increasing public influence and control because elections provide the accepted standard of citizen influence. These critics are not opposed to representative government, but they are critical of a political system that stops at representation and limits other (and perhaps more effective) methods of citizen influence.

The linkage between the public and the political decision makers is one of the essential questions for the study of democratic political systems. The commitment to popular rule is what sets democracies apart from other political systems. Although we cannot resolve the debate on the merits of representative government, we can address how well the representation process functions in Western democracies today.

COLLECTIVE CORRESPONDENCE

In the broadest sense of the term, the *representativeness* of elite attitudes is measured by their similarity to the overall attitudes of the public. Robert Weissberg (1978) referred to this comparison as *collective correspondence*: when the public's policy preferences are matched by the preferences of elites, the citizenry as a collective is well represented by elites as a collective.

The complexity of the representation process obviously goes beyond a definition based simply on citizen-elite agreement. Some elected officials may

TABLE 11.1 Distribution of Opinions for the American Public and Elites

	Citizens	Members of Congress	Difference
1986–1987			
Liberal/conservative position	4.26	4.05	–.21
Government provide services	3.57	4.14	.57*
Government guarantee living standard	4.47	4.01	–.46*
Government should aid minorities	4.17	3.34	–.83*
Spend more on defense	3.82	3.58	–.24
Cooperate more with Russia	4.35	3.58	–.77*
Intervene in Central America	3.31	2.98	.33
Attitudes toward abortion	2.13	1.69	–.44*
1998 (percentages)			
Maintain government programs	57	45	
Liberal/conservative position			
Conservative	37	47	
Moderate	40	31	
Liberal	19	7	

SOURCES: For the top panel, 1987 House of Representatives Survey (Herrera, Herrera, and Smith 1992) and 1986 ANES; for the bottom panel, 1998 Pew Center Survey of members of Congress (PEW Center 1998b).

NOTE: Entries in the top panel are mean scores on a 7-point scale, with 1 = the liberal position; the abortion item is measured on a 4-point scale; differences marked by an asterisk are significant at .01 level. Entries in the bottom panel are percentages agreeing with policy statement and self-identifying on a partisan scale.

stress their role in educating the public instead of merely reflecting current public preferences. When voters hold contradictory opinions, the policy-making role of elites may lead them to adopt more consistent, but less representative, positions. Policy preferences also are not necessarily equivalent to policy outcomes. We could add other qualifiers to this list. Still, citizen-elite agreement is a basic standard for judging the representativeness of a democratic system. Agreement is a meaningful test because it determines whether decision makers approach policymaking with the same policy preferences as the public, and as such it is a critical goal of representative democracy.

Cross-national data comparing the opinions of top-level political elites and the public are fairly rare. More common are studies that focus on public-elite comparisons in a single nation.[3] This chapter assembles a diverse mix of evidence comparing elite and public opinion within and across nations.

We begin with evidence from the United States. The top panel in table 11.1 compares the American public to members of Congress in 1987 and 1998. In 1987 the American public was more conservative than these elites on the issue of minority aid (–.83), for example, but more liberal than elites on the government providing needed services (+.57) (Herrera, Herrera, and Smith

1992). On overall liberal/conservative positions, the match between the public and elites was quite close, which is appropriate because this measure summarizes political positions on many policy matters.

In 1998 the Pew Center (1998b) surveyed members of Congress, but this study included just a few items that were comparable to questions in public opinion surveys. Only 45 percent of members of Congress said that federal government programs should be maintained to deal with important problems, but 57 percent of the American public supported this position. On the standard liberal/conservative scale, Congress had more self-identified conservatives than the public at large, and fewer liberals, but the percentage differences were modest on each response. These findings suggest that the balance of elite opinions had shifted away from the liberal tendencies of the 1986–1988 Democratic Congress with a Republican majority in the 1996–1998 Congress.

Although the public and elites differed somewhat in their policy views, the survey did not find a large and systematic bias in the direction of these differences. In addition, previous comparisons of public opinion and opinions of members of Congress in 1978 and 1982 found that the two groups differed by only a few percentage points (Bishop and Frankovic 1981; Erikson and Tedin 2001, 267). Therefore, the fit between the American public and congressional elites generally shows a high level of collective correspondence.

Cross-national studies of mass and elite opinions in Europe are quite rare. Researchers survey European public opinion and European elite opinions—but they do not regularly ask the same questions to both groups.[4] Consequently, we compare citizen and elite opinions on Left/Right orientations as a broad measure of political orientations (figure 11.1).

Reading left to right, the first two bars in each group show the percentage leftist among citizens in Britain, France, and Germany during the 1994 and 1999 European Parliament elections.[5] There is some variability in where the average citizen places himself across time, and this is part of the normal ebb and flow of politics as issues and conditions change over time. But the percentage leftist is roughly within 10 percentage points between both elections. As we saw in chapter 6, the French public is more to the left than either the British or German public.

The other bars in figure 11.1 display Left/Right positions from two elite surveys. The next bar presents the percentage leftist among members of the European Parliament (MEPs) elected in 1994.[6] The large gap between British MEPs and the British public reflects a combination of the possible bias in this elite sample because of the small number of MEPs and the distorting effects of the British single member electoral districts. As the largest vote-getter, the Labour Party was substantially overrepresented in the MEP sample. The French MEPs were broadly representative of the public, in part because the European Parliament elections used proportional representation. The citizen-elite consistency in Germany is also closer than in Britain, presumably because Germans use a proportional electoral system.

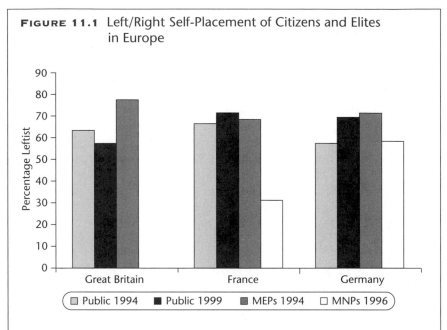

FIGURE 11.1 Left/Right Self-Placement of Citizens and Elites in Europe

SOURCE: The citizen data are from the 1994 and 1999 European Election Studies; the 1994 candidates to the European Parliament (MEPs) and 1996 members of the National Parliament (MNPs) are from Schmitt and Thomassen (1999); and Katz and Wessels (1999).

NOTE: The figure presents the percentage placing themselves to the Left on the Left/Right scale.

The last bar for France and Germany shows the percentage Left among members of their respective national parliaments (MNPs) surveyed in 1996 (British MNPs were not interviewed). Again, the match to the voters is closer in Germany with its proportional representation system. France uses a modified form of single-member district than can distort the election results, so the gap to MNPs is greater. In short, the collective correspondence is substantial at the start of the electoral process, but it can be transformed by the nature of the electoral system.

National studies have compared citizens and elites on specific issue opinions. The 1997 British election study found that the average British citizen and member of the British Parliament position themselves at virtually the same position on the Left/Right scale (Norris 1999d). On traditional economic issues—taxes versus services, privatization, and jobs versus prices—the MPs are slightly to the right of the British public. On two noneconomic issues—European integration and the role of women—the British MPs are to the left of the public. When Bernhard Wessels (1993) compared the issue opinions of Bundestag deputies and the German public, he found close agreement on Old Politics issues such as economic growth and public order, and somewhat lower levels of agreement on New Politics goals.

In summary, collective correspondence on broad political orientations and most issues opinions is fairly common in established democracies. This result should be expected because the logic of the electoral process is to select legislators who are broadly consistent with public preferences. These patterns may, however, vary across issues and be affected by the nature of the electoral system. Therefore, we turn to the processes of representation in the next section.

DYADIC CORRESPONDENCE

Collective correspondence between the opinions of the public and the political elites does not occur by chance. Some degree of popular control is necessary to ensure the responsiveness of elites. Citizen-elite agreement without popular control is representation by luck, not democracy. One method of popular control makes political elites electorally dependent on a specific geographic district. Robert Weissberg (1978) defined the pairing of district opinion and elites as *dyadic correspondence*—in simple terms, liberal districts presumably select liberal representatives, and conservative districts select conservative representatives.

In studying the connection between citizens and elites, researchers initially treated the individual legislator as the basis of dyadic linkage. This approach derived from the historical development of political theory on representation. Traditionally, a *delegate* model defined the legislator's role in a deterministic fashion. Representative government implied that voters would formally instruct the delegates on district preferences before they went to parliament, and the legislator was obliged to follow the district's mandate. Edmund Burke's classic "Speech to the Electors of Bristol" in 1774 offered a new model of representation that still influences modern political science. Burke proposed a more independent *trustee* role for legislators. He argued that once elected, legislators should be allowed to follow their own beliefs about what they thought was best for their constituency and the nation.

Modern research on political representation reinforced this emphasis on the individual legislator, especially American research that treated the legislator as the basis of political linkage (Miller and Stokes 1963). In part, this focus reflected the weakness of American parties and the open structure of the American political process, in which many legislators seem to act as individual entrepreneurs. And, in part, it reflected the use of a single-member-district electoral system in Britain and the United States, where one legislator was elected to represent the district.

Warren Miller and Donald Stokes (1963) conducted the seminal study of political representation in America based on the trustee and delegate models of representation. They interviewed a small sample of the public in a set of congressional districts after the 1958 elections as well as the members of the

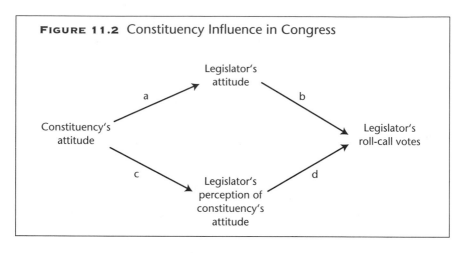

FIGURE 11.2 Constituency Influence in Congress

House of Representatives from these same districts. They also assembled the voting records of the members of Congress for the next legislative session, which allowed them to compare citizen opinions to the opinions and votes of these representatives.

Miller and Stokes used this information to build a model of the representation process (figure 11.2). Broadly speaking, these researchers envisioned two pathways by which a district could influence the legislative voting of its representative. One pathway defined the trustee model of representation: the district selects a legislator who shares its views (path *a*), so that in following his or her convictions (path *b*) the legislator represents the district's will. In this case, the district's opinion and the legislator's actions are connected through the legislator's policy attitudes. A second pathway traces the delegate model. A legislator turns to citizens in his or her district for cues on their policy preferences (path *c*) and then follows these cues in making voting choices (path *d*). In this case, the legislator's perception of district attitudes provides the linkage between actual district opinion and the legislator's voting behavior.

Miller and Stokes applied the model to three policy areas: civil rights, social welfare, and foreign policy. They found a strong relationship between constituency opinion and the legislator's voting record for civil rights and social welfare issues and a weaker connection for foreign policy. In addition, the path of constituency influence varied between policy areas. Civil rights issues functioned primarily by a delegate model. Members of Congress accurately perceived the opinions of their constituents and voted in accord with these opinions. For social welfare issues, the trustee path through the legislator's own attitude was the most important means of district influence.

This study provided evidence of the representation process at work. Moreover, the process seemed to work fairly well: most liberal districts were represented by liberal legislators, and most conservative districts chose conservative representatives. Many have criticized the methodology of this study,

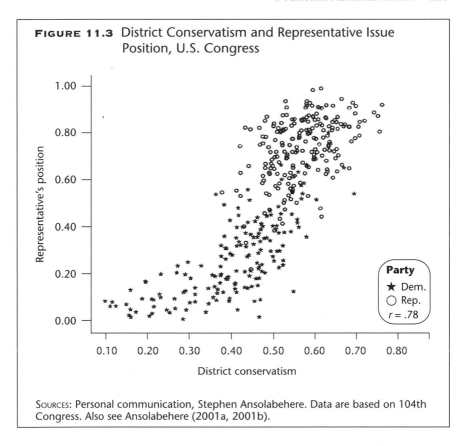

FIGURE 11.3 District Conservatism and Representative Issue Position, U.S. Congress

SOURCES: Personal communication, Stephen Ansolabehere. Data are based on 104th Congress. Also see Ansolabehere (2001a, 2001b).

but most political scientists still support its essential conclusions (for further discussion, see Erikson and Tedin 2001, ch. 10; Warren Miller et al. 1999).

Cheryl Lyn Herrera, Richard Herrera, and Eric Smith (1992) partially repeated the Miller and Stokes analyses for the 1986–1988 Congress. They compared the opinions of members of Congress from thirty-three districts to the opinions of their constituents. They found that the fit between districts and their representatives was fairly high on most issues, especially those with sizable issue publics and polarized public opinion, such as abortion, minority aid, and government services. They concluded that "dyadic representation is better today than was true 30 years ago" (p. 201), implying that the democratic process in the United States was working even better than during the Miller and Stokes study in the late 1950s.

Another example of dyadic congruence comes from a study by Stephen Ansolabehere, James Snyder, and Charles Stewart (2001a; 2001b). They measured the positions of congressional candidates from surveys conducted by the *Vote Smart* project in the mid-1990s, and then compared these candidate positions to measures of district opinions and the roll-call votes of the elected representatives during the next Congress. Figure 11.3 depicts the relationship between the liberal/conservative opinions of each district on the horizontal axis and the liberal/conservative opinions of the district's representative on the vertical axis.[7] The congruence between district and representative opinions is very strong, as one would expect if the democratic process is functioning. Moreover, when these researchers examined the next step in the representation process—path *b* in figure 11.2—they found an equally strong link between the representatives' attitudes and their overall voting pattern ($r = .88$ for Republicans and .85 for Democrats).[8] Elections thus provide a means for voters to select candidates who broadly share their political values, and who then take these orientations to Washington.

The Miller and Stokes model was extended to representation studies in nearly a dozen other Western democracies (Miller et al. 1999), but these studies typically found limited policy agreement between districts and their legislators. Samuel Barnes (1977) found virtually no correspondence between the issue opinions of Italian deputies and public opinion in their respective districts. Barbara Farah (1980) documented a similar lack of correspondence between district opinions and the policy views of district-elected deputies in the German Bundestag. The French representation study found a weak linkage between district and legislator opinions on specific policy issues (Converse and Pierce 1986, ch. 22).[9] It appeared that either political representation did not occur in these European democracies or that it worked through other means.

THE PARTY GOVERNMENT MODEL

Research on political representation in non-American political systems gradually deemphasized a model based on individual legislators and focused instead on the actions of political parties as collectives. This model of representation through parties—*responsible party government*—is built upon several principles:

- Elections should provide competition between two or more parties contending for political power.
- Parties must offer distinct policy options so voters have meaningful electoral choices.
- Voters should recognize these policy differences among the parties.
- At the least, voters should be sufficiently informed to reward or punish the incumbent parties based on their performance.

National elections therefore serve as evaluations of the political parties and their activities, and representation occurs through parties rather than individual candidates. In many ways, these principles are similar to the principles of issue voting discussed in chapter 10, now applied to parties as a collective.

The party government model seems more relevant for parliamentary systems with strong political parties. In most European systems, candidates are selected by party elites rather than through open primaries, so they are first and foremost representatives of their parties. The responsible party government model presumes that members of a party's parliamentary delegation act in unison. Parties vote as a bloc in parliament, although the members may have an internal debate before the party position is decided. Parties exercise control over the government and the policymaking process through party control of the national legislature. In sum, the choice of parties—rather than constituency-based representation—provides the electorate with a means to control over the actions of legislators and the affairs of government.

Political representation in Europe largely follows the party government model. In comparison to the United States, the multiparty systems of most European democracies offer the voters greater diversity in party programs, which gives more meaning to party labels (see chapter 7). Most democracies are parliamentary systems with unified legislative parties. Party cohesion in European legislatures is considerably higher than in the U.S. Congress (Bowler 2000). When a party votes as a united bloc, it makes little sense to discuss the voting patterns of individual legislators. Giovanni Sartori (1968, 471) maintains that "citizens in Western democracies are represented *through* and *by* parties. This is inevitable" (emphasis in original).

The party government model therefore directs the voters' attention to parties as political representatives rather than individual legislators. Indeed, many Europeans (including Germans) vote directly for party lists. Dyadic correspondence is based more on a voter-party model than a district-legislator model. The voter half of the dyad is composed of all party supporters in a nation, even if the country is organized by geographic electoral districts, and the representative half is composed of party officials as a collective. If the party government model holds, we should expect a close match between the policy views of party voters and party elites taken as collectives.

We should stress one other point about dyadic correspondence. We occasionally speak in causal terms—voter opinions presumably influence party positions—but the causal flow works in both directions. Voters influence parties, as parties try to persuade voters, which is why researchers have adopted the causally neutral term *correspondence*. The essence of the democratic marketplace is that like-minded voters and parties search out each other and join forces. Even if one cannot determine the direction of causal flow, the similarity of opinions between party voters and party elites is a meaningful measure of the representativeness of parties.

Cross-national evidence of the correspondence between voters and their parties comes from the 1994 European Parliament Election Study (Schmitt and Thomassen 1999). We previously compared elites and public Left/Right preferences by nation from this study (figure 11.1). Figure 11.4 compares the Left/Right position of voters and elites within each party. The horizontal axis in the figure plots the average position of a party's supporters; the vertical axis plots the average opinion of the party's elites. These two coordinates define a party's location in the figure. The 45-degree line represents perfect

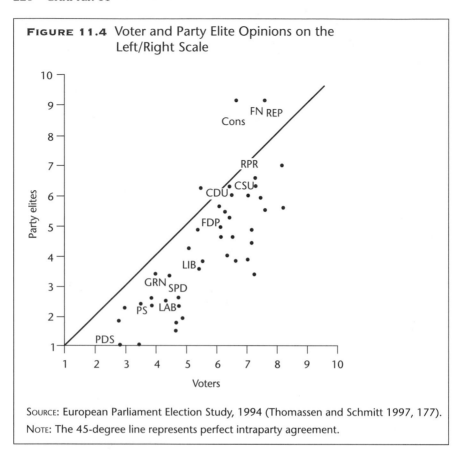

FIGURE 11.4 Voter and Party Elite Opinions on the Left/Right Scale

SOURCE: European Parliament Election Study, 1994 (Thomassen and Schmitt 1997, 177).

NOTE: The 45-degree line represents perfect intraparty agreement.

intraparty agreement—when the opinions of party elites exactly match those of their supporters.

This figure shows two important patterns. The first is the strong relationship between voter and elite opinions by party. Voters with leftist preferences and elites who share these views come together in the traditional leftist parties, such as the German SPD, the British Labour Party, and the French Socialists; and the congruence on the right is similar. This pattern provides the evidence of party differences that underlie the party government model of representation. Second is the systematic tendency for party elites to say they are more leftist than their own voters (in the figure most parties lie below the diagonal line).

Unfortunately, the 1994 EP Election Study contained very few issues, so we turned to other data sources to examine the patterns of issue agreement. In chapter 7 we used expert judgments to plot the party positions on Old Politics and New Politics policies. To measure voter opinions, we found comparable issue questions in the International Social Survey Program for both policies. Then we compared the opinions of party voters to the experts' judgments

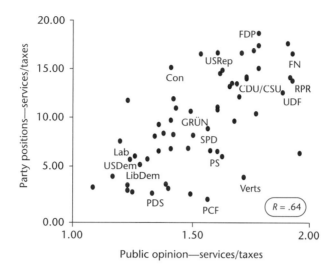

FIGURE 11.5 Relationship between Party Placement and Voters' Opinions on Taxes versus Social Services Dimension

Sources: The fifty-nine dyads represent position of party supporters on the services/taxes question in the 1996 International Social Survey and party positions from Benoit and Laver (2006) on the taxes/services dimension. The party groups come from thirteen democracies, and the positions of the major parties in the United States, Great Britain, France, and Germany are noted in the figure.

of party positions in a diverse set of nations available from the public opinion study.

Figure 11.5 displays party patterns on the Old Politics issue of cutting taxes versus support for the social services (see figure 7.2, p. 136). We have voter and party positions for fifty-nine parties in thirteen advanced industrial democracies, which demonstrate a strong correspondence on this issue. The socialist and communist parties tend toward the lower-left quadrant, and their voters also hold liberal opinions on taxes/services issue. For example, the voters for the German PDS and the party itself are positioned at the bottom left corner of the figure. Conversely, the economically conservative Free Democrats (FDP) are located at the opposite corner of this continuum.[10] The correlation between voters and parties is quite high. And, because economic and religious issues are so important in structuring political conflict, research generally suggests that congruence on these issues remains high (Dalton 1985; Miller et al. 1999).

Asking whether the government should spend more on environmental protection is a good measure of public support for a New Politics program. The voter opinions on environmental spending are then compared to the expert judgments of party positions on this dimension (see figure 7.2, p. 136).

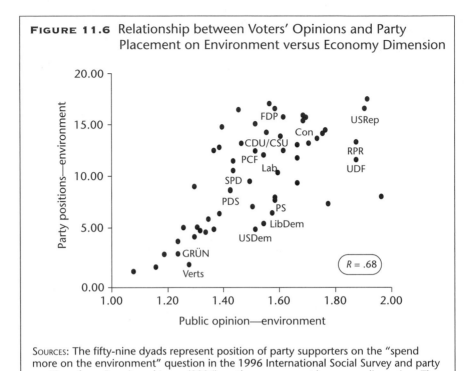

FIGURE 11.6 Relationship between Voters' Opinions and Party Placement on Environment versus Economy Dimension

SOURCES: The fifty-nine dyads represent position of party supporters on the "spend more on the environment" question in the 1996 International Social Survey and party positions from Benoit and Laver (2006) on the envronment/economy dimension. The party groups come from thirteen democracies, and the positions of the major parties in the United States, Great Britain, France, and Germany are noted in the figure.

Figure 11.6 also shows a basic correspondence between party voters and party elites on this issue: a voter bloc that wants more spending on the environment is represented by party elites who generally share the voters' concern for the environment.

Party alignment on the environmental issue is significant for several reasons. First, in comparing results to those in the previous edition of this book, we see that party polarization on the environmental dimension has strengthened over time, as voters and elites become more congruent. In addition, the Left/Right Old Politics alignment is not fully repeated for environmental issues. The British Labour Party, the French Communist Party, and the German SPD all are located close to the German CDU/CSU. The distinctly pro-environment parties are the German Greens and the French Verts. Party alignments on the environment and other New Politics issues still tend to cut across the traditional Left/Right party lines defined by Old Politics issues.

Just as important as the overall level of dyadic correspondence are the factors affecting voter-party agreement. Some parties consistently achieve a close match between the opinions of voters and party elites, while other parties display less correspondence. These variations in party representation determine the efficiency of the party-linkage process.

An earlier study found that characteristics that clarify party positions make it easier for voters to select a compatible party (Dalton 1985). Centrally organized parties tend to be in closer agreement with their supporters. In addition, voter-party agreement is higher among ideological parties (of either the Left or Right). Apparently these characteristics make it easier for voters to identify and select a party consistent with their issue opinions. A centralized party is more likely to project clear party cues, and an ideological image helps voters identify a party's general political orientation.

At the national level, Bernhard Wessels (1999) found that majoritarian systems, such as the United States and Great Britain, place a greater emphasis on elites representing the typical voter in society, which normally pulls elites toward the center of the political spectrum. In contrast, elites in proportional representation systems are more closely tied to their party's voters. The greater degree of party choice in most such electoral systems facilitates this partisan focus. This systemic distinction reinforces the conclusion drawn from our previous evidence: the style of representation is affected by the institutional structures of the nation.

PATTERNS OF POLITICAL REPRESENTATION

This chapter describes two distinct patterns of representative government among Western democracies. Political representation in the United States is largely dependent on the relationship between individual legislators and their constituencies. Citizens in most other democracies are primarily represented through their choice of political parties at election time. Some research, however, suggests that this American/European contrast may be lessening. Warren Miller (1987, ch. 4) discusses the important role that parties play in American representation (see also Erikson and Tedin 2001, ch. 11), but our own analyses suggest that the party government model is weakening in Europe (chapter 9; Dalton and Wattenberg 2000). Still, the contrasts between the American and European patterns of representation will probably continue to hold.

Both models can provide effective means of citizen-elite linkage, but they emphasize different aspects of representation. The American system of representative government based on individual legislators allows for greater responsiveness to the interests of each legislative district. The political process is also more open to new political interests and the representation of minority groups because electoral control at the constituency level is more easily accomplished than control of an entire party.

The flexibility of the American style of representation also involves some costs. An entrepreneurial style of representation makes it more difficult for the public to monitor and control the actions of their representatives between elections, and it encourages campaigns to focus on personalities and district service, rather than on policy and ideological orientations. Indeed, studies of congressional elections suggest that personality and constituency service are important influences on voting patterns.

Nevertheless, empirical research shows that policy outcomes in the United States generally reflect the preferences of the public—although obviously this result is, and probably should be, an imperfect linkage. Alan Monroe (1998) found a broad agreement between American policy preferences and policy outcomes in the several hundred specific cases he examined. Benjamin Page and Robert Shapiro (1983; 1992) also described a significant correspondence between public preferences for policy change and actual changes in public policy.[11] Sophisticated new empirical analyses are providing fresh insights into the overall impact of public opinion on the policy process and how this influence interacts with the institutional structure of American politics (Stimson, McKuen, and Erikson 1995; Burstein 2003; Wlezien 2004).

Research projects working within the party-government framework also find that party choices have clear policy consequences. Hans-Dieter Klingemann, Richard Hofferbert, and Ian Budge (1994) analyzed whether the programs that parties offer to the voters are translated into policy after the election. They found that parties are meaningful vehicles for policy control in most democracies. More recent research demonstrates a general congruence between public policy preferences and government outcomes across a range of nations and across different policy domains (Brettschneider 1996; Franklin and Wlezien 1997). And, after demonstrating that changes in citizen spending preferences are generally translated into shifts in government spending across different policy domains in the United States, Britain, and Canada, Stuart Soroka and Christopher Wlezien (2003) come to a simple conclusion: "Democracy works."

But many roadblocks and pitfalls still stand in the way of representation, even within a democratic system. In these times of change and political turmoil, the evidence of government failures and party failures is often obvious. Moreover, even close citizen-elite policy agreement is not proof that public opinion is efficiently and effectively represented in modern democracies. A large part of the observed correspondence must be attributed to an interactive process. Voters migrate to the party (candidate) that best represents their views, and the party convinces supporters to adopt these policies. Congruence therefore does not prove that the public can control government. Beyond the general patterns described here, one can think of a host of specific policies on which the impact of public preferences is uncertain. Still, congruence indicates an agreement between public preferences and public policy that is expected under a democratic system. Moreover, congruence underscores our belief that there is a rationality in public action that elitist theories of democracy doubt exists.

SUGGESTED READINGS

Converse, Philip, and Roy Pierce. *Representation in France.* Cambridge, Mass.: Harvard University Press, 1986.

Erikson, Robert, Michael MacKuen, and James Stimson. *The Macro Polity.* Cambridge: Cambridge University Press, 2002.

Erikson, Robert, Gerald Wright, and John McIver. *State House Democracy: Public Opinion and Public Policy in the American States.* New York: Cambridge University Press, 1994.

Esaiasson, Peter, and Sören Holmberg. *Representation from Above: Members of Parliament and Representative Democracy in Sweden.* Aldershot, Hants, England, and Brookfield, Vt.: Dartmouth Publishing, 1996.

Miller, Warren, et al. *Policy Representation in Western Democracies.* Oxford: Oxford University Press, 1999.

Page, Benjamin, and Robert Shapiro. *The Rational Public: Fifty Years of Trends in Americans' Policy Preferences.* Chicago: University of Chicago Press, 1992.

NOTES

1. Ironically, there was pressure to delay the film's release, which coincided with the outbreak of World War II, because the film depicted political corruption and appeared to paint an unflattering picture of the U.S. government and its inner workings.

2. The development of two-way cable television, teleconferencing, and other communication advances may lead democracies to reconsider the physical limits on direct citizen participation in large collectives. Indeed, the technology exists for instantaneous national referendums and national town meetings (Bimber 2003).

3. Previous studies include the following: for the United States, Miller and Jennings (1986) and Miller (1987); for Germany, Herzog, Rebenstorf, and Wessels (1993); for France, Converse and Pierce (1986).

4. Earlier editions of this book compare the opinions of citizens and elites in the 1979 European Parliament election study, but these data are now nearly three decades old (Dalton 1985).

5. The citizen data are from the 1994 and 1999 European Election Studies (http://www.europeanelectionstudies.net). The elite surveys are drawn from the 1996 Member of the European Parliament and Member of the National Parliament studies described in Schmitt and Thomassen (1999). The elite samples are weighted to reflect the percentage each party gained in the previous election to adjust for different response rates across parties. Figure 11.1 plots the percentage of the public and elites who position themselves on the Left (points 1–5) on a 10-point Left/Right scale.

6. To maximize comparability, we weighted responses to reflect each party's vote share in the 1994 EP election. The 1994 MEP results are based on a relatively small number of delegates elected from each party, and this is not a fully representative sample within or between parties because of nonresponse. The 1996 MNP sample is larger and more representative. For additional analyses, see Schmitt and Thomassen (1999) and Katz and Wessels (1999).

7. The median district opinion was based on the difference between the percentages of the presidential vote in the district for the Democratic and the Republican candidates in 1996. The candidate position is an average of opinions on more than two hundred policy questions. See Ansolabehere, Snyder, and Stewart (2001a).

8. These data were provided by Steve Ansolabehere, and we greatly appreciate his assistance.

9. The power of Philip Converse and Roy Pierce's analysis (1986, ch. 23) was to specify the conditions that strengthen or retard the representation process. These

researchers found that citizen/elite congruence varied by policy domain, competitiveness of the district, and the legislator's role conceptions.

10. Figure 11.5 also shows some interesting anomalies. The voters of the French PCF and PS have moved toward a centrist position on this dimension, as has the German SPD. Supporters of the Verts in France were surprisingly conservative in their opinions, at least in 1996.

11. State-level comparisons provide another opportunity to study the congruence between public opinion and public policy. A study by Robert Erikson and his colleagues shows a strong policy correspondence (Erikson, Wright, and McIver 1994).

PART FOUR

DEMOCRACY AND THE FUTURE

CHAPTER 12

Citizens and the Democratic Process

Politics today is like the opening line in a Dickens novel: We seem to live in the best of times—and the worst of times—for the democratic process. In the last decade of the twentieth century, a wave of democratization swept across the globe. The citizens of Eastern Europe, South Africa, and several East Asian nations rose up against their authoritarian governments. The Soviet Empire collapsed, and millions of people enjoyed new democratic freedoms. These events led a noted political analyst, Francis Fukuyama (1992), to claim that we were witnessing "the end of history." Humankind's historical evolution was converging on a single form of government—democracy—as the culmination of human development. Even some who had previously proclaimed the end of democracy's international expansion now trumpeted this third wave of democratization.[1]

The 1990s also brought unprecedented affluence and economic well-being to the United States, as Americans experienced their longest period of sustained economic growth in peacetime. Crime rates dropped, and progress was made on many policy fronts. To a lesser degree, our allies in Western Europe also enjoyed a peace dividend of economic stability and a new era of international security. This was, it seemed, a positive time for Western democracy. The cold war was over, and we had won. In addition, the citizens in the former authoritarian states of the Soviet Empire had won.

Despite these advances, public opinion surveys indicate that people are critical of politicians, political parties, and political institutions (Dalton 2004; Norris 1999b; Listhaug, Aardal, and Ellis 2008; Nye, Zelikow, and King 1997). The malaise appeared first in the United States. Beginning with the crises and political scandals of the 1960s and 1970s—Vietnam, urban unrest, and Watergate—Americans' trust in their politicians sank steadily lower. In 1979 Jimmy Carter warned that declining public confidence "was a fundamental threat to American democracy." The Reagan administration tried to instill a new sense of political purpose and renew the political spirit by evoking uplifting images of "morning in America" and America as the "shining city on the hill." By the end of the Reagan-Bush administrations in 1992, however, public skepticism had revived, fueled by new crises and new scandals. These trends have stimulated a chorus of voices claiming that American democracy is at risk (Macedo et al. 2005; Wolfe 2006).

Political dissatisfaction is also common in other advanced industrial societies. As scandals strained Britons' faith in their democratic institutions in the mid-1990s, Parliament formed the Standards in Public Life Committee,

---

Internet Resource

Visit the Freedom House Web site for information on the extent of democracy around the globe:

http://www.freedomhouse.org

---

also called the Nolan Committee, before which Ivor Crewe (1995) testified: "There is no doubt that distrust and alienation has risen to a higher level than ever before. It was always fairly prevalent; it is now in many regards almost universal." The British Social Attitudes surveys have tracked a decrease in political trust over time (Curtice and Jowell 1997; Curtice, Fisher, and Lessard-Phillips 2007). During the 1990s Germany achieved a historic ambition: unification as a free and democratic nation. And yet, political trust sank among the German public. President Richard von Weizsäcker (1992, 164) chastised Germany's political elites, claiming that politicians and political parties were "power-crazed for electoral victory and powerless when it comes to understanding the content and ideas required of political leadership." Similarly, if one is fortunate enough to browse through Paris bookshops, one sees titles such as *France in Freefall, Gallic Illusions,* and *France's Misfortune.* "Declinism" has become a school of thought among French intellectuals.

Admittedly, anxiety about the health of democracy is a regular feature of political science and political punditry. An important discussion about the nation's postwar goals took place during the Eisenhower administration, and the next president, John Kennedy, asked Americans to renew their commitment to state and nation (see Mueller 1999, ch. 7). A prominent academic study of the 1970s nearly forecast democracy's demise (Crozier, Huntington, and Watanuki 1975). These earlier pessimistic accounts of democracy's future fortunately proved to be overstatements.

It does seem, however, that contemporary attitudes toward government are changing in fundamental ways, and citizens in most Western democracies are no longer deferential and supportive of political elites. This development leads us to ask whether such changes in the political culture put democracy at risk and how they are affecting the democratic process.

In this chapter we look at how citizens judge the democratic process today. How is it that as democracy celebrates its success at the beginning of the new millennium, its citizens are apparently expressing deep doubts about their political systems? In addition, we consider how the new style of citizen politics may contribute to these misgivings and what the implications are for the future functioning of the democratic process.

ASPECTS OF POLITICAL SUPPORT

Political support is a term with many possible meanings. Gabriel Almond and Sidney Verba (1963) referred to attitudes toward politics and the political system as the *political culture* of a nation. Political culture encompasses everything from beliefs about the legitimacy of the system itself to beliefs about the adequacy and appropriateness of structures for political input, government policies, and the role of the individual in the political process. The most important of these attitudes is a generalized feeling toward the political system, or *system affect*. Such feelings are presumably socialized early in life (Easton and Dennis 1969), representing a positive attitude toward the political system that is relatively independent of the actions of the current government. Almond and Verba felt that affective feelings toward the political system assure the legitimacy of democratic governments and limit expressions of discontent with the political system.

David Easton (1965; 1975) developed a theoretical framework describing the various objects of political support: political authorities, the regime, and the political community.

- *Political authorities support* encompasses the public's opinions toward the incumbents of political office or, in a broader sense, the pool of political elites from which government leaders are drawn. Support for political authorities focuses on specific individuals or groups of individuals.
- *Regime support* refers to attitudes toward the institutions and offices of government rather than the present officeholders—such as respect for the presidency rather than any particular president. Regime support also involves attitudes toward the procedures of government and political institutions, such as the principles of pluralist democracy and support for parliamentary government.
- *Political community support* implies a basic attachment to the nation and political system beyond the present institutions of government. A sense of being "English" or "Scottish" exemplifies these attachments.

The differences among these levels of support are very significant. Discontent with the political authorities normally has limited implications for the overall political process. People often become dissatisfied with political officeholders and act on these feelings by voting the rascals out and selecting new officials at the next election. Dissatisfaction with authorities, within a democratic system, is not usually a signal for basic political change. Negative attitudes toward political officials can and does exist with little loss in support for the office itself or the institutional structure encompassing the office.

When the object of dissatisfaction becomes more general—shifting to the regime or the political community—the political implications increase. A decline in regime support might provoke a basic challenge to political institutions or calls for reform in the procedures of government. Weakening ties to the political community might foretell eventual revolution, civil war, or the loss of democracy. As Easton says, "Not all expressions of unfavorable orientations have the same degree of gravity for a political system. Some may be consistent with its maintenance; others may lead to fundamental change" (1975, 437).

In addition to the objects of political support, Easton identified two kinds of support: diffuse and specific. According to Easton, *diffuse support* is a state of mind—a deep-seated set of attitudes toward politics and the political system that is relatively impervious to change. For example, the sentiment "America, right or wrong" reflects a commitment to the nation's political system that is distinct from the actual behavior of the government. In contrast, *specific support* is closely related to the actions and performance of the government or political elites. This kind of support is object-specific in two senses. First, it normally applies to evaluations of political authorities, and it is less relevant to support for the regime and political community. Second, specific support is typically based on the actual policies and governing style of political authorities.

The distinction between diffuse and specific support is important in understanding the significance of attitudes toward the political process. Democratic political systems must keep the support of their citizens if they are to remain viable. But, because all governments occasionally fail to meet public expectations, short-term political failures must not directly erode diffuse support for the regime or political community. In other words, a democratic political system requires a reservoir of diffuse support independent of immediate policy outputs (specific support) if it is to weather periods of public disaffection and dissatisfaction.

German history in the twentieth century illustrates the significance of diffuse support. The Weimar Republic (1918–1933) was built on an unstable foundation. Many Germans felt that the creation of this government at the end of World War I had contributed to Germany's wartime defeat; from the outset, the regime was stigmatized as a traitor to the nation. Important sectors of the political establishment—the military, civil service, and the judiciary—and many citizens questioned the legitimacy of the new regime and favored the political system of the former German Empire. The fledgling democratic state then faced a series of major crises: postwar economic hardships, attempted right-wing and left-wing coups, explosive inflation in the early 1920s, and the French occupation of the Ruhr. Because the political system was never able to build up a pool of diffuse support for the republic, the dissatisfaction created by the Great Depression in the 1930s easily eroded support for political authorities and the democratic regime. Communists and Nazis argued that the democratic political system was at fault, and the Weimar Republic succumbed to these attacks.[2]

The democratic transition in the German Democratic Republic in 1989–1990 also illustrates the importance of cultural and institutional congruence. Surveys of East German youth found a marked decrease in support for the communist principles of the German Democratic Republic during the 1980s (Friedrich and Griese 1990). These youths led the populist revolt in the East that weakened the regime in the fall of 1989. Revelations in early 1990 about the Communist Party's abuses of power eroded the regime's popular base still further and spurred the race toward unification with the West.

Early cross-national opinion studies argued that political support was a requisite of stable democracy. Almond and Verba (1963) found that system affect in the late 1950s was most widespread in the long-established democracies of the United States and Great Britain. For example, 85 percent of Americans and 46 percent of Britons spontaneously mentioned their political system as a source of national pride. These sentiments suggested that diffuse support had developed over the long democratic histories of these two nations. Satisfaction with the policy outputs of government was also common in both nations. In contrast, system support was more limited in West Germany and Italy: only 7 percent of West Germans and 3 percent of Italians mentioned their political system as a source of national pride. The limited diffuse support in these systems raised fears that democracy was still fragile in these two formerly fascist states. The early years of the Federal Republic were closely watched by those who worried that the Bonn Republic would follow the same course as Weimar (Baker, Dalton, and Hildebrandt 1981).

A cross-national study by Hadley Cantril (1965) found a similar pattern in public opinion: positive national self-images were more common in the stable, well-run democracies than in fledgling democracies. A more recent set of comparative studies has similarly demonstrated that a democratic political culture is strongly correlated with the stability of a democratic system (Inglehart 1990; 1997, ch. 6; Putnam 1993). Although one can never be certain whether stable government produces popular support, or whether popular support produces stable government, these two are interrelated.

An authoritarian state may endure without the support of its public, but popular support is essential for a democracy to survive. This chapter assesses the breadth and depth of popular support for democratic governance as a crucial element in diagnosing democracy's future.

DECLINING CONFIDENCE IN AUTHORITIES

A few years ago I was visiting Germany during its national elections. On the weekend before the vote, I went to the town square with a friend to talk to the parties' representatives about the election. At one booth I was given a nice pen with a picture of the local candidate down the side. My friend leaned over and whispered: "Hurry up and use the pen now, because after the election it will stop working—just like the politician." Such public skepticism of elected officials and other political authorities has become a common part of contemporary politics in most advanced industrial democracies.

Rather than focus on individual officeholders, we examine citizen images of political leaders in general. A variety of evidence points to Americans'

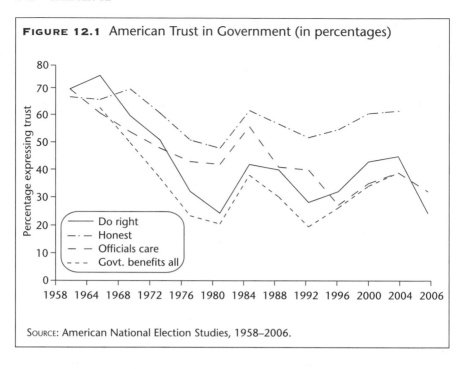

FIGURE 12.1 American Trust in Government (in percentages)

Percentage expressing trust

— Do right
—·— Honest
— — Officials care
- - - Govt. benefits all

1958 1964 1968 1972 1976 1980 1984 1988 1992 1996 2000 2004 2006

SOURCE: American National Election Studies, 1958–2006.

growing skepticism about their leaders. The American National Election Study (ANES) has measured feelings toward political officials and the government over time (figure 12.1). The early readings depicted a largely supportive public. In 1958 most Americans believed that one can trust the government to do what is right (71 percent), that people in government are honest (68 percent), and that officials care what people think (71 percent). These positive feelings remained relatively unchanged until the mid-1960s and then declined precipitously.

Distrust of government officials reached a low point in 1980, after which the upbeat presidency of Ronald Reagan temporarily improved Americans' image of politics. But, by the end of the Reagan-Bush era, trust in government was as low as it had been in 1980. The Clinton administration had a mixed record. By 1994 these indicators had hit historic lows, but steady economic growth and relative international stability began a partial revival of confidence in government. Trust grew from 1994 until the end of the decade, according to the ANES surveys. Yet even with the unprecedented economic growth of the 1990s and the consolidation of democracy around the globe, Americans' trust in government rebounded only to the levels of Reagan's first administration (even while Clinton was being impeached). Support for incumbents and the government briefly spiked upward after the September 2001 terrorist attacks on the United States, but soon faded. By the 2006 elections, trust had again decreased to the levels of the early 1990s.

Virtually all long-term public opinion series show similar downward trends (Nye, Zelikow, and King 1997; Hibbing and Theiss-Morse 2002). For example, since 1966 the Harris poll has tracked sentiments on two measures of political alienation: "The people running the country don't really care what happens to you," and "Most people with power try to take advantage of people like yourself." Rising levels of assent on both items reflect the public's growing cynicism from the 1960s to the 1990s. The Pew Center for Media and the Press (1998a) extended an earlier trend on evaluations of the ethical and moral practices of federal government officials: 34 percent of Americans were critical in 1964; by 1997 that number had doubled to 68 percent.

Looking back at this span of American history, it is easy to cite reasons for the public's growing doubts about their leaders. Over any four-year electoral cycle, one can identify multiple events that have diminished the reputations of Congress and the executive branch: Watergate, the House banking scandal, Iran-contra, the Jack Abramoff lobbying scandal, and so on. Candidates promise one thing at election time, but they regularly fail to deliver and may even violate their promises once in office (for example, George H. W. Bush's promise "Read my lips, no new taxes"). In addition, some of the most distinguished members of Congress have resigned from office and offered stinging indictments of the institution. As one former representative said upon leaving the U.S. House, "May your mother never find out where you work."

Such explanations of decreasing trust focus on the peculiar history of American politics, but the same trends are occurring in Great Britain, France, Germany, and most other Western democracies. Figure 12.2 tracks the decline in the belief that politicians in our set of four nations care what people think.[3] In 1977, 53 percent of the French public believed politicians cared what they thought; by 1997, only 19 percent shared this opinion. Other trends from these four nations generally display the same pattern of decreasing trust in elected officials (Bromley, Curtice, and Seyd 2002; Kepplinger 1996; Mayer 2000).

Even more significant, public skepticism about politicians and government officials is spreading to virtually all the advanced industrial democracies. A recent study assembled a cross-national inventory of questions that measure support for politicians and government from national surveys in sixteen Western democracies (Dalton 2004; also see Norris 1999b; Pharr and Putnam 2000). Typically beginning in the late 1960s or early 1970s, these trends show a downward slide in political support *in fourteen of sixteen countries for which systematic long-term data are available*. Decreasing trust in government and elected officials has become a common feature of contemporary democracies.

Ironically, the puzzle is that this trend has occurred at a time when the political systems of most advanced industrial societies have made real advances in addressing the policy challenges facing their nations (e.g., Bok 1996). In

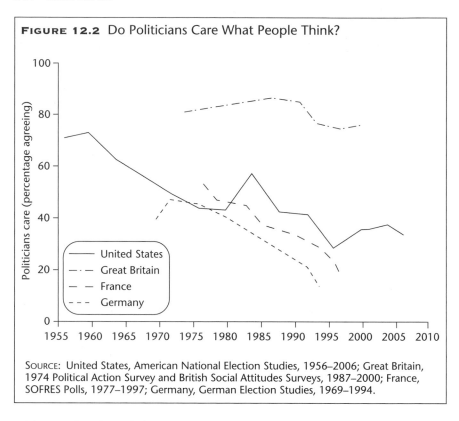

FIGURE 12.2 Do Politicians Care What People Think?

SOURCE: United States, American National Election Studies, 1956–2006; Great Britain, 1974 Political Action Survey and British Social Attitudes Surveys, 1987–2000; France, SOFRES Polls, 1977–1997; Germany, German Election Studies, 1969–1994.

addition, these trends have paralleled an apparent decrease in political corruption and an increase in citizen access to politics. It is the best of times and the worst of times.

VIEWS OF POLITICAL INSTITUTIONS

Although skepticism about political elites is now common, political scientists disagree on whether these opinions reflect doubts about political authorities or more fundamental questions about the regime and the structure of government.

The debate was first taken up by Arthur Miller (1974a; 1974b) and Jack Citrin (1974). Miller argued that Americans were generalizing their dissatisfaction with the repeated policy failures and political scandals of government officials into broader criticism of the political process as a whole. He spelled out the potentially grave consequences the loss of regime support could have for the American political process.

Citrin felt that Miller was overstating the problem. He interpreted the declines in political support as a sign of disenchantment with specific government authorities or politicians in general, not distrust in the system of American government. Citrin claimed that "political systems, like baseball teams, have slumps and winning seasons. Having recently endured a succession of losing seasons, Americans boo the home team when it takes the field" (1974, 987). He maintained that these boos do not show opposition to the process of democratic government, but only to the players in the lineup and their recent performance on the field. Given a few new stars or a winning streak, the decline in public confidence would reverse.

Citrin's cautiousness seemed warranted in 1974, but now, more than three decades later, public disenchantment continues. In addition, distrust has spread to the institutions of democratic government. One standard set of survey questions taps public confidence in the people running major social, economic, and political organizations. These items indicate that confidence in the leadership of virtually every U.S. institution has tumbled downward. The data in table 12.1 show that in 1966 many Americans expressed a fair amount of confidence in the executive branch (41 percent) and Congress (42 percent), but these positive evaluations dropped substantially over time. In 2006 only 14 percent of Americans had confidence in the executive branch, and Congress fared even worse (11 percent). Confidence in business, labor, higher education, organized religion, the press, and the medical profession have suffered similar declines over the past four decades.

The American National Election Study examines the perceived responsiveness of government and political institutions. Respondents' answers show a trend of waning confidence in parties, elections, and the government in general. Other survey series document increasing public doubts about Congress as a political institution. In 1996 the Harris poll found that 42 percent of Americans had great confidence in Congress; in 2007 only 10 percent felt that way.

Furthermore, the erosion of public confidence in the institutions of representative democracy is not unique to the United States. Trends from the other advanced industrial democracies show that trust in the national legislature is falling in twelve of sixteen nations for which long-term data are now available—including all four of our core nations (Dalton 2004, 37–39). The Gallup poll found that 48 percent of the British public expressed "quite a lot" of confidence in the House of Commons in 1981, compared to only 24 percent in 1996. Similar evidence is available for Germany and France.

The 2005–2008 World Values Survey compared confidence in institutions across our four nations (see table 12.2).[4] The question wording and set of institutions differ from those in table 12.1, so the results are not directly comparable to that table. Still, the data present a familiar pattern: the public displays little confidence in the institutions of representative democracy. Roughly a third in each nation expresses "a great deal" or "quite a lot" of confidence in the national government or the national legislature. Perceptions of political parties are even more critical. A 2004 Eurobarometer study found that confidence in political parties averages only 18 percent across the European Union—far below the average confidence levels for a dozen or more other social and political institutions examined. In addition, despite the downward

TABLE 12.1 Confidence in Leadership of American Institutions (in percentages)

	1966	1971	1973	1976	1980	1984	1988	1993	1998	2000	2004	2006
Medicine	72	61	54	54	52	52	51	39	45	44	36	39
Higher education	61	37	37	38	30	29	30	22	27	27	28	28
Military	62	27	32	39	28	37	34	42	37	40	57	47
Organized religion	41	27	35	31	35	32	20	23	28	29	24	25
Supreme Court	50	23	32	35	25	35	35	30	33	34	30	32
Major corporations	55	27	29	22	27	32	25	21	28	29	17	17
Press	29	18	23	28	22	17	18	11	10	10	9	11
Executive branch	41	23	29	14	12	19	16	12	14	14	21	14
Congress	42	19	24	14	9	13	15	7	11	13	13	11
Organized labor	22	14	16	12	15	9	10	8	12	14	11	11
Average	48	28	31	29	26	28	25	22	25	25	25	24

SOURCES: 1966 and 1971, Harris Poll; 1973–2006, NORC (National Opinion Research Center) General Social Surveys.

NOTE: Table entries are the percentages expressing a "great deal" of confidence in the people running each institution.

TABLE 12.2 Cross-National Confidence in Social Institutions (in percentages)

	United States	Great Britain	France	Germany
National government	41	34	29	27
National legislature	36	36	35	26
Courts	66	60	40	60
Civil service	61	46	54	34
Political parties	22	18	16	15
Press	26	14	39	34
Major companies	32	37	40	26
Labor unions	36	30	⸜ 39	34
Environmental groups	59	70	65	60

SOURCE: 2005–2008 World Values Survey.
NOTE: Table entries are the percentages expressing "a great deal" or "quite a lot" of confidence in each institution. Missing data were excluded from the calculation of percentages.

trend in political support in all four nations, Americans remain more trustful of political institutions.

People express more confidence in nonpolitical institutions of government, such as the judicial system or the civil service, than in the institutions of representative democracy. This finding is ironic. The members of the U.S. Supreme Court are not subject to election, and the justices serve for life, but Americans are more positive about the Court than about the government officials they elect. What these numbers may suggest is a growing public dissatisfaction with the style of representative government and politicians who act on narrow self-interest or group interest. It is illuminating to see that all four publics have more confidence in environmental groups than in their elected officials.

Are these changes in political trust important? Decreasing political support is changing citizen attitudes and behavior. In place of the habitual party support of the past, more citizens are now skeptical of parties, which contributes to the increased variability in voting choices. And citizens who are skeptical about politicians and parties are less likely to vote, which contributes to the downward slide in election turnout.

Political distrust also encourages protest and other forms of unconventional political action (chapter 4). These new forms of activism often strain the democratic process, as demonstrators challenge established political elites and current government structures. The rise of new social movements and citizen interest groups further institutionalizes the changing nature of citizen politics.

A skeptical public is also likely to act differently from a trusting public (Dalton 2004; Norris 1999c; Hetherington 2005). Public opinion surveys suggest that people who think their government wastes tax money and is unresponsive to their interests may feel they are justified in fudging a bit on their taxes or bending the law in other ways. The skeptical citizen may also be hesitant to serve on a jury or perform other public service activities. In short, political support is part of the social contract that enables democracies to act without coercion and with the voluntary compliance of the citizenry. Decreasing support erodes this part of the social contract.

SUPPORT FOR A DEMOCRATIC REGIME

The loss of trust in government and political institutions can have even more fundamental implications. Returning to Citrin's baseball analogy, it is not just that the home team has had a losing season (or two, or three); rather, it is that people see most politicians and governments in most nations as on a long-term losing streak. Presidents, prime ministers, and chancellors alike have been replaced during this losing streak, but the skepticism continues.

At some point, we must worry that dissatisfaction about the team (the government or the political institutions) generalizes to dissatisfaction with the game itself (democracy and its values). If contemporary publics begin to have such doubts, they may demand more fundamental changes in the democratic process.

In earlier historical periods, dissatisfaction with politicians or political institutions often led to (or arose from) disenchantment with the democratic process itself. This was the case with the antidemocratic challenges that faced the United States and many European democracies in the 1920s and 1930s. Even during the years immediately following World War II, dissatisfaction with democracy in Europe was often concentrated among antidemocratic extremists on the Left or Right. If people lose faith in the norms and principles of the democratic process, they may reject government authority or question whether democracy is sustainable or desirable. Such sentiments would place democracy at risk.

But the news is not all bad. The available data suggest that the current situation is different from these historical examples. Support for democratic norms and procedures has actually grown over the past generation—even while trust in government has decreased. For example, long-term trends indicate that people became more politically tolerant during the postwar period. Americans' tolerance of five potentially antisystem groups has trended upward over the past three decades, and expressed support for civil liberties is more common (Dalton 2007a, ch. 5; Nie, Junn, and Stehlik-Barry 1996).[5] The extension of democratic rights to women, racial and ethnic minorities, and homosexuals has profoundly altered the politics of advanced industrial democracies in a relatively short time (also see chapter 6). At least in principle, there is widespread public endorsement of the political values and norms that underlie the democratic process.

In addition, contemporary publics now emphasize a more participatory style and a greater willingness to challenge authority. Ronald Inglehart's research on postmaterial value change—with its emphasis on participatory val-

TABLE 12.3 Support for Democracy (in percentages)

Nation	Democratic system is good	Democracy is better than other governments
Australia	87	87
Austria	96	97
Belgium	89	92
Canada	88	87
Denmark	98	98
Finland	87	91
France	90	93
Germany	95	97
Great Britain	88	78
Greece	98	97
Ireland	90	92
Italy	97	94
Japan	92	92
Netherlands	96	96
New Zealand	91	87
Norway	96	95
Portugal	90	93
Spain	95	93
Sweden	97	94
Switzerland	93	91
United States	89	88

SOURCE: 1999–2002 World Values Survey/European Values Survey.

NOTE: Table entries are the percentages agreeing with each statement. Missing data were excluded from the calculation of percentages.

ues as a measure of postmaterialism—reinforces these points (1990; 1997). Inglehart finds the growing emphasis on political and social participation as core value priorities. Other evidence points to the breadth of democratic values among contemporary publics, especially among the young (Dalton 2007a; Thomassen 2007).

To tap regime values, opinion surveys typically ask whether democracy is the best form of government. Although we have no long cross-national time series for this question, the current high degree of support suggests no major erosion in these sentiments (table 12.3).[6] On average, about 90 percent of the public in advanced industrial democracies agree that democracy is better than other forms of government (also see Klingemann 1999; Dalton 2004, ch. 2). Another question in the World Values Survey was less evaluative, asking public support for the idea of democracy. Assent to the statement "The democratic system is good" shows that support is nearly universal within Western democracies. Moreover, in comparison to a Eurobarometer survey of the late 1980s, support for democratic government has strengthened in most West European nations.

In summary, the evidence suggests that political dissatisfaction is not a critique of democracy, as it was in the past, but exists among citizens who remain deeply committed to the democratic ideal.

COMMUNITY SUPPORT

A final aspect of political support concerns orientations toward the political community and society. System support involves the system affect described by Almond and Verba (1963). A strong emotional attachment to the nation presumably provides a reservoir of diffuse support that can maintain a political system through temporary periods of political stress. Most Western democracies endured at the start of the Great Depression because people had faith that democracy would address the problems, and such a reservoir of popular identification helps a political system endure during periods of crisis.

One measure of such feelings is pride in one's nation. Figure 12.3 displays the percentages of citizens who felt very proud of their nation within the advanced industrial democracies in the early 1980s and again in the 2000s.[7] Overall, feelings of national pride are relatively high, but with significant national differences (Elkins and Sides 2004).

National pride is exceptionally high in the United States: 97 percent of the public in 1981 and 96 percent in 1999 felt "very proud" or "proud" to be an American. Those chants of "USA! USA! USA!" are not limited to Olympic competition; they signify a persistent feeling among Americans.

Most Europeans voice their national pride in more moderate tones. Germans are hesitant in their expressions of national pride, for the trauma of the Third Reich burned a deep scar in the German psyche in both West and East. Young Germans especially feel that the nationalist excesses of the past must never be repeated. The Federal Republic therefore has avoided many of the emotional national symbols that are common in other industrial nations. Germany celebrates few political holidays or memorials; the national anthem is seldom played; and even the anniversary of the founding of the Federal Republic attracts little public attention. Although most citizens are proud to be German, they refrain from any unquestioning emotional attachment to the state.

Beyond these cross-national variations, it is clear that national pride has not eroded over the past two decades. Indeed, the World Values Survey suggests that national pride is generally growing, which is surprising given the high baseline of opinions in the first survey in the early 1980s. When longer time series are available for specific nations, they too show a pattern or relative stability or growth in national pride over time (e.g., Topf, Mohler, and Heath 1989). As one should expect from affective feelings of community attachment, these sentiments have been relatively impervious to the erosion in other aspects of political support.

FIGURE 12.3 Feelings of National Pride

1981–1983		1999–2002
	100	
Australia		Australia/Ireland
United States		**United States**
Ireland		Canada
Canada		Finland
		Denmark
	90	**Great Britain/France**
Great Britain		Italy/Norway
		Sweden
Finland		
France/Italy	80	Netherlands
Belgium		
Norway		
Denmark		Belgium
Sweden		
		Norway
	70	
		Finland
		Germany
W. Germany		
Japan/Netherlands		
	60	
		Japan

SOURCES: 1981–1983 World Values Survey; 1999–2002 World Values Survey/European Values Survey.

NOTE: Figure entries are the percentages feeling "very proud" and "proud." Missing data were excluded from the calculation of percentages.

DISSATISFIED DEMOCRATS

By some measures, the present may be considered the golden age of democracy. At the beginning of the twenty-first century, more nations in the world have become or strive to be democracies than at any other point in human history. Furthermore, most of the other political ideologies that once stood as major rivals to democracy, such as fascism and communism, seem to have lost their legitimacy. Democracy has brought peace, freedom, and prosperity to the advanced industrial societies.

At the same time, people have grown more critical of political elites, more negative toward political parties, and less confident of political institutions—and their attitudes represent fundamental changes in the political orientation of democratic publics. The deference to authority that once was common in many of these nations has been partially replaced by skepticism about elites. In most democracies, the public has grown cynical about political parties and the other institutions of democratic governance. Yet, as citizens are criticizing the incumbents and institutions of government, they are simultaneously expressing strong support for the democratic creed.

These mixed sentiments produce a new pattern of "dissatisfied democrats"—a public that is dissatisfied with political institutions but supportive of democratic principles (Klingemann 1999). Dissatisfied democrats appear to be another characteristic of the new style of citizen politics, although researchers debate this point.

The significance of the trends rests in part on what is producing them, what is shaping the new citizen orientations. Although they acknowledge these trends in public opinion, political scientists interpret them in dramatically different ways. The remainder of this section discusses the two major contrasting views of the changes.

The Democratic Elitist Perspective

One group of scholars cites the new dissatisfied democrats as evidence of a crisis of democracy (Zakaria 2003; Macedo et al. 2005; Wolfe 2006; Huntington 1981). Some researchers claim that excessive public demands are overtaxing governments' ability to satisfy them. Ironically, others claim that government is demanding too much of its citizens, who simply want to be left alone and not involved in politics (Hibbing and Theiss-Morse 2002).

Consequently, some analysts use the elitist theory of democracy (see chapter 2) to offer a solution to this crisis. In a crude exaggeration of democratic theory, they maintain that if a supportive and quiescent public ensures a smoothly functioning political system, then we must redevelop these traits in contemporary publics. The centrifugal tendencies of democratic politics (and the demands of the public) must be controlled, and political authority must be reestablished. Samuel Huntington assumed the ermine robes as spokesperson for this position:

> The problem of governance in the United States today stems from an "excess of democracy." . . . [T]he effective operation of a democratic political system usually requires some measure of apathy and non-involvement on the part of some individuals and groups. The vulnerability of democratic government in

the United States comes . . . from the internal dynamics of democracy itself in a highly educated, mobilized, and participatory society. (1975, 37–38)

More recently, Fareed Zakaria (2003, 248) is even blunter in his critique of American democracy: "What we need in politics today is not more democracy, but less." In short, these analysts maintain that the crisis of democracy has developed because too many people want to apply its creed of egalitarian values to themselves, but democratic systems cannot meet these expectations. They contend that democracy has become overloaded because minorities are no longer apathetic, women are demanding equality, students are no longer docile, and the average citizen is no longer deferential. If these groups would only leave politics to the politicians—and their expert advisers—"democracy" would again be secure.[8]

Another element of the elitist perspective calls for a reduction in the scale of government. These theorists argue that governments have assumed too large a role in society, which contributes to the overload. This tenet was one of the theoretical underpinnings of Thatcher's, Reagan's, and other neoconservatives' attempts to limit the size of government. Such administrations, however, are often biased in determining which programs the government should no longer support; usually targeted for cuts are social services or environmental programs, rather than programs that benefit conservative constituencies.

Those who claim that people want to be less involved in government suggest that democracy be reformed to spare them the burdens of democratic citizenship (Hibbing and Theiss-Morse 2002). This is a provocative argument, but it runs counter to the study's own evidence as well as the evidence presented here. John Hibbing and Elizabeth Theiss-Morse's survey of American public opinion found that 86 percent favored more ballot initiatives and an expansion of democracy (2002, 75).

Taken together, the cures offered by the elitist theorists are worse than the problem it addresses; democracy's very goals are ignored in its defense. The critics of citizen politics forget that democracy means popular control of elites, not elite control over the populace.

The New Politics Perspective

The New Politics perspective offers a contrasting image of contemporary democracy. Political dissatisfaction has increased the most not among the poor and those at the margins of politics who might be suffering economically or who feel that politics is too demanding. Instead, dissatisfaction has increased the most among the young and the better educated—those who disproportionately hold New Politics values and who benefit most from the social modernization of advanced industrial societies (Dalton 2004, ch. 5). These individuals have higher expectations of government: they are more demanding of politicians and more critical of how the process functions. Because they follow politics and are more concerned about what government does, they hold government to a higher standard than citizens did in the past.

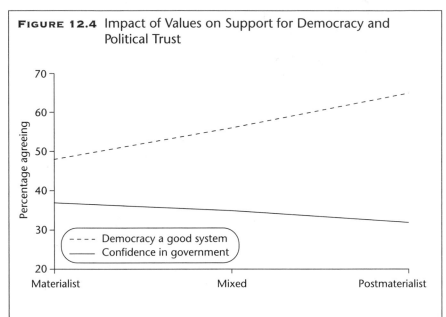

FIGURE 12.4 Impact of Values on Support for Democracy and Political Trust

Legend:
- - - - Democracy a good system
——— Confidence in government

SOURCE: Combined data from the United States, Great Britain, France, and Germany from the 2005–2008 World Values Survey.

NOTE: Figure plots the percentages of those strongly agreeing that democracy is a good system of government and those who have confidence in the national government.

From this perspective, the current dissatisfied democrats may represent another historic step in democracy's progress toward its ideals. Just as earlier periods of dissatisfaction led to the expansion of the mass franchise, the granting of voting rights to women, and populist reforms that strengthened the democratic process, we may be in a new period of democratic reform.

One illustration of the present mix of orientations is seen in the relationship of postmaterial values to political trust and support for the democratic ideal. Figure 12.4 shows that postmaterialists are distinctly less likely than materialists to express confidence in government. At the same time, postmaterialists are much more likely to support democratic ideals. Only 48 percent of materialist respondents in our four core nations strongly agree that democracy is a good form of government, compared to 65 percent of postmaterialists.[9] Postmaterialists therefore illustrate the creedal passion in support for democracy that Huntington laments—but which offers the potential for democracy to move toward its theoretical ideal, on the horizon.

In short, the New Politics approach offers a different diagnosis of current patterns of political support. Contemporary publics are better informed and more highly skilled than previous electorates, and they carry different expectations about how the democratic process should function. People today are also more conscious of their political rights and more demanding in their individualism (Dalton 2007a). The new style of citizen politics encourages a diversity of political interests (issue publics), instrumental and flexible voting choices, and more direct styles of political action.

In addition, there has been an explosion of citizen interest groups, social movements, and other social groups in recent decades (Meyer and Tarrow 1998; Berry 1999). These groups represent a new style of interest representation, as citizens can focus their attention and their activity on specific policy concerns—and work through methods of direct action. The groups signify a new way of organizing and mobilizing public opinion. (One might add the creation of an omnipresent mass media to this change in the pattern of politics.) But public interest groups also present a challenge to political parties and the established processes of representative government. The structures of representative democracy that were created in the late 1800s often seem illsuited to deal with the plethora of new interests, articulated in new ways and functioning by new rules.

Democratic governments need to accommodate the changing patterns of citizen politics. For example, the structured system of representative democracy limits the potential for citizen participation, especially in Western Europe. Opportunities for electoral input are scandalously low for most Europeans; the option to cast only a few votes during a multiyear electoral cycle is not a record of citizen input that should be admired. Moreover, beyond elections, these political systems have offered their citizens few ways to participate in the decisions of government that affect their lives. Indeed, governments often shielded themselves from public scrutiny and intentionally limited the direct impact of the citizenry—as in the constitutional structure initially devised by the Founders of the United States (or the constitutional structure of many European parliamentary systems). The fundamental structure of contemporary democratic institutions was developed in the nineteenth century—and society has changed a good deal since then.

The emphasis on new forms of citizen access and influence is not simply a call for participation for participation's sake. Expanding citizen participation can open up political systems that have become sclerosized by corporatist policymaking and bureaucratized administration. The triumvirate of businesslabor-government in many advanced industrial democracies often restricts the political interests of other groups. A system that distorts access to the political process is necessarily inefficient in meeting all of society's needs. One can see elements of these problems in the struggles of contemporary party systems in many of these democracies.

Opening up the political process is also a method to ensure that governments become more responsive to a broader spectrum of political demands. This method does not increase the quantity of political demands—the needs of the environment, women, consumers, and other groups exist—but it ensures that the demands receive fair attention from the government and thereby improves the government's ability to address all societal needs.

Greater political involvement also educates citizens in the democratic process. James Wright (1976, 260) noted a basic irony in the elitists' criticisms of citizen participation. The democratic elitists believe that governments can generate more support by convincing citizens of a lie (a sense of political efficacy that is fictitious) than by encouraging citizens to participate and learn of the necessary limits to their influence. The "big lie" may work for a while, but as soon as someone points out the gap between myth and reality, the political credibility of the system falters. It happened to the East European governments in 1989–1991. Call it co-optation, pragmatism, or Jeffersonian idealism, but involving citizens in the democratic process is one method to increase their identification with the process.

Finally, greater citizen input ultimately ensures the quality of government decision making. As we noted in chapter 1, Jefferson viewed the public as the major constraint of the potential excesses of government officials. Citizen participation is not, however, a panacea for all of modern society's ills: even educated, informed, and politically involved citizens will still make errors in judgment. As Benjamin Barber (1984, 151) also noted:

> Democracy does not place endless faith in the capacity of individuals to govern themselves, but it affirms with Machiavelli that the multitude will on the whole be as wise or wiser than princes, and with Theodore Roosevelt that "the majority of plain people will day in and day out make fewer mistakes in governing themselves than another smaller body of men will make in trying to govern them."

Since I presented this evaluation of contemporary democratic politics in the first edition of *Citizen Politics,* the calls for political reform have become the new catchphrases of politics. And there are encouraging signs that politicians and governments are responding.

Even more significant is that institutional reforms are actually restructuring the democratic process (Cain, Dalton, and Scarrow 2003). Many nations are reforming administrative procedures to give citizen groups access to the formerly closed processes of policy administration. In Germany local citizen action groups have won changes in administrative law to allow for citizen participation in local administrative processes. Similar reforms in the United States offer individual citizens and citizen groups greater access to the political process (Ingram and Smith 1993). New Freedom of Information laws and ombudsman offices are making government more transparent and accessible to its citizens (Cain, Fabrinni, and Egan 2003).

Other forms of direct democracy are also more apparent. Citizen groups in the United States and Europe are making greater use of referendums to involve the public directly in policymaking (Gallagher and Uleri 1996; Bowler and Glazer 2008). Another important development is that citizens are turning to the courts to guarantee their rights of democratic access and influence (Stone Sweet 2000; Cichowski and Stone Sweet 2003). Environmentalists in many nations have gained legal standing in the courts so they can sue to curb the harmful actions of municipalities or government agencies.

Reforms can be seen within the structured system of party government. The formation of new parties is one sign of adaptation, but even the established parties are changing internally to give their members more influence (Scarrow, Webb, and Farrell 2000). The term limits movement is one expression of these reformist sentiments. A majority of U.S. states have now enacted some type of term limits legislation, normally through citizen initiatives.

These institutional changes are difficult to accomplish. They proceed at a slow pace and often have unintended consequences. But once implemented, they restructure the whole process of making policy that extends beyond a single issue or a single policy agenda. And when such reforms are taken together, they work. We find evidence that the degree of institutional change during the past three decades rivals the reformist surge of the Populist movement of the early 1990s (Cain, Dalton, and Scarrow 2003). The processes of contemporary democracies are being transformed to reflect the new style of citizen politics.

Indeed, these adaptations reflect the ability of democracy to grow and evolve, for the lack of such adaptivity is what brought about the downfall of communism. As German sociologist Ralf Dahrendorf noted:

> What we have to do above all is to maintain that flexibility of democratic institutions which is in some ways their greatest virtue: the ability of democratic institutions to implement and effect change without revolution—the ability to react to new problems in new ways—the ability to develop institutions rather than change them all the time—the ability to keep the lines of communication open between leaders and led—and the ability to make individuals count above all. (1975, 194)

Such change in the style of representative democracy is not without risk. The political process may experience some growing pains as it adjusts to greater citizen participation, especially in the more tightly structured European political systems. One potential problem is the possibility of a growing participation gap between sophisticated and unsophisticated citizens (see chapter 3). Because the resources required to lobby government directly or to organize a public interest group are greater than those required to vote, a change in the style of political activity may leave behind those in society who lack the education and other skills and resources needed for direct-action politics.

Democracies must also face the challenge of balancing greater responsiveness to specific interests against the broader interests of the nation (Bok 2001; Dalton 2004, ch. 9). In the vernacular of political science, we have seen a dramatic increase in interest articulation over the past generation but an erosion of interest aggregation within the polity. In other words, citizen interest groups, social movements, individual citizens, and various political groups are now more vocal about their political interests and have greater access to the democratic process. At the same time, the ability of political institutions to balance contending interests—and to make interest groups sensitive to the collective needs of society—has diminished. The collective interest is more than just the sum of individual interests, and one of the pressing needs for contemporary democracies is to find new ways to bring diverse interests together.

Participatory democracy can generate political overkill, but it also contains an equilibrium mechanism to encourage political balance. In the United States, the process has generally succeeded in retaining the benefits of new ideas while avoiding the ominously predicted excesses of democracy. We should remember that democratic politics is not supposed to maximize government efficiency or to increase the autonomy of political elites. Just the opposite. In fact, efficiency is partially sacrificed to ensure a more important goal: popular control of elites. Expanding participation is not a problem but an opportunity for the advanced industrial democracies to come closer to matching their democratic ideals.

In summary, the current crisis of democracy is really just another stage in the ongoing history of democracy's development. Democracies need to adapt to present-day politics and to the new style of citizen politics. As Dahrendorf (2000, 311) has observed, "Representative government is no longer as compelling a proposition as it once was. Instead, a search for new institutional forms to express conflicts of interest has begun." This process of democratic experimentation and reform may be threatening to some, and it does present a risk—but change is necessary. The challenge to democracies is to discover whether they can continue to evolve, to guarantee political rights, and to increase the ability of citizens to control their lives. Can we move democracy closer to its theoretical ideals?

SUGGESTED READINGS

Bok, Derek. *The Trouble with Government.* Cambridge: Harvard University Press, 2001.

Dalton, Russell. *Democratic Challenges, Democratic Choices: The Erosion of Political Support in Advanced Industrial Democracies.* Oxford: Oxford University Press, 2004.

Hetherington, Marc. *Why Trust Matters: Declining Political Trust and the Demise of American Liberalism.* Princeton: Princeton University Press, 2005.

Hibbing, John, and Elizabeth Theiss-Morse. *Stealth Democracy: Americans' Beliefs about How Government Should Work.* New York: Cambridge University Press, 2002.

Norris, Pippa, ed. *Critical Citizens: Global Support for Democratic Governance.* Oxford: Oxford University Press, 1999.

Nye, Joseph, Philip Zelikow, and David King. *Why People Don't Trust Government.* Cambridge, Mass.: Harvard University Press, 1997.

Pharr, Susan, and Robert Putnam, eds. *Disaffected Democracies: What's Troubling the Trilateral Countries?* Princeton: Princeton University Press, 2000.

Putnam, Robert. *Making Democracy Work.* Princeton: Princeton University Press, 1993.

NOTES

1. In the mid-1980s Samuel Huntington (1984) was explaining why there would be no more democracies in the world, a theme consistent with his elitist view of democracy. By the end of the decade, he was describing democratization as a wave that was transforming the international order (Huntington 1991).
2. The argument is also made that diffuse regime support existed in most other Western democracies in the 1930s and that dissatisfaction focused on the performance of political elites in these systems. These feelings were channeled within the political process, and the basic structure of democratic government persisted in the United States, Britain, and France.
3. The question wording and coding categories were slightly different in each nation, so one should not directly compare the levels of support across nations in this figure. For such comparisons, see Klingemann (1999) and tables 12.2 and 12.3 in this chapter.
4. For a more extensive comparison of confidence in institutions, see Dalton (2004) and Klingemann (1999).
5. Some counter evidence is apparent for Britain, where the British Social Attitudes survey shows a drop in tolerance and civil liberties in 2005 (Johnson and Gearty 2007). But a good deal of time has passed since the previous survey, and the 2005 result may have been affected by the July 7 terrorist attacks in London that occurred in the midst of the interviewing for the survey. More study is needed to see if tolerance is affected by international terrorist incidents.
6. The two questions were as follows: "Would you say it is a very good, fairly good, fairly bad, or very bad way of governing this country: Having a democratic political system?" and "Democracy may have problems but it's better than any other form of government. Do you agree or disagree?"
7. The 2005–2008 World Values Survey shows little change for the four core nations: United States (93 percent), Britain (86 percent), France (86 percent), and Germany (68 percent). The question asked, "How proud are you to be (nationality)?" The responses were: (1) very proud, (2) quite proud, (3) not very proud, and (4) not at all proud. The figure presents the "very proud" and "proud" responses.
8. Samuel Huntington's advice on limiting political demands overlooks the possibility of constraining the input of Harvard professors, corporate executives, and the upper class. His focus solely on the participation of average citizens suggests that he has confused the definitions of plutocracy and democracy.
9. These results are from the 2005–2008 World Values Survey combining results from the United States, Britain, France, and Germany. The democracy item asks about approval of a democratic form of government; the confidence in government question is the same as presented in table 12.2.

APPENDIX A

Statistical Primer

Most newspapers report on public opinion polls and publish tables and graphs to illustrate the results. The informed citizen needs to know how to read and interpret these tables and graphs.

This book provides this kind of information to describe the attitudes and behavior of contemporary publics. The tables and figures I present generally follow one of two patterns. The first pattern describes the differences in citizen opinions or behaviors across the four core nations in this study. As examples, table 2.1 describes the sources of information for citizens in each nation, and table 3.4 summarizes patterns of political participation. Surveys estimate public opinion, and typically the results in such a table are within a few percentage points of what the entire public actually thinks or does (Asher 2007).

In the second pattern, tables or figures describe the relationships between two or more questions from a public opinion survey. For example, what factors are related to different types of political participation, what are the correlates of voting choice, or what attitudes are related to trust in government? I often present these relationships in graphic terms; showing, perhaps, that as education goes up, so does voting turnout (figure 4.1), or, as church attendance increases, so does the share of the vote going to conservative parties (table 8.3). Implicitly, at least, there is a presumption of causality: when education is related to higher turnout, we can infer that education provides the skills and resources that allow people to be more politically active.

These presentations of relationships in a table or figure typically have the presumed predictor aligned along the horizontal axis, with categories of the predictor marked in the table or figure. The effect is arrayed along the vertical axis. In figure 4.1, the least educated group (less than a high school diploma) is on the left of the horizontal axis, and the most educated age group (some college or more) is on the right side of this axis. The figure then presents the voting turnout rates on the vertical axis. A separate line plots the increase in turnout with education for each of the four nations.

Often tables and figures include multiple comparisons, such as many levels of education or church attendance—and it can become difficult to see the overall pattern amid a blur of numbers. Therefore, I often use correlation statistics to summarize relationships. Statistics are tools to help you understand relationships, even if you are not numerically inclined. These correlations summarize the extent to which responses on one survey question (such has higher levels of education) are related to responses on another question (such as higher turnout).

Statistics is a complex field, and data analysis is a complicated research methodology, and statisticians might disapprove of the quick summaries that follow and the limited attention devoted to the assumptions underlying the use of these statistics. Nevertheless, this primer provides a guide on how to use the statistics presented in this book, with the hope that it helps you understand the presentation of findings.

I most commonly use three correlation statistics:

- **Cramer's V correlation.** This correlation measures the relationship between two variables when at least one of them is a "categoric" variable, that is, a set of categories with no distinct order. Examples of a categoric variable are region, race, religious denomination, or other measures that do not follow a natural order from low to high, agree to disagree, or some other underlying order.
- **Pearson's r correlation.** This correlation measures the relationship between two variables when both have an ordered pattern of categories, such as from low to high or agree to disagree. This statistic is more powerful and demanding, because it does not just see if categories differ on the predicted variable, but it presumes an ordered pattern to these differences. See figure 4.1 for an example: as education level increases, the vote turnout also should increase. The larger differences by education in the United States imply that education has a stronger impact (correlation) than for the three European countries.

  The Pearson's r also measures the *direction* of a relationship because there is a distinction between higher and lower values. For example, age is positively related to voting turnout, but protest decreases with age. The first example would produce a positive correlation, and the second, a negative correlation.

  Several tables and figures present correlations to summarize relationships across different nations or groups, rather than display each relationship in a separate graph. Figure 8.2 presents the relationship between social class and voting choice in seventeen nations. Figure 8.5 presents the relationship between postmaterial values and vote choice for a set of nations.
- **Regression coefficient (β).** This statistic is the most complex. Often we want to examine the relationship between two variables, but we think the relationship might partially depend on one or more other variables. Multiple regression is a statistical method to simultaneously examine the relationships of several variables with a dependent variable, so that we can assess the separate effects of each. The regression coefficient describes the relationship between two variables, while "statistically controlling for" the other variables in the model. For example, we can determine the effect of education on turnout while simultaneously controlling for (or statistically removing) age differences or ideological differences in turnout because all three variables are interrelated.

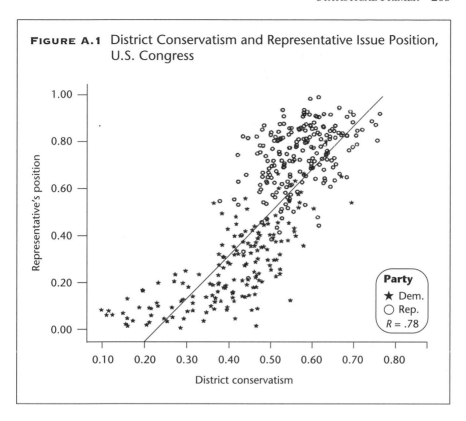

FIGURE A.1 District Conservatism and Representative Issue Position, U.S. Congress

This book presents standardized regression coefficients from several such models (e.g., figure 4.3 and table 4.1). These statistics are comparable to the Pearson's r and are calculated in similar ways. They signify the direction and strength of a relationship, and the differences between a Pearson's r and a regression coefficient indicate how much a relationship changes by controlling for the other variables in the model.

A simple example from this book illustrates the logic of regression analysis. We begin with the example of figure A.1, which is similar to figure 11.3. The ideological position of a district (the horizontal axis) is used to predict the ideological position of the member of Congress from that district (the vertical axis). The figure shows that there is a strong relationship between these two variables. The slanted line in this version of the figure summarizes the overall pattern, and shows that as district ideology changes there is a marked change in the predicted ideology of the elected member of Congress. In addition, the points in the figure are relatively close to this summary line. The Pearson's r is .78, which signifies a very strong relationship. (In part, the correlation is so high because we are dealing with aggregated units, electoral districts, and most relationships among individual attitudes are not so strong.)

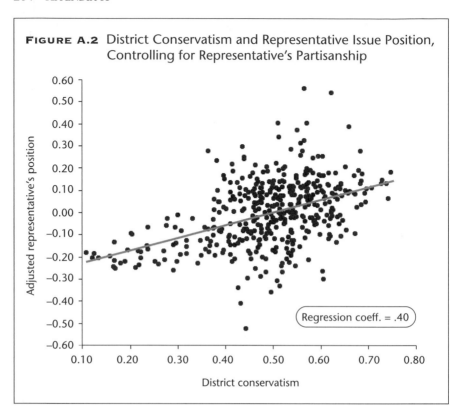

FIGURE A.2 District Conservatism and Representative Issue Position, Controlling for Representative's Partisanship

Regression coeff. = .40

If we stopped here, we would conclude that voters can perceive the ideological position of the candidates, and therefore most districts pick representatives who share their views. Liberal districts generally pick liberal candidates, and conservative districts generally pick conservative candidates. There is some variation, so points are spread out a bit in the figure. But the variation is limited, and hence the strong correlation.

One might ask, however, whether voters are really aware of the ideology of candidates, or whether they are using political party as a cue. That is, if you look closely at the original figure 11.3, you see that Democratic representatives tend toward the liberal end of the dimension, and Republican representatives toward the conservative end. In other words, both party and district ideology may predict the ideology of the elected representative. This potential joint effect of party and ideology produces a two-variable regression model, using these two predictors.

The figure above (figure A.2) graphically illustrates the outcome from these analyses. The figure presents the ideology of the district and the ideology of the representative—while statistically holding constant party effects. One can see that the fit between the two variables is still substantial, but the line summarizing this relationship is now flatter, and the spread of points around the line is more dispersed. The statistic summarizing this relationship drops from the .78 correlation in the previous figure to the $\beta = .40$ regression coefficient. The effect of district ideology has weakened by controlling for party, but it is still a significant predictor of the ideology of representatives. This, in brief, is the logic of multiple regression—to examine the independent impact of one variable while controlling for the effect of other variables.

WHAT IS BIG?

Correlations are designed to summarize the strength of the relationship between two variables. This raises the question of what is a strong relationship versus a weak relationship. I primarily rely on the three correlation statistics in this text because they give comparable values for similar relationships, even if they are calculated differently:

- **Cramer's V correlation.** This statistic ranges from a value of 0.0 when there are no differences across categories (that is, each comparison in a table has the same percentage distribution) to a values of 1.00 when categories in a table differ by a maximum possible 100 percent. Typically, we interpret coefficients of .10 or less as a weak relationship, .10–.20 as a modest relationship, and .20 or larger as a strong relationship.
- **Pearson's r correlation.** This statistic measures three properties that are apparent in figure A.1. First, how strongly does one variable predict differences in the dependent variable; in figure A.1 this means how steep is the angle of the line describing this relationship. Second, how closely are points clustered around this line; in other words, how well does the line represent the overall pattern. The points are more tightly clustered around the line in figure A.1 than in figure A.2. Third, relationships can be positive or negative. For example, voting turnout can increase with age (a positive relationship), while protest participation decreases with age (a negative relationship).

  Thus, the Pearson's r ranges from a value of –1.0 when there is a perfect negative relationship (a sharp negatively sloped line with all the points clustered on the line), to 0.0 when there are no differences across categories (that is, scores of the predictor variable are unrelated to the dependent variable), to a value of 1.00 when there is a perfect positive correlation. As with Cramer's V, we interpret coefficients of .10 or less as a weak relationship, .10–.20 as a modest relationship, and .20 or larger as a strong relationship.
- **Regression coefficient (β).** This statistic is comparable to the Pearson's r, except that it measures the relationship between two variables while controlling for the relationships shared by other variables in the model. Like the Pearson's r, it ranges from –1.0 for a perfect negative relationship to 1.0 for a perfect positive relationship. As with the other two statistics, we

interpret coefficients of .10 or less as a weak relationship, .10–.20 as a modest relationship, and .20 or larger as a strong relationship.

Statistics, graphs, and tables can sometimes seem complex, but they are simply a shortcut for summarizing how much one variable is related to another. With this guide, these relationships should be easier to interpret than trying to understand all the percentages in a statistical table or points in a graph.

APPENDIX B

Major Data Sources

In 1948 researchers at the University of Michigan conducted one of the first national election surveys based on scientific sampling methods. The four scholars who eventually directed the early surveys—Angus Campbell, Philip Converse, Warren Miller, and Donald Stokes—wrote the landmark study of American electoral behavior, *The American Voter*. Since then, this election study series has been repeated at each biennial national election. The American National Election Studies (ANES) is a national resource in the social sciences and is used by researchers in hundreds of universities worldwide.

David Butler and Donald Stokes began a comparable series of British election studies with the 1964 election. These scholars continued the series through the 1966 and 1970 elections, and then a team of researchers at the University of Essex, led by Ivor Crewe, continued the series in 1974 and 1979. Between 1983 and 1997, Anthony Heath, Roger Jowell, and John Curtice of Social and Community Planning Research (SCPR) in London conducted the British Election Studies. A new research team at the University of Essex directed by Harold Clarke conducted the 2001 and 2005 British Election Studies.

Academic studies of German elections trace their roots back to the 1961 study conducted by Gerhard Baumert, Erwin Scheuch, and Rudolf Wildenmann from the University of Cologne. The Cologne researchers and their students have established this series through the work of Max Kaase, Hans-Dieter Klingemann, Franz Pappi, and the Forschungsgruppe Wahlen (Manfred Berger, Wolfgang Gibowski, Dieter Roth, Mattias Jung, et al.) in Mannheim. A new academic group at the Wissenschaftszentrum Berlin für Sozialforschung (WZB) has continued this election series.

France has a less institutionalized series of surveys that are publicly available. A number of individual scholars have conducted surveys of specific French elections: Roland Cayrol and his associates; Philip Converse and Roy Pierce; and Michael Lewis-Beck, Nonna Mayer, and Daniel Boy and their colleagues. The emerging series of election studies provides an opportunity to track the evolution of French political behavior during the Fifth Republic.

Most of the data analyzed in this volume were drawn from the data sources mentioned above and specifically listed below. We acquired most of these data from the Inter-university Consortium for Political and Social Research (ICPSR) at the University of Michigan in Ann Arbor. Additional data were made available by the Economic and Social Data Service at the University of Essex, England, and the Zentralarchiv für empirische Sozialforschung

(ZA), University of Cologne, Germany. Neither the archives nor the original collectors of the data bear responsibility for the analyses presented here.

American National Election Studies (ANES)

1948   American National Election Study (N = 622). Angus Campbell and Robert Kahn.

1952   American National Election Study (N = 1,899). Angus Campbell, Gerald Gurin, et al.

1956   American National Election Study (N = 1,762). Angus Campbell, Philip Converse, et al.

1960   American National Election Study (N = 1,181). Angus Campbell, Philip Converse, et al.

1964   American National Election Study (N = 1,571). Political Behavior Program.

1968   American National Election Study (N = 1,557). Political Behavior Program.

1972   American National Election Study (N = 2,705). Warren Miller, Arthur Miller, et al.

1976   American National Election Study (N = 2,248). Warren Miller, Arthur Miller, et al.

1980   American National Election Study (N = 1,614). Warren Miller et al.

1984   American National Election Study (N = 2,257). Warren Miller et al.

1988   American National Election Study (N = 2,040). Warren Miller et al.

1992   American National Election Study (N = 2,485). Warren Miller et al.

1996   American National Election Study (N = 1,714). Steven Rosenstone et al.

2000   American National Election Study (N = 1,807). Nancy Burns et al.

2004   American National Election Study (N = 1,212). Nancy Burns et al.

British Election Studies

1964   British Election Study (N = 1,769). David Butler and Donald Stokes.

1966   British Election Study (N = 1,874). David Butler and Donald Stokes.

1970   British Election Study (N = 1,885). David Butler and Donald Stokes.

1974   British Election Study, February (N = 2,462). Ivor Crewe, Bo Saarlvik, and James Alt.

1974   British Election Study, October (N = 2,365). Ivor Crewe, Bo Saarlvik, and James Alt.

1979   British Election Study (N = 1,893). Ivor Crewe, Bo Saarlvik, and David Robertson.

1983   British Election Study (N = 3,955). Anthony Heath, Roger Jowell, and John Curtice.

1987   British Election Study (N = 3,826). Anthony Heath, Roger Jowell, John Curtice, and Sharon Witherspoon.

1992   British Election Study (N = 3,534). Anthony Heath, Roger Jowell, and John Curtice.

1997   British Election Study (N = 3,615). Anthony Heath, Roger Jowell, John Curtice, and Pippa Norris.

2001   British Election Study (N = 3,223). Harold Clarke, David Sanders, Marianne Stewart, and Paul Whiteley.

2005   British Election Study (N = 4,971). David Sanders, Paul Whitely, Harold Clarke and Marianne Stweart.

German Election Studies

1953   The Social Bases of West German Politics (N = 3,246). UNESCO Institute.

1961   West German Election Study (N = 1,679; 1,633; 1,715). Gerhart Baumert, Erwin Scheuch, and Rudolf Wildenmann.

1965   West German Election Study, October (N = 1,305). DIVO Institut.

1965   West German Election Study, September (N = 1,411). Rudolf Wildenmann and Max Kaase.

1969   West German Election Study (N = 1,158). Hans-Dieter Klingemann and Franz Pappi.

1972   West German Election Study (N = 2,052). Manfred Berger, Wolf-gang Gibowski, Max Kaase, Dieter Roth, Uwe Schleth, and Rudolf Wildenmann.

1976   West German Election Study (N = 2,076). Forschungsgruppe Wahlen.

1980   West German Election Study (N = 1,620). Forschungsgruppe Wahlen.

1983   West German Election Study (N = 1,622). Forschungsgruppe Wahlen.

1987   West German Election Study (N = 1,954). Forschungsgruppe Wahlen.

1990   German Election Study, November (West = 984; East = 1,095). Forschungsgruppe Wahlen.

1994   German Election Study, September (West = 1,013; East = 1,068). Forschungsgruppe Wahlen.

1998   German Post-election Study (West = 978; East = 1,041). Mannheimer Zentrum für Europäische Sozialforschung (MZES), the Wissenschaftszentrum Berlin für Sozialforschung (WZB), the Zentralarchiv für empirische Sozialforschung, and the Zentrum für Umfragen, Methoden und Analysen (ZUMA), Mannheim.

2002   German Election Study (N = 2,000). Hermann Schmitt and Bernhard Wessels.

2005   German Election Study (N = 2,018). Hermann Schmitt and Berhard Wessels.

French Election Studies

1958   French Election Study (N = 1,650). Georges Dupeux. Available ICPSR.

1967   French Election Study (N = 2,046). Philip Converse and Roy Pierce.

1968   French Election Study (N = 1,905). Ronald Inglehart.

1978   French Election Study (N = 4,507). Jacques Capdevielle, Elisabeth Dupoirier, Gerard Grunberg, Etienne Schweisguth, and Colette Ysmal.

1988   French Presidential Election Survey (N = 1,013). Roy Pierce.

1995   French National Election Study (N = 4,078). Michael Lewis-Beck, Nonna Mayer, Daniel Boy, et al.

1997   French National Election Study (N = 3,010). Centre d'Etudes de la Vie Politique Française (CEVIPOF), Centre d'Informatisation des Données Socio-Politiques (CIDSP), and Centre de Recherches Administratives, Politiques et Sociales (CRAPS).

2002   French Comparative Study of Electoral Systems (N = 1,000). Thomas Gschwend and Hermann Schmitt.

2002   French National Election Study (N = 4017). CIDSP-IEP de Grenoble, Centre for studies of French Political Life (CEVIPOF), Centre for Computerized socio-political databases (CECOP).

Major Cross-National Studies

1959   The Civic Culture Study (USA = 970; Great Britain = 963; West Germany = 955). Gabriel Almond and Sidney Verba.

1970   European Community Surveys/Eurobarometers (an ongoing series of opinion surveys conducted by the Commission of the European Union).

1974   Political Action Study (USA = 1,719; Great Britain = 1,483; West Germany = 2,307). Samuel Barnes, Max Kaase, et al.

1981–   World Values Survey (USA = 1,729; Great Britain = 1,231; West
1983   Germany = 1,305; France = 1,200).

1985   International Social Survey Program (a coordinated series of public opinion surveys conducted by various sociological institutes in the U.S. and Europe).

1990–   World Values Survey (USA = 1,839; Great Britain = 1,484; West
1991   Germany = 2,101; France = 1,002; East Germany = 1,336). Ronald Inglehart and the European Values Systems Study Group.

1995–   World Values Survey (USA = 1,542; Great Britain = 1,093; West
1998   Germany = 1,017; East Germany = 1,009). Ronald Inglehart, Hans-Dieter Klingemann, et al.

1999–   World Values Survey/European Values Survey (USA = 1,200; Great
2002   Britain = 994; France = 1,615; Germany = 2,036).

1996–   Comparative Study of Electoral Systems, module I (USA = 1,714; Great Britain = 3,615; Germany = 2,021).

2002   European Social Survey (Great Britain = 2,052; Germany = 2,919).

2000–   Comparative Study of Electoral Systems, module II (USA = 1534; Great Britain = 842; France 1,000; Germany = 2,000).

2005–   World Values Survey (USA = 1,493; Great Britain = 1,041; France = 1,001; Germany = 2,064).

2004 International Social Survey Codebook

One of the main sources of public opinion data in this book is the International Social Survey Program (ISSP). To assist students and instructors in understanding the causes and correlates of public opinion, we have prepared a subset of the data from the 2004 ISSP for instructors to use in connection with *Citizen Politics*. For ease of student usage, these data have been extensively recoded and reformatted. One example is the merging of categories to ensure reasonable group sizes in tabular analyses. Students can use these data for small research exercises designed by the instructor or for longer-term research projects that explore the themes in this book or other elections of public opinion.

This appendix includes a brief description of the 2004 International Social Survey Program and an abbreviated codebook that describes the variables included in this subset. Portable files for the *Statistical Package in the Social Sciences* (SPSS) can be downloaded from the CQ Press Web site for this book (www.cqpress.com/cs/dalton). There are four files containing data for the four core nations of this book (the United States, Great Britain, France, and Germany). The following codebook describes these data.

THE INTERNATIONAL SOCIAL SURVEY

The International Social Survey Program is a continuing, annual program of cross-national collaboration. On a nearly annual basis, the collaborating research institutes collect a common research module on a specific topic, such as the role of government, religion, work orientations, social inequality, or the environment.

The 2004 module focused on the meaning of citizenship and its causes. Portions of this module have been analyzed in Russell Dalton, *The Good Citizen: How Young People Are Reshaping American Politics* (CQ Press, 2007).

The ISSP evolved from a bilateral collaboration between the ALLBUS survey of the Zentrum für Umfragen, Methoden, und Analysen (ZUMA) in Mannheim, Germany, and the General Social Survey (GSS) of the National Opinion Research Center, University of Chicago. The ISSP now includes more than three dozen nations spanning the established democracies and new emerging and consolidating democracies. Additional information about the ISSP can be found on the Web site (www.issp.org). The full set of surveys is available from the Zentralarchiv für empirische Sozialforschung at the University of Cologne, the Inter-university Consortium for Political and Social Research at the University of Michigan, and other national social science data archives.

Variable List

V001   COUNTRY
V002   WEIGHT

Defining Good Citizenship

V003   GOOD CITIZEN ALWAYS VOTE
V004   GOOD CITIZEN DOESNT EVADE TAXES
V005   GOOD CITIZEN OBEY LAWS
V006   GOOD CITIZEN WATCH GOVERNMENT
V007   GOOD CITIZEN ACTIVE IN ASSOCIATIONS
V008   GOOD CITIZEN UNDERSTAND OTHERS
V009   GOOD CITIZEN CHOOSE PRODUCTS
V010   GOOD CITIZEN HELP OTHERS—COUNTRY
V011   GOOD CITIZEN HELP OTHERS—WORLD
V012   GOOD CITIZEN SERVE IN MILITARY
V013   CITIZEN DUTY INDEX
V014   ENGAGED CITIZEN INDEX

Political Tolerance

V015   ALLOW MEETINGS—RELIG EXTREMISTS
V016   ALLOW MEETINGS—OVERTHROW GOVT
V017   ALLOW MEETINGS–RACISTS
V018   POLITICAL TOLERANCE INDEX

Political Interest

V019   INTEREST IN POLITICS
V020   POLITICAL DISCUSSION—FREQUENCY
V021   POL DISCUSSION—CONVINCE FRIENDS

Political Participation

V022   VOTED IN ELECTION
V023   SIGN A PETITION
V024   BOYCOTT CERTAIN PRODUCTS
V025   PARTICIPATE IN DEMONSTRATION
V026   ATTEND POLITICAL MEETING
V027   CONTACT POLITICIAN

V028   DONATE MONEY
V029   CONTACT MEDIA
V030   JOIN INTERNET FORUM
V031   PROTEST INDEX
V032   CONVENTIONAL PARTICIPATION INDEX
V033   TOTAL PARTICIPATION INDEX

Group Membership

V034   BELONG TO POLITICAL PARTY
V035   BELONG TO TRADE UNION
V036   BELONG TO CHURCH
V037   BELONG TO SPORTS GROUP
V038   BELONG TO OTHER GROUP
V039   NUMBER OF GROUPS

Democratic Rights

V040   ADEQUATE LIVING STANDARD
V041   GOVERNMENT RESPECT MINORITIES
V042   GOVERNMENT EQUAL TREATMENT
V043   CITIZEN ORIENTED DECISIONS
V044   CITIZENS INVOLVED IN DECISIONS
V045   CIVIL DISOBEDIENCE ACTS
V046   DEMOCRATIC RIGHTS INDEX

Political Efficacy

V047   NO INFLUENCE ON WHAT GOVT DOES
V048   GOVERNMENT DOES NOT CARE WHAT I THINK
V049   GOVERNMENT RESPONSIVE INDEX
V050   GOOD UNDERSTANDING OF ISSUES
V051   MOST PEOPLE ARE BETTER INFORMED
V052   PERSONAL EFFICACY INDEX
V053   UNJUST LAW LIKELY ACTION
V054   UNJUST LAW LIKELY ATTENTION

Political Trust

V055   CAN TRUST PEOPLE IN GOVERNMENT
V056   POLITICIANS ONLY PROFIT

Social Trust

V057   PEOPLE TAKE ADVANTAGE
V058   PEOPLE CAN BE TRUSTED

Democratic Performance

V059   DEMOCRACY TODAY
V060   DEMOCRACY 10 YEARS AGO
V061   DEMOCRACY 10 YEARS FUTURE
V062   GOVERNMENT RESTRICT RIGHTS

International Opinions

V063   OPINION UNITED NATIONS
V064   OPINION INTERNAT ORGANIZATIONS
V065   OPINION UN INTERVENTION

Attitudes toward Political Parties

V066   PARTIES ENCOURAGE ACTIVITY
V067   PARTIES—NO REAL CHOICES
V068   REFERENDUM A GOOD METHOD

Image of Elections

V069   LAST ELECTION HONEST
V070   LAST ELECTION FAIR

Party Preference

V071   LEFT/RIGHT PARTY PREFERENCE
V072A   PARTY: UNITED STATES
V072B   PARTY: BRITAIN
V072C   PARTY: FRANCE
V072D   PARTY: GERMANY

Image of Public Service

V073   PUBLIC SERVICE COMMITTED TO PUBLIC
V074   PUBLIC SERVICE CORRECTS MISTAKES
V075   PUBLIC SERVICE CORRUPT

Demographic Variables

V076   GENDER
V077   GENERATION
V078   MARITAL STATUS
V079   STEADY LIFE-PARTNER
V080   EDUCATION LEVEL
V081   EMPLOYMENT STATUS
V082   WEEKLY HOURS

V083   R OCCUPATION
V084   R MIDDLE/WORKING CLASS
V085   PUBLIC/PRIVATE SECTOR
V086   SUPERVISE OTHERS
V087   UNION MEMBER
V088   SPOUSE EMPLOYMENT
V089   SPOUSE OCCUPATION
V090   SPOUSE MIDDLE/WORKING CLASS
V091   SPOUSE PUBLIC/PRIVATE
V092   R INCOME
V093   HOUSEHOLD SIZE
V094   HOUSEHOLD COMPOSITION
V095   RELIGION
V096   RELIGIOUS ATTENDANCE
V097   SOCIAL STATUS
V098A   REGION—USA
V098B   REGION—BRITAIN
V098C   REGION—FRANCE
V098D   REGION—GERMANY
V099A   SIZE COMMUNITY—USA
V099B   SIZE COMMUNITY—BRITAIN
V099C   SIZE COMMUNITY—FRANCE
V099D   SIZE COMMUNITY—GERMANY
V100   TYPE OF COMMUNITY
V101   ETHNICITY/RACE—USA

Codebook

V001   COUNTRY

1.   United States (Unweighted N = 1472; weighted N = 1485)
2.   Britain (Unweighted N = 853; weighted N = 833)
3.   France (Unweighted N = 1419; weighted N = 1421)
4.   Germany (Unweighted N = 1332; weighted N = 1342)

V002   WEIGHT

All four nations provide a weight variable used to correct the sample to reflect national distributions of key variables or to adjust for different sampling fractions for population groups. For example, East German respondents were oversampled, and their responses should be weighted to yield a representative national sample. The SPSS can use this weight variable to construct a representative sample; the weight should be used for each nation.

V003   GOOD CITIZEN ALWAYS VOTE

There are different opinions as to what it takes to be a good citizen. As far as you are concerned personally on a scale of 1 to 7, where 1 is not at all important and 7 is very important, how important is it: Always to vote in elections
1.   Not at all important (1–3)
2.   Somewhat important (4–5)
3.   Important (6)
4.   Very important (7)
9.   Don't know

V004   GOOD CITIZEN DOESNT EVADE TAXES

(How important) Never try to evade taxes?
[See V003 for response categories]

V005   GOOD CITIZEN OBEY LAWS

(How important) Always obey laws and regulations?
[See V003 for response categories]

V006   GOOD CITIZEN WATCH GOVERNMENT

(How important) To keep watch on the actions of government?
[See V003 for response categories]

V007   GOOD CITIZEN ACTIVE IN ASSOCIATIONS

(How important is) To be active in social or political associations?
[See V003 for response categories]

V008   GOOD CITIZEN UNDERSTAND OTHERS

(How important) To try to understand the reasoning of people with other opinions?
[See V003 for response categories]

V009   GOOD CITIZEN CHOOSE PRODUCTS

(How important) To choose products for political, ethical or environmental reasons, even if they cost a bit more?
[See V003 for response categories]

V010   GOOD CITIZEN HELP OTHERS—COUNTRY

(How important) To help people in (COUNTRY) who are worse off than yourself?
[See V003 for response categories]

V011   GOOD CITIZEN HELP OTHERS—WORLD

(How important) To help people in the rest of the world who are worse off than yourself?
[See V003 for response categories]

V012   GOOD CITIZEN SERVE IN MILITARY

(How important) To be willing to serve in the military at a time of need?
[See V003 for response categories]

V013   CITIZEN DUTY INDEX

[This index was constructed from the items that emphasize citizen duty, such as obeying the law, not evading taxes, serving in the military, and voting. For more information, see Dalton (2007a).]
1.   Low importance for citizen duty
2.
3.
4.   High importance for citizen duty
9.   Don't know

V014   ENGAGED CITIZEN INDEX

[This index was constructed from the items that emphasize citizen engagement, such as concern with others, participation in society, and keeping watch on government. For more information, see Dalton (2007a).]
1.   Low importance for engaged citizenship
2.
3.
4.   High importance for engaged citizenship
9.   Don't know

V015   ALLOW MEETINGS—RELIG EXTREMISTS

There are a number of groups in society. Should religious extremists be allowed to hold public meetings?
1.   Should definitely be allowed
2.   Should probably be allowed
3.   Should probably not be allowed
4.   Should definitely not be allowed
9.   Don't know

V016   ALLOW MEETINGS—OVERTHROW GOVT

Should people who want to overthrow the government by force be allowed to hold public meetings?
[See V015 for response categories]

V017   ALLOW MEETINGS—RACISTS

Should people prejudiced against any racial or ethnic group be allowed to hold public meetings?
[See V015 for response categories]

V018   POLITICAL TOLERANCE INDEX

[This variable is a count of the number of groups tolerated in V015–V017:]
0.   No groups tolerated
1.   One group
2.   Two groups
3.   All three groups
9.   Don't know

V019   INTEREST IN POLITICS

How interested would you say you personally are in politics?
1.   Very interested
2.   Fairly interested
3.   Not very interested
4.   Not at all interested
9.   Missing data

V020   POLITICAL DISCUSSION—FREQUENCY

When you get together with your friends, relatives or fellow workers how often do you discuss politics?
1.   Often
2.   Sometimes
3.   Rarely
4.   Never
9.   Missing data

V021   POL DISCUSSION—CONVINCE FRIENDS

When you hold a strong opinion about politics, how often do you try to persuade your friends, relatives or fellow workers to share your views?
1.   Often
2.   Sometimes
3.   Rarely
4.   Never
9.   Missing data

V022   VOTED IN ELECTION

Did you vote in the last national elections
1.   Voted
2.   Did not vote
9.   Missing data

V023   SIGN A PETITION

Here are some different forms of political and social action that people can take. Please indicate, for each of one, whether: you have done any of these things in the past year; you have done it in the more distant past; you have not done it but might do it; or have not done it and would never, under any circumstances, do it. Signed a petition?
1.   Have done in the past year
2.   Have done in the more distant past
3.   Have not done, but might do it
4.   Have not done, and would never do it
9.   Missing data

V024   BOYCOTT CERTAIN PRODUCTS

(Have you) Boycotted, or deliberately bought, certain products for political, ethical, or environmental reasons:
[See V023 for response categories]

V025   PARTICIPATE IN DEMONSTRATION

(Have you) Took part in a demonstration?
[See V023 for response categories]

V026   ATTEND POLITICAL MEETING

(Have you) Attended a political meeting or rally?
[See V023 for response categories]

V027   CONTACT POLITICIAN

(Have you) Contacted, or attempt to contact, a politician or a civil servant to express your views?
[See V023 for response categories]

V028   DONATE MONEY

(Have you) Donated money or raised funds for a social or political activity?
[See V023 for response categories]

V029 CONTACT MEDIA

(Have you) Contacted or appeared in the media to express your views?
[See V023 for response categories]

V030 JOIN INTERNET FORUM

(Have you) Joined an Internet political forum or discussion group?
[See V023 for response categories]

V031 PROTEST INDEX

[This variable is a count of the number of protest activities the respondent has done in last year V023–V025, V030.]
0.   No protest activities
1.   One
2.   Two
3.   Three or more
9.   Missing data

V032 CONVENTIONAL PARTICIPATION INDEX

[This variable is a count of the number of nonprotest activities the respondent has done in V022, V027–V029.]
0.   No political activities
1.   One
2.   Two
3.   Three or more
9.   Missing data

V033 TOTAL PARTICIPATION INDEX

[This variable is a count of the number of all political activities the respondent has done in V023–V030.]
0.   No activities
1.   One
2.   Two
3.   Three
4.   Four
4.   Five or more
9.   Missing data

V034   BELONG TO POLITICAL PARTY

People sometimes belong to different kinds of groups or associations.
For each type of group, please indicate whether you: belong and actively participate; belong but don't actively participate; used to belong but do not any more; or have never belonged to it. A political party:
1.   Belong and actively participate
2.   Belong but don't participate
3.   Used to belong
4.   Never belonged
9.   Don't know

V035   BELONG TO TRADE UNION

(Belong to) A trade union, business, or professional association?
[See V034 for response categories]

V036   BELONG TO CHURCH

(Belong to) A church or other religious organization?
[See V034 for response categories]

V037   BELONG TO SPORTS GROUP

(Belong to) A sports, leisure, or cultural group?
[See V034 for response categories]

V038   BELONG TO OTHER GROUP

(Belong to) Another voluntary association?
[See V034 for response categories]

V039   NUMBER OF GROUPS

Number of organizations to which the respondent belongs (V034–V038):
0.   No group
1.   One group
2.   Two groups
3.   Three or more groups
9.   Missing data

V040   ADEQUATE LIVING STANDARD

There are different opinions about people's rights in a democracy. On a scale of 1 to 7, where 1 is not at all important and 7 is very important, how important is it that all citizens have an adequate standard of living?
1.   Not at all important (1–3)
2.   Somewhat important (4–5)

3.   Important (6)
4.   Very important (7)
9.   Don't know

V041   GOVERNMENT RESPECT MINORITIES

(How important) that government authorities respect and protect the rights of minorities?
[See V040 for response categories]

V042   GOVERNMENT EQUAL TREATMENT

(How important) that government authorities treat everybody equally regardless of their position in society?
[See V040 for response categories]

V043   CITIZEN ORIENTED DECISIONS

(How important) that politicians take into account the views of citizens before making decisions?
[See V040 for response categories]

V044   CITIZENS INVOLVED IN DECISIONS

(How important) that people be given more opportunities to participate in public decision making?
[See V040 for response categories]

V045   CIVIL DISOBEDIENCE ACTS

(How important) that citizens may engage in acts of civil disobedience when they oppose government actions?
[See V040 for response categories]

V046   DEMOCRATIC RIGHTS INDEX

[This variable is a count of the number of all democratic rights items that the respondent rated as very important in V040–V044; V045 is not included.]
0.   No items mentioned
1.   One item
2.   Two items
3.   Three items
4.   Four items
5.   Five items mentioned
9.   Missing data

V047   NO INFLUENCE ON WHAT GOVT DOES

To what extent do you agree or disagree with the following statements:
People like me don't have any say about what the government does?
1.   Strongly agree
2.   Agree
3.   Neither agree/disagree
4.   Disagree
5.   Strongly disagree
9.   Missing data

V048   GOVERNMENT DOESNT CARE WHAT I THINK

(Do you agree or disagree) I don't think the government cares much what
people like me think?
[See V047 for response categories]

V049   GOVERNMENT RESPONSIVE INDEX

The variable measures feelings that the government is responsive. [The variable is a count of the number of efficacious replies (disagree or strongly disagree for V047–V048.]
0.   None (low)
1.   One
3.   Two (high)
9.   Missing data

V050   GOOD UNDERSTANDING OF ISSUES

(Do you agree or disagree) I feel I have a pretty good understanding of the
important political issues facing (COUNTRY)?
[See V047 for response categories]

V051   MOST PEOPLE ARE BETTER INFORMED

(Do you agree or disagree) I think most people in (COUNTRY) are better informed about politics and government than I am?
[See V047 for response categories]

V052   PERSONAL EFFICACY INDEX

The variable measures feelings of personal efficacy [The variable is a count of
the number of efficacious replies for V050–V051.]
0.   None (low)
1.   One
3.   Two (high)
9.   Missing data

V053   UNJUST LAW LIKELY ACTION

Suppose a law were being considered by parliament that you considered to be unjust or harmful. If such a case arose, how likely is it that you, acting alone or together with others, would be able to try to do something about it?
1. Very likely
2. Fairly likely
3. Not very likely
4. Not at all likely
9. Missing data

V054   UNJUST LAW LIKELY ATTENTION

Suppose a law were being considered by parliament that you considered to be unjust or harmful. If you made an effort, how likely is it that parliament would give serious attention to your demands?
1. Very likely
2. Fairly likely
3. Not very likely
4. Not at all likely
9. Missing data

V055   CAN TRUST PEOPLE IN GOVERNMENT

To what extent do you agree or disagree with the following statements?
Most of the time we can trust people in government to do what is right.
1. Strongly agree
2. Agree
3. Neither agree/disagree
4. Disagree
5. Strongly disagree
9. Missing data

V056   POLITICIANS ONLY PROFIT

(Do you agree or disagree) Most politicians are in politics only for what they can get out of it personally?
1. Strongly agree
2. Agree
3. Neither agree/disagree
4. Disagree
5. Strongly disagree
9. Missing data

V057   PEOPLE TAKE ADVANTAGE

How often do you think that people would try to take advantage of you if they got the chance, and how often would they try to be fair?
1.   Advantage all the time
2.   Advantage most of time
3.   Fair most of time
4.   Fair all the time
9.   Missing data

V058   PEOPLE CAN BE TRUSTED

Generally speaking, would you say that people can be trusted or that you can't be too careful in dealing with people?
1.   Always trust
2.   Usually trust
3.   Usually be careful
4.   Always be careful
9.   Missing data

V059   DEMOCRACY TODAY

On the whole, on a scale of 0 to 10, where 0 is very poorly and 10 is very well, how well does democracy work in (COUNTRY) today?
1.   Very poorly (0–3)
2.   Poorly (4, 5, 6)
3.   Well (7, 8)
4.   Very well (9, 10)
9.   Don't know

V060   DEMOCRACY 10 YEARS AGO

And what about 10 years ago? How well did democracy work in (COUNTRY) then?
[See V059 for response categories]

V061   DEMOCRACY 10 YEARS FUTURE

And how about 10 years from now? How well do you think democracy will work in (COUNTRY)?
[See V059 for response categories]

V062   GOVERNMENT RESTRICT RIGHTS

Here are some views regarding (COUNTRY's) political system. Which of these statements is closer to your view?
1. Under no circumstances should democratic rights be restricted by government
2. When the government thinks it is necessary it should restrict democratic rights
9. Missing data

V063   OPINION UNITED NATIONS

Now we would like to ask your opinion about international issues. Thinking about the United Nations, which comes closest to your view?
1. Too much power
2. Right amount of power
3. Too little power
9. Missing data

V064   OPINION INTERNAT ORGANIZATIONS

Which of these two statements comes closer to your view?
1. In international organizations, decisions should be left to national government representatives
2. In international organizations, citizens' organizations should be involved directly in the decision-making process
9. Missing data

V065   OPINION UN INTERVENTION

Which of these two statements comes closer to your view?
1. If a country seriously violates human rights, the United Nations should intervene
2. Even if human rights are seriously violated, the country's sovereignty must be respected, and the United Nations should not intervene
4. Missing data

V066   PARTIES ENCOURAGE ACTIVITY

Thinking now about politics in (COUNTRY), to what extent do you agree or disagree with the following statements? Political parties encourage people to become active in politics
1. Strongly agree
2. Agree
3. Neither agree/disagree
4. Disagree
5. Strongly disagree
9. Missing data

V067   PARTIES—NO REAL CHOICES

(Do you agree or disagree) Political parties do not give voters real policy choices
[See V066 for response categories]

V068   REFERENDUM A GOOD METHOD

(Do you agree or disagree) Referendums are a good way to decide important political questions
[See V066 for response categories]

V069   LAST ELECTION HONEST

Thinking of the last national election in (COUNTRY), how honest was it regarding the counting and reporting of the votes?
1.   Very honest
2.   Somewhat honest
3.   Neither honest nor dishonest
4.   Somewhat dishonest
5.   Very dishonest
9.   Missing data

V070   LAST ELECTION FAIR

Thinking of the last national election in (COUNTRY), how fair was it regarding the opportunities of the candidates and parties to campaign?
1.   Very fair
2.   Somewhat fair
3.   Neither fair nor unfair
4.   Somewhat unfair
5.   Very unfair
9.   Missing data

V071   LEFT/RIGHT PARTY PREFERENCE

This item measures the respondent's party preference. Different questions were used in each nation that either tapped general party preference or current vote choice. This variable recodes responses into either Left or Right party preference.
1.   Left party
2.   Right party
9.   Missing data (including no party preference)

V072A PARTY—UNITED STATES

Generally speaking, do you usually think of yourself as a Republican, Democrat, Independent, or what? (If Republican or Democrat) Would you call yourself a strong or not a very strong Republican or Democrat? (If Independent) Do you think of yourself as closer to the Republican or Democratic party?

1.   Strong Democrat
2.   Weak Democrat
3.   Independent—Lean Democrat
4.   Independent
5.   Independent—Lean Republican
6.   Weak Republican
7.   Strong Republican
9.   Missing data (including no party preference)

V072B   PARTY—BRITAIN

If there were a general election tomorrow, which political party do you think you would be most likely to support?

1.   Conservatives
2.   Labour
3.   Liberal Democrats
6.   Scottish National Party (SNP)
7.   Plaid Cymru
8.   Greens
9.   Missing data (including no party preference)

V072C   PARTY—FRANCE

Can you tell me of which party or political movement you feel the closest or at least the least far away?

1.   Communist party (PCF)
2.   Extreme Left
3.   Socialist party (PS)
4.   Greens (Verts)
5.   Union for French Democracy (UDF)
6.   UMP/RPR (Gaullist party)
7.   National Front (FN)
9.   Missing data (including no party preference)

V072D   PARTY—GERMANY

If there is a general election next Sunday, which party would you vote for with your second vote (for a party)?

1.   Christian Democrats (CDU/CSU)
2.   Social Democrats (SPD)

3.   Free Democrats (FDP
4.   Greens
5.   Republikaner (REP)
6.   Party of Democratic Socialism (PDS)
9.   Missing data (including no party preference)

V073   PUBLIC SERVICE COMMITTED TO PUBLIC

Thinking of the public service in (COUNTRY), how committed is it to serve the people?
1.   Very committed
2.   Somewhat committed
3.   Not very committed
4.   Not at all committed
9.   Missing data

V074   PUBLIC SERVICE CORRECTS MISTAKES

When the public service makes serious mistakes in (COUNTRY) how likely is it that they will be corrected?
1.   Very likely
2.   Somewhat likely
3.   Not very likely
4.   Not at all likely
9.   Missing data

V075   PUBLIC SERVICE CORRUPT

How widespread do you think corruption is in the public service in (COUNTRY)?
1.   Hardly anyone is involved
2.   A small number of people are involved
3.   A moderate number of people are involved
4.   A lot of people are involved
5.   Almost everyone is involved
9.   Missing data

V076   GENDER

Sex of respondent:
1.   Male
2.   Female
9.   Missing data

V077   GENERATION

Can you tell me your year of birth, please? 19___ This means you are ____ years old. (We code generation not by when respondent was born, but when they reached age 18.)

1.   Pre–World War II (age 77 and over in 2004)
2.   Postwar Boomers (age 62–76)
3.   Flower Generation (age 47–61)
4.   Generation X (age 32–46)
5.   Generation Y (up to age 31)
9.   Missing data

V078   MARITAL STATUS

Are you currently . . . (READ OUT AND CODE ONE ONLY)

1.   Married/Living together as married
2.   Widowed
3.   Divorced
4.   Separated but married
5.   Single, never married
9.   Missing data

V079   STEADY LIFE-PARTNER

Do you live together with a steady partner?

1.   Yes
2.   No
9.   Missing data

V080   EDUCATION LEVEL

What is the highest educational level that you have attained? (each nation used differently worded questions):

1.   Primary education or less
2.   Primary school plus
3.   Complete secondary technical
4.   Secondary school plus
5.   University with degree
9.   Missing data

V081   EMPLOYMENT STATUS

Respondent: Current employment status, current economic position, main source of living:

1.   Full time paid employment
2.   Part time
3.   Retired/pensioned

5.   Housewife not otherwise employed
6.   Student
7.   Unemployed
9.   Missing data

V082   WEEKLY HOURS

How many hours did you work last week, how many hours do you usually work a week, at all jobs?
1.   1–20 hours
2.   21–30 hours
3.   31–40 hours
5.   40 or more hours
9.   Missing data; not employed

V083   R OCCUPATION

What kind of work do/did you normally do? What do/did you actually do in that job? [ILO/ISCO 1988 coding]:
1.   Professional
2.   Technical/clerical
3.   Services/sales
4.   Manual worker
9.   Missing data; other occupation; not employed

V084   R MIDDLE/WORKING CLASS

[This variable collapses the categories of V083.]
1.   Middle class (codes 1–3)
2.   Working class (code 4)
9.   Other occupations; no answer

V085   PUBLIC/PRIVATE SECTOR

Do you work at present or did you work in your last job in the private or public sector?
1.   Work for government
2.   Public firm
3.   Private firm
4.   Self-employed
9.   Missing data; not employed

V086   SUPERVISE OTHERS

In your main job, do you supervise anyone or are you directly responsible for the work of other people?
1.   Yes
2.   No
9.   Missing data; not employed

V087   UNION MEMBER

Are you a member of trade unions at present?
1.   Currently member
2.   One member
3.   Never member
9.   Missing data; not employed

V088   SPOUSE EMPLOYMENT

Spouse: Current employment status, current economic position, main source of living:
1.   Full time paid employment
2.   Part time
3.   Retired/pensioned
5.   Housewife not otherwise employed
6.   Student
7.   Unemployed
9.   Missing data

V089   SPOUSE OCCUPATION

What kind of work does/did your spouse normally do? What does/did your spouse actually do in that job? [ILO/ISCO 1988 codes]
1.   Professional
2.   Technical/clerical
3.   Services/sales
4.   Manual worker
9.   Missing data; other occupation; not employed

V090   SPOUSE MIDDLE/WORKING CLASS

[This variable collapses the categories of V089.]
1.   Middle class (codes 1–3)
2.   Working class (code 4)
9.   Other occupations; no answer

V091   SPOUSE PUBLIC/PRIVATE

Do you work at present or did you work in your last job in the private or public sector?
1.   Work for government
2.   Public firm
3.   Private firm
4.   Self-employed
9.   Missing data; not employed

V092   R INCOME

Did you earn any income from the job you worked in 2003?
1.   Lowest quartile
2.   Second quartile
3.   Third quartile
4.   Highest quartile
9.   Missing data; not employed

V093   NUMBER OF PEOPLE

What is the composition of your household?
1.   One
2.   Two
3.   Three or four
4.   Five or more persons
9.   Missing data

V094   HOUSEHOLD COMPOSITION

What is the composition of your household?
1.   One adult, no children
2.   Two adults, no children
3.   One adult, children
4.   Two adults, children
5.   Other composition
9.   Missing data; not employed

V095   RELIGION

(IF Religious, denomination:) Which one?
1.   No religion
2.   Roman Catholic
3.   Protestant
4.   Jewish
5.   Other religion
9.   Missing data

V096   RELIGIOUS ATTENDANCE

How often do you attend religious services?
1.   Weekly or more often
2.   Monthly or more often
3.   Less frequently
4.   Never
9.   Missing data

V097   SOCIAL STATUS

In our society there are groups of people which tend to be towards the top and groups which tend to be towards the bottom. Below is a scale that runs top to bottom. Where would you put yourself on this scale?
1.   Lowest (1–3)
2.   Low-middle (4–5)
3.   Middle-high (6–7)
4.   High (8–10)
9.   Missing data; not asked in Britain

V98A   REGION—USA

USA: Region where the interview was conducted:
0.   Not available: all other countries
1.   New England
2.   Middle Atlantic
3.   East North Central
4.   West North Central
5.   South Atlantic
6.   East South Central
7.   West South Central
8.   Mountain
9.   Pacific

V098B   REGION—BRITAIN

Britain: Region where interview was conducted:
0.   Not available: all other countries
1.   Scotland
2.   North, North West, Yorkshire Hbs
3.   West, East Midlands
4.   Wales
5.   East Anglia, South West, SE
6.   Greater London

V098C   REGION—FRANCE

France: Region where interview was conducted:
0. Missing data; other nation
1. Paris Basin
2. Center-East
3. East
4. Ile de France
5. Mediterranean
6. North
7. West
8. South West

V098D   REGION—GERMANY

Region (Land) in Germany where interview was conducted:
0. Not available: all other countries
1. Schleswig-Holstein
2. Hamburg
3. Niedersachsen
4. Bremen
5. Nordrhein-Westfalen
6. Hessen
7. Rheinland-Pfalz
8. Baden-Wuerttemberg
9. Bayern
10. Saarland
11. Berlin-Ost
12. Mecklenburg-Vorpommern
13. Brandenburg
14. Sachsen-Anhalt
15. Thueringen
16. Sachsen
17. Berlin-West

V099A   SIZE OF TOWN—USA

US: Size of town:
0. Missing data; other nations
1. 1–9 million inhabitants
2. 500,000–999,999 inhabitants
3. 100,000–499,999 inhabitants
4. 50,000–99,999 inhabitants
5. 10,000–49,999 inhabitants
6. 1,000–9,999 inhabitants
7. Less than 1,000 inhabitants

V099B   SIZE OF TOWN—BRITAIN

Britain: Size of town:
0.   Missing data; other nations
1.   Less than 3 persons per square hectare
2.   3 to 18.37 persons per square hectare
3.   8.37 to 31.3 persons per square hectare
4.   More than 31.3 persons per square hectare

V099C   SIZE OF TOWN—FRANCE

France: Size of town:
0.   Missing data; other nations
1.   Greater Paris
2.   More than 500,000 inhabitants
3.   100,001–500,000 inhabitants
4.   50,001–100,000 inhabitants
5.   20,001–50,000 inhabitants
6.   10,001–20,000 inhabitants
7.   2,001–10,000 inhabitants
8.   2,000 inhabitants or less

V099D   SIZE OF TOWN—GERMANY

Germany: Size of town:
0.   Missing data; other nations
1.   500,000 inhabitants and more
2.   100,000–499,999 inhabitants
3.   50,000–99,999 inhabitants
4.   20,000–49,999 inhabitants
5.   5,000–19,999 inhabitants
6.   2,000–4,999 inhabitants
7.   Up to 1,999 inhabitants

V100   TYPE OF COMMUNITY

Type of community:
1.   Urban area, a big city
2.   Suburbs of a big city (not used in France)
3.   Small city or town
4.   Country village, farm (not used in USA)
9.   Missing data

V101   RACE/ETHNIC GROUP—USA

Are you Spanish, Hispanic, or Latino? What is your race? Indicate one or more races that you consider yourself to be (region of the world was coded):

1.   American
2.   African
3.   Asian
4.   Hispanic
5.   Native American
9.   Not included in British, French, or German survey

References

Aardal, Bernt, and Pieter van Wijnen. 2005. Issue voting. In *The European Voter*, ed. J. Thomassen. Oxford: Oxford University Press.

Aarts, Kees, André Blais, and Hermann Schmitt. 2005. *Political Leaders and Democratic Elections*. Oxford: Oxford University Press.

Abramson, Paul. 1979. Developing party identification. *American Journal of Political Science* 23:79–96.

Abramson, Paul, John Aldrich, and David Rohde. 2005. *Change and Continuity in the 2004 Elections*. Washington, D.C.: CQ Press.

Abramson, Paul, and Ronald Inglehart. 1995. *Value Change in Global Perspective*. Ann Arbor: University of Michigan Press.

Abramson, Paul, and Charles Ostrom. 1991. Macropartisanship: An empirical reassessment. *American Political Science Review* 85:181–192.

———. 1994. Question wording and partisanship. *Public Opinion Quarterly* 58:21–48.

Alba, Richard, Peter Schmidt, and Martina Wasmer, eds. 2003. *Germans or Foreigners? Attitudes toward Ethnic Minorities in Post-reunification Germany*. New York: Palgrave Macmillan.

Almond, Gabriel, G. Bingham Powell, Russell Dalton, and Kaare Strom, eds. 2007. *Comparative Politics Today*. 9th ed. New York: Longman.

Almond, Gabriel, and Sidney Verba. 1963. *The Civic Culture*. Princeton: Princeton University Press.

Alvarez, R. Michael, and Thad Hall. 2004. *Point, Click, and Vote: The Future of Internet Voting*. Washington, D.C.: Brookings Institution Press.

Anand, Sowmya, and Jon A. Krosnick. 2003. The impact of attitudes toward foreign policy goals on public preferences among presidential candidates. *Presidential Studies Quarterly* 33:31–71.

Anderson, Christopher. 1995. *Blaming the Government: Citizens and the Economy in Five European Democracies*. Armonk, N.Y.: M. E. Sharpe.

———. 2000. Economic voting and political context. *Electoral Studies* 19:151–170.

Anderson, Christopher, and Carsten Zelle, eds. 1998. *Stability and Change in German Elections: How Electorates Merge, Converge, or Collide*. Westport, Conn.: Praeger.

Anderson, Christopher, et al. 2005. *Losers' Consent: Elections and Democratic Legitimacy*. Oxford: Oxford University Press.

Ansolabehere, Stephen, James Snyder, and Charles Stewart. 2001a. The effects of party and preferences on congressional roll-call voting. *Legislative Studies Quarterly* 26:533–572.

———. 2001b. Candidate positioning in the U.S. House elections. *American Journal of Political Science* 45:136–159.

Armingeon, Klaus. 2007. Political participation and associational involvement. In *Citizenship and Involvement in European Democracies*, ed. J. van Deth, J. Montero, and A. Westholm. London: Routledge.

Arnold, Douglas. 1990. *The Logic of Congressional Action*. New Haven: Yale University Press.

Asher, Herbert. 2007. *Polling and the Public: What Every Citizen Should Know*. 7th ed. Washington, D.C.: CQ Press.

Bagehot, Walter. 1978. *The English Constitution*. Oxford: Oxford University Press.

Baker, Kendall, Russell Dalton, and Kai Hildebrandt. 1981. *Germany Transformed: Political Culture and the New Politics*. Cambridge: Harvard University Press.

Barber, Benjamin. 1984. *Strong Democracy*. Berkeley: University of California Press.

Barker, David, and Susan Hansen. 2005. All things considered: Systematic cognitive processing and electoral decision making. *Journal of Politics* 64:319–344.

Barnes, Samuel. 1977. *Representation in Italy*. Chicago: University of Chicago Press.

Barnes, Samuel, Max Kaase, et al. 1979. *Political Action*. Beverly Hills, Calif.: Sage.

Barnum, David, and John Sullivan. 1989. Attitudinal tolerance and political freedom in Britain. *British Journal of Political Science* 19:136–146.

Bartels, Larry. 2000. Partisanship and voting behavior. *American Journal of Political Science* 44:35–50.

———. 2003. Democracy with attitudes. In *Electoral Democracy*, ed. M. MacKuen and G. Rabinowitz. Ann Arbor: University of Michigan Press.

Bartolini, Stefano, and Peter Mair. 1990. *Identity, Competition and Electoral Availability*. New York: Cambridge University Press.

Bauer-Kaase, Petra. 1994. German unification. In *German Unification*, ed. D. Hancock and H. Welsh. Boulder: Westview.

Baum, Matthew. 2003. *Soft News Goes to War: Public Opinion and American Foreign Policy in the New Media Age*. Princeton: Princeton University Press.

Baum, Matthew, and Angela Jamison. 2005. Oprah effect: How soft news helps inattentive citizens vote consistently. *Journal of Politics* 68:946–959.

Bean, Clive, and Anthony Mughan. 1989. Leadership effects in parliamentary elections in Australia and Britain. *American Political Science Review* 83:1165–79.

Beck, Paul Allen, et al. 1992. Patterns and sources of ticket-splitting in subpresidential voting. *American Political Science Review* 86:916–928.

Beedham, Brian. 1993. What next for democracy? *The Economist*, September 11; special supplement: *The Future Surveyed*.

Bell, Daniel. 1973. *The Coming of Post-industrial Society*. New York: Basic Books.

Benoit, Kenneth, and Michael Laver. 2006. *Party Policy in Modern Democracies*. New York: Routledge.

Berelson, Bernard, Paul Lazarsfeld, and William McPhee. 1954. *Voting*. Chicago: University of Chicago Press.

Berger, Manfred. 1977. Stabilität und Intensität von Parteieneigung. *Politische Vierteljahresschrift* 18:501–509.

Berglund, Frode, et al. 2005. Partisanship: Causes and consequences. In *The European Voter*, ed. J. Thomassen. Oxford: Oxford University Press.

Berry, Jeffrey. 1999. *The New Liberalism: The Rising Power of Citizen Groups*. Washington, D.C.: Brookings Institution Press.

Bimber, Bruce. 2003. *Information and American Democracy: Technology in the Evolution of Political Power*. New York: Cambridge University Press.

Bimber, Bruce, and Richard Davis. 2003. *The Internet and U.S. Elections*. New York: Oxford University Press.

Bishop, George, and Kathleen Frankovic. 1981. Ideological consensus and constraint among party leaders and followers in the 1978 election. *Micropolitics* 1:87–111.

Blais, André. 2000. *To Vote or Not to Vote: The Merits and Limits of Rational Choice Theory*. Pittsburgh: University of Pittsburgh Press.

Bok, Derek. 1996. *The State of the Nation: Government and the Quest for a Better Society*. Cambridge: Harvard University Press.

———. 2001. *The Trouble with Government*. Cambridge: Harvard University Press.

Borre, Ole, and Daniel Katz. 1973. Party identification and its motivational base in a multiparty system. *Scandinavian Political Studies* 8:69–111.

Borre, Ole, and Elinor Scarbrough, eds. 1995. *The Scope of Government*. Oxford: Oxford University Press.

Bowler, Shaun. 2000. Party cohesion. In *Parties without Partisans*, ed. R. Dalton and M. Wattenberg. Oxford: Oxford University Press.

Bowler, Shaun, and Todd Donovan. 1998. *Demanding Choices: Opinion, Voting, and Direct Democracy*. Ann Arbor: University of Michigan Press.

Bowler, Shaun, David Farrell, and Richard Katz, eds. 1999. *Party Discipline and Parliamentary Government*. Columbus: Ohio State University Press.

Bowler, Shaun, and Amihai Glazer, eds. 2008. *Directing Democracy*. New York: Macmillan Palgrave.

Boy, Daniel, and Nonna Mayer, eds. 1993. *The French Voter Decides*. Ann Arbor: University of Michigan Press.

Braithwaite, Valerie, T. Makkai, and Y. Pittelkow. 1996. Inglehart's materialism-postmaterialism concept: Clarifying the dimensionality debate through Rokeach's model of social values. *Journal of Applied Social Psychology* 26:1536–55.

Brettschneider, Frank. 1996. Public opinion and parliamentary action: Responsiveness of the German Bundestag in comparative perspective. *International Journal of Public Opinion Research* 8:292–311.

Brody, Richard. 1978. The puzzle of political participation in America. In *The New American Political System,* ed. A. King. Washington, D.C.: American Enterprise Institute.

———, et al. 1994. Accounting for divided government. In M. Kent Jennings and T. Mann, eds., *Elections at Home and Abroad.* Ann Arbor: University of Michigan Press.

Bromley, Catherine, and John Curtice. 2003. Where have all the voters gone? In Alison Park et al., *British Social Attitudes, 19th Report.* Newbury Park, Calif.: Sage.

Bromley, Catherine, John Curtice, and Ben Seyd. 2002. Confidence in government. In Roger Jowell et al., *British Social Attitude Survey.* Brookfield, Vt.: Dartmouth Publishing.

Bryce, James. 1921. *Modern Democracies.* Vol. 1. New York: Macmillan.

Budge, Ian, Ivor Crewe, and David Farlie, eds. 1976. *Party Identification and Beyond.* New York: Wiley.

Burstein, Paul. 2003. The impact of public opinion on public policy: A review and an agenda. *Political Research Quarterly* 56(1): 29–40.

Butler, David, and Donald Stokes. 1969. *Political Change in Britain.* New York: St. Martin's.

Cain, Bruce, Russell Dalton, and Susan Scarrow, eds. 2003. *Democracy Transformed? Expanding Political Access in Advanced Industrial Democracies.* Oxford: Oxford University Press.

Cain, Bruce, Sergio Fabrinni, and Patrick Egan. 2003. Toward more open democracies: The expansion of freedom of information laws. In *Democracy Transformed?* eds. B. Cain, R. Dalton, and S. Scarrow. Oxford: Oxford University Press.

Campbell, Angus, et al. 1960. *The American Voter.* New York: Wiley.

———. 1966. *Elections and the Political Order.* New York: Wiley.

Campbell, David. 2006. *Why We Vote: How Schools and Communities Shape our Civic Life.* Princeton: Princeton University Press.

Cantril, Hadley. 1965. *The Patterns of Human Concern.* New Brunswick, N.J.: Rutgers University Press.

Caplan, Bryan. 2007. *The Myth of the Rational Voter: Why Democracies Choose Bad Policies.* Princeton: Princeton University Press.

Carmines, Edward, and James Stimson. 1980. The two faces of issue voting. *American Political Science Review* 74:78–91.

Carty, Kenneth. 2002. Canada's nineteenth-century cadre parties at the millennium. In *Political Parties in Advanced Industrial Democracies,* ed. P. Webb, D. Farrell, and I. Holliday. Oxford: Oxford University Press.

Caul, Miki, and Mark Gray. 2000. From platform declarations to policy outcomes. In *Parties without Partisans,* ed. R. Dalton and M. Wattenberg. Oxford: Oxford University Press.

Central Intelligence Agency. 2007. *World Fact Book.* http://www.odci.gov/cia/publications/factbook/index.html.

Charlot, Monica. 1980. Women in politics in France. In *The French National Assembly Elections of 1978*, ed. H. Penniman. Washington, D.C.: American Enterprise Institute.

Cichowski, Rachel, and Alec Stone Sweet. 2003. Participation, representative democracy, and the courts. In *Democracy Transformed?* ed. B. Cain, R. Dalton, and S. Scarrow. Oxford: Oxford University Press.

Citrin, Jack. 1974. Comment. *American Political Science Review* 68: 973–988.

Claggett, William, and Philip Pollack. 2006. Models of political participation revisited. *Political Research Quarterly* 59:593–600.

Clark, Terry Nichols, and Seymour Martin Lipset, eds. 2001. *The Breakdown of Class Politics: A Debate on Post-industrial Stratification*. Baltimore: Johns Hopkins University Press.

Clark, Terry Nichols, and Vincent Hoffmann-Martinot, eds. 1998. *The New Political Culture*. Boulder: Westview.

Clarke, Harold, and Nitish Dutt. 1991. Measuring value change in western industrialized societies. *American Political Science Review* 85:905–920.

Clarke, Harold, and Marianne Stewart. 1998. The decline of parties in the minds of citizens. *Annual Review of Political Science* 1:357–378.

Clarke, Harold, et al. 1999. The effect of economic priorities on the measurement of value change: New experimental evidence. *American Political Science Review* 93:637–647.

———. 2004. *Political Choice in Britain*. Oxford: Oxford University Press.

———. 2008. *Performance Politics: The British Voter*. New York: Cambridge University Press.

Conover, Pamela, and Stanley Feldman. 1984. How people organize the political world. *American Journal of Political Science* 28:95–126.

Conradt, David. 2004. *The German Polity*. 8th ed. New York: Longman.

Converse, Philip. 1964. The nature of belief systems in mass publics. In *Ideology and Discontent*, ed. D. Apter. New York: Free Press.

———. 1966. The normal vote. In *Elections and the Political Order*. Angus Campbell et al. New York: Wiley.

———. 1969. Of time and partisan stability. *Comparative Political Studies* 2:139–171.

———. 1970. Attitudes and nonattitudes. In *The Quantitative Analysis of Social Problems*, ed. E. Tufte. Reading, Mass.: Addison-Wesley.

———. 1972. Change in the American electorate. In *The Human Meaning of Social Change*, ed. A. Campbell and P. Converse. New York: Russell Sage Foundation.

———. 1976. *The Dynamics of Party Support*. Beverly Hills, Calif.: Sage.

———. 1990. Popular representation and the distribution of information. In *Information and Democratic Processes*, ed. J. Ferejohn and J. Kuklinski. Urbana: University of Illinois Press.

Converse, Philip, and Greg Markus. 1979. Plus ça change . . . The new CPS election study panel. *American Political Science Review* 73:32–49.

Converse, Philip, and Roy Pierce. 1986. *Representation in France.* Cambridge: Harvard University Press.

Conway, Mary Margaret. 2000. *Political Participation in the United States.* 3rd ed. Washington, D.C.: CQ Press.

Crepaz, Markus. 1990. The impact of party polarization and postmaterialism on voter turnout. *European Journal of Political Research* 18:183–205.

Crewe, Ivor. 1981. Electoral participation. In *Democracy at the Polls,* ed. D. Butler et al. Washington, D.C.: American Enterprise Institute.

———. 1995. Oral evidence in "Standards in Public Life: First Report of the Committee on Standards in Public Life." In vol. 2 of *Transcripts of Evidence,* CM 2850-II. London: HMSO.

Crewe, Ivor, and J. Denver, eds. 1985. *Electoral Change.* Oxford: Oxford University Press.

Crewe, Ivor, and Donald Searing. 1988. Mrs. Thatcher's crusade: Conservatism in Britain, 1972–1986. In *The Resurgence of Conservatism in the Anglo-American Countries,* ed. B. Cooper et al. Durham: Duke University Press.

Crozier, Michel, Samuel Huntington, and Joji Watanuki. 1975. *The Crisis of Democracy.* New York: New York University Press.

Curtice, John, and Sören Holmberg. 2005. Leadership and voting decision. In *The European Voter,* ed. J. Thomassen. Oxford: Oxford University Press.

Curtice, John, Stephen Fisher, and Laurence Lessard-Phillips. 2007. Proportional representation and the disappearing voter. In *British Social Attitudes: Perspectives on a Changing Society,* ed. A. Park et al. London: Sage Publications.

Curtice, John, and Roger Jowell. 1997. Trust in the political system. In *British Social Attitudes—the 14th Report.,* eds. R. Jowell et al. Brookfield, Vt.: Dartmouth Publishing.

Curtice, John, and Ben Seyd. 2002. Is there a crisis of political participation? In *British Social Attitudes: Public Policy, Social Ties,* ed. A. Park et al. Newbury Park, Calif.: Sage.

Cyert, Richard, and James March. 1963. *A Behavioral Theory of the Firm.* Englewood Cliffs, N.J.: Prentice-Hall.

Dahl, Robert. 1971. *Polyarchy.* New Haven: Yale University Press.

Dahrendorf, Ralf. 1975. Excerpts from remarks on the ungovernability study. In *The Crisis of Democracy,* M. Crozier et al. New York: New York University Press.

———. 2000. Afterword. In *Disaffected Democracies,* ed. S. Pharr and R. Putnam. Princeton: Princeton University Press.

Dalton, Russell. 1984. Cognitive mobilization and partisan dealignment in advanced industrial democracies. *Journal of Politics* 46:264–284.

———. 1985. Political parties and political representation. *Comparative Political Studies* 17:267–299.

———. 2000. The decline of party identification. In *Parties without Partisans*, eds. R. Dalton and M. Wattenberg. Oxford: Oxford University Press.

———. 2004. *Democratic Challenges, Democratic Choices: The Erosion of Political Support in Advanced Industrial Democracies*. Oxford: Oxford University Press.

———. 2007a. *The Good Citizen: How a Younger Generation Is Reshaping American Politics*. Washington, D.C.: CQ Press.

———. 2007b. Politics in Germany. In *Comparative Politics Today*, ed. G. Almond, G. Powell, R. Dalton, and K. Strom. New York: Addison Wesley Longman.

———. 2007c. Partisan mobilization, cognitive mobilization and the changing American electorate. *Electoral Studies* 26:274–286.

———. 2008. Environmentalism and party alignments: A research note on electoral change in advanced industrial democracies. *European Journal of Political Research*.

Dalton, Russell, and Wilhelm Bürklin. 2003. Wähler als Wandervögel: Dealignment and the German voter. *German Politics and Society* 21: 57–75.

Dalton, Russell, Scott Flanagan, and Paul Beck, eds. 1984. *Electoral Change in Advanced Industrial Democracies*. Princeton: Princeton University Press.

Dalton, Russell, and Mark Gray. 2003. Expanding the electoral marketplace. In *Democracy Transformed?* ed. B. Cain, R. Dalton, and S. Scarrow. Oxford: Oxford University Press.

Dalton, Russell, and Hans-Dieter Klingemann, eds. 2007. *The Oxford Handbook of Political Behavior*. Oxford: Oxford University Press.

Dalton, Russell, and Robert Rohrschneider. 1998. The greening of Europe: Environmental values and environmental behavior. In *British—and European—Social Attitudes: The 15th Report*, ed. Jowell et al. Brookfield, Vt.: Ashgate.

Dalton, Russell, and Martin Wattenberg. 1993. The not so simple act of voting. In *The State of the Discipline*, ed. A. Finifter. Washington, D.C.: American Political Science Association.

———, eds. 2000. *Parties without Partisans: Political Change in Advanced Industrial Democracies*. Oxford: Oxford University Press.

Dalton, Russell, and Steve Weldon. 2005. Public images of political parties: A necessary evil? *West European Politics* 28: 931–951.

Damon, William. 2001. To not fade away: Restoring civil identity among the young. In *Making Good Citizens: Education and Civil Society*, ed. D. Ravitch and J. Viteritti. New Haven: Yale University Press, 2001.

Delli Carpini, Michael, and Scott Keeter. 1996. *What Americans Know about Politics and Why It Matters*. New Haven: Yale University Press.

Downs, Anthony. 1957. *An Economic Theory of Democracy*. New York: Wiley.

Duch, Raymond, and Michael Taylor. 1993. Postmaterialism and the economic condition. *American Journal of Political Science* 37:747–779.

———. 1994. A reply to Abramson and Inglehart's "Education, security, and postmaterialism." *American Journal of Political Science* 38:815–824.

Dye, Thomas, and Harmon Ziegler. 1970. *The Irony of Democracy.* Belmont, Calif.: Duxbury.

Easton, David. 1965. *A Systems Analysis of Political Life.* New York: Wiley.

———. 1975. A reassessment of the concept of political support. *British Journal of Political Science* 5:435–457.

Easton, David, and Jack Dennis. 1969. *Children in the Political System.* New York: McGraw-Hill.

Eichenberg, Richard. 2007. Citizen opinion on foreign policy and world politics. In *The Oxford Handbook of Political Behavior,* ed. R. Dalton and H. Klingemann. Oxford: Oxford University Press.

Elkins, Zachary, and John Sides. 2004. In search of the unified nation-state: National attachment among distinctive citizens. Paper presented at the annual meeting of the Midwest Political Science Association, Chicago.

Erikson, Robert, Michael MacKuen, and James Stimson. 2002. *The Macro Polity.* Cambridge: Cambridge University Press.

Erikson, Robert, and Kent Tedin. 2001. *American Public Opinion.* 6th ed. New York: Allyn and Bacon.

Erikson, Robert, Gerald Wright, and John McIver. 1994. *State House Democracy: Public Opinion and Public Policy in the American States.* New York: Cambridge University Press.

Evans, Geoffrey, ed. 1999. *The End of Class Politics? Class Voting in Comparative Context.* New York: Oxford University Press.

———. 2000. The continued significance of class voting. *Annual Review of Political Science* 3:401–417.

Evans, Jocelyn. 2004. *Voters and Voting: An Introduction.* Thousand Oaks, Calif.: Sage.

Farah, Barbara. 1980. *Political representation in West Germany.* PhD diss., University of Michigan.

Feldman, Stanley. 1989. Reliability and stability of policy positions. *Political Analysis* 1:25–60.

Fiorina, Morris. 1981. *Retrospective Voting in American National Elections.* New Haven: Yale University Press.

———. 2002. Parties and partisanship: A forty year retrospective. *Political Behavior* 24:93–115.

———. 2005. *Culture War? The Myth of a Polarized America.* New York: Pearson Longman.

Flanagan, Scott. 1982. Changing values in advanced industrial society. *Comparative Political Studies* 14:403–444.

———. 1987. Value change in industrial society. *American Political Science Review* 81:1303–19.

Flanagan, Scott, and Aie-Rie Lee. 2003. The new politics, culture wars, and the authoritarian-libertarian value change in advanced industrial democracies. *Comparative Political Studies* 36:235–270.

Florida, Richard, 2003. *The Rise of the Creative Class: And How It's Transforming Work, Leisure, Community, and Everyday Life.* New York: Basic Books.

Franklin, Mark. 2004. *Voter Turnout and the Dynamics of Electoral Competition in Established Democracies since 1945.* New York: Cambridge University Press.

Franklin, Mark, Tom Mackie, and Henry Valen, eds. 1992. *Electoral Change.* New York: Cambridge University Press.

Franklin, Mark, and Christopher Wlezien. 1997. The responsive public: Issue salience, policy change, and preferences for European unification. *Journal of Theoretical Politics* 9:247–263.

———, eds. 2002. *The Future of Election Studies.* Amsterdam: Elsevier.

Friedrich, Walter, and Hartmut Griese. 1990. *Jugend und Jugendforschung in der DDR.* Opladen: Westdeutscher Verlag.

Fuchs, Dieter, and Hans-Dieter Klingemann. 1989. The Left-Right schema. In *Continuities in Political Action,* ed. M. K. Jennings and J. van Deth. Berlin: deGruyter.

———. 1995. Citizens and the state. In *Citizens and the State,* ed. H. Klingemann and D. Fuchs. Oxford: Oxford University Press.

Fuchs, Dieter, and Robert Rohrschneider. 1998. Postmaterialism and electoral choice before and after German unification. *West European Politics* 21:95–116.

Fukuyama, Francis. 1992. *The End of History and the Last Man.* New York: Free Press.

Funk, Carolyn. 1999. Bringing the candidate into models of candidate evaluation. *Journal of Politics* 61:700–720.

Gallagher, Michael, and Pier Vincenzo Uleri, eds. 1996. *The Referendum Experience in Europe.* Basingstoke, Hants.: Macmillan.

Gallup, George. 1976a. *International Public Opinion Polls: Britain.* New York: Random House.

———. 1976b. *International Public Opinion Polls: France.* New York: Random House.

Geer, John. 2005. *Public Opinion and Polling around the World.* 2 vols. Santa Barbara, Calif.: ABC-CLIO.

German Marshall Fund. 2007. *Transatlantic Trends: Key Findings 2007.* www.transatlantictrends.org.

Gershkoff, Amy. 2005. Not "Non-attitudes" but rather "non-measurement." Paper presented at the Southern Political Science Association Meeting, New Orleans.

Glass, David. 1985. Evaluating presidential candidates: Who focuses on their personal attributes? *Public Opinion Quarterly* 49:517–534.

Goldthorpe, John. 1987. *Social Mobility and Class Structure in Modern Britain.* Oxford: Clarendon Press.

Gordon, Stacy, and Gary Segura. 1997. Cross-national variation in the political sophistication of individuals: Capability or choice? *Journal of Politics* 59:126–147.

Gray, Mark, and Miki Caul. 2000. Declining voter turnout in advanced industrial democracies 1950–1997. *Comparative Political Studies* 33: 1091–1122.

Green, Donald, Bradley Palmquist, and Eric Schickler. 2002. *Partisan Hearts and Minds: Political Parties and the Social Identities of Voters.* New Haven: Yale University Press.

Gurr, T. Robert. 1970. *Why Men Rebel.* Princeton: Princeton University Press.

Haegel, Florence. 1993. Partisan ties. In *The French Voter Decides,* ed. D. Boy and N. Mayer. Ann Arbor: University of Michigan Press.

Hall, Peter. 2002. Social capital in Britain. In *Democracies in Flux,* ed. R. Putnam. Oxford: Oxford University Press.

Heath, Anthony, Roger Jowell, and John Curtice. 1991. *Understanding Political Change: The British Voter 1964–1987.* New York: Pergamon.

———. 1994. *Labour's Last Chance: The 1992 Election and Beyond.* Brookfield, Vt.: Dartmouth Publishing.

Heath, Anthony, and Dorren McMahon. 1992. Changes in values. In R. Jowell et al. *British Social Attitudes: The 9th Report.* Brookfield, Vt.: Dartmouth Publishing.

Heath, Anthony, and Roy Pierce. 1992. It was party identification all along. *Electoral Studies* 11:93–105.

Herrera, Cheryl Lyn, Richard Herrera, and Eric R. A. N. Smith. 1992. Public opinion and congressional representation. *Public Opinion Quarterly* 56:185–205.

Herzog, Dietrich, Hilke Rebenstorf, and Bernhard Wessels. 1993. *Parlament und Gesellschaft: Eine Funktionsanalyse der reprasentativen Demokratie.* Opladen: Westdeutscher Verlag.

Hess, Robert, and Judith Torney. 1967. *The Development of Political Attitudes in Children.* Chicago: Aldine.

Hetherington, Marc. 2005. *Why Trust Matters: Declining Political Trust and the Demise of American Liberalism.* Princeton: Princeton University Press.

Hibbing, John, and Elizabeth Theiss-Morse, eds. 2001. *What Is It about Government that Americans Dislike?* New York: Cambridge University Press.

———. 2002. *Stealth Democracy: Americans' Beliefs about How Government Should Work.* New York: Cambridge University Press.

Hollifield, James. 1993. *Immigrants, Markets, and States.* Cambridge: Harvard University Press, 1993.

Holmberg, Sören. 1994. Party identification compared across the Atlantic. In *Elections at Home and Abroad,* ed. M. K. Jennings and T. Mann. Ann Arbor: University of Michigan Press.

Hout, Michael, et al. 1995. The democratic class struggle in the United States, 1948–1992. *American Sociological Review* 60:805–828.

Huntington, Samuel. 1974. Postindustrial politics: How benign will it be? *Comparative Politics* 6:147–177.

———. 1975. The democratic distemper. *Public Interest* 41:9–38.

———. 1981. *American Politics: The Promise of Disharmony.* Cambridge: Harvard University Press.

———. 1984. Will more countries become democratic? *Political Science Quarterly* 99:193–218.

———. 1991. *The Third Wave.* Norman: University of Oklahoma Press.

———. 2004. *Who Are We? The Challenges to America's National Identity.* New York: Simon and Schuster.

Hurwitz, Jon, and Mark Peffley. 1987. How are foreign policy attitudes structured? *American Political Science Review* 81:1099–1120.

Hutchings, Vincent. 2003. *Public Opinion and Democratic Accountability.* Princeton: Princeton University Press.

Ignazi, Piero. 2003. *Extreme Right Parties in Western Europe.* Oxford: Oxford University Press.

Inglehart, Ronald. 1977. *The Silent Revolution.* Princeton: Princeton University Press.

———. 1981. Post-materialism in an environment of insecurity. *American Political Science Review* 75:880–900.

———. 1984. Changing cleavage alignments in Western democracies. In *Electoral Change in Advanced Industrial Democracies,* ed. R. Dalton, S. Flanagan, and P. Beck. Princeton: Princeton University Press.

———. 1990. *Culture Shift in Advanced Industrial Society.* Princeton: Princeton University Press.

———. 1995. Political support for environmental protection. *PS—Political Science and Politics* 28:57–72.

———. 1997. *Modernization and Postmodernization: Cultural, Economic and Political Change in 43 Nations.* Princeton: Princeton University Press.

Inglehart, Ronald, and Pippa Norris. 2003. *A Rising Tide: Gender Equality and Cultural Change around the World.* New York: Cambridge University Press.

Inglehart, Ronald, and Christian Welzel. 2005. *Modernization, Cultural Change, and Democracy: The Human Development Sequence.* New York: Cambridge University Press.

Ingram, Helen, and Steven Smith, eds. 1993. *Public Policy for Democracy.* Washington, D.C.: Brookings Institution Press.

Jackman, Robert. 1972. Political elites, mass publics, and support for democratic principles. *Journal of Politics* 34:753–773.

———. 1987. Political institutions and voter turnout in the industrialized democracies. *American Political Science Review* 81:405–424.

Jacoby, William. 1991. Ideological identification and issue attitudes. *American Journal of Political Science* 35:178–205.

Jelen, Ted, Sue Thomas, and Clyde Wilcox. 1994. The gender gap in comparative perspective. *European Journal of Political Research* 25:171–186.

Jennings, M. Kent. 2007. Political socialization. In *Oxford Handbook of Political Behavior,* ed. R. Dalton and H. Klingemann. Oxford: Oxford University Press.

Jennings, M. Kent, and Thomas Mann, eds. 1994. *Elections at Home and Abroad.* Ann Arbor: University of Michigan Press.

Jennings, M. Kent, and Greg Markus. 1984. Partisan orientations over the long haul. *American Political Science Review* 78:1000–18.

Jennings, M. Kent, and Richard Niemi. 1973. *The Character of Political Adolescence.* Princeton: Princeton University Press.

———. 1981. *Generations and Politics.* Princeton: Princeton University Press.

Jennings, M. Kent, and Jan van Deth, eds. 1989. *Continuities in Political Action.* Berlin: deGruyter.

Jennings, M. Kent, et al. 1979. Generations and families. In *Political Action,* S. Barnes, M. Kaase et al. Beverly Hills, Calif.: Sage.

Johnson, Mark, and Conor Gearty. 2007. Civil liberties and the challenges of terrorism. In *British Social Attitudes: Perspectives on a Changing Society,* ed. A. Park et al. London: Sage Publications.

Jowell, Roger, et al., eds. 1998. *British—and European—Social Attitudes: The 15th Report.* Brookfield, Vt.: Ashgate.

Judis, John, and Ruy Teixeira. 2002. *The Emerging Democratic Majority.* New York: Scribner.

Kaase, Max, and Kenneth Newton. 1998. Commitment to the welfare state. In *British—and European—Social Attitudes: The 15th Report.* ed. R. Jowell et al. Brookfield, Vt.: Ashgate.

Katz, Richard, and Bernhard Wessels, eds. 1999. *The European Parliament, National Parliaments, and European Integration.* Oxford: Oxford University Press.

Keith, Bruce, et al., 1992. *The Myth of the Independent Voter.* Berkeley: University of California Press.

Kepplinger, Hans Mathias. 1996. Skandale und Politikverdrossenheit—ein Langzeitvergleich. In O. Jarren et al., *Medien und Politische Prozeß.* Opladen: Westdeutscher Verlag.

Key, V. O. 1966. *The Responsible Electorate.* Cambridge: Belknap Press.

Kinder, Donald, and D. R. Kiewiet. 1981. Sociotropic politics. *British Journal of Political Science* 11:129–161.

Kinder, Donald, et al. 1980. Presidential prototypes. *Political Behavior* 2:315–337.

Klein, Markus, et al., eds. 2000. *50 Jahre empirische Wahlforschung in Deutschland: Entwicklung, Befunde, Perspektiven, Daten.* Opladen: Westdeutscher Verlag.

Klingemann, Hans-Dieter. 1999. Mapping political support in the 1990s. In *Critical Citizens,* ed. P. Norris. Oxford: Oxford University Press.

————, ed. 2008. *The Comparative Study of Electoral Systems.* Oxford: Oxford University Press.

Klingemann, Hans-Dieter, Richard Hofferbert, and Ian Budge, eds. 1994. *Parties, Policy and Democracy.* Oxford: Oxford University Press.

Klingemann, Hans-Dieter, et al. 2006. *Mapping Policy Preferences II: Estimates for Parties, Electors, and Governments in Eastern Europe, European Union, and OECD 1990–2003.* Oxford: Oxford University Press

Knutsen, Oddborn. 1995a. Left-Right materialist value orientations. In *The Impact of Values,* ed. J. van Deth and E. Scarbrough. New York: Oxford University Press.

————. 1995b. Party choice. In *The Impact of Values,* ed. J. van Deth and E. Scarbrough. New York: Oxford University Press.

————. 2006. *Class Voting in Western Europe: A Comparative Longitudinal Study.* Lanham, Md.: Lexington Books.

Knutsen, Oddbjorn, and Staffan Kumlin. 2005. Value orientations and party choice. In *The European Voter,* ed. J. Thomassen. Oxford: Oxford University Press.

Koch, Achim, Martina Wasmer, and Peter Schmidt, eds. 2001. *Politische Partizipation in der Bundesrepublik Deutschland: Empirische Befunde und theoretische Erklärungen.* Opladen: Leske + Budrich.

Kohut, Andrew, et al. 2000. *The Diminishing Divide: Religion's Changing Role in American Politics.* Washington, D.C.: Brookings Institution Press.

Kornhauser, William. 1959. *The Politics of Mass Society.* New York: Free Press.

Krosnick, Jon. 1990. Government policy and citizen passion: A study of issue publics in contemporary America. *Political Behavior* 12:59–92.

Kuklinski, James, and Buddy Peyton. 2007. Belief systems and political decision-making. In *Oxford Handbook of Political Behavior,* ed. R. Dalton and H. Klingemann. Oxford: Oxford University Press.

Kuklinski, James, and Paul Quirk. 2000. Reconsidering the rationale public. In *Elements of Reason,* ed. A. Lupia, M. McCubbins, and S. Popkin. New York: Cambridge University Press.

Lane, Robert. 1962. *Political Ideology.* New York: Free Press.

————. 1973. Patterns of political belief. In *Handbook of Political Psychology,* ed. J. Knutson. San Francisco: Jossey-Bass.

Langenbacher, Eric, ed. 2006. The 2005 Bundestag elections. Special issue of *German Politics and Society* 24.

Lau, Richard, and David Redlawsk. 2006. *How Voters Decide: Information Processing during Election Campaigns.* New York: Cambridge University Press.

Layman, Geoffrey. 2001. *The Great Divide.* New York: Columbia University Press.

Lazarsfeld, Paul, Bernard Berelson, and Hazel Gaudet. 1948. *The People's Choice.* New York: Columbia University Press.

LeDuc, Lawrence. 1981. The dynamic properties of party identification. *European Journal of Political Research* 9:257–268.

LeDuc, Lawrence, Richard Niemi, and Pippa Norris, eds. 2002. *Comparing Democracies: New Challenges in the Study of Elections and Voting.* 2nd ed. Thousand Oaks, Calif.: Sage.

Leege, David, et al. 2002. *The Politics of Cultural Differences: Social Change and Voter Mobilization Strategies in the Post–New Deal Period.* Princeton: Princeton University Press.

Lewis-Beck, Michael. 1988. *Economics and Elections.* Ann Arbor: University of Michigan Press.

———. ed. 1999. *How France Votes.* New York: Chatham House.

———. et al. 2008. *The American Voter Revisited.* Ann Arbor: University of Michigan Press.

Lewis-Beck, Michael, and Martin Paldam, eds. 2000. *Electoral Studies* 19, special issue, *Economics and Elections.*

Lewis-Beck, Michael, and Andrew Skalaban. 1992. France. In *Electoral Change.* ed. M. Franklin et al. New York: Cambridge University Press.

Lijphart, Arend. 1999. *Patterns of Democracy: Government Forms and Performance in Thirty-six Countries.* New Haven: Yale University Press.

Lippmann, Walter. 1922. *Public Opinion.* New York: Harcourt, Brace.

Lipset, Seymour Martin. 1981. *Political Man: The Social Bases of Politics.* Baltimore: Johns Hopkins University Press.

Lipset, Seymour Martin, and Everett Ladd. 1980. Public opinion and public policy. In *The United States in the 1980s,* ed. P. Duignan and A. Rabushka. Stanford, Calif.: Hoover Press.

Lipset, Seymour Martin, and Stein Rokkan, eds. 1967. *Party Systems and Voter Alignments.* New York: Free Press.

Listhaug, Ola. 2005. Retrospective voting. In *The European Voter,* ed. J. Thomassen. Oxford: Oxford University Press.

Listhaug, Ola, Bernt Aardal, and Ingunn Opheim Ellis. 2008. Institutional variation and political support. In *The Comparative Study of Electoral Systems,* ed. H. Klingemann. Oxford: Oxford University Press.

Lovenduski, Joni, and Pippa Norris, eds. 1996. *Women in Politics.* New York: Oxford University Press.

Lupia, Arthur. 1994. Shortcuts versus encyclopedias. *American Political Science Review* 88:63–76.

Lupia, Arthur, and Mathew McCubbins. 1998. *The Democratic Dilemma: Can Citizens Learn What They Need to Know?* Cambridge: Cambridge University Press.

Lupia, Arthur, Mathew McCubbins, and Samuel Popkin, eds. 2000. *Elements of Reason: Cognitions, Choice and the Bounds of Rationality.* New York: Cambridge University Press.

Macedo, Stephen, et al. 2005. *Democracy at Risk: How Political Choices Undermine Citizen Participation, and What We Can Do About It.* Washington, D.C.: Brookings Institution Press.

MacKuen, Michael, Robert Erikson, and James Stimson. 1989. Macropartisanship. *American Political Science Review* 83:1125–42.

———. 1992. Peasants or Bankers? *American Political Science Review* 86: 597–611.

MacRae, Duncan. 1967. *Parliament, Parties, and Society in France, 1946–1958.* New York: St. Martin's.

Manza, Jeff, and Clem Brooks. 1999. *Social Cleavages and Political Change.* New York: Oxford: Oxford University Press.

Maslow, Abraham. 1954. *Motivations and Personality.* New York: Harper and Row.

Mayer, Nonna. 2000. The decline of political trust in France. Paper presented at the meetings of the International Political Science Association, Quebec, Canada.

Mayer, Nonna, and Vincent Tiberj. 2004. Do issues matter? In *The French Voter,* ed. M. Lewis-Beck. Basingstoke: Palgrave Macmillan.

McAllister, Ian. 1996. Leadership. In *Comparing Democracies,* ed. L. LeDuc, R. Niemi, and P. Norris. Newbury Park, Calif.: Sage.

McClosky, Herbert, and Alida Brill. 1983. *Dimensions of Tolerance: What Americans Think about Civil Liberties.* New York: Russell Sage Foundation.

McCrone, David, and Paula Surridge. 1998. National identity and national pride. In *British—and European—Social Attitudes: The 15th Report.* ed. R. Jowell et al. Brookfield, Vt.: Ashgate.

McDonald, Michael, and Samuel Popkin. 2001. The myth of the vanishing voter. *American Political Science Review* 95:963–974.

Meyer, David, and Sidney Tarrow, eds. 1998. *The Social Movement Society: Contentious Politics for a New Century.* Lanham, Md.: Rowman and Littlefield.

Miller, Arthur. 1974a. Political issues and trust in government. *American Political Science Review* 68:951–972.

———. 1974b. Rejoinder. *American Political Science Review* 68:989–1001.

Miller, Arthur, and Martin Wattenberg. 1985. Throwing the rascals out. *American Political Science Review* 79:359–372.

Miller, Arthur, Martin Wattenberg, and Oksana Malanchuk. 1986. Schematic assessments of presidential candidates. *American Political Science Review* 80:521–540.

———. 1987. *Without Consent: Mass-Elite Linkages in Presidential Politics.* Lexington: University Press of Kentucky.

Miller, Warren, and M. Kent Jennings. 1986. *Parties in Transition: A Longitudinal Study of Party Elites and Party Supporters.* New York: Russell Sage Foundation.

Miller, Warren, and J. Merrill Shanks. 1996. *The New American Voter.* Cambridge: Harvard University Press.

Miller, Warren, and Donald Stokes. 1963. Constituency influence in Congress. *American Political Science Review* 57:45–56.

Miller, Warren, et al. 1999. *Policy Representation in Western Democracies.* Oxford: Oxford University Press.

Miller, William, and Richard Niemi. 2002. Voting: Choice, conditioning, and constraint. In *Comparing Democracies,* ed. L. LeDuc, R. Niemi, and P. Norris. 2nd ed. Newbury Park, Calif.: Sage.

Monroe, Alan. 1998. Public Opinion and public policy, 1980–1993. *Public Opinion Quarterly* 62:6–28.

Morris, Richard. 1995. What informed public? *Washington Post National Weekly Edition,* April 10–16, 36.

Mueller, John. 1999. *Capitalism, Democracy, and Ralph's Pretty Good Grocery.* Princeton: Princeton University Press.

Nadeau, R., Richard Niemi, and A. Yoshinaka. 2002. A cross-national analysis of economic voting. *Electoral Studies* 21:403–423.

National Conference on Citizenship. 2006. *America's Civic Health Index: Broken Engagement.* Washington, D.C.: National Conference on Citizenship.

Nevitte, Neil. 1996. *The Decline of Deference.* Petersborough, Canada: Broadview.

Nie, Norman, Jane Junn, and Kenneth Stehlik-Barry. 1996. *Education and Democratic Citizenship in America.* Chicago: University of Chicago Press.

Nie, Norman, Sidney Verba, and John Petrocik. 1979. *The Changing American Voter.* Cambridge: Harvard University Press.

Niedermayer, Oskar, and Richard Sinnott, eds. 1995. *Public Opinion and International Governance.* New York: Oxford University Press.

Niemi, Richard, and M. Kent Jennings. 1991. Issues and inheritance in the formation of party identification. *American Journal of Political Science* 35:970–988.

Niemi, Richard, and Herbert Weisberg, eds. 2001. *Controversies in Voting.* 4th ed. Washington, D.C.: CQ Press.

Nieuwbeerta, Paul. 1995. *The Democratic Class Struggle in Twenty Countries 1945–90.* Amsterdam: Thesis Publishers.

Nieuwbeerta, Paul, and Nan Dirk de Graaf. 1999. Traditional class voting in 20 postwar societies. In *The End of Class Politics?* ed. G. Evans. New York: Oxford University Press.

Norpoth, Helmut. 1992. *Confidence Regained: Economics, Mrs. Thatcher, and the British Voter.* Ann Arbor: University of Michigan Press.

Norris, Pippa. 1999a. A gender-generation gap. In *Critical Elections,* ed. G. Evans and P. Norris. London: Sage.

———. 1999b. *Critical Citizens: Global Support for Democratic Governance,* ed. P. Norris. Oxford: Oxford University Press.

———. 1999c. Conclusions: The growth of critical citizens and its consequences. In *Critical Citizens,* ed. P. Norris. Oxford: Oxford University Press.

———. 1999d. New politicians? Changes in party competition at Westminster. In *Critical Elections,* ed. G. Evans and P. Norris. London: Sage.

———. 2000. *Virtuous Circle: Political Communications in Postindustrial Societies*. Cambridge: Cambridge University Press.

———, ed. 2001. *Britain Votes 2001*. Oxford: Oxford University Press.

———. 2002. *Democratic Phoenix: Reinventing Political Activism*. Cambridge: Cambridge University Press.

———. 2004. *Electoral Engineering: Voting Rules and Political Behavior*. New York: Cambridge University Press.

Norris, Pippa, and Ronald Inglehart. 2004. *Sacred and Secular: Religion and Politics Worldwide*. New York: Cambridge University Press.

Norris, Pippa, et al. 1999. *On Message: Communicating the Campaign*. London: Sage.

Norton, Philip. 2000. *The British Polity*. 4th ed. New York: Longman.

Nye, Joseph, Philip Zelikow, and David King, eds. 1997. *Why People Don't Trust Government*. Cambridge: Harvard University Press.

Offe, Claus, and Susanne Fuchs. 2002. A decline of social capital? The German case. In *Democracies in Flux*, ed. R. Putnam. Oxford: Oxford University Press.

Ohr, Dieter. 2000. Wird das Wählerverhalten zunehmend personalisierter, or ist jede Wahl anders? In *50 Jahre empirische Wahlforschung in Deutschland*, ed. M. Klein et al. Opladen: Westdeutscher Verlag.

Oskarson, Maria. 2005. Social structure and party choice. In *The European Voter*, ed. J. Thomassen. Oxford: Oxford University Press.

Page, Benjamin. 1978. *Choices and Echoes in Presidential Elections*. Chicago: University of Chicago Press.

Page, Benjamin, and Charles Jones. 1979. Reciprocal effects of policy preferences, party loyalties and the vote. *American Political Science Review* 73: 1071–89.

Page, Benjamin, and Robert Shapiro. 1983. Effects of public opinion on public policy. *American Political Science Review* 77:175–190.

———. 1992. *The Rational Public: Fifty Years of Trends in Americans' Policy Preferences*. Chicago: University of Chicago Press.

Palmer, Harvey. 1995. Effects of authoritarian and libertarian values on Conservative and Labour party support. *European Journal of Political Research* 27:273–292.

Parry, Geraint, George Moyser, and Neil Day. 1992. *Political Participation and Democracy in Britain*. Cambridge: Cambridge University Press.

Patterson, Thomas. 1993. *Out of Order*. New York: Knopf.

———. 2003. *The Vanishing Voter: Public Involvement in an Age of Uncertainty*. New York: Vintage.

Pattie, Charles, Patrick Seyd, and Paul Whiteley. 2004. *Citizenship in Britain: Values, Participation, and Democracy*. New York: Cambridge University Press.

Peffley, Mark, and Jon Hurwitz. 1985. A hierarchical model of attitude constraint. *American Journal of Political Science* 29:871–890.

Petrocik, John. 1996. Issue ownership in presidential elections, with a 1980 case study. *American Journal of Political Science* 40:825–850.

Pew Center for People and the Press. 1998a. *Deconstructing Distrust: How Americans View Government.* http://people-press.org/reports.

———. 1998b. *Public Appetite for Government Misjudged: Washington Leaders Wary of Public Opinion.* http://people-press.org/reports.

———. 2002. *What the World Thinks in 2002.* http://people-press.org/pgap.

———. 2003. *Views of a Changing World 2003.* http://people-press.org/pgap.

Pharr, Susan, and Robert Putnam, eds. 2000. *Disaffected Democracies: What's Troubling the Trilateral Countries?* Princeton: Princeton University Press.

Pierce, John, et al. 1992. *Citizens, Political Communication, and Interest Groups.* New York: Praeger.

Piven, Frances Fox, and Richard Cloward. 2000. *Why Americans Don't Vote: And Why Politicians Want It That Way,* rev. ed. Boston: Beacon Press.

Poguntke, Thomas. 1993. *Alternative Politics.* Edinburgh: University of Edinburgh Press.

Poguntke, Thomas, and Paul Webb, eds. 2005 *The Presidentialization of Politics: A Comparative Study of Modern Democracies.* New York: Oxford University Press.

Popkin, Samuel. 1991. *The Reasoning Voter.* Chicago: University of Chicago Press.

Powell, G. Bingham. 1986. American voting turnout in comparative perspective. *American Political Science Review* 80:17–44.

———. 2000. *Elections as Instruments of Democracy: Majoritarian and Proportional Visions.* New Haven: Yale University Press.

Prior, Markus. 2007. *Post-Broadcast Democracy: How Media Choice Increases Inequality in Political Involvement and Polarizes Elections.* New York: Cambridge University Press.

Putnam, Robert. 1993. *Making Democracy Work.* Princeton: Princeton University Press.

———. 2000. *Bowling Alone: The Collapse and Renewal of American Community.* New York: Simon and Schuster.

———. ed. 2002. *Democracies in Flux: The Evolution of Social Capital in Contemporary Society.* Oxford: Oxford University Press.

RePass, David. 1971. Issue saliency and party choice. *American Political Science Review* 65:389–400.

Richardson, Dick, and Chris Rootes, eds. 1995. *The Green Challenge: The Development of Green Parties in Europe.* London and New York: Routledge.

Rohrschneider, Robert, and Russell Dalton, eds. 2003. Judgment day and beyond: The 2002 Bundestagswahl. Special issue, *German Politics and Society,* Summer.

L

Rokeach, Milton. 1973. *The Nature of Human Values*. New York: Free Press.

Rootes, Christopher, ed. 1999. *Environmental Politics* 8, special issue: *Environmental Movements: Local, National, and Global*.

Rose, Richard, ed. 1969. *Electoral Behavior*. New York: Free Press.

———. 1990. *The Loyalties of Voters: A Lifetime Learning Model*. Newbury Park, Calif.: Sage.

Rose, Richard, and Derek Urwin. 1969. Social cohesion, political parties, and strains in regimes. *Comparative Political Studies* 2:7–67.

Rosenstone, Steven, and John Hansen. 1993. *Mobilization, Participation and Democracy in America*. New York: Macmillan.

Safran, William. 2002. *The French Polity*. 6th ed. New York: Longman.

Saggar, Shamit. 2007. Race and political behavior. In *The Oxford Handbook of Political Behavior*, ed. R. Dalton and H. Klingemann. Oxford: Oxford University Press.

Saggar, Shamit, and Anthony Heath. 1999. Race: Towards a multicultural electorate? In *Critical Elections*, ed. G. Evans and P. Norris. Thousand Oaks, Calif.: Sage.

Sartori, Giovanni. 1968. Representational systems. *International Encyclopedia of the Social Sciences* 13:470–475.

Scarrow, Susan, Paul Webb, and David Farrell. 2000. From social integration to electoral contestation. In *Parties without Partisans*, ed. R. Dalton and M. Wattenberg. Oxford: Oxford University Press.

Schattschneider, E. E. 1942. *Party Government*. New York: Rinehart.

Schickler, Eric, and Donald Green. 1997. The stability of party identification in Western democracies. *Comparative Political Studies* 30:450–483.

Schlozman, Kay, Nancy Burns, and Sidney Verba. 1994. Gender and the pathways to participation. *Journal of Politics* 56:963–990.

Schmitt, Hermann, and Jacques Thomassen, eds. 1999. *Political Representation and Legitimacy in the European Union*. Oxford: Oxford University Press.

Schoen, Harald. 2000. Stimmensplitting bei Bundestagswahlen. In *50 Jahre empirische Wahlforschung in Deutschland*. ed. M. Klein et al. Wiesbaden: Westdeutscher Verlag.

Schuman, Howard, et al. 1997. *Racial Attitudes in America: Trends and Interpretations*. Rev. ed. Cambridge: Harvard University Press.

Schumpeter, Joseph. 1943. *Capitalism, Socialism and Democracy*. London: Allen and Unwin.

Schwartz, Shalom, and A. Bardi. 2001. Value hierarchies across cultures. *Journal of Cross-Cultural Psychology* 32:268–290.

Scott, Jacqueline, Michael Braun, and Duane Alwin. 1998. Partner, parent, worker: Family and gender roles. In *British—and European—Social Attitudes: The 15th Report*, eds. R. Jowell et al. Brookfield, Vt.: Ashgate.

Semetko, Holli, and Klaus Schoenbach. 1994 *Germany's Unity Election*. Cresskill, N.J.: Hampton Press.

Shanks, J. Merrill, and Warren Miller. 1990. Policy direction and performance evaluations. *British Journal of Political Science* 20:143–235.

Shively, W. Phillips. 1979. The development of party identification among adults. *American Political Science Review* 73:1039–54.

Skocpol, Theda, and Morris Fiorina, eds. 1999. *Civic Engagement in American Democracy*. Washington, D.C.: Brookings Institution Press.

Smith, Tom, and Paul Sheatsley. 1984. American attitudes toward race relations. *Public Opinion* 7:14ff.

Sniderman, Paul, Richard Brody, and James Kuklinski. 1984. Policy reasoning and political values. *American Journal of Political Science* 28:74–94.

Sniderman, Paul, Richard Brody, and Philip Tetlock. 1991. *Reasoning and Choice*. New York: Cambridge University Press.

Sniderman, Paul, and Louk Hagendoorn. 2007. *When Ways of Life Collide: Multiculturalism and Its Discontents in the Netherlands*. Princeton: Princeton University Press.

Sniderman, Paul, and Thomas Piazza. 1993. *The Scar of Race*. Cambridge: Harvard University Press.

Sniderman, Paul, et al. 1991. The fallacy of democratic elitism. *British Journal of Political Science* 21:349–370.

———. 2001. *The Outsider: Prejudice and Politics in Italy*. Princeton: Princeton University Press.

Soroka, Stuart, and Christopher Wlezien. 2003. Degrees of democracy: Public preferences and policy in comparative perspective. Paper presented at the annual meeting of the American Political Science Association, Philadelphia, August.

Stanley, Harold, and Richard Niemi. 2000. *Vital Statistics of American Politics*. 7th ed. Washington, D.C.: CQ Press.

Stimson, James. 1975. Belief systems: Constraint, complexity and the 1982 election. *American Journal of Political Science* 19:393–417.

———. 1999. *Public Opinion in America: Moods, Cycles, and Swings*. 2nd ed. Boulder: Westview.

Stimson, James, Michael McKuen, and Robert Erikson. 1995. Dynamic representation. *American Political Science Review* 89:543–565.

Stokes, Donald. 1963. Spatial models of party competition. *American Political Science Review* 57:368–377.

Stolle, Dietlind, Marc Hooghe, and Michele Micheletti. 2005. Politics in the supermarket: Political consumerism as a form of political participation. *International Political Science Review* 26:245–270.

Stone Sweet, Alec. 2000. *Governing with Judges*. Oxford: Oxford University Press.

Stouffer, Samuel. 1955. *Communism, Conformity, and Civil Liberties*. New York: Doubleday.

Studlar, D., Ian McAllister, and B. Hayes. 1998. Explaining the gender gap in voting: A cross-national analysis. *Social Science Quarterly* 79:779–798.

Surowiecki, James. 2004. *The Wisdom of Crowds.* New York: Doubleday.

Swanson, David, and Paolo Mancini, eds. 1996. *Politics, Media, and Modern Democracy.* Westport, Conn.: Praeger.

Taagepera, Rein, and Matthew Shugart. 1989. *Seats and Votes: The Effects and Determinants of Electoral Systems.* New Haven: Yale University Press.

Taber, Charles, and Milton Lodge. 2006. Motivated skepticism in the evaluation of political beliefs, *American Journal of Political Science* 50: 755–769.

Taylor-Gooby, Peter. 1998. Commitment to the welfare state. In *British—and European—Social Attitudes: The 15th Report.* ed. R. Jowell et al. Brookfield, Vt: Ashgate.

Teixeira, Ruy. 1992. *The Disappearing American Voter.* Washington, D.C.: Brookings Institution Press.

Teorell, Jan, Mariano Torcal, and José Ramon Montero. 2007. Political participation: Mapping the terrain. In *Citizenship and Involvement in European Democracies,* ed. J. van Deth, J. Montero, and A. Westholm. London: Routledge.

Thomassen, Jacques. 1995. Support for democratic values. *Citizens and the State,* ed. H. Klingemann and D. Fuchs. Oxford: Oxford University Press.

———, ed. 2005. *The European Voter: A Comparative Study of Modern Democracies.* Oxford: Oxford University Press.

———. 2007. Democratic values. In *Handbook of Political Behavior,* ed. R. Dalton and H. Klingemann. Oxford: Oxford University Press.

Tocqueville, Alexis de. 1966. *Democracy in America.* Reprint of 1835, 1840 editions. New York: Knopf.

Topf, Richard, Peter Moeller, and Anthony Heath. 1989. Pride in one's country: Britain and West Germany. In *British Social Attitudes: Special International Report,* ed. R. Jowell, S. Witherspoon, and L. Brook: Brookfield, Vt.: Gower.

Uhlaner, Carole. 1989. Rational turnout. *American Journal of Political Science* 33:390–422.

van Deth, Jan. 2001. Soziale und politische Beteiligung: Alternativen, Ergänzungen oder Zwillinge? In *Politische Partizipation in der Bundesrepublik Deutschland,* ed. A. Koch, M. Wasmer, and P. Schmidt. Opladen: Leske + Budrich.

van Deth, Jan, and Elinor Scarbrough, eds. 1995. *The Impact of Values.* New York: Oxford University Press.

van Deth, Jan, et al., eds. 1999. *Social Capital and European Democracy.* New York: Routledge.

———. 2007. *Citizenship and Involvement in European Democracies: A Comparative Analysis.* London: Routledge.

Verba, Sidney, and Norman Nie. 1972. *Participation in America.* New York: Harper and Row.

Verba, Sidney, Norman Nie, and J. O. Kim. 1978. *Participation and Political Equality.* New York: Cambridge University Press.

Verba, Sidney, Kay Schlozman, and Henry Brady. 1995. *Voice and Equality: Civic Voluntarism in American Politics.* Cambridge: Harvard University Press.

von Weizsäcker, Richard. 1992. *Richard von Weizsäcker im Gespräch mit Gunter Hofmann und Werner Perger.* Frankfurt: Eichborn.

Wald, Kenneth. 2003. *Religion and Politics in the United States.* 4th ed. Lanham, Md.: Rowman and Littlefield.

Wattenberg, Martin. 1991. *The Rise of Candidate-centered Politics.* Cambridge: Harvard University Press.

———. 1998. *The Decline of American Political Parties, 1952–1996.* Cambridge: Harvard University Press.

———. 2002. *Where Have All the Voters Gone?* Cambridge: Harvard University Press.

———. 2006. *Is Voting for Young People?* New York: Longman.

Webb, Paul. 2002. Conclusion: Political parties and democratic control in advanced industrial societies. In *Political Parties in Advanced Industrial Democracies,* ed. P. Webb, D. Farrell, and I. Holliday. Oxford: Oxford University Press.

Webb, Paul, David Farrell, and Ian Holliday, eds. 2002. *Political Parties in Advanced Industrial Democracies.* Oxford: Oxford University Press.

Weisberg, Herbert, and Steve Greene. 2003. The political psychology of party identification. In *Electoral Democracy,* ed. M. MacKuen and G. Rabinowitz. Ann Arbor: University of Michigan Press.

Weisberg, Herbert, and Jerold Rusk. 1970. Dimensions of candidate evaluation. *American Political Science Review* 64:1167–85.

Weissberg, Robert. 1978. Collective versus dyadic representation in Congress. *American Political Science Review* 72:535–547.

Wessels, Bernhard. 1993. Politische Repräsentation als Prozeß gesellschaftlich-parlamentarischer Kommunikation. In *Parlament und Gesellschaft.,* ed. D. Herzog et al. Opladen: Westdeutscher Verlag.

———. 1994. Gruppenbindung und rationale Faktoren als Determinaten der Wahlentscheidung in Ost- und West Deutschland. In *Wahlen und Wähler,* ed. H. Klingemann and M. Kaase. Opladen: Westdeutscher Verlag.

———. 1999. System characteristics matter: Empirical evidence from ten representation studies. In *Policy Representation in Western Democracies.* ed. W. Miller et al. Oxford: Oxford University Press.

Whiteley, Paul, and Patrick Seyd. 2002. *High-intensity Participation: The Dynamics of Party Activism in Britain.* Ann Arbor: University of Michigan Press.

Whitten, Guy, and Harvey Palmer. 1999. Cross-national analyses of economic voting. *Electoral Studies* 18:49–67.

Wlezien, Christopher. 2004. Patterns of representation: Dynamics of public preferences and policy. *Journal of Politics* 66:1–24.

Wlezien, Christopher, Mark Franklin, and Daniel Twiggs. 1997. Economic perceptions and vote choice. *Political Behavior* 19:7–17.

Wolfe. Alan. 2006. *Does American Democracy Still Work?* New Haven: Yale University Press.

Wolfinger, Raymond, and Steven Rosenstone. 1980. *Who Votes?* New Haven: Yale University Press.

World Bank. 2001. *World Development Report 2001.* Washington, D.C.: World Bank.

Wright, Erik. 1997. *Class Counts: Comparative Studies in Class Analysis.* Cambridge: Cambridge University Press.

Wright, James. 1976. *The Dissent of the Governed.* New York: Academic Press.

Wuthrow. 2002. United States: Bridging the privileged and marginalized? In *Democracies in Flux: The Evolution of Social Capital in Contemporary America,* ed. R. Putnam. Oxford: Oxford University Press.

Zakaria, Fareed. 2003. *The Future of Freedom: Illiberal Democracy at Home and Abroad.* New York: Norton.

Zaller, John. 1992. *The Nature and Origins of Mass Opinion.* New York: Cambridge University Press.

Zelle, Carsten. 1995. Social dealignment vs. political frustration. *European Journal for Political Research* 27:319–345.

Zimmerman, Michael. 1990. Newspaper editors and the creation-evolution controversy. *Skeptical Inquirer* 14:182–195.

———. 1991. A survey of pseudoscientific sentiments of elected officials: A comparison of federal and state legislators. *Creation/Evolution* 29:26–45.

Zuckerman, Alan, and Martin Kroh. 2006. The Social Logic of Bounded Partisanship in Germany. *Comparative European Politics* 4:65–93.

Zukin, Cliff, et al. 2006. *A New Engagement? Political Participation, Civic Life, and the Changing American Citizen.* New York: Oxford University Press.

Index